Agamben and the Existentialists

Agamben and the Existentialists

EDITED BY
MARCOS ANTONIO NORRIS
AND
COLBY DICKINSON

EDINBURGH
University Press

Edinburgh University Press is one of the leading university presses in the UK. We publish academic books and journals in our selected subject areas across the humanities and social sciences, combining cutting-edge scholarship with high editorial and production values to produce academic works of lasting importance. For more information visit our website: edinburghuniversitypress.com

© editorial matter and organisation Marcos Antonio Norris and Colby Dickinson, 2021, 2023
© the chapters their several authors, 2021, 2023

Edinburgh University Press Ltd
The Tun – Holyrood Road
12(2f) Jackson's Entry
Edinburgh EH8 8PJ

First published in hardback by Edinburgh University Press 2021

Typeset in 11/13 Adobe Garamond by
Servis Filmsetting Ltd, Stockport, Cheshire

A CIP record for this book is available from the British Library

ISBN 978 1 4744 7877 9 (hardback)
ISBN 978 1 4744 7878 6 (paperback)
ISBN 978 1 4744 7879 3 (webready PDF)
ISBN 978 1 4744 7880 9 (epub)

The right of Marcos Antonio Norris and Colby Dickinson to be identified as the editors of this work has been asserted in accordance with the Copyright, Designs and Patents Act 1988, and the Copyright and Related Rights Regulations 2003 (SI No. 2498).

Contents

Notes on Contributors   vii

1. Introduction: Agamben, Nothingness and Existentialism   1
   Marcos Antonio Norris

Part I: Agamben and the Sovereign Exception

2. The Many Faces of a Hidden God: Agamben's Relations to Kierkegaard Reconsidered   25
   Lucas Lazzaretti

3. Biopolitics and Probability: Modifications on Life's Way   46
   Virgil W. Brower

4. Kierkegaard and the Figure of Form-of-Life   65
   Tom Frost

Part II: Agamben and the Death of God

5. The Work of Art and the Death of God in Nietzsche and Agamben   83
   Vanessa Lemm

6. Whither the Divine? Nietzsche, Heidegger and the End of Metaphysics in Agamben's Thought   100
   Colby Dickinson

7. Sartre and Agamben: Confronting Nothingness and the (Apparent) Death of God   115
   John Gillespie

Part III: Existentialist Themes in Agamben

8. Death and the Negative in Agamben and Beauvoir　　139
   Beatrice Marovich

9. Endless Ontology: Agamben and Sartre on Death　　155
   Andrew Welch

10. Destituent Potential and Camus's Politics of Rebellion　　174
    Tim Christiaens

11. A Politics Like No Other: Agamben, Fanon and the
    Colonial Fracture　　191
    Susan Dianne Brophy

12. Dis/Belief in Agamben and de Silentio　　212
    Marcos Antonio Norris

13. The Existential Situation and Christian Experience:
    Messianism and Eschatological Salvation　　237
    Daniel Minch

Index　　253

Notes on Contributors

Susan Dianne Brophy received her PhD in Social and Political Thought from York University (Canada) and is serving as Chair of the Department of Sociology and Legal Studies at St. Jerome's University in the University of Waterloo (Canada). Her research focuses on the theory and history of law and capitalism as well as anti-colonialist methodology and analysis, and she has published in such journals as *Constellations, European Journal of Political Theory, Labour/Le Travail, Law and Critique* and *Settler Colonial Studies*.

Virgil W. Brower is Research Fellow on the Human Condition in the Digital Age in the Faculty of Protestant Theology at Charles University in Prague and currently serves as coordinating speaker for the media philosophy working group of the Gesellschaft für Medienwissenschaft. His research analyses intersections of phenomenology, deconstruction, political theory and radical empiricism.

Tim Christiaens is a postdoctoral researcher at the Institute of Philosophy in Leuven. He works primarily on Italian critical theory and neoliberalism with publications in *Theory, Culture & Society, Cultural Critique* and *The European Journal of Social Theory*.

Colby Dickinson is Associate Professor of Theology at Loyola University Chicago. He is the author of *Agamben and Theology* (T&T Clark, 2011), *Words Fail: Theology, Poetry, and the Challenge of Representation* (Fordham University Press, 2016), *Theology and Contemporary Continental Philosophy: The Centrality of a Negative Dialectics* (Rowman & Littlefield, 2019) and, most recently, *The Fetish of Theology: The Challenge of the Fetish-Object to Modernity Theology* (Palgrave Macmillan, 2020).

Tom Frost is Lecturer in Law at the University of Leicester. He is the author of a number of publications on Agamben, and is working on a monograph looking at the relationship between Agamben and Emmanuel Levinas, focusing on Agamben's form-of-life. He is also a member of the Advisory Board of the *Journal of Italian Philosophy*.

John Gillespie is Professor of French Language and Literature (Emeritus) at Ulster University and an Executive Editor of *Sartre Studies International*. His research focuses on the interactions between literature, philosophy, theology and belief (particularly in relation to Christianity) in the twentieth century. He has published widely: on Gide, Sartre, Camus, Beckett and applied linguistics, and been involved in developing language policy and strategy. His recently published book (written with Piotr Blumczynski), *Translating Values* (Palgrave, 2016), examines the importance of evaluative concepts in translation.

Lucas Lazzaretti is a postdoctoral researcher at Universidade Estadual de Campinas (UNICAMP). He received the Kierkegaard House Foundation Fellowship (2018–2019) at St. Olaf College. His research explores the intersections of Kierkegaard, German Idealism and continental philosophy.

Vanessa Lemm is Professor of Philosophy and Executive Dean of the Faculty of Arts and Education at Deakin University. She is the author of *Homo Natura: Nietzsche, Philosophical Anthropology and Biopolitics* (Edinburgh University Press, 2020), *Nietzsche's Animal Philosophy: Culture, Politics and the Animality of the Human Being* (Fordham University Press, 2009) and numerous publications on Nietzsche and contemporary philosophy. She is the editor of *Nietzsche-Studien* (De Gruyter).

Beatrice Marovich is Assistant Professor of Theology in the Department of Theological Studies at Hanover College. She has written about Agamben and the work of Simone Weil in *Agamben's Philosophical Lineage* (Edinburgh University Press, 2020), edited by Adam Kotsko and Carlo Salzani, and *Simone Weil and Continental Philosophy* (Rowman & Littlefield, 2019), edited by Rebecca Roselle-Stone. She is currently working on a book project called *Sister Death: Political Theology in an Age of Extinctions*.

Daniel Minch is Assistant Professor of Dogmatic Theology at the Institute of Systematic Theology and Liturgical Studies, University of Graz, Austria. Minch is the author of 'Our Faith in Creation, God's Faith in Humanity: Edward Schillebeeckx and Pope Francis on Human Transcendence and an

Anthropocentric Cosmos', *Theological Studies*, 80, 4 (2019); *Eschatological Hermeneutics: The Theological Core of Experience and Our Hope for Salvation* (T&T Clark, 2018); and the co-editor (with Stephan van Erp) of the *T&T Clark Handbook of Edward Schillebeeckx* (T&T Clark, 2019).

Marcos Antonio Norris is a Crown Fellow of English at Loyola University Chicago, where he is completing a dissertation on 'Hemingway, Sartre, and Secularization: Reconsidering the Lost Generation'. Norris is the author of numerous peer-reviewed articles, most recently including 'The Failed Atheism of Jean-Paul Sartre' with *The Heythrop Journal*, 'Gender Pronoun Use in the University Classroom: A Posthumanist Perspective' with *Transformation in Higher Education*, 'Bibliographical Approaches to D. H. Lawrence's "Odour of Chrysanthemums"' with *Textual Cultures*, and '"Her voice is full of money": Mechanical Reproduction and a Metaphysics of Substance in F. Scott Fitzgerald's *The Great Gatsby*' with *English Studies*.

Andrew Welch completed his PhD in 2018 at Loyola University Chicago and continues to teach at Loyola. He is the co-author with Marcos Norris of 'Gender Pronoun Use in the University Classroom: A Posthumanist Perspective' with *Transformation in Higher Education*. His research explores the poetics of death and dying in romantic and post-romantic literature and philosophy.

Chapter 1

Introduction: Agamben, Nothingness and Existentialism

Marcos Antonio Norris

In *The Kingdom and the Glory* (2011), Agamben argues that *nothingness* is concealed at the heart of democratic society's sovereign political structures. This negative ontology at the heart of existence is symbolised in Western theology by an empty throne, a vacant seat of power that, in Agamben's reading of the Christian tradition, represents the absolute freedom to convert potentiality into actuality, *anomie* into *nomos*, through a kind of legal illegality that conceals nothingness within being. Agamben famously argues that modern democratic leaders inhabit unique politico-juridical stations that are both inside and outside of the law, stations that allow sovereign leadership to essentially dictate the law at will. This secular form of governance grows out of a theological paradigm that, according to the Nazi legal theorist Carl Schmitt, rightly equips the sovereign leader of the state with the miraculous power of God. But, as Agamben seeks to demonstrate at various points in the *Homo Sacer* series and beyond, this God is an ontological void, or pure potentiality, whose absence is essential to the nature of law itself. He writes in the preface of *The Kingdom and the Glory* that the 'center of the governmental machine is empty', so the empty throne, or '*hetoimasia tou thronou* that appears on the arches and apses of the Paleochristian and Byzantine basilicas, is perhaps, in this sense, the most significant symbol of power' we have, as modern democratic societies enforce their laws through lawlessness, or the unrestricted free will of a sovereign decision maker.[1] 'The empty throne', Agamben writes, 'is what we need to profane in order to make room, beyond it, for something that, for now, we can only evoke with the name *zoē ainoios*, eternal life.'[2] Agamben goes on to describe this form-of-life in the final instalment of the *Homo Sacer* series as an *impotentiality* that does not convert into actuality and that, by remaining impotent, deprives the law of its ontic force.

This profanation of the law, as Agamben calls it, returns the transcendent to common use by exposing the nothingness concealed within our representational constructs; profanation reveals the law to be non-essential and contingent rather than a metaphysical reality. Agamben advances this *coming* philosophy to combat the inherent violences of sovereign political power.

What perplexes the editors of the current volume is why Agamben has not been studied in the context of existentialism, or, to put things more directly, why the major figures of existentialist thought have not been engaged with as obvious interlocutors of the philosopher. To be sure, Adam Kotsko and Carlo Salzani's 2017 edited volume, *Agamben's Philosophical Lineage*, offers short chapters on the existentialist philosophers Martin Heidegger and Friedrich Nietzsche, but the respective authors of these chapters, Matthew Abbott and Vanessa Lemm (the latter of whom makes up for this deficit in the volume at hand), do not engage with what is particularly existentialist about the parties involved. For this reason, their contributions merely accentuate the paucity of research on this topic. One might readily assume, in light of the missing scholarship, that Agamben bears little resemblance to the major figures of existentialism. But it is our belief that Agamben's existentialist tendencies run deep. The current volume makes up for this critical lacuna by reading Agamben in conversation with Søren Kierkegaard, Friedrich Nietzsche, Martin Heidegger, Jean-Paul Sartre, Simone de Beauvoir, Albert Camus and Frantz Fanon, in addition to important existentialist themes.

Like Gilles Deleuze and their shared philosophical predecessor, Baruch Spinoza, Agamben envisions the world as absolutely immanent, a world that is completely bereft of transcendental realities and which therefore lacks the metaphysical divisions that follow – the most important of which include, for Agamben, the division between potentiality and actuality, existence and essence. This is why Agamben calls for a general *profanation* of the sacred, or that which divides the transcendent from the immanent; it is only by profaning the sacred through a *division of division itself* – a key gesture that Agamben credits to Paul in his 2005 study *The Time That Remains* – that one may escape the force of law and thereby deauthorise the metaphysical impositions of sovereign power and exclusionary truth. In this regard, Agamben follows the tradition of Spinoza and Deleuze, but it should be noted that his vision of absolute immanence also bears a striking resemblance to Jean-Paul Sartre's materialist atheism. According to Sartre, God's absence in the world transforms how we perceive the ontological nature of reality by bringing into vision the nothingness at the core of our being. Under this atheistic purview, the human subject 'is left among things and is not set apart from them by a divine consciousness that contemplates them and causes them to exist'.³ Rather, humankind lacks a predetermined purpose in the world and, consequently, they are free to make of this life – and of themselves – whatever they will. The meaning of humanity is up for grabs.

Existentialism and the God of Nothingness

Kate Kirkpatrick takes up this aspect of Sartre's philosophy in her 2018 publication *Sartre on Sin: Between Being and Nothingness*. She argues that sin, in the Augustinian tradition inherited by Sartre through the Catholic mystic of nothingness Pierre de Bérulle, is the privation, or absence, of being. In the French theological tradition, to exist without God is to exist as an absence because, as Kirkpatrick observes, God is the originary source of being. This is why, for Sartre and other existentialists, the death of God is of primary philosophical importance. Like Agamben, they imagine human life as no longer captive to transcendental values or fixed, ontological identities. In following the Sartrean dictum that *existence precedes essence*, the existential subject appears to embody Agamben's form-of-life, which he describes in *The Use of Bodies* as a pure potentiality, or 'void of representation', who prioritises its contingency over against its actualisation as an ontic being through, what Agamben calls, a deactivation of the anthropological machine.⁴ Here, the existentialist idea of nothingness and Agamben's notion of absolute immanence operate as parallel concepts; what appears in Agamben as a profanation of transcendental authority, appears in Sartre, Nietzsche, Heidegger, Beauvoir, Camus and others as the death of God. Drawing this parallel is important to the study of Agamben's work because it illuminates the atheistic undertones of his political theology as well as his decades-long engagement with the Christian tradition. What appears in such texts as *The Coming Community* (1990), *The Time That Remains* (2005), *The Highest Poverty* (2011) and *The Use of Bodies* (2014) as an ostensibly Christian ethic harkens back to his earlier, 1982 publication, *Language and Death: The Place of Negativity*, where he describes the Judaeo-Christian god as 'the negative ground on which all ontology rests, the originary negativity sustaining every negation'.⁵ This early study lays the groundwork for Agamben's political analyses in the decades to follow by uncovering a notion of divine being, already latent in Hebrew mysticism, that structures, for Agamben, the history of metaphysics, as well as its Christian theological heritage in the West.

Following Heidegger's description of *Dasein* as a placeholder for nothingness, or existential possibility in the face of one's mortality, Agamben traces the concept of being-there to the Aristotelean division between the first essence, *prote ousia*, and the second essences, *deuterai ousiai*. 'Agamben insists that to understand Dasein as the being that stands outside of itself, we must follow the itinerary of its [grammatical] shifter – we must pass through *there*. It is *there*, in the utterance, that Dasein experiences the system of language as a living event,' writes Andrew Welch in his chapter contribution to the present volume; 'Drawing this argument forward towards Agamben's analysis of potentiality, we might revise yet again: Dasein is language speaking itself.' For Plato, Aristotle and Dionysus of Thrace (as for Agamben), grammatical categories were inseparable from the philosophical categories of being that would go on to inform the theological perspectives of Thomas Aquinas, John of Damascus and Alain de Lille. The connection between grammar and ontology took on even greater currency with grammarians in the second half of the fifth century AD who identified the pronoun with *prote ousia*, or 'pure being in itself, before and beyond any qualitative determination'.[6] The basic idea, Agamben explains, was that pronouns remained indeterminate, or *empty*, until entering discourse, where they would subsequently take on a determinate meaning as semantic content. Noting the influence of the pronominal category on medieval Christian theology, Agamben writes that:

> The link between grammar and theology is so strong in medieval thought that the treatment of the problem of the Supreme Being cannot be understood without reference to grammatical categories. In this sense, despite the occasional polemics of theologians opposed to the application of grammatical methods to sacred scripture (Donatum non sequimur), theological thought is also grammatical thought, and the God of the theologians is also the God of the grammarians.[7]

In light of the pronominal category, medieval Christian theologians would interpret the divine nature as a kind of nothingness, according to Agamben, an originary potential that passes into actuality through divisive, signifying acts of creation. This capacity to create *ex nihilo* cuts to the heart of the divine nature which, as the '*negative foundation of human discourse*', is paradoxically natureless, being prior to signification and the representational divisions that bring intelligibility to our world.[8] The medieval notion that God is nothingness – or the pure potentiality of being – resulted from theologians engaging with the Greek philosophical tradition, but it also harkens back to the secret and unspeakable name of God, the tetragrammaton, Agamben says, which Thomas Aquinas, John of Damascus and Alain de Lille all identified with God's prelinguistic nature, the originary potential from which all determinate entities would finally emerge. '[A]t this extreme fringe of ontological thought', Agamben writes, 'where the taking-place of being is grasped as shadow, Christian theological reflection incorporates Hebrew mystical notions of the *nomen tetragrammaton*, the secret and unpronounceable name of God.'⁹ On this basis, the ancient Hebrews would conclude that God was 'no longer an experience of language but language itself, that is, its taking place in the removal of the voice'.¹⁰

This 'privileged status of the pronoun' would re-emerge in modern linguistic theories by Roman Jakobson and Émile Benveniste who described pronouns as empty signifiers pointing to the very event of language itself, its mere taking place in the form of pure existence before any determinate essence has been attributed to it.¹¹ Pronouns 'become "full" as soon as the speaker assumes them in an instance of discourse. Their scope', Agamben writes, 'is to enact "the conversion of language into discourse" and to permit the passage from *langue* to *parole*.'¹² Later, in *Infancy and History*, Agamben describes the ontological distinction between existence and essence, language and discourse, respectively, as the distinction between humankind's infancy and its interpellation into subjecthood. 'Animals do not enter language', Agamben writes, 'they are already inside it. Man, instead, by having an infancy, by preceding speech, splits this single language and, in order to speak, has to constitute himself as the subject of language – he has to say *I*. Thus, if language is truly man's nature, . . . then man's nature is split at its source.'¹³ This internal division between language and discourse, infancy and subjecthood becomes spiritually significant for the Christian believer, Agamben argues in *The Time That Remains* (2005), because it marks yet an additional distinction between the law and faith. Nothingness/Being, existence/essence, language/discourse, *langue/parole*, potentiality/actuality and faith/law traverse Agamben's oeuvre as parallel – and even synonymous – concepts. As Agamben would have it, the Pauline faith of early Christianity sought to deactivate *nomos*, or law, which he describes in *The Time That Remains* as Jewish law, Roman law, but also as the constative logic of discourse. In Agamben's reading, faith returns believers to the pure potentiality of human infancy by uniting them with God, the negative ground of ontology, or language before its divisive articulation as discourse – three seemingly disparate categories that Agamben regards as synonymous.

As he explains, *pistis*, the Greek word for faith, refers to the magical, pre-law agreement formed between God and Abraham prior to the juridical division of Jew and Gentile, a distinction the Israelites legally authorised through the practice of circumcision. This pre-law agreement, Agamben says, activates one's proximity to *the Word*, 'Jesus Messiah', whom Agamben identifies with the pure potentiality concealed within our divisive representations.¹⁴ According to Agamben, the Pauline faith represents a proximity to the creative potential of language, which he ties to spirit, or *breath*, and the circumcision of the heart. This messianic division of flesh and spirit cuts across the lawful division of Jew and Gentile to deactivate juridical authority of all kinds. 'The criteria for how this division works is both clear (circumcised/foreskin) and exhaustive, for it divides all "men" into two subsets', Agamben explains; 'Paul cuts this division in two via a new division, that of the flesh/breath. This partition does not coincide with that of the Jew/non-Jew, but it is not external to it either; instead, it divides the division itself' to reveal a nothingness, or pure potentiality, which breeds forth differential articulations that carry within them the structural antinomies that both constitute and threaten their existence.[15] Faith in Jesus Messiah therefore reveals the self-division, or constructed nature, of all earthly vocations, deactivating their lawful authority while retaining their functional use. Paul's theology thus renders the law inoperative without abolishing it, presenting all people as both inside and outside of the law, as both concrete-specific and subject to potential change. Agamben champions a return to a form-of-life, or life before the exclusionary violence of political representation. If Agamben's Christian ethics are founded on nothingness, as a comparative analysis of his works suggest, it may be fair to say that Agamben's project is thoroughly existentialist. The present volume explores this possibility as its central concern. By engaging with both theistic and atheistic strains of existentialism, we hope to illuminate the peculiar a/theological nature of Agamben's project.

Agamben and the Kierkegaardian Exception

But the question lingers: why hasn't this study been taken up before? If the parallels between Agamben's scholarship and existentialism are as remarkable as we claim, one could expect to see extensive literature on the topic. The complete lack of scholarship in this area is partly because existentialism today is widely considered a cultural relic with which no respectable philosopher would seriously align themselves. Like psychoanalysis, existentialism is often dismissed as a bygone twentieth-century movement that significantly impacted its cultural moment, but which has since been recognised as outmoded and even naive, despite its continued popularity in undergraduate programmes and mainstream culture. George Cotkin, author of *Existential America* (2003), argues that cultural appropriations of existentialism eclipsed the philosophy itself, especially in the United States, where magazines 'reduced it to a passing philosophical fancy, an object for consumption and disposal' by faddish, middle-brow culture.[16] According to Cotkin:

> The continuing allure of France, of things French, in American culture must not be underestimated as a factor in the popularity of French existentialism. ... Between 1946 and 1948, American audiences were introduced to French existentialism in the pages of *Life*, the *New York Times Magazine*, *Time*, *Newsweek*, and fashion magazines such as *Vogue* and *Harper's Bazaar*. These popular discussions stressed Simone de Beauvoir's lifestyle and Jean-Paul Sartre's attachment to the bohemian café scene more than their ideas. A cult of personality developed whereby the general renown of existentialism became intimately connected to the personal life of the philosopher and even to the circumstances of the nation he or she represented.[17]

For this reason, existentialism was regarded as more cultural attitude than serious philosophy, as more fashion statement than intellectual practice, and so became a sort of epithet among academics. Of course, the term was popularised in association with Sartre who first rejected the appellation and later embraced it; but this led Heidegger, Camus and others to repudiate the term in order to distance themselves from Sartre for reasons philosophical, political and interpersonal. In the coming decades, the increased popularity of structuralism, poststructuralism, deconstruction and the associated schools of contemporary continental thought would force existentialism into the background as not only passé but as intellectually and politically dangerous. For continental philosophers of the late twentieth century, existentialism promoted the sovereign subject under a metaphysics of language that was responsible for longstanding cultural hierarchies and so-called systems of oppression. Commenting on this point, Colby Dickinson writes in his chapter contribution to the present volume that:

> Sartre's French Catholic heritage ... led him to divinise language itself, the Words with which he crafted his own singular existence. ... The metaphysics of language that Sartre developed as motivation for his writing was nothing new to the period in which he wrote. It was in fact something of the *lingua franca* for the literary artist. As his lifelong companion, Simone de Beauvoir, would suggest on more than one occasion, putting one's life into words was, in part, an effort to give meaning to life itself when viewed through the short lens of death – something which elevated the act of writing to a metaphysical principle.

According to Dickinson, signification, for Sartre and Beauvoir, was a creative act of volition operating with metaphysical and even divine-like authority. That contemporary continental philosophers – among whom we find Agamben – are prone to reject without even engaging with the philosophies of Sartre and Beauvoir is therefore unsurprising. But their lack of engagement – which may result more from their sheer indifference to the topic than from a principled refusal to consider Agamben in relationship to existentialism – leaves untapped a wellspring of research with the potential to illuminate both Agamben and the legacy of existentialism in novel ways.

Of course, Agamben directly engages with certain existentialists, including Heidegger, Nietzsche and Franz Kafka; he also makes indirect contact with Kierkegaard via Carl Schmitt, Agamben's primary opponent in the realm of political philosophy. But, as we have already noted, Agamben's engagement with these thinkers has not been studied in the context of existentialism or from an existentialist perspective. The significant impact of Kierkegaard on Schmitt's theory of the sovereign exception – and the important philosophical role it plays in Schmitt's defence of fascist governmentality – has itself gained considerable scholarly treatment over the years. Yet, in spite of the obvious nexus formed in Schmitt's *Political Theology* (1922) between Kierkegaard and Agamben – that is, Agamben critiques a definition of sovereignty that Schmitt bases on the Kierkegaardian exception – there remains an unaccounted for and rather surprising lacuna in the scholarship.[18] Virtually no one has addressed Agamben's relationship to Kierkegaard, in part because Agamben and his philosophical progenitor Jacob Taubes blindly accept Schmitt's reading of the Kierkegaardian exception. Taubes writes in *The Political Theology of Paul* (2004), for example, that there is a clear 'trajectory between [the] Kierkegaardian exception and Schmitt's definition of sovereignty'[19] – that is, constitutional law depends upon the unrestricted decisions of a sovereign political leader just as the universal laws of nature depend upon the poetic young man of Kierkegaard's *Repetition*, who 'explains the universal and himself', the pseudonymous author Constantin Constantius writes, through a 'temporary suspension' of the natural order.[20] Following Taubes, Agamben adopts Schmitt's reading of Kierkegaard, which naturally forces Kierkegaard into the background as the indirect target of Agamben's political theological critique. Subsequent readers of Agamben have simply followed suit, leaving Agamben's relationship to Kierkegaard largely unexamined.

To my knowledge, the only exception to this rule is Leif Bork Hansen's 2011 essay 'Giorgio Agamben: State of Exception'.[21] Hansen reads Kierkegaard's *Fear and Trembling*, *The Sickness unto Death* and *A Literary Review* in conversation with Agamben's *Homo Sacer*, *The Coming Community* and *Remnants of Auschwitz* to argue that exceptionality refers not to a sovereign political force but to the human individual stripped of his political identity. For Hansen, the individual before God in Kierkegaard is comparable to Agamben's *whatever being*, for both Kierkegaard and Agamben see 'danger in reducing the single human being to a citizen of the state'.[22] Doing so separates *bare life* from the legally protected citizen, and absorbs both into *Sittlichkeit*, or the hegemonic structures of the government. But Hansen is not alone in his reading of Kierkegaard. Bartholomew Ryans, for one, writes that 'Kierkegaard's exception' refers to 'the individual being governed rather than to the powers that govern'.[23] Saitya Brata Das likewise argues that Kierkegaardian exceptionalism models a '*Kenosis* that empties out the "normative representations" . . . of an established hegemony'[24] through the political dissidence of individual citizens rather than the miraculous power of an omnipotent lawmaker. It is only Hansen, however, who reads Kierkegaard in light of Agamben, and though he does well to establish positive relations between the two thinkers, Hansen is not able to counter Schmitt's Kierkegaardian reading of sovereignty. As Hansen and others suggest, Kierkegaard may certainly have in mind the governed individual rather than a sovereign lawmaker when discussing the suspension of normative laws, but Hansen's individualist approach to Kierkegaard still models the decisionist philosophy that Agamben finds to be so problematic in Schmitt.

Through its various contributions, this volume aims to complicate Agamben's antagonistic stance towards the Kierkegaardian exception, a foundational existentialist concept that extends well beyond Kierkegaard to the decisionist philosophies of other existentialist thinkers, with whom the book seeks to deepen Agamben's ties. Of course, Kierkegaard's pseudonymous authorship presents a challenge to anyone hoping to approximate a clear understanding of the writer himself, but a cursory reading of *The Sickness unto Death* by Anti-Climacus (of which Kierkegaard lists himself as the editor) reveals a possible overlap with Agamben's depiction of the Pauline faith. For Agamben, anthropogenesis embeds human life within representational constructs that, when taken as lawful and binding, conceal the nothingness, or pure potentiality, lurking within them – what Agamben identifies variously with God, or the negative ground of ontology. The faithful individual, by contrast, inhabits these same representational constructs but, in recognising the pure potentiality concealed within them – dwelling, as it were, in close proximity to *the Word* – the faithful deactivates the legal force of representation, and so comes to regard his earthly vocation not as lawful and binding, but as one possible mode of being among others. This modal ontology, or monadic *form-of-life*, as Agamben refers to it in *The Use of Bodies*, is 'inseparable from its form, [as] an indissoluble unity in itself', but it is also, at the same time, 'inseparable from its context, precisely because it is not in relation but in contact with it'.[25] To be in *relation* with one's context is to regard representational divisions as juridical; whereas to be in *contact* with one's context is to regard those same representational divisions as constructed. 'A form-of-life is, in this sense, that which ceaselessly deposes the social conditions in which it finds itself to live, without negating them, but simply by using them.'²⁶ Only by attending to the pure potentiality of *langue* can faithful individuals perform the divisions of a representational economy without losing sight of their arbitrariness and contingency. 'Only if act is never totally separated from potential' can 'a form of life . . . become, in its very facticity and thingliness, *form-of-life*, in which it is never possible to isolate something like a bare life.'²⁷ Looked at from this perspective, the faithful individual can be understood as a synthesis of *langue* and *parole*, potentiality and actuality that, in the writings of Kierkegaard's Anti-Climacus, might be reframed as the synthesis of infinitude and finitude, for, as Anti-Climacus writes:

> The self is the conscious synthesis of infinitude and finitude which relates itself to itself, whose task is to become itself, a task which can be performed only by means of a relationship to God. But to become oneself is to become concrete. But to become concrete means neither to become finite nor infinite, for that which is to become concrete is a synthesis. Accordingly, the development consists in moving away from oneself infinitely by the process of infinitizing oneself, and in returning to oneself infinitely by the process of finitizing.²⁸

Thus, according to Anti-Climacus, selfhood – which is discovered only in relationship to God – is neither finite nor infinite, but a synthesis of the two. Likewise, it is in *Jesus Messiah*, Agamben says, that one gains a conscious awareness that both potentiality and actuality comprise human nature, that the concrete conditions of existence are, in fact, a synthesis of counteracting forces. In a paper delivered at the UNESCO colloquium on Kierkegaard in 1946, Sartre wonders how a philosopher committed to Christian dogma could, at the same time, accept Kierkegaard's constructivist historiography, which in effect relativises the universal truths of Christianity as mere historical constructions limited to time and place. The answer, Sartre explains, is that truth is subjective for Kierkegaard; it is manifested through the will as an absolute in the midst of the relative. But unlike the sovereign decisionism promoted by Carl Schmitt, this leap of faith constitutes itself as law without concealing its underlying contingency. The self-constituting subject, for Kierkegaard, becomes a 'law for others and for himself . . . But . . . the content of this universality remains his contingency', Sartre writes; 'In short, this universality has two sides to it: . . . it raises contingency to the level of concrete universality.'²⁹ From Sartre's perspective, then, Kierkegaard envisions lawmaking decisions that preserve their contingency even as concrete universals. As Anti-Climacus would have it, the concrete conditions of existence are a synthesis of finitude and infinitude; one is confronted with the limitless possibilities of infinity but nevertheless housed within the functional spaces of everyday life, where an individual 'return[s] to oneself infinitely', the pseudonymous author writes, 'by the process of finitizing'. Of course, whether finitude and infinitude can be respectively aligned with actuality and potentiality as parallel concepts is a matter of debate in need of further corroboration. This is a task that a number of our contributors have taken up directly, Tom Frost writing in his chapter that Agamben's depiction of subject formation concretises 'Kierkegaard's claim that the human being is a synthesis with the possibility of becoming a self'.

The A/Theism of Existential Choice

Indeed, before readily committing ourselves to these ostensible overlaps in Agamben's work and existentialism as a whole, it would behove us to remember that the prolific scholar of existentialism Walter Kaufmann famously argued that this so-called philosophical school is a heterogeneous set of 'revolts against traditional philosophy' that are more dissimilar than they are alike.[30] 'Most of the living "existentialists" have repudiated this label', Kaufmann wrote in 1956, 'and a bewildered outsider might well conclude that the only thing they have in common is a marked aversion for each other.'[31] There is certainly no question about it – there are considerable differences among Kierkegaard, Nietzsche, Heidegger, Sartre, Beauvoir, Camus and the other major figures of existentialism, but the same can be said of any major philosophical school, be it poststructuralist, phenomenologist, Marxist, feminist or what have you. What allows us to group together divergent thinkers into philosophical schools of thought is not that they share entirely identical worldviews, but that they share a set of core beliefs, the fundamental tenets that mark out their philosophy as distinct from other philosophies.

Often, the existentialists are grouped together around concepts like *anxiety*, *dread*, *alienation*, *rebellion* and *authenticity*, but we feel that even these concepts are a step removed from the core structure of existentialism. We believe with Sartre that existentialism 'can be easily defined. What complicates the matter is that there are two kinds of existentialists: on the one hand, the Christians . . . and on the other hand, the atheistic existentialists . . . What they have in common is simply their belief that existence precedes essence.'[32] According to the well-known Sartrean dictum, human beings have no predetermined essence and must therefore define themselves through acts of free choice. At the core of both theistic and atheistic accounts of existentialism, then, is the shared belief that free will determines the nature of human identity. As Kierkegaard scholar Gordon Marino writes, 'Kierkegaard, Gabriel Marcel, Miguel de Unamuno y Jugo, and other non-atheist existentialists would disagree with Sartre's claim that there is no underlying plan in our lives, but all the existentialists concur that it is through our choices that we become who we are.'[33] Thus, the sovereign individual – commonly referred to as the Kierkegaardian exception – lies at the heart of existentialism. Truth, identity and the meaning of life begins with the individual subject, even for the religiously devout Kierkegaard, 'who rejects belief in the eternal verities, as well as Plato's trust in reason as a kind of second sight. Ethics is for him not a matter of seeing the good', Marino writes, 'but of making a decision.'[34] As Thomas Flynn asserts in *Existentialism: A Brief Insight*, 'truth is more a matter of decision than discovery' for the existentialists, so 'the nature of choice is criterion-*constituting* rather than criterion*less*'.[35] This is why Carl Schmitt is quick to align the decisionist politics of the state with the Kierkegaardian exception; it is not human value, natural law or a transcendental ethic that determines the boundaries of human identity and legal protection, for Schmitt, but the sovereign decision-maker alone, who suspends constitutional law in order to constitute laws of his own. The question is whether these lawmaking decisions can be authorised as universally binding, or whether they lack such authority, being founded – for Agamben and the existentialists alike – on nothingness, a concept appearing in both theistic and atheistic forms.

What appears in Kierkegaard as a teleological suspension of the ethical appears in the works of Nietzsche, Heidegger, Sartre, Beauvoir and Camus as the death of God, a suspension of universal morality that, in at least one interpretation, instils human decision making with the metaphysical authority of law. Just as Abraham in *Fear and Trembling* and the poetic exception in *Repetition* suspend the universal through sovereign, self-originating choices, so too does Nietzsche's overman transvalue the normative ethics of Christianity by creating his own moral values in a world without God. According to Taubes, one cannot fully understand Paul's Letter to the Romans without also understanding Nietzsche's 'nihilistic'[36] suspension of moral law. One might therefore expect Agamben's follow-up to *The Political Theology of Paul* in *The Time That Remains* to engage with Nietzsche's atheism in a more explicit way. After all, Nietzsche's transvaluation of the law resembles Agamben's division of division itself, an act that deauthorises the juridical division between Jew and Gentile through a contradiction that reveals the pure potentiality of God's non-being – what Agamben describes in multiple works as nothingness, or the negative ground of ontology. It would appear, on this basis, that Agamben advances a Nietzschean reading of Pauline Christianity that paradoxically announces the death of God through the nominal syntagma *Jesus Messiah*, a phrase that drops the definite article, Agamben says, in order to suspend the constative logic of non-contradiction.

The current volume explores Agamben's relationship to Nietzsche, especially as it pertains to God's death as the suspension of normative laws. Does Agamben's division of division neutralise the decisionist metaphysics of Nietzsche's will to power? Or, in communion with Nietzsche, does it give way to a form-of-life that grounds the religious exception on the negative ontology of God's non-being? In the former case, we would say that Agamben and Nietzsche are clearly at odds; when it comes to the death of God, however, Agamben and Nietzsche appear deeply in tune, as both would prefer to envision the world as devoid of transcendence and therefore as absolutely immanent.

Anke Snoek makes note in *Agamben's Philosophical Lineage* of a similar conflict in the writings of the existentialist Franz Kafka, with whom Agamben engages at length. Snoek reads Agamben in conversation with the Marxist literary theorist and political philosopher Walter Benjamin, who sees in Kafka's parables a 'messianic gesture' that 'inverts imperfect nihilism into perfect nihilism, or the virtual state of exception into a real state of exception'.[37] The difference between perfect and imperfect nihilism is also the difference, Snoek explains, between the lawmaking decisions of a sovereign political power and decisions that have been emptied of their lawmaking force in the wake of God's death as the end of metaphysics. Snoek writes:

> what characterizes the state of exception is the fact that the law is preserved in its suspension; its content has been removed but it is in force all the more, just like the law Kafka describes. . . . Herein lies Kafka's profound insight into the law, stressing that the force of the law seems to be more important than its content. Agamben even calls Kafka a prophet, stressing how the state of exception, or the law's being in force without content, has become increasingly dominant in our modern times.[38]

This force of law without content characterises, at least in one reading, a Nietzschean will to power in the face of nothingness. Under this rubric of imperfect nihilism, the law has been stripped of a determinate form and recast as unbridled decisionism. But, according to Snoek, Kafka is after a perfect nihilism that empties the law of not only its content but its force. This messianic nihilism, as Benjamin calls it, reduces the law to a *plaything* by divesting sovereign decisionism of its metaphysical authority. Following Benjamin, Agamben advances a religious alternative that builds upon the death of God with the death of authority per se. Borrowing Snoek's terms, it would appear that Agamben's perfect nihilism suspends the authoritarian tendencies of an imperfect nihilism that instils the sovereign exception with the metaphysical authority of law. Following Carl Schmitt, there is a tendency to read sovereign exceptionalism – and so too existentialism as a whole – as a model of imperfect nihilism.

Existentialism as Ontotheology

So there is another side to the Agamben–existentialist dialogue. Under a Schmittian framework, the sovereign exception passes from potentiality into actuality and from nothingness into being through self-originating choices that establish free will as the active origin of ontic reality. The sovereign decision, Agamben writes, 'is that through which Being founds itself *sovereignly* . . . without anything preceding or determining it (*superiorem non recognoscens*) other than its own ability not to be'.[39] Self-origination is thus the highest expression of ontotheology, for Agamben, who argues that sovereign leadership operates under this metaphysical paradigm to justify its violation of constitutional law. Executive powers and legislative powers – potentiality and actuality – combine as a single force in this 'zone of indistinction'[40] to police the laws that it alone has the ability to create. Returning to Sartre, it could likewise be said that existence precedes essence as a force of law without content that, under Sartre's existentialist account of freedom, actualises potentiality through self-originating choices. That Sartre describes every person as a 'legislator'[41] should therefore come as little surprise, despite the strong parallels we identified earlier between a Sartrean understanding of nothingness and Agamben's vision of the absolutely immanent. It may be that Sartre, more so than Kierkegaard, models the metaphysical view of sovereign decision-making extolled by Carl Schmitt.

Arguably, then, what distinguishes Sartre from Agamben is not the unbridled freedom that Sartre attributes to the existential subject, for we see a parallel figure carved out by Agamben in the *whatever* singularities of *The Coming Community*. Rather, what distinguishes Sartre from Agamben is his provocative, somewhat authoritarian claim that the free individual is a lawmaker not only for himself but for everyone. As he announces in his 1946 lecture *Existentialism is a Humanism*, 'the first effect of existentialism is to make every man . . . solely responsible for his own existence. And when we say that man is responsible for himself, we do not mean that he is responsible only for his own individuality, but that he is responsible for all men.'[42] One may certainly argue that, by extending the power to self-determine beyond his own identity to the identity of every individual, Sartre positions himself as the sovereign administrator of what Agamben calls the anthropological machine, constructed divisions between the lawful citizen and bare life, humanity and the non-human other. This atheistic account of freedom is itself a secularised theological view, for '[t]he key consequence of not believing in God', Sartre scholar and contributor to the current volume John Gillespie writes in a 2013 article for *Sartre Studies International*, is tantamount to 'be[coming a] God for oneself'.[43] It is assuming the power, in the aftermath of God's disappearance, to create moral laws in much the same way that a sovereign political leader creates new laws during an emergency state. For this reason, readers may be more inclined to associate Sartre with Carl Schmitt than with Agamben, who seeks to combat the sovereign decisionism that so many of us have come to associate with existentialism and its major figures. This volume challenges Agamben's misappropriation of the Kierkegaardian exception in order to forge the lines of communication between Agamben and the existentialist tradition, but Agamben's relationship to the major figures of existentialism is nevertheless complicated, so, in the collection of essays commissioned for this volume, we have attempted to offer a measured approach that thoroughly takes these complications into account.

Volume Overview

We have organised the volume around three questions: Why hasn't this topic been taken up before (Part I), why is this topic a worthwhile pursuit (Part II), and if the topic is indeed worthy of scholarly attention, in what directions can we take it moving forward (Part III)? The first part, 'Agamben and the Sovereign Exception', begins with a chapter by Lucas Lazzaretti that challenges the traditional pathway from Kierkegaard to Agamben via Schmitt by establishing an alternate trajectory through Walter Benjamin. Agamben's relations to Kierkegaard have been overshadowed, Lazzaretti says, by Schmitt's secularisation of the Kierkegaardian exception as a model for totalitarian state authority, the primary target of Agamben's political-theological critique. But, as Lazzaretti explains, Schmitt's reading of the Kierkegaardian exception is based on one specific work, *Repetition*, which provides only a limited understanding of Kierkegaard's complete philosophical project. For a more comprehensive view of the matter, Lazzaretti brings Kierkegaard's *Fear and Trembling* into conversation with Benjamin's *Critique of Violence* to reconceive sovereign exceptionalism from, what Lazzaretti considers, a truly Kierkegaardian point of view.

In similar manner, Virgil W. Brower's chapter, 'Biopolitics and Probability: Modifications on Life's Way', addresses the complicated genealogy traced from Kierkegaard to the bare life, state of exception and biopower of Agamben's corpus. Not only is there inattention paid to Kierkegaard's pseudonymous method of indirect communication, Brower says, but there are important omissions of which to take note in the treatment of Kierkegaard that further develop, perpetuate and compound from Carl Schmitt to Jacob Taubes and, eventually, to Agamben. As Brower observes, Schmitt does not give a textual citation for *Repetition* and refers to the author as *a Protestant theologian* who is never directly identified as Kierkegaard. Moreover, Schmitt's deceptively simple block quote of *Repetition* omits four sentences, with no indicative ellipsis of the omission. Taubes does not mention the omission, Brower says, and nor does he cite *Repetition* as the text proper. Instead, the citation is recited and the identification is again evoked (and, again, left undocumented) in his 1987 lectures, delivered in Heidelberg, on the political theology of Paul: 'You see the trajectory between Kierkegaardian exception and Schmitt's definition of sovereignty.'[44] But, as Martin Buber says to Taubes, 'Taubes, you know *Being and Time*, you don't know Heidegger.'[45] The accused concedes that 'he was right' and confesses similar shortcomings with regard to his early readings of Kierkegaard. Thus, a similar critique could be levelled at Schmitt, Taubes and, by proxy, Agamben: *Political theology, you may know a few lines from* Repetition, Brower very cleverly states, *but you don't necessarily know Kierkegaard*. Brower concludes that precious opportunity is lost by Agamben to address the kinds of law, legitimacy and biopower that emerge from and beyond the Kierkegaardian exception. In the same paragraph of *Repetition* – which neither Schmitt, Taubes nor Agamben address – one finds Kierkegaard already grappling with political struggle, law and legitimacy.

Part I closes with a chapter by Tom Frost, 'Kierkegaard and the Figure of Form-of-Life', which also seeks to correct Agamben's misappropriation of Kierkegaard. According to Frost, Agamben's work is driven by a desire to explore a politics of pure means, which is best modelled by his form-of-life figure. Form-of-life needs to be read through an existentialist lens, Frost says, that Kierkegaard's writings can help to illuminate. Through contact with other forms-of-life, and in living a life of contemplative use, form-of-life deactivates the appropriative biopolitics that constantly divide and separate us. According to Frost, however, Agamben's form-of-life cannot account for the liminal figures of bare life. Rather than consider this a flaw in the construction of form-of-life, Frost concludes that form-of-life should be read as a new interpretation of Kierkegaard's claim that the human being is a synthesis of the infinite and the finite. Advancing this existentialist reading of form-of-life, Frost illustrates how form-of-life is subject to a continual process of repetition, an existential process that is always already happening.

Having challenged Agamben's misappropriation of Kierkegaard through Schmitt and Taubes in Part I, in Part II we present three chapters that further justify our line of research as a worthwhile pursuit, beginning with Vanessa Lemm's contribution, 'The Work of Art and the Death of God in Nietzsche and Agamben'. Of course, Agamben's engagement with

Nietzsche's philosophy is continuous and ongoing throughout his work, but Lemm focuses in on one Nietzschean concept that appears to hold special purchase for Agamben: the work of art without the artist, which she presents as a variant of God's death, a central existentialist theme. Agamben confirms in a 2004 interview that 'Nietzsche was important for me also', Lemm notes, and when asked about his vision of the philosophical life, Agamben answers: 'Nietzsche's idea of a work of art without the artist.'[46] Agamben's first critical engagement with Nietzsche concludes on the same note, Lemm records, with a citation from Nietzsche's posthumous work, where he writes: 'The work of art, where it appears without an artist' and where 'the artist is only a preliminary stage' – this should be our model for 'The world as a work of art that gives birth to itself.'[47] Lemm explores this concept of the work of art with no artist, or the world in God's absence that gives birth to itself, to better ascertain the unique shape of Agamben's atheistic worldview.

Following Lemm, Dickinson argues in his chapter that the line of critique offered by both Nietzsche and Heidegger concerning the death of God and the end of metaphysics is one that stresses the role of the will in overcoming the sheer contingency of human existence. But Agamben's discussion of the will, Dickinson explains, opens the door towards critiques of a particular nominalist strand of thought, Nietzsche's emphasis on the will to power and various forms of nihilism in the modern period alike. Positing an ontology of *command* – which Dickinson aligns with the sovereign exception – in deliberate contrast with an ontology of *demand*, Agamben develops a modal ontology that is able think the possibility of divine existence only by pushing beyond the theism/atheism binary (as with Being/Nothing in Heidegger). 'The ontology of command that rests upon a metaphysics of the will and that transforms language into a metaphysical platform for the construction of the sovereign subject', Dickinson states, 'is subsequently contrasted by Agamben with an ontology of demand that respects only the singularity of each individual life (as a form-of-life) and which demands to be heard from within the contingency of its own existence'. Agamben advances beyond the existentialist tradition by deauthorising its exalted view of the will – what Dickinson frames as a division of existentialism from within.

The final chapter in this part, 'Sartre and Agamben: Confronting Nothingness and the (Apparent) Death of God', written by noted Sartre scholar John Gillespie, likewise considers the sovereign subject in light of Agamben's identification of God with nothingness. The extent to which Agamben's theology resembles Sartre's atheism, and the significance of that resemblance is carefully examined. In a seeming reversal of Dickinson's stance, however, Gillespie concludes that Agamben's project remains firmly within the context of God's death and existentialism, rather than moving positively beyond it. Sartre's preoccupation with God, theology and religious themes, Gillespie says, has been researched more fully and frequently in recent years. In particular, the death of God has shown to be central to Sartre's thought, notably his rejection of transcendence, the importance of nothingness for the individual's freedom and his dependence on theological concepts. Gillespie argues that Sartre's concept of nothingness is a form of negative theology which is held in opposition to the idea of God, who is therefore not as dead as Sartre would judge him to be. This chapter outlines Sartre's move from the individual sovereignty of the for-itself, in which the individual becomes God for themselves, to Sartre's championing of social and political ethics, which calls into question his initial stance and its implications.

Whether one aligns Agamben with the existentialist tradition or chooses to view him as an opponent and critic, *nothingness* remains an important concept for both himself and various existentialist thinkers, be they theistic or atheistic. Having established this point in Part II, we conclude the volume with a third part titled 'Existentialist Themes in Agamben' that opens the floor to various explorations of Agamben in relationship to existentialism, generally speaking. We begin the section with an essay by Beatrice Marovich, 'Death and the Negative in Agamben and Beauvoir'. According to Marovich, Heidegger's presentation of *Dasein* as a being-towards-death has exerted significant influence over various accounts of existentialism. In *Language and Death*, Agamben marks a break with the sacrificial and nihilistic dimensions of Heidegger's negative orientation, and yet Agamben is no vitalist, Marovich states; he does not offer figures of life as a curative, or a tonic, to soothe or quell this negativity with an affirmation. Instead, the negative dimensions typically associated with death are differently arranged in Agamben's thinking. This chapter evokes a resonance between Agamben's figuration of the relation between life and death, and the figurations that appears in the work of the existentialist thinker Simone de Beauvoir. Both Agamben and Beauvoir think death within a site of suspension – as if imbricated with the embryonic or the infantile. For both thinkers, in different ways and to different degrees, death appears alongside of life as a figure that not only evokes decay and destruction but also germination and fermentation. Thus, in the work of Beauvoir and Agamben, neither the powers of life nor the powers of death are ascendant, Marovich concludes.

The next chapter, by Andrew Welch, 'Endless Ontology: Agamben and Sartre on Death', revisits Agamben's readings of Montaigne and Heidegger in, respectively, *Infancy and History* and *Language and Death*. In these engagements, Agamben suggests an understanding of death as the condition of form, rather than its undoing – a line of thinking that will become important for the later concept of bare life. Yet this invocation of death poses a specific challenge for Agamben's project via the concept of potentiality, Welch states, for thinking death as the *telos* of life opens new possibilities for the construction of meaning, but it also risks fastening life to a narrative logic that may extinguish potentiality by actualising life in advance of itself. Through his reading of Heidegger, Agamben aims to preserve death's formative power while undoing its *telos* by positioning death as the beginning, rather than at the end, of *Dasein*. Having established these points, Welch then argues that Agamben's revisions of death in Montaigne and Heidegger find an antecedent in Sartre's *The Transcendence of the Ego*, which develops an understanding of consciousness set against the teleologies of the ego by rethinking consciousness as something self-generating and self-contained. The result is a set of conceptual tools for the maintenance of potentiality both in relation to, and against, the end of life.

One of the central tenets of Agamben's political philosophy, Tim Christiaens notes in his chapter, 'Destituent Potential and Camus's Politics of Rebellion', is his defence of destituent potential as an escape from the dialectic of constituent and constituted power. In order to cultivate their inoperativity, human beings should allegedly not try to reform the political system or replace it with a better one through revolutionary action. They should rather, like Bartleby or Paul, withdraw from socio-political life in a life *hos me*. But this proposal disappoints on three levels, according to Christiaens: (1) this ethic of self-subtraction does not produce an impetus for change in actual politics; (2) the messianic tone leads to an all-or-nothing choice between redemption or perdition; and (3) Agamben presumes to derive a positive form of intersubjective praxis from nothing but negatives, such as 'in-operativity' or 'im-potentiality'. In response to these shortcomings, Christiaens presents Camus's politics of rebellion as a viable alternative reading of destituent potential. According to Christiaens, the experience of suffering induces people to rebel against evil and thereby create a better world without necessarily leading to either reform or revolution, in Camus's perspective. The focus is on combatting suffering rather than installing a particular form of life. In contrast to Agamben's life *hos me*, Camus's politics of rebellion, Christiaens concludes, affirms the actual, present world, values small-scale improvements and gives positive guidelines for collective conduct.

Transitioning from a generalised politics to the politics of postcolonialism, Susan Dianne Brophy examines Agamben's understanding of the exception through the framework of Fanonian existentialism in her chapter, 'A Politics Like No Other: Agamben, Fanon and the Colonial

Fracture'. Here, Brophy brings the limits of Agamben's writings about the being/praxis relation into relief. In Sartre's 'Orphée noir', Brophy begins, the detached posture that necessitates objectivity emanates from the white man's ability to see from an 'uncomplicated' standpoint. Fanon, however, insists that Sartre's existentialist position – radical in so far as it universalises the possibility of a will to freedom – cannot account for the overarching factors that differentiate experiences of alienation and complicate the will to freedom. Though he rebukes Sartre on this point, Fanon nevertheless adheres to a degree of Sartrean nihilism, Brophy argues, which is necessary in order to destroy the shackles of alienation forged by colonialism. As a result of this decolonisation imperative, Fanonian existentialism is multivalent in a manner that extends beyond Agamben's framework of negation. According to Brophy, Fanon's existentialism calls for an *emancipatory* understanding of being/praxis, which is meant to chase away the detachment of presumed superiority that perpetuates relations of oppression and provide an avenue of empowerment through which self-knowledge can translate into political action.

This is followed by a chapter under my authorship, 'Dis/Belief in Agamben and de Silentio', that a few years ago first inspired the project at hand. Straddling theistic and atheistic worldviews, I was taken with Agamben's peculiar, a/theistic depiction of God and shortly thereafter realised how the philosopher's work might speak to the fractured origins of existentialism, which is sometimes traced back to Kierkegaard and other times traced back to Nietzsche. *Agamben and the Existentialists* is, in some ways, a culmination of that project, but it is also a first step towards discerning how Agamben might be reimagined in the context of existentialism, and likewise how existentialism, which is currently experiencing something of a resurgence, may find novel expression in the works of Agamben. Offering a bridge to more explicit discussions of Christian existentialism, my chapter paves the way for the final chapter of our volume, 'The Existential Situation and Christian Experience: Messianism and Eschatological Salvation', by Daniel Minch. Agamben has drawn heavily on Christian sources to reframe contemporary philosophical discussions of economics, government and law, Minch writes. But Agamben's reflections on Christianity almost completely ignore many of the important voices shaping contemporary theological discourse and Christian self-understanding post Vatican II. Making up for this oversight, Minch brings Agamben's formulation of messianic time into a constructive dialogue with the eschatological hermeneutics of the existentialist Dominican theologian Edward Schillebeeckx. Schillebeeckx's attention to the 'existential situation' of contemporary people was a key part of his development of an eschatological framework. This chapter presents a constructive dialogue between Agamben's notion of 'messianism' and a hermeneutically based Christian eschatology that rounds out our study of *Agamben and the Existentialists*.

Notes

1. Giorgio Agamben, *The Omnibus Homo Sacer* (Stanford: Stanford University Press, 2017), pp. 370–1.
2. Ibid.
3. Ibid. p. 438.
4. Ibid. p. 1243.
5. Giorgio Agamben, *Language and Death* (Minneapolis: University of Minnesota Press, 1991), p. 36.
6. Ibid. p. 20.
7. Ibid. p. 27.
8. Ibid. p. 30.
9. Ibid.
10. Ibid.
11. Ibid. p. 20.
12. Ibid. p. 24.
13. Giorgio Agamben, *Infancy and History: The Destruction of Experience*, trans. Liz Heron (London and New York: Verso, 1993), p. 52.
14. Giorgio Agamben, *The Time That Remains: A Commentary on the Letter to the Romans* (Stanford: Stanford University Press, 2005), p. 137.
15. Ibid. p. 49.
16. George Cotkin, *Existential America* (Baltimore and London: Johns Hopkins University Press, 2003), p. 91.
17. Ibid. p. 92.
18. Apart from Leif Bork Hansen's article, discussed in the next paragraph, the closest we get are Rebecca Gould's 'Laws, Exceptions, Norms: Kierkegaard, Schmitt, and Benjamin on the Exception', *Telos: A Quarterly Journal of Politics, Philosophy, Critical Theory, Culture, and the Arts* 162 (2013); Bartholomew Ryan's 'Carl Schmitt: Zones of Exception and Appropriation', in *Kierkegaard's Influence in Social-Political Thought*, ed. Jon Stewart (London: Routledge, 2011); and Collin McQuillan's 'The Real State of Emergency: Agamben on Benjamin and Schmitt', *Studies in Social and Political Thought* 18 (2010). Gould's article focuses on the relationship between Kierkegaard and Schmitt, while Ryan's and McQuillan's articles focus on the relationship between Schmitt and Agamben; neither, however, consider the relationship between Kierkegaard and Agamben.
19. Jacob Taubes, *The Political Theology of Paul* (Stanford: Stanford University Press, 2004), p. 65.
20. Søren Kierkegaard, *Fear and Trembling: Repetition* (Princeton: Princeton University Press, 1983), pp. 227, 229.
21. Leif Bork Hansen, 'Giorgio Agamben: State of Exception', in *Kierkegaard's Influence on Social-Political Thought*, ed. Jon Stewart (London: Routledge, 2011).
22. Ibid. pp. 24–5.
23. Bartholomew Ryans, *Kierkegaard's Indirect Politics: Interludes with Schmitt, Benjamin, and Adorno* (New York: Rodopi, 2014), p. 95.
24. Ibid. p. 4.
25. Agamben, *The Omnibus*, p. 1248.
26. Ibid. p. 1275.
27. Ibid. p. 1217.

28. Søren Kierkegaard, *Fear and Trembling, The Sickness unto Death*, trans. Walter Lowrie (Garden City, NY: Doubleday & Company, Inc.), pp. 162–3.
29. Jean-Paul Sartre, 'Kierkegaard: The Singular Universal', *We Have Only One Life to Live: The Selected Essays of Jean-Paul Sartre, 1939–1975*, ed. Ronald Aronson and Adrian van den Hoven (New York: New York Review of Books, 2013), p. 424.
30. Walter Kaufmann, *Existentialism from Dostoevsky to Sartre* (Royal Oak, Auckland: Pickle Partners Publishing, 2016), p. 7.
31. Ibid.
32. Jean-Paul Sartre, *Existentialism is a Humanism*, trans. Carol Macomber, ed. John Kulka (New Haven and London: Yale University Press, 2007), p. 20.
33. Gordon Marino, ed., *Basic Writings of Existentialism* (New York: Modern Library, 2004), p. xiv.
34. Ibid.
35. Thomas Flynn, *Existentialism: A Brief Insight* (New York and London: Sterling, 2006), p. 14.
36. Taubes, *The Political Theology of Paul*, p. 72.
37. Anke Snoek, 'Frans Kafka', in *Agamben's Philosophical Lineage*, ed. Adam Kotsko and Carlo Salzani (Edinburgh: Edinburgh University Press, 2007), p. 157.
38. Ibid. p. 156.
39. Agamben, *The Omnibus*, p. 42.
40. Ibid.
41. Jean-Paul Sartre, *Existentialism is a Humanism*, ed. John Kulka, trans. Carol Macomber (New Haven and London: Yale University Press, 2007), p. 25.
42. Sartre, *Existentialism is a Humanism*, p. 23.
43. John Gillespie, 'Sartre and God: A Spiritual Odyssey? Part 1', *Sartre Studies International* 19.1 (2013): 82.
44. Jakob Taubes, *The Political Theology of Paul*, trans. D. Hollander (Stanford: Stanford University Press, 2003), 65.
45. Ibid. p. 108.
46. Ulrich Rauff, 'An Interview with Giorgio Agamben', *German Law Journal* 5.5 (2004): 612–13.
47. Giorgio Agamben, *The Man without Content*, trans. Georgia Albert (Stanford: Stanford University Press, 1999), p. 93.

1
Agamben and the Sovereign Exception

Chapter 2

The Many Faces of a Hidden God: Agamben's Relations to Kierkegaard Reconsidered

Lucas Lazzaretti

Blind Paths and Point of View

Agamben's relations to Kierkegaard seem already to have a well-known path that goes from Agamben, through Carl Schmitt, to Kierkegaard. Yet, Agamben's relations to Kierkegaard would not be simply mediated by Schmitt (and Jacob Taubes, to some extent) but would be determined by the concept of the exception and the field of political theology as a whole. It is true that part of Agamben's philosophical project deals with the concept of the exception in a careful and cautious way, and it is equally true that Schmitt, among all of the political, social, metaphysical and ontological philosophers, was the one who accurately presented what could be taken as the most rigorous analysis of the relation between our modern states' constitutions and the concept of 'exception'. It is also true that Agamben, knowing Schmitt's importance in these matters, starts his *Homo Sacer* project with the German philosopher's insights on politics and his thesis on political theology, a consideration intended to surpass Schmitt's analysis and, most of all, Schmitt's teleology in defence of a total state. Finally, it is also true that Schmitt himself brought Kierkegaard into this debate when, in his *Political Theology*, he mentioned, in a rather suggestive and mysterious way, that a 'protestant theologian who demonstrated the vital intensity possible in theological reflection'[1] understood the real meaning of 'exception'. Schmitt quotes Kierkegaard's *Repetition*, a book that is in the middle of all possible Agamben–Kierkegaard relations, partially because of the word 'exception' and partially because of Schmitt's reading of it.

It is perhaps strange that Agamben's relations to Kierkegaard are solely determined by Schmitt once it is known that the Italian philosopher was influenced by many thinkers who had dealt with Kierkegaard's philosophy, such as Heidegger, Benjamin, Blanchot and so on. Someone with such notorious erudition, as Agamben frequently demonstrates in his books, would probably be aware of Kierkegaard's works beyond this predetermined field, knowing more than just one book and one concept. Nonetheless, why do we accept that Agamben is opposed and contrary to Kierkegaard? If Kierkegaard's view of the concept of the exception is determined by Schmitt's interpretation, then the Danish philosopher becomes almost a fundamentalist theologian who takes God's side at any time. Oddly enough, if that were the case, all Kierkegaard's careful comments on the complexities of human existence would lose their weight and importance. In order to indicate Kierkegaard's concept of exception in its existential potentiality – a potentiality that puts his works in relation to Agamben – we need to show how the exception can be understood not only as determined by God's perspective. We need to show the many faces of a hidden God in order to see how the exception can be treated existentially.

Considering this problematic beginning, this chapter intends to present three particular points: (1) To consider the problematic consequences of an interpretation that assumes Agamben's relations to Kierkegaard through Schmitt, showing how this is not only unproductive for readings of Agamben and Kierkegaard, but also with regard to the concept of the exception. (2) To show that Agamben himself presents an alternative path to his relations with Kierkegaard in his writings, that is, the possible mediation that Benjamin represents. Benjamin is one important influence of Agamben's analysis of the concept of exception and, just like Schmitt, was also influenced by Kierkegaard. Considering Benjamin's *Critique of Violence* and establishing a comparison between the point of view in this text and the one presented in *Fear and Trembling*, it is possible to bring Agamben near to Kierkegaard in another way. (3) To analyse Agamben's relations to Kierkegaard in a new perspective, considering how Agamben's reflections on the concept of exception are not opposed to Kierkegaard's existential philosophy, demonstrating not only the proximity but also the complementarity of these two authors.

Kierkegaard through Schmitt: Between the Poet and God's Exception

The first sentence of Schmitt's *Political Theology* establishes the core of his philosophical analysis on the issue of politics: 'Sovereign is he who decides on the exception.'² Schmitt's philosophical project focused at the same time on two different realms: on the one hand, he tries to analyse the political-juridical situation of the State, both in a theoretical and in a historical-practical way; on the other hand, he tries to compose a project that would solve the problems of an unstable and unsatisfactory modern state. Schmitt's criticism of a 'pluralistic state',³ the kind of political arrangement found in the parliamentary legislative state of his time, takes him to a point where the practical fragility and insecurity of the State is considered in opposition to its theoretical position, where this essentially political institution would present itself as a stable juridical term. The sovereign is the figure that should deal with the fact that a state is a *situation*, a contingency that can fall and decay at any moment.⁴

The sovereign presented by Schmitt is the one who decides when the 'state of exception' (*Ausnahmenzustand*) begins precisely because he is aware of the *situational* feature of the State. Because of this double standard revealed by the concept of sovereign, Schmitt had to recognise that the exception, as something simultaneously both *inside* and *outside* the State, is a 'borderline concept', something *in-between*.⁵ Being between the Law and the No-Law, between the political and juridical, this is the essence of exception. However, when Schmitt determines that the sovereign is the one to decide when the exception begins and ends, he inevitably instantiates the sovereign as being exceptional on his own terms.⁶ This could be seen as a fundamental problem, as Agamben will eventually do himself, but instead is taken by Schmitt as being the very essence of his philosophical project. When Schmitt tries to find the legitimate justification of his concepts of the sovereign and the exception, he intensifies this fundamental problem to a maximum degree.

This is precisely the point where Schmitt quotes Kierkegaard, where the exception must find its legitimate ground in order to justify the sovereign's place and function in his theory of the State. Preparing his argumentation and the proper space to quote a 'protestant theologian', Schmitt starts to talk about the exception in a broader way, metaphysically, and pointing to an 'existential' level where concreteness and life are intertwined. He does so after criticising the 'rationalist' position that he traces from Locke to Kelsen, a rationalism considered insufficient to deal with the actuality (*Wirklichkeit*) of concrete life.⁷ Taking a critical position against 'rationalism' allows Schmitt to go even further into a metaphysical basis: 'precisely a philosophy of concrete life must not withdraw from the exception and the extreme case, but must be in it to the highest degree.'⁸ This is not the realm of a political philosophy, but it is certainly the realm of an *existential philosophy*. With this in mind, Schmitt can suggest that the 'exception is more interesting than the rule', because 'the rule proves nothing; the exception proves everything'.⁹ In this 'philosophy of concrete life' the relation between sovereign and exception was suddenly set aside and a new relation was now established between the exception and the 'general' or the 'universal', a relation that substitutes identity (sovereign = exception) through differentiation (exception ≠ universal). It is only through the passage from a political to an 'existential' realm that Schmitt can provide the adequate space to quote Kierkegaard concerning a conditioned and previously determined term that would fit his intentions. The passage quoted is taken from *Repetition*, a book signed by 'Constantin Constantius', a pseudonym:

> The exception explains the general and itself. And if one wants to study the general correctly, one only needs to look around for an actual exception [*wirkliche Ausnahme*]. It reveals everything more clearly than does the general. Endless talk about the general becomes boring; there are exceptions. If they cannot be explained, then the general also cannot be explained. The difficulty is usually noticed because the general is not thought about with passion but with a comfortable superficiality. The exception, on the other hand, thinks the general with intense passion.¹⁰

As Bartholomew Ryan has shown, 'Schmitt has modified and edited his quotation from Kierkegaard's *Repetition*' in a way that 'is not to be found in any German editions', an alteration intensified by the fact that Schmitt substituted the political term 'legitimate' (*berettiget*) – the term used by Kierkegaard – for the more philosophical term 'actual' (*wirklich*).¹¹ If 'legitimate' is a term closer to a political discourse, why should Schmitt change it for 'actual', a concept that is deeply entrenched in the whole history of philosophy in a metaphysical sense? Because Schmitt is looking at Kierkegaard as if he can find with him the justification for a universal concept of *exception* that is created in a metaphysical/existential ground. But when Schmitt comes to the point of trying to gain this conceptual ground, he has already started with assumptions about the sovereign, the decision and the political that will necessarily determine the concept of exception that Schmitt wants to extract from Kierkegaard's text.

In the way Schmitt interprets *Repetition*, the exception is not only a concept with its own determinations, but it also operates as a determination of the 'general' or 'universal' (*Allgemeine*). Schmitt speaks therefore about an 'actual exception' since he wants to assert that his idea of the exception, precisely because it is a concrete actuality, should be regarded as the fundamental principle to all universality. What is actual (*wirklich*) is concrete; what is concrete must be particular. If the universal cannot explain the particular or the exception, then the exception should be able to explain itself and the universal at the same time. But in the moment that Schmitt argues that this should be the case, he assumes something that is completely foreign to Kierkegaard's existential philosophy. Schmitt ends up transforming his concept of exception through the measure and mediation of the concept of the universal in such a way that the exception's 'legitimacy' – that word that Schmitt hid – becomes a 'generality'. More than that, the concept of the exception receives its legitimacy when it is able to determine itself *and* the 'universal', a movement that necessarily takes the particularity of the exception.

Schmitt's argument here faces a crucial problem: the confusion between particular and general leads to a confusion between exception and universal. Initially, he states that the exception is apprehended from the particular, a case in which the particular is the phenomenon that allows the analysis and the conceptualisation to occur. However, as soon as the concept of the exception is determined as some sort of ground to itself *and* to the universal, then the exception starts to receive its determination not from the particular, but from the general. This only happens because Schmitt's whole point of view is that of someone or something that is superior, elevated, transcendental and exterior to the distinction between the particular and the general. To this Godlike type, the particular will be at some point subsumed to a 'total set' in the sense that the 'particular' is still part of a set that is defined by something universal. There is no particular-general to the God–sovereign relation because all it can envision is the dynamic that unveils the unity between the exception and the universal. This is the consequence of Schmitt's conceptualisation: the exception becomes the rule or the 'main state' because in its metaphysical basis this exception forces its way to the universal's place and role. Schmitt grounds this metaphysical basis using his interpretation of Kierkegaard's idea of exception.

This Schmittian conceptual structure has an important consequence to the way Kierkegaard's concept of exception is understood by Agamben. Kierkegaard is comprehended as the philosopher who provided a metaphysical basis for legitimising the God–sovereign relationship. The first sentence in Agamben's *Homo Sacer* defines this situation both in analytical and critical ways: 'The paradox of sovereignty consists in the fact the sovereign is, at the same time, outside and inside the juridical order.'[12] For this reason, Kierkegaard would be on the opposite side of Agamben's intentions since Kierkegaard would be allegedly grounding this paradox through his idea of exception.

If one considers *Repetition* in the context of Kierkegaard's works, the first thing to note is the fact that this is a text signed by a pseudonym, Constantin Constantius, who discusses the concept of repetition by analysing the example of a Young Man. As he relates, this particular Young Man's story is somewhat trivial: he had fallen in love with a girl, proposed to her and she accepted, and now that he should be able to fulfil his desire and get married he has changed his mind and wants to break up with his bride. The Young Man confides his situation to Constantius. What the pseudonym sees in the whole story, however, is something completely determined by his own interest to consider the fact that the Young Man is between the position of a naive creature without interiority and the position of a *poet*. According to Constantius, the Young Man wants to break up because the girl was the 'occasion' for him to feel the power of his own interiority sprouting; the occasion for him to become a poet. But following the path opened by the occasion demands from the Young Man that he reinforce his interiority in opposition to the rules of exteriority, that is, the social conventions that impose upon him values such as honour, loyalty and the importance of marriage. The opposition that Constantius creates is one between this general rule of exteriority assumed as the rules of convention and the power and self-determinacy of one's own interiority and personality.

As the book progresses, we can feel that this possibility-of-a-poet agrees that marital love is only another form of constraint imposed from an 'exteriority'. But the Young Man also recognises that he is unable to become the poet or the aesthetician that Constantius wants him to be.[13] From one side, the Young Man sees himself as stuck between two positions, unable to establish the determination of his own differentiation in some absolute way. From another side, Constantius wants to see something already singular in the poetic potentiality of this Young Man, pointing out how 'a poetic productivity [*digterisk Productivitet*] awakened in him on a scale I had never believed possible'.[14] The Young Man's sin, according to Constantius, was to dedicate his poetic potency to that one girl and not to himself and, as a result, to the production of a 'poetry' that would be beneficial to everybody. These two positions are essential if we want to comprehend Kierkegaard's way of indicating the nuances and perspectives that are taking place. In terms of a relation between particular and universal, the Young Man recognises his incapability to find a self-determination in order to differentiate himself as particular in opposition to the universal. Constantius, however, is trying to demonstrate a strange structure in which the Young Man's poetical potentiality would be perceived as a particular that differentiates itself from the universal only in the sense that this same 'particular' would be later transformed in the convenient ground to the universal. Constantius's position is not the one to be followed, Kierkegaard indicates through subtle argumentation. Rather, Constantius's position is the one to be regarded as suspicious because of the way the pseudonym moves from his 'wishes' of a poetic potentiality to be fulfilled in actuality to the thesis on an idea of the 'exception' presented at the end of the book. The Young Man perceives the difficulty of finding anything sufficiently grounded to support him in determining his interiority. When he asks in a letter, 'how did I get involved [*Interessent*] in this big enterprise called actuality [*Virkeligheden*]?',[15] he is acknowledging his position of being in-between (*inter-esse*). The Young Man then turns to God in his considerations of Job, looking for an example of this lack of determination. In a way, the Young Man can see the reasons behind his troubled situation, but because he is immersed in his own 'immediacy' he cannot overcome his condition. He indicates that a governance could help him, but once he is *in-between*, any determination would be still eternally far from a hidden God that insistently does not show his face.[16] Kierkegaard thus presents how the Young Man's decision is not located in the right place.

It is Constantius, however, who delivers the last word in his 'concluding letter', trying to solve the problem left by the Young Man. The solution would be Constantius's concept of exception: an attempt to overcome the *in-between* situation by creating a structure that would legitimise the 'particular' as a self-determining potency that could substitute for the lack of a 'universal' determination. According to Constantius, 'such an exception is a poet, who constitutes the transition to the truly aristocratic exceptions, to the religious exception'.[17] Constantius sees the possibility of a relation to God, but he sees that only as a mere possibility, due to God's hidden face. The poet's exception is a 'false exception' since it is determined only by the poet in his immanent position of being a 'particular' and not a 'universal'. The poet that Constantius takes as the 'exception' puts himself in the position of ideality in order to overcome the immediacy of his ungrounded actuality, but, in doing so, the poet establishes a self-determination that takes the hidden God's place. The poet tries to take God's place but because this is impossible his exception relies on a mistake.

Schmitt's exception seems to fall precisely into Constantius's trap. Schmitt assumes, with Constantius, that he is dealing with a real exception in which the absolute determination makes of itself an exception by the power of its own absolute character. In other words, Schmitt thinks he is dealing with a Godlike position that he will identify with the sovereign. However, because Constantius's position is not the one of a Godlike type, being rather the poet-like type, Schmitt's exception ends up incurring the same 'romantic' or 'aesthetic' error that is proper to the pseudonym. In political terms, if the sovereign is the one who decides on the exception, then he necessarily is already not a 'particular', but is also not a 'universal'. The sovereign is a 'universal' that produces the exception of his own universality in an attempt to legitimise its own total self-determination. The consequence of this structure would be the tendency to understand the sovereign, the State and the political realm as a sort of teleological totalitarianism.

Agamben's critique of Schmitt's exception targets this point. Agamben agrees that, if we go beyond the juridical excuses proper to a certain legal positivism in which the Law and the State excludes politics in order to create a non-conflictual and bureaucratic reality, then we will find that the modern state is violently and continually inserting exceptions to its rules in order to maintain its own power. Yet, Agamben sees Schmitt's theory as a phenomenon of this logic of power, control, violence and oppression. According to Agamben, Schmitt's praising of an idea of exception does not present a critique of this structure. Therefore, Agamben's critique of Schmitt's exception points out the paradox indicated before:

> The situation created in the exception has the peculiar characteristic that it cannot be defined either as a situation of fact or as a situation of right, but instead institutes a paradoxical threshold of indistinction between the two. It is not a fact, since it is only created through the suspension of the rule. But for the same reason, it is not even a juridical case in point, even if it opens the possibility of the force of law. This is the ultimate meaning of the paradox that Schmitt formulates when he writes that the sovereign decision 'proves itself not to need law to create law.'[18]

As it was demonstrated, this critique could also be applied to Constantius's case. The paradox, taken as the 'threshold of indistinction between the two', perfectly describes the problematic issue around Constantius's idea of the exception: neither a particular (fact) nor a universal (right); something that posits itself between the two as a self-exception that assumes the place of an absolute and, precisely because of that, tends to convert its desire for an *absolute* into the production of a *self-referential totality*. The poet that Kierkegaard portrays and that Constantius venerates in his idea of the exception is an attempt of a 'self-referential totality' that could only have as its *telos* the paradoxical condition in which the poet is entangled. As Kierkegaard sees it: aesthetically the poet can be a wonderful thing, given his power of ideality, but existentially and subjectively this Romantic poet is problematic because he inevitably will try to take a Godlike position to justify his own viewpoint.

Agamben's critique helps to make evident something that is already implied in Kierkegaard: politically, the poet can be dangerous since his tendency to take himself as an absolute reference for its own determination leads to a legitimisation of a totalitarian postulate. In this sense, Kierkegaard would agree with Agamben's critique because the exception presented in *Repetition* is Constantius's point of view and not Kierkegaard's. If we want to go further in our understanding on the concept of exception, however, we must also take *Fear and Trembling* into consideration. If Schmitt's exception guided us into Constantius's exception, it will be Benjamin's critique of violence that will make it possible to see Kierkegaard's presentation of exception through another angle altogether, one that likewise illuminates Agamben's stake in the game.

Benjamin: Violence and Exception

Agamben's analysis of Schmitt's notion of the exception critically addresses the problem that is inherent to the modern state's constitution. However, in order to provide the conceptual approach required to overcome a first round of analysis, Agamben searches for a criticism that shares with Schmitt certain basic assumptions, though, at the same time, for a criticism that indicates a different perspective. Walter Benjamin's essay 'Critique of Violence' allows Agamben to find the passage from a 'negative critique' – where the target should unveil itself – to a 'positive critique' – where some new element will appear coming from the previous unveiling. As Adam Kotsko points out, 'in *Homo Sacer*, Agamben devotes a crucial "threshold" to an extremely compressed reading of Benjamin's "Critique of Violence" one that provides a transition between his elaboration of the logic of sovereignty and his analysis of the concept of *homo sacer* or "bare life."'[19] According to Agamben, Benjamin's essay demonstrates a 'dialectical oscillation between the violence that posits law and the violence that preserves it'.[20] At the time of his composition of the essay in 1920, Benjamin had not read Schmitt's *Political Theology*, and for that reason the term 'exception' was not as present in 'Critique of Violence', as evidently as it appears, for example, in his later 'Theses on the Philosophy of History'. However, even if the term 'exception' is not evident, the essay's first sentence already establishes the *in-between* situation: 'The task of a critique of violence can be summarized as that of expounding its relation to law [*Recht*] and justice [*Gerechtigkeit*].'[21] Agamben noticed that even though 'exception' is not clearly addressed in Benjamin's essay, the consequences of this relation between 'law' and 'justice' would necessarily reach the paradoxical point in which the exception finds its place. According to Agamben, when Benjamin discusses the violence that posits law and the violence that maintains law he already implies the *in-between* situation where the differentiating lines are blurred and a new state or condition seems to appear. Interpreting Benjamin in that way allows Agamben to insert a consideration of the 'state of exception' in Benjamin's critique of violence:

> Sovereign violence and the state of exception, therefore, do not appear in the essay, and it is not easy to say where they would stand with respect to the violence that posits law and the violence that preserves it. The root of

the ambiguity of divine violence is perhaps to be sought in precisely this absence. The violence exercised in the state of exception clearly neither preserves nor simply posits law, but rather conserves it in suspending it and posits it in excepting itself from it. In this sense, sovereign violence, like divine violence, cannot be wholly reduced to either one of the two forms of violence whose dialectic the essay undertook to define. This does not mean that sovereign violence can be confused with divine violence. The definition of divine violence becomes easier, in fact, precisely when it is put in relation with the state of exception.[22]

Agamben here performs an argumentative trick. The difficulty of Benjamin's essay is presented in the idea of a 'divine violence'. Clarifying this idea should allow Agamben to think how the 'exception' could be approached in Benjamin's terms. Because it is difficult to see where 'sovereign violence' and the 'state of exception' enter the essay, Agamben assumes that it would be better if they were related to 'divine violence', the third element that makes the relation in itself possible. 'Sovereign violence' is not identical to 'divine violence', Agamben cautions, but since 'sovereign violence' is more immediately concrete and evident than 'divine violence', one can easily assume that establishing some sort of analogy between one and the other would be beneficial. As Agamben says, 'the definition of divine violence becomes easier, in fact, precisely when it is put in relation with the state of exception.'[23] Agamben inverts the argument to his own benefit: initially, he was interested in how Benjamin's essay could allow him to critically analyse the idea of exception in a more profound form; now it seems that his own analysis will benefit Benjamin's essay, at least regarding the idea of 'divine violence'.

With Schmitt, the exception moves from one specific and exceptional case to the rule and determination of everything. With Benjamin, as Agamben interprets matters, the direction is completely the opposite. We start in a limited and contingent position in order to be able to understand 'divine violence'. In other words, we change from a sovereign point of view to a merely existent point of view, a position that could be understood as a being that simply exists.

Benjamin's position is not a simple change of direction; it is a true change of perspective. Instead of occupying the location of a theoretically conceived sovereign – as Schmitt does – it occupies the position of a subject who lives within the unlawful condition of an exception. The sovereign is never the target of violence and consequently this Godlike figure does not have to analyse the 'divine' features of suffering the conditions of violence. As Benjamin asserts:

> one might perhaps consider the surprising possibility that the law's interest in a monopoly of violence vis-à-vis individuals is explained not by the inten-

tion of preserving legal ends but, rather, by the intention of preserving the law itself; that violence, when not in the hands of the law, threatens it not by the ends that it may pursue but by its mere existence outside the law.[24]

According to Benjamin's analysis, there are two types of exceptions: one that takes the sovereign's position and one that takes the divine's position. Once the Schmittian sovereign exception reveals an in-between situation on a theoretical level exempted from suffering violence, the divine exception considered by Benjamin shows the concreteness of its reality. There is an opposition between a transcendental and an immanent type of exception. Meanwhile, though the transcendence of a sovereign exception does not help us to understand the determination of a concrete violent exception, the divine exception allows us to draw a line, moving, as Agamben noticed, to a more concrete notion of 'bare life':

> The violence that Benjamin defines as divine is instead situated in a zone in which it is no longer possible to distinguish between exception and rule. It stands in the same relation to sovereign violence as the state of actual exception, in the eighth thesis, does to the state of virtual exception. This is why (that is, insofar as divine violence is not one kind of violence among others but only the dissolution of the link between violence and law) Benjamin can say that divine violence neither posits nor conserves violence, but deposes it. Divine violence shows the connection between the two violences – and, even more, between violence and law – to be the single real content of law. . . . This is why it is not by chance that Benjamin, with a seemingly abrupt development, concentrates on the bearer of the link between violence and law, which he calls 'bare life' (*blosses Leben*), instead of defining divine violence. The analysis of this figure – whose decisive function in the economy of the essay has until now remained unthought – establishes an essential link between bare life and juridical violence.[25]

The characteristic of *being in* or *merely being* a 'bare life' can only be comprehended when it is linked with a manifestation of violence that always correlates itself, on one hand, to a power that is hiding its face and, on the other hand, to a concretely existent human being who depends on unveiling the hidden face in order to break up with an unjustified, unbearable and incomprehensible violence. A 'bare life' faces the condition of being simultaneously 'sacred' and 'not-sacred'. 'Divine violence' establishes a line whereby the existing individual can distinguish between the Law and the Un-Law. At the same time as this *borderline* appears, the evidence of 'bare life' also appears. However, 'divine violence' cannot be directly addressed as an exception given its character of immanence. It definitely demonstrates to the individual the condition of exception, but only as a glimpse of it.

Once 'divine violence' helps us to see the borderline and the condition of 'bare life', it also helps us to see that there is something beyond that line, something that is not sovereign. Because Benjamin's perspective is opposed to Schmitt's, he cannot simply transform the immanence of divine violence into a problematic transcendence. Benjamin writes about a mythical violence, the one that 'in its archetypal form is a mere manifestation of the gods'.[26] Mythical violence is in the realm of transcendence but merely as an original violence. This is a primeval image that brings forth the idea of *lawmaking* as a power of what posits the law and still holds out the possibility of suspending it. As Benjamin writes, 'lawmaking is powermaking, assumption of power, and to that extent an immediate manifestation of violence'.[27]

Mythical violence is the clearest evidence of an exception because it is at the same time inside and outside the law through its determination of power. The continuation of the law is based on the god's capacity to punish and fulfil its power. As an original image of all violence, mythical violence partially solves the problem of a sovereign who tries to elevate itself to a position of transcendence. More than this, mythical violence provides a way for concrete individuals to understand how, in the exception, rules are determined contingently and how they, as actual targets of violence, will be the ones to suffer the exception. In Benjamin's essay, as Agamben explores, an inversion of perspectives allows us to see how the universal posits the particular as an exception. It is the one who occupies the position of universality who determines who are the ones that will be taken as an exception, not the other way around.

This is the reason why Agamben sees in Benjamin's idea of 'bare life' something unique, because it demonstrates the concreteness of a phenomenon that opens itself to the analysis of its genealogical structure, and is secured precisely through the passage from divine to mythical violence. It is here that a structure is guaranteed in terms of its transcendence as well. However, Benjamin's bare life ends up not being explored in existential terms. For his part, Benjamin is able to invert the perspective concerning violence and its relation to the exception, but he remains in a position where analysis is centred on the general structures of Law and not on the existential consequences to concrete individuals.[28] Agamben, however, tries to address this existential realm in his own work, and, for this reason, a new interpretation of Kierkegaard's exception can provide a different path to their relations.

Kierkegaard: Exception and Suffering

Once we highlight how Constantius's exception should not be confused with 'Kierkegaard's idea of exception', then we should ask what other ideas of exception he can present us with. Kierkegaard had repeatedly juxtaposed his pseudonym authors really close to each other, sometimes publishing two different books in the same day. This is the case with *Repetition* and *Fear and Trembling*, both published on 16 October 1843. Publishing them as such inevitably meant that these books were somehow related. More than that, I would suggest, they are actually in dialogue with each other.

Repetition's idea of exception tries to assume the poet's point of view or, to be more precise, it tries to elevate the poet to being the one who posits himself as an exception, though all of this activity is presented by a pseudonym that is not himself a poet. *Fear and Trembling*, however, is written by *Johannes de Silentio*, a pseudonym that is, in fact, a poet. Precisely because of this situation, the pseudonym does not start with the assumption of his own elevation. On the contrary, knowing by his own experience the insufficiency of a poet-like position in its relation to the Absolute, he wants to indicate the exception in a more concrete and existential way, that is, as an exception that is imposed on the existing being by the Absolute.

The first thing to be mentioned in this regard is that in *Fear and Trembling* the term *Undtagelsen* is not used as it is in *Repetition*. There is no theoretical discussion on a 'conceptual exception', and Johannes de Silentio does not intend to push forward an 'analytical agenda' in the same way that Constantius does with the concept of repetition. The idea of exception is presented in *Fear and Trembling* through the considerations and reflections on Abraham's 'temptation', faith and myth. Silentio's intention seems to be dialectical in the sense that he introduces different perspectives in order to show how the meaning of Abraham's story can be perceived.

Silentio's dialectic inverts the meaning of things according to Abraham's singular condition. Usually, to be strong is a sign of being powerful, but, in Abraham's case, being powerless is the true strength because only when all the power is taken from him can the strength of his faith be revealed. The pseudonym's discourse assumes *faith's point of view*, and his eulogy of Abraham is, in fact, a eulogy of 'Abraham's faith', two things Silentio will conveniently differentiate and identify according to his own interests: Abraham's faith and Abraham himself. It is in this dialectic that the exception appears. On the one hand, Silentio's discourse considers how unique and magnificent Abraham's faith is because it not only established the pattern or the rule for all faith in the Judaeo-Christian sense, but it also shows how this rule is based on the fulfilling of an interior-subjective determination rather than an exterior-objective one. On the other hand, Silentio deals with Abraham as a concretely existing human being, someone to whom the demand of faith is also a form of suffering. By juxtaposing both of these approaches, Silentio will indicate already in the preliminary expectoration that 'what is omitted from Abraham's story is the anxiety, because to money I have no ethical obligation, but to the son the father has the highest and holiest'.[29] The ground where these positions meet will be in the discussion about the *teleological suspension of the ethical*. Silentio starts the first *problemata* indicating how the 'exception' will be understood with regard to Abraham's character. This first *problemata* is dedicated to explaining and interpreting Abraham's faith, as well as Abraham himself, through the perspective of a relation between the universal and the singular. The first paragraph is worth being quoted in its totality since it is in this context that the 'exception' is indirectly indicated:

> The ethical as such is the universal, and as the universal it applies to everyone, which from another angle means that it applies at all times. It rests immanent in itself, has nothing outside itself that is its τέλοζ [end, purpose] but is itself the τέλοζ for everything outside itself, and when the ethical has absorbed this into itself, it goes not further. The single individual, sensately and psychically qualified in immediacy, is the individual who has his τέλοζ in the universal, and it is his ethical task continually to express himself in this, to annul his singularity in order to become the universal. As soon as the single individual asserts himself in his singularity before the universal, he sins, and only by acknowledging this can he be reconciled again with the universal. Every time the single individual, after having entered the universal, feels an impulse to assert himself as the single individual, he is in a spiritual trial [*Anfægtelse*], from which he can work himself only by repentantly surrendering as the single individual in the universal. If this is the highest that can be said of man and his existence, then the ethical is of the same nature as a person's eternal salvation, which is his τέλοζ forevermore and at all times, since it would be a contradiction for this to be capable of being surrendered (that is, teleologically suspended), because as soon as this is suspended it is relinquished, whereas that which is suspended is not relinquished but is preserved in the higher, which is its τέλοζ.[30]

Silentio's critique of ethics as the element, practice or theory that can fulfil human existence is grounded in the contradiction between the universal and the singular. Assuming that ethics is necessarily universal, as a rule, then human singularities would not be singular in the sense of a differentiation from the rule. In fact, if ethics is taken as the universality that should determine a human's singularity, the concretely existing human beings would only be singular if they were universal, a contradiction that would annihilate 'singularity'. In other words, when one assumes an ethical viewpoint the whole determination comes only from the universal, to the degree that the singular becomes a mere circumscription within the total scope of universality. Silentio's critique, however, made clear that this contradiction inherent to ethics leads not only to the elimination of all possible 'singularities', but also to the potential oblivion of the particular's relation to the absolute. In order to be determined as a singularity, the particular entity must be able to differentiate itself from the universal, not only existing as the non-universal, but as being the other-from-the-universal. Otherwise, there would be a 'particular *ens*', but never a 'singular *ens*'. Meanwhile constructing his critique, Silentio introduced the idea of a *singularity* that was not evidently present in Constantius's *Repetition*. The particular has a dubious relation to the universal within the poetic point of view due to the fact that it is a contingent 'particular *ens*' that arrogates itself to the universal position, being then a universal-particular or a particular-universal, depending on the way it is seen. In the ethical point of view, however, the particular's relation to the universal loses its ambiguity and it is one-sidedly determined as a mere part of a totality. Consequently, both of them (the ethical and the poetic) posit an impossibility of singularity. The pseudonym in *Fear and Trembling* is talking about Abraham, who is in neither of these positions. Bringing up this issue concerning 'singularity' within a critique of ethics as a teleological universal determination is a way to indicate that a different form of positing the relation between particular and universal is the intended target.

'Faith', Silentio says, 'is namely this paradox that the single individual is higher than the universal.'[31] The pseudonym is careful to specify that the paradox posits the 'singularity' out of the universal power of determination. Since *Fear and Trembling* has a mirror relation with *Repetition*, it is not a surprise that Silentio provides the dialectics for that differentiation through an idea of repetition. As the pseudonym explains, the singular individual can only be higher than the universal 'in such a way that the movement repeats itself, so that after having been in the universal he as the single individual isolates himself as higher than the universal'.[32] Silentio tries to assure the basis for his analysis of a different form of relation between particular and universal, a form that should keep the 'particular's particularity' and the 'universal's universality' in order to reveal the singularity. To do so, Silentio must abolish the tendency of mediation proper to the 'general', a mediation that inserts a third element into the relation between the particular and the universal, one that perverts the relation, transforming and subsuming it to the determinations of generality.

Ethics is teleological by its nature, as Silentio illustrated. Any kind of relation between the concrete individual and the Absolute will be taken by the ethical point of view as an exterior third element. In Abraham's case, the ethical point of view would take God's absurd commandment as a 'spiritual trial', subverting the absurdity and singularity that could preserve the relation between particular and universal. The suspension of the ethical entails the suspension of all mediation, the suspension of all external teleology and the suspension of 'in-differentiation'. But without the ethical, the rule and the general, how can we understand Abraham's actions, since there is no ground for any judgement? Silentio's answer calls us back to the relation between the concrete human being (Abraham) and the Absolute (God), but in such a way that the relation is paradoxically abolished in order to be preserved:

> Why, then, does Abraham do it? For God's sake and – the two are wholly identical – for his own sake. He does it for God's sake because God demands this proof of his faith; he does it for his own sake so that he can prove it. The unity of the two is altogether correctly expressed in the word already used to describe this relationship. It is an ordeal, a temptation.[33]

Establishing an identity between Abraham's action and God's will would necessarily abolish the difference between particular and universal if the ethical or the poetical viewpoint were the centre of this determination. However, from faith's point of view, that is, from the paradox's point of view, it is only through such unity that Abraham can be preserved as a particular, not being subsumed to the universal's determination. And this can only be the case because the determination comes from the Absolute and it is the Absolute's singularity that determines Abraham as an exception. This is the difference between the 'exception' presented in *Fear and Trembling* and that defended by Constantius in *Repetition*. In order to preserve the exception as a singularity, that is, as an exception that cannot be annihilated in the generality and cannot transform itself in the terms of its own universality, Silentio had to indicate that the determination is posited by the Absolute, this strange figure that brings the paradoxical condition of being in and out of universality, this figure that constitutes the universality preserving its own singularity. Without showing its face, the Absolute determines that now this one particular individual is an exception, that he is *in* the exception. The manifestation of this exception – of being an exception – comes to this particular individual as a 'temptation', and it is here that the exception confronts its existential consequences. If we consider things from Abraham's faith-based point of view, the 'temptation' is actually a blessing, because it is through this temptation that the paradox of faith finds the unity between the individual's action and the Absolute's will. More than that, the temptation is the manifestation or evidence of Abraham's singularity, though it is a type of singularity that is determined by the Absolute when it posits the individual as an exception. Silentio had argued that, through temptation, the singular individual finds their singular way of existing:

> But if the ethical is teleologically suspended in this manner, how does the single individual in whom it is suspended exist? He exists as the single individual in contrast to the universal.... How did Abraham exist? He had

faith. This is the paradox by which he remains at the apex, the paradox that he cannot explain to anyone else, for the paradox is that he as the single individual places himself in an absolute relation to the absolute. Is he justified? Again, his justification is the paradoxical, for if he is, then he is justified not by virtue of being something universal but by virtue of being the single individual.[34]

According to Silentio, Abraham's existence as a single individual depends on Abraham's faith. But we know that Abraham's faith depends on Abraham's temptation, and we also know that this temptation is determined by God, and the singularity here is partial once it is only God who determines it. However, Abraham's faith should not be identified with Abraham himself, at least if we want to preserve the possibility of singularity. When we consider Abraham himself, the blessing becomes something completely different: a violence. The determination of Abraham as an exception, even though perpetrated through the relation, is an act of unidimensional violence imposed by God. If the existence is not considered through faith, that is, if existence is not determined by faith, then becoming an exception in these terms cannot be anything but a violence. Even when existence is determined by faith, the violence is potentially there because the beginning of this relation and this determination comes from God, in the sense that it is God who defines if it can be a blessing or a violence. The duality of faith is expressed by the pseudonym's testimony when he indicates the inherent passivity in it: 'Faith is a marvel, and yet no human being is excluded from it; for that which unites all human life is passion [*lidenskab*], and faith is a passion.'[35] The word *lidenskab* brings in its root the verb *at lide*, meaning 'to suffer', that is, the passive position of being affected by someone or something. If faith is a 'passion', then faith is actively determined for human beings by God and passively received by them. Silentio does not escape this complicated situation. He admits that any analysis of Abraham's case would always face the impossibility of overcoming this paradoxical situation, and in such a way that 'one approaches him with a *horror religiosus*'.[36] Silentio tries to understand the existential suffering of Abraham, that is, his condition of being a concrete individual, but he returns to the paradoxical situation in which this analysis of existence can only be done through the analysis of God's violence. This violence, however, shows us the individual's impossibility of determining himself as an exception when he remains under the determination of a transcendental Absolute.

Considering this paradoxical situation, we can now bring Kierkegaard closer to Benjamin. As mentioned previously, Benjamin does not explore the existential consequences of his idea of 'bare life', an idea that is essential to Agamben's project. Kierkegaard's presentation of the exception through

Abraham's case not only reveals a form of exception that is opposed to the one determined by a sovereign point of view (Constantius/Schmitt), but it also reveals the fact that the single individual, the concretely existing human being, in their relation to the Absolute-type figure (God, sovereign and so on), has their existence determined by an imposition that presents itself as a form of violence. The dialectical relation between 'blessing' and 'violence' is, by its own structure, a reflection of an original violence that belongs to the God–human relation, an *original* violence in the sense of a *lawmaking* power as Benjamin states. Receiving the blessing is the evidence of a violence posited by God upon human beings, in the sense that this is not an actual blessing, but merely a violence. Kierkegaard cannot hide the fact that 'blessing', 'grace', 'ordeal' and 'temptation' also mean 'passion', '*pathos*', 'passivity' and 'suffering'. There is no temptation without suffering because there is no blessing without violence. The existential characteristic that is present in *Fear and Trembling* is that of faith; but we understand faith existentially only if we grasp the nuance of suffering and violence. Silentio asserts this in a subtle way throughout the entire book:

> Should we, then, not dare to speak about Abraham? I surely think we can. If I were to speak about him, I would first of all describe the pain of the ordeal. To that end, I would, like a leech, suck all the anxiety and distress and torment out of a father's suffering in order to describe what Abraham suffered, although under it all he had faith.[37]

Silentio announces that Abraham suffered, *although under it all he had faith*, but we can also perceive that being made an exception through God's determination is the situation with respect to violence and not as in the case of a blessing. Faith appears in relation to blessing as the rule appears in relation to law, but violence is under faith and law, as Benjamin's insight has shown. If we consider Kierkegaard's idea of the exception as it is presented in *Fear and Trembling*, we can see that 'bare life' is the violent determination imposed by this Absolute-type figure (God, sovereign). Abraham's case is surely emblematic, but this sort of structure follows Kierkegaard's works and ideas. The exception as a potential violence is present in all of his philosophical considerations, always noting too that the poet-like and the Godlike position is something into which we must not fall. Just as we should not take the poet-like position, because this is a false exception unable to determine our singularity, we cannot depend on God's determination because it excludes us from the relation and, consequently, from singularity. Kierkegaard gives us a paradox to solve, the type of paradox that can be useful when we bring Agamben's philosophy unto an existential ground.

Hidden Faces and Forms of Life

In the last book of the *Homo Sacer* project, *The Use of Bodies*, Agamben considers the theory of hypostases as a way to show that there is no external determination to the forms of life that can assure to themselves the role of substance. If that is the case, life's modes of being cannot find an external element to their existence that would determine life through the paradox of being both inside and outside life in itself. At a certain point, Agamben reaches the theological concept of trinity as some sort of consequence developing from out of this theory of hypostases. Agamben analyses Augustine's argument about the relation (*omnis essentia quae relative dicitur est etiam aliquid excepto relativo*) showing how the logic of exception creates a condition in which human existence becomes something that depends on an 'excepto relativo', that is, an exception that is relative to the relation that establishes the relation, then keeping the elements in relation as foreigners to the relation itself:

> Hence the decisive importance of the formula excepto relativo: it is to be read according to the logic of the exception that we have defined in Homo Sacer I (Agamben 4, pp. 21–22/17–19): the relative is at once included and excluded in the absolute, in the sense that – according to the etymology of the term *ex-ceptio* – it has been 'captured outside', which is to say, included by means of its exclusion. The relativity and the singularity of the persons have been captured in the unitary essence-potential of God, in such a way that they are both excluded and included in it.[38]

Hypostases also have the meaning of 'individual existence', and Agamben's critique of a certain type of exception indicates that we can only think about a 'singularity' of modes of being in life if we overcome the vicious circle of a determination that is external to life/existence itself. This is a determination that posits itself through violence and that maintains its own predominance and hegemony by hiding and covering its face, presenting itself as a blessing with the intention of creating an illusion that introduces violence and dependency as the only possible conditions.

Kierkegaard's analysis of the exception can be interesting if considered in relation to Agamben's philosophical project in two ways: (1) it critiques a certain type of 'exception' that eludes the analysis of life/existence; (2) it shows the paradoxical position that any attempt of forming a conceptual analysis of an *existential exception* will face. Because Kierkegaard understands existence as a tensional relation between extremes (immanence and transcendence), he allows us to establish an analysis that does not have to depend on either of them. Kierkegaard makes it evident that the tensions of existence cannot avoid encountering the exception if one wants to consider the singularity of modes of being as part of existence's potentiality.[39] Everything depends on how the relation between singularity and exception can be established and determined, an issue that Kierkegaard stresses when he makes it clear that, if the determination of an exception comes from the Absolute-like standpoint, then either the individual is fictionally trying to assume this position (as with the poet) or he is suffering with the consequences of it. Assuming this interpretation allows us to reconsider Agamben's relations to Kierkegaard in such a way that some existential interpretations could be reinforced in Agamben's work. In *The Coming Community*, considering the role of ethics, for example, Agamben states that 'there is in effect something that humans are and have to be, but this something is not an essence nor properly a thing: *It is the simple fact of one's own existence as possibility or potentiality.*'[40] That this 'existence as possibility or potentiality' would be, in the end, some form of 'exception', this he seems to understand with a clear intuition. The case is, yet, to find the ground to this new structure of the exception. Maybe, through Kierkegaard, we could consider this ground not only as 'possibility *or* potentiality', but as a 'possibility *of* potentiality'.

Notes

1. Throughout, references will indicate first the original edition and subsequently the English translation. Carl Schmitt, *Politische Theologie: Vier Kapitel zur Lehre von der Souveränität* (Berlin: Duncker & Humblot, 1979), p. 22; *Political Theology*, trans. George Schwab (Chicago: The Chicago University Press, 1985), p. 15.
2. Schmitt, *Politische Theologie*, p. 5; *Political Theology*, p. 11.
3. In order to consider Schmitt's views on the 'pluralistic state', see Carl Schmitt, 'Staatsethik und pluralistischer Staat', *Kant-Studien* 35 (1930).
4. 'All law is "situational law" [*Situationsrecht*].' Schmitt, *Politische Theologie*, p. 13; *Political Theology*, p. 20.
5. 'Only this definition can do justice to a borderline concept [*Grenzbegriff*]. Contrary to the imprecise terminology that is found in popular literature, a borderline concept is not a vague concept, but one pertaining to the outermost sphere.' Schmitt, *Politische Theologie*, p. 5; *Political Theology*, p. 11.
6. Schmitt states that 'it is precisely the exception that makes relevant the subject of sovereignty.' *Politische Theologie*, p. 6; *Political Theology*, p. 12.
7. Schmitt, *Politische Theologie*, p. 14; *Political Theology*, p. 21.
8. Schmitt, *Politische Theologie*, p. 15; *Political Theology*, p. 22.
9. Ibid.
10. This is quoted by Schmitt: *Politische Theologie*, p. 15; *Political Theology*, p. 22. It loosely represents the passage also found in Søren Kierkegaard, *Gjentagelsen- Frygt og Bæven – Philosophiske Smuler – Begrebet Angst – Forord*, Søren Kierkegaards Skrifter IV (Copenhagen: Gads Forlag, 1998) [henceforth *SKS* 4], p. 93; *Fear and Trembling / Repetition*, Kierkegaard Writings VI, trans. Howard V. Hong and Edna H. Hong (Princeton: Princeton University Press, 1983) [henceforth *Repetition*], p. 227.
11. Bartholomew Ryan, *Kierkegaard's Indirect Politics: Interludes with Lúkacs, Schmitt, Benjamin, and Adorno* (Amsterdam: Rodopi, 2014), p. 92.

12. Giorgio Agamben, *Homo Sacer: il potere sovrano e la nuda vita* (Turin: Giulio Einaudi Editore, 2005), p. 19; *Homo Sacer: Sovereign Power and Bare Life*, trans. Daniel Heller-Roazen (Stanford: Stanford University Press, 1998), p. 15.
13. Kierkegaard, *SKS* 4, pp. 59–60; *Repetition*, p. 190.
14. Kierkegaard, *SKS* 4, p. 15; *Repetition*, p. 138.
15. Kierkegaard, *SKS* 4, p. 68; *Repetition*, p. 200.
16. Kierkegaard, *SKS* 4, p. 80; *Repetition*, p. 213.
17. Kierkegaard, *SKS* 4, p. 93; *Repetition*, p. 228.
18. Agamben, *Homo Sacer: Il potere* . . ., p. 23; *Homo Sacer: Sovereign Power* . . ., pp. 18–19.
19. Adam Kotsko, 'Reading the "Critique of Violence"', in *Agamben's Coming Philosophy: Finding a New Use for Theology*, ed. Colby Dickinson and Adam Kotsko (London: Rowman & Littlefield, 2015), p. 41.
20. Agamben, *Homo Sacer: Il potere* . . ., p. 72; *Homo Sacer: Sovereign Power* . . ., p. 63.
21. Walter Benjamin, 'Zur Kritik der Gewalt', in *Gesammelte Schriften* II.1, ed. Rolf Tiedemann and Hermann Schweppenhäuser (Frankfurt am Main: Suhrkamp, 1977), p. 179; 'Critique of Violence', in *Selected Writings*, vol. 1: 1913–1926, ed. Marcus Bullock and Michael W. Jennings. (Cambridge, MA: The Belknap Press of Harvard University Press, 1996), p. 236.
22. Agamben, *Homo Sacer: Il potere* . . ., p. 73; *Homo Sacer: Sovereign Power* . . ., p. 64.
23. Agamben, *Homo Sacer: Il potere* . . ., p. 73; *Homo Sacer: Sovereign Power* . . ., p. 64.
24. Benjamin, 'Zur Kritik der Gewalt', p. 183; 'Critique of Violence', p. 239.
25. Agamben, *Homo Sacer: Il potere* . . ., pp. 74–5; *Homo Sacer: Sovereign Power* . . ., p. 65.
26. Benjamin, 'Zur Kritik der Gewalt', p. 197; 'Critique of Violence', p. 248.
27. Benjamin, 'Zur Kritik der Gewalt', p. 198; 'Critique of Violence', p. 248.
28. It is true that Benjamin attempted to present some considerations about certain 'figures of exception', such as in his work 'On Hashish' or in his analysis of prostitution and the dispossessed.
29. Kierkegaard, *SKS* 4, p. 124; *Fear and Trembling*, p. 28.
30. Kierkegaard, *SKS* 4, p. 148; *Fear and Trembling*, p. 54.
31. Kierkegaard, *SKS* 4, p. 149; *Fear and Trembling*, p. 55.
32. Kierkegaard, *SKS* 4, p. 149; *Fear and Trembling*, p. 55.
33. Kierkegaard, *SKS* 4, p. 153; *Fear and Trembling*, pp. 59–60.
34. Kierkegaard, *SKS* 4, p. 155; *Fear and Trembling*, pp. 61–2.
35. Kierkegaard, *SKS* 4, p. 159; *Fear and Trembling*, pp. 66–7.
36. Kierkegaard, *SKS* 4, p. 154; *Fear and Trembling*, p. 61.
37. Kierkegaard, *SKS* 4, p. 146; *Fear and Trembling*, p. 53.
38. Giorgio Agamben, *L'uso dei corpi*, Homo Sacer IV.2 (Vicenza: Neri Pozza Editore, 2014), p. 190; *The Use of Bodies*, trans. Adam Kotsko (Stanford: Stanford University Press, 2016), p. 144.
39. Potentiality is understood as the potency of becoming. Kierkegaard's concept of existence, *tilværelse*, means the movement of becoming that is potentially inherent to existence.
40. Giorgio Agamben, *La communità che viene* (Turin: Giulio Einaudi Editore, 1990), p. 30; *The Coming Community*, trans. Michael Hardt (Minneapolis: University of Minnesota Press, 2007), p. 42.

Chapter 3

Biopolitics and Probability: Modifications on Life's Way

Virgil W. Brower

> Despite everything people ought to have learned from my maieutic carefulness . . . they will probably bawl out . . . that I know nothing about sociality
> . . .
>
> Kierkegaard's journal[1]

This project retraces activations of Kierkegaard in the development of political theology. It suggests alternative modes of states of exception attributed to him. Several Kierkegaardian themes open themselves to 'something like pure potential'[2] in Agamben, namely: living death, animality, criminality, auto-constitution, modification, liturgy, love and certain articulations of improbabilities.

Genealogy of Infatuations

It is almost comical, distinctly short of divine. The Dane and Dante are thought together. Something borders on humour about the way Agamben twice invokes Kierkegaard in an early essay devoted to the radical naming of the divine as '*Comedy*'. He is included among a solemn few who appreciate the tragic-comic distinction in the development of modern philosophy. But this early engagement seems to strand Kierkegaard exclusively on the tragic stage – as if lacking any laughter on his side[3] – associating *Fear and Trembling* with the Abraham of Averroes: 'the tragic situation par excellence'.[4]

Something is no less tragic about another way Agamben later invokes Kierkegaard as a prophet of the state of exception, by which a delimited extreme becomes a norm. In §2.4 of *Remnants of Auschwitz*, the 'extreme situation' or 'limit situation' . . . is analogous to the function ascribed by some jurists to the state of exception . . . As Kierkegaard writes, 'the exception explains the general as well as itself. And when one wants to really study the general, one need only look around for a real exception.'[5]

Agamben does not find it necessary to cite or reference the text in question. This is already an anxious tic symptomatic of an overgeneralised and unnuanced deployment of Kierkegaard within political theology. Agamben is not *the first* to exhibit this symptom. This deployment becomes a self-perpetuating – perhaps even tactical (considering its dissemination in wartime) – feedback loop of repeated self-reinforcements that verges upon regulatory 'capture'.[6] The primary concern would be critical consideration of what remains uncaptured: beginning with the serious omissions that have been made to Kierkegaard's text.

For a thinker so allegedly attuned towards style[7] as Agamben, there is tragic inattention to the meticulous pains and 'maieutic carefulness' Kierkegaard devotes to the pseudonymous perspectives[8] of respective texts through his signature mode of indirection. The deference which Agamben's political theology grants to 'the anonymous ones we call artists [seeking] to constitute their life as a form of life', specifically, 'one who signs [a "work"] with an ironic false name'[9] must be extended Kierkegaard's singular style.

Such referential haste in *Remnants* is likely self-pardoned by Agamben because he is simply extracting the first two sentences from a larger quotation already canonised by Schmitt in the first chapter of *Political Theology*.

> *A Protestant theologian* [*Ein protestantischer Theologe*] who demonstrated the vital intensity possible in theological reflection in the nineteenth century stated: 'The exception explains the general and itself. And if one wants to study the general correctly, one need only look around for a true exception. [Here, Agamben stops.] It reveals everything more clearly than does the general. Endless talk about the general becomes boring; there are exceptions. If they cannot be explained, then, the general also cannot be explained. The difficulty is usually not noticed because the general is not thought about with passion but with a comfortable superficiality. The exception, on the other hand, thinks the general with intense passion.'[10]

In *Homo Sacer* Agamben identifies this 'theologian . . . as none other than Søren Kierkegaard'.[11] Schmitt not only omits the title of the text in question, but even Kierkegaard's name (the omission of which is, ironically, perhaps the most astute aspect of the quotation).

Besotted Repetitions

Something almost criminal is at hand. As if constituting a kind of sovereign command or expropriating control over another's words, Schmitt's block quote effaces four additional sentences from the text with no indicative ellipsis of the omission. These lines are drawn from *Repetition*. Equally important to the discussion (if not more so) is its supplemental descriptions of an ambivalent 'conflict' and 'struggle' between the exception and the universal (translated 'general', above). This results from what Constantin Constantius (an ethicist in the Kierkegaardverse) calls the universal's 'besotted infatuation with the exception', in which the universal 'delights' despite its 'impatience and anger . . . in relation to' it.[12] These lines are found earlier in the same paragraph from which Schmitt selectively borrows. Constantius writes of force, sin, love and wrath, and claims that the universal 'will not reveal its infatuation with the exception until the exception forces it to do so'.[13]

In a 1986 address given in Paris, Jakob Taubes also cites Schmitt's citation and immediately identifies that '*Der Autor, der Schriftsteller, ist Sören Kierkegaard*' and continues to emphasise the influence of Kierkegaard on Adorno, Lukács and Schmitt.[14] Taubes also does not attribute the lines to *Repetition*, nor mention Schmitt's omission. This is repeated (and, again, left undocumented) in his 1987 lectures delivered in Heidelberg on *The Political Theology of Paul*. These underscore 'the trajectory between Kierkegaardian exception and Schmitt's definition of sovereignty'[15] and the collateral liberal *Rechtslehre* that develops from it.

Taubes further suggests Kierkegaard's influence to extend over others, especially Heidegger and his alleged tactical ambition to 'neutralize the Christian in Kierkegaard . . . [But] . . . *everything revolves around this Kierkegaard of the exception*, whether in Rosenzweig, in Ebner, or in Schmitt. This is what they have in common.'[16] As such, the 'political potential of Kierkegaard had been long underestimated',[17] but is reported to exercise its sway in Karl Löwith's claim that no longer are there rulers or kings, 'there remains only the image of the martyr'.[18] This point is then overdetermined to be subtly at work in a secret 1934 meeting in Rome between Schmitt, Heidegger and Mussolini, specifically in the latter's imperative: 'Save the state from the party!'[19] A sloppy *Repetition* citation metamorphoses into a clandestine command by *Il Duce* over the course of a few anecdotal paragraphs.

There is certainly something profound – if not prescient – about the genealogical possibility of 'this Kierkegaard of the exception' performing (or, being made to perform) as the nodal point around which 'everything revolves' in the 'liberal' or larval 'ordoliberal'[20] political legalism slouching towards Germany circa the 1930s. But if there is anything resembling a fascist imperative to be conflated there, it would be imperative to note the truncated caricature of Kierkegaard (above) and the oversimplification of the words extracted from *Repetition* by Schmitt's primal citation. A counter-revolutionary power might be identified in this command of words, rather than what is attributed to the words themselves.

Martin Buber once said, 'Taubes, you know *Being and Time*, [but] you don't know Heidegger.'[21] Only after substantial development along Taubes's lifeway does he eventually concede, Buber 'was right'.[22] He confesses shortcomings regarding his early readings of Kierkegaard. 'In my youth I had difficulties in really understanding Kierkegaard; I didn't understand this play of masks . . .'[23] For example, Taubes proclaims, 'Kierkegaard has made it absolutely clear that Christian life is *inwardness* and must therefore be . . . *anti-worldly*',[24] despite Kierkegaard clearly signing: '*The work of praising love must be done outwardly* . . . must essentially be regarded as struggling in this world.'[25]

An analogue to Buber's critique (and Taubes's later self-criticism) could be levelled arguably at Schmitt and, by consequence, Agamben: 'Political theology, you may know some lines from *Repetition*, but you don't necessarily know Kierkegaard.' Something meta-repetitive emerges in this Germanic telephone game (like a return of something repressed). Nascent political theology follows an uncanny script already directed by Marx and Engels critiquing Saint Max of the Leipzig Council. 'The peculiarity and uniqueness of [Schmitt's] attitude to [legal] history consists in . . . being transformed into *a "clumsy" copier* of [Kierkegaard].'[26] '[Taubes's] trivial creative work in his copy of [Kierkegaardian exception] is restricted to establishing his *ignorance even of what he copies.*'[27]

Auto-Constitution of Hetero-Constantius

This illocutionary comedy borders on intellectual tragedy. Still, one might smile.[27] Kierkegaard's indirect style has a gift for setting the stage on which lessons to learn disclose themselves without being overtly written or directly stated. Do readers experience irony or humour in this unwitting performance of impossible iterability? We are led through repeated attempts – no less than four times, through three authors (and Taubes suggests several more) – to politically apprehend and publicly recite Kierkegaard's thinking. Schmitt and Taubes capture, activate and utilise niche lines from *Repetition* – the very text in which Kierkegaard satirises the ways a naive autonomous self stubbornly insists himself capable of forcing repetition to happen – all while they ignore the role of 'force' in the same text. Under a veil of ignorance (in a hypothetical historical vacuum) well-versed Kierkegaard readers might suspect that 'Schmitt' and 'Taubes' (perhaps even 'Agamben') were themselves Kierkegaardian pseudonyms performing, misrepresenting, mis-repeating, yet indirectly insinuating the solemn stakes at hand . . . as well *or better* than Constantius himself.

What emerges as exception is undecidable indistinction between legitimacy or illegitimacy. For Constantius, exception comes about from the law and yet is always beyond the bounds of law. It becomes exceptional because of its constitutive illegitimacy. In the closing letter to the reader, he confronts 'the dialectical battle through which the exception emerges from the universal, the extended and incredibly complicated procedure through which the exception fights for and asserts its legitimacy, because the illegitimate exception is recognizable in that it wants to bypass the universal'.[29]

'The exception thus explains the universal' in *Repetition*, as it exposes the illegitimate legitimacy of the law performed through a besotted auto-constitution[30] of the political state, in Agamben. It is auto-constituting because it 'explains the universal *and itself*'.[31] The law, grounded, conditioned, activated and determined by its universal presumptions must assert itself by force of law as legally legitimated precisely because from its own legalised perspective, it is only recognisable as illegal, anomic, illegitimate and exceptional to its own universal criteria.

If one felt determined to finding 'the first',[32] then it is worth noting that the first passage Kierkegaard writes on exception (for publication) is a discussion on love.[33] Through the course of his written stages, the concept of love will modify itself alongside (in much the same way as) the self, itself, that feels, practises and works it. As an aesthete might become a self, *erotic love* might become *works of love* (by which the latter becomes indifferent to any consequential counter-love sought by the former). As such, love is a proto-Schmittian conception of exception that both private and (eventually) public selves discover along their developmental lifeways. Love, self and faith come to constitute themselves in a singular hybridity. This is nothing less than a Kierkegaardian exception to the state of exception itself.

Living Death

Agamben does not overtly suggest nor uncritically espouse the political interpretation of Kierkegaard by Taubes (although his immediate association of Kierkegaard with Karl Barth in §2.4 of *Remnants* bears an uncanny signature with Taubes's lectures). In inheritance of the Schmittian straw man of an alleged Kierkegaardian exception, precious opportunities are lost by Agamben to engage the Dane's own articulations of law, legitimacy and biopowers that emerge from – and beyond – sovereign powers. The disjunctions of *killing* or *letting-live* and *making-live* or *letting-die* (*Homo Sacer*, Pt 1, §1.1) are at least insinuated in *Repetition* more than a century before Foucault.

The same paragraph from which Schmitt and Agamben borrow grapples not only with exception but also the political struggle that emerges around a strange simultaneity of living one's own killing. Constantine writes of an 'incredibly complicated procedure through which *the exception fights* for and asserts its *legitimacy*, because the *legitimate exception* . . . wants to bypass the universal'.[34] This 'is, in a word, *as difficult as killing a man while letting him live*'.[35] Though in no way simply equivalent to bare life (whatever it might be), Kierkegaard resists the cultural attitude 'in which life . . . is articulated and divided',[36] evincing prescient appreciation of the 'incredibly complicated' procedures that blossom into biopower in Foucault, lifedeath in Derrida (or Pynchon)[37] and 'the undecidability of life . . . that must each time be decided politically and singularly'[38] in Agamben.

Kierkegaard's writings often preferentially opt for the poor[39] and unfortunate groups of marginalised people banned to half-lives of biopolitical zombies (neither dead nor killable nor completely living). One of his dangerous leitmotifs encourages a form of life that endeavours to exist and live beyond colloquial delimitations of life and death. One is to die to the world (even crucify one's understanding) in hopes of exceeding or breeching aesthetic, immediate, ethical, universalist and solipsist shortcomings along with their collateral political proclivities. Such a self endeavors living, loving, and thinking both oneself and others as not – *hos me*[40] – merely alive but as though already dead. 'To think oneself dead is earnestness.'[41]

> One who is living can indeed be mistaken, can be changed, can be stamped in a moment . . . The living person may favor you too much – perhaps too little . . . It does not *disappear* until you conduct yourself with [another] as with one already dead.[42]

Bewildering disappearance acts appear throughout both Kierkegaard and Agamben.

One of several ways to think such a relation is one thereby no longer incentivised to earn due reciprocal rewards determined by economy, duty, ethics, morality or even religious salvation. This oddity of living death is perhaps best articulated in Notebook 36, akin to the 'modal ontology' developed in *The Use of Bodies*. 'Spirit is: *to live as though dead* (to die away from the world). Now, this *mode of existence* is so distant from the natural hum[an] being that for him it is quite literally worse than dying pure and simple.'[43]

Love Crimes

Kierkegaard is at heart a crypto-criminal. His subhuman crimes are indissociable with his ventures to become a lover or to effectuate love (which might be a human impossibility and only possible for god). He longs to love as he dreams of anomy, ever faithful to *that one* executed by the Roman state. Readers receive one of his many confessions in Notebook 33: 'I can truly say that I have an inborn genius with respect to criminality.'[44] Kierkegaard purrs and 'play[s] with the law'[45] like Agamben's 'cat who plays with a ball of yarn . . . just as the child plays with ancient religious symbols . . . that once belonged to the economic sphere'.[46] This deactivates and modifies both oneself and the plaything.

Love can learn much from the criminal who no longer lives by the juridico-proprietary distinction between mine and yours. A self may, thereby, inversely modify crime into effectuated '*aneconomic*'[47] works. Criminality suffers a sacrificial kind of curse on the way to a possibility of revolutionary love:

> The more profound the *revolution*, the more completely the distinction '*mine and yours*' *disappears*, the more perfect is the *love* . . . the *thief*, the *robber*, the *swindler*, the *assailant*, will acknowledge no *yours* at all. But for this very reason the distinction '*mine*' also disappears entirely for him. Even if *the criminal does not understand* it . . . justice understands that the criminal has no *mine* . . . It is the *curse* resting on the criminal that his *mine* disappears because he wants to do away entirely with *yours*. It is a blessing resting on the truly loving one that the specification '*yours*' disappears; thus everything becomes the true lover's. As Paul says, 'All things are yours.' . . . [This is] a divine secret, since humanly speaking the truly loving one, the *sacrificing*, the *self-giving* one who loves . . . is humanly speaking *the injured one*, the most injured of all, even if *he makes himself that* by continually giving himself. Thus he is exactly the very opposite of the criminal.[48]

The passage deserves patient analysis alongside curses of sacred bare life in *Homo Sacer*, common uses beyond ownership in *The Highest Poverty* and self-modifications in *The Use of Bodies*.[49] Love deactivates ownership as the possessive distinction of its very terminology 'disappears', anticipating Agamben's fascination with 'mysterious disappearance'.[50]

Kierkegaard's post-criminal lifeway of love (supplemented, altered and modified by crime) achieves a mode akin to the 'messianic life'[51] Agamben finds in Paul. It discovers and discloses 'the mystery of anomy'[52] and 'radicalizes the condition of the state of exception, whereby law is applied in disapplying itself . . . rendering law inoperative while carrying it to its fulfillment'.[53] Enacting a singular form of liturgy, 'even if they were criminal', works of love 'would not for this reason lose [their] validity'.[54] In an effectual ontology, the criminality of such acts might be the very element that validates them as public works of love.

State Crimes

Philosophical Crumbs begins on a singular crime against the state. The necropolitics of the death penalty executed by political power soon follows. Its 'author', Johannes Climacus, is a humourist, on the edge of (yet still within) the ethical sphere at the threshold between duty and religiousness. Climacus 'would not wish . . . to commit an ἀπραμοσύνη, which is always a crime against the state . . . since in olden times it was prohibited on pain of death'.[55] This crime would be a non-pragmatics[56] – or, after Agamben, perhaps a non-liturgics – of *apragmosyné*: refusing to participate in public affairs or civic life. It specifically evokes the exceptional movement Agamben finds set in motion by Odo Casel: 'the liturgical mystery's pragmatic character . . . the problem of the relationship between [such pragmatic] liturgy and law'.[57]

To live love (or love life) demands becoming effectuated into an effectiveness beyond efficacy by *Wirklichkeit*.[58] These sacramentalised actions or praxes transform one's life into liturgy. Liturgical life as such rediscovers 'consistency with the etymological meaning of the term *leitourgia*'.[59] 'Public work' thought as works of love is where *ergon* becomes devoted to *laos*. It works love and lives love towards one's neighbouring laity[60] (beyond any ethicised and politicised *laicité* of secular fundamentalism).

But if liturgical practice, as such, seems prone to a religiofied complacency of metaphysical universalism, then Climacus wishes to disrupt it (as if already critically anticipating the global politics of contemporary laicism). He asks the reader to consider an even higher crime than this uncivil counter-pragmatics committed against the state that no longer services or applies 'to the interests of the general public'.[61] Suppose instead 'that one, by one's interference, was guilty of a greater crime, to the extent that he caused only confusion . . .'[62]

Greater crimes would transgress any ethical legitimacy and exceed any utilitarian calculus for the greater public good. This rearticulates the qualitative distinction drawn between Abraham and Agamemnon by Johannes de Silentio (another ethicist persona) in *Fear and Trembling*. The sovereign's sacrifice of Iphigenia makes ethical common sense to observers who measure the action by universal, utilitarian or deontological standards for the sake (or glory) of the greater numbers of the nation-state. But 'Abraham's situation is different. By his act he transgressed the ethical altogether . . . It is not to save a nation, not to uphold the idea of the state that Abraham does it; it is not to appease the angry gods.'[63]

Existential Becoming as Self-Modification

This singular faith converges with Agamben's move beyond colloquial ethics by way of supplemental ontologies. The mode of living needed is, itself, 'a threshold of indifference between ontology and ethics'.[64] The existential becoming indirectly oriented by Kierkegaard through life's stages might be considered a form of self-modification. One possible way to consider a Kierkegaardian modification of the self is through the dense and complicated self-relation affected in *The Sickness unto Death*.

This text opens on 'a relation that relates itself to itself and in relating itself to itself relates itself to another'.[65] This 'other' element would be 'that which has established the entire relation'[66] beyond any mere autonomous self (that is, beyond an ethical, Kantian or unified subject). After Agamben, the possibility of such a supplementary mode of living oneself 'is no longer an ontology but an ethics (on the condition that we add that the ethics of modes is no longer an ethics but an ontology)'.[67] In response to this mode of ethics suggested by Agamben, a Kierkegaardian might offer a life of faith and love: a life lived no longer in mere aesthetic immediacy. It becomes an other-oriented ethical existence (on the condition that we add that such life is no longer bound by universal ethics, duty or even direct communication and language more broadly).

The silence attributed to Johannes de Silentio when confronted with meta- or para-ethical Abrahamic faith – as well as Abraham's own silent incapacity to communicate it to Sarah, Isaac or the general public – is an exemplary performative of Agamben's suspicion: 'It is possible . . . that the mechanism of the exception is constitutively connected to the event of language that coincides with anthropogenesis.'[68] Be they Abrahamic articulations, ethical confoundment or practising the pseudonymous style itself, the diffuse silences of indirection exceed any generalised communicative action grounded in universalised language (or the generative grammar of rationalist inneism based on laws of logic). As such, Kierkegaardian faith seems called to follow Agamben towards '*a pure demand held in tension between language and world*'.[69]

Agamben's exceptional ethical endeavour draws attention to the presumed divisions between private life and public life. He criticises the cultural attitude that elides a complex understanding of life that is 'time after time articulated and divided into *bios* and *zoē*, politically qualified life and bare life, public life and private life . . .'[70] Whereas Agamben suspects it 'is as if each of us obscurely felt that precisely the opacity of our clandestine life held within it a genuinely political element',[71] Kierkegaard encourages an existential becoming through which any genuinely political life (if there is such a thing) – or simply loving others – eventually rediscovers its initially clandestine subjective self (by which it was made possible), but was, at that stage, over-personalised prior to discovering (and relating to) oneself, that, thereby, eventually endeavours to live with, towards and for others.

Kierkegaard ultimately tries to think and write out the complex hybridity made possible by way of existential becoming through three stages on life's way towards *Works of Love*.[72] For '*love* does not alter the beloved, rather it *alters itself*'.[73] Its self-modified lifeway is akin to what Agamben briefly considers 'loving life together'.[74] In the macrocosm of public works performed by the church, he recognises the effectiveness of works. In Agambenian terms, a Kierkegaardian self no longer 'depend[s] on the subject who sets it to work [as had been the case for an ethicist] and nonetheless needs the subject [which had been lacking in the aesthete] as an "animate instrument" to be actualized and rendered effective',[75] now, through works of love. Both thinkers suspect that such a lifestyle might not be possible to live by delimited human potencies (at least, as they have been defined by classical ontology or political theory).

Supplemental to the division between Agamemnon and Abraham (ethics and faith), Agamben's public and private lives are rearticulated by the ethicist of *Either/Or*, Judge Wilhelm, as civic and personal lives. As one ventures through the stages (of Agamben's 'way of life')[76] from (1) aesthetic personal life into (2) ethical public life and *then*, upon becoming a self, revisits personal life, (3) one's previous personal perspective will have been altered by its public engagement and finds itself in a zone of indistinction that no longer properly adheres to either the public or the personal (neither merely aesthetic nor properly ethical).

In the Judge's words, one 'transfers himself from personal life to civic life [and then] from this to personal life. Personal life as such was an isolation and therefore imperfect, but when he turns back into his personality through the civic life, the personal life appears in a higher form.'[77] Through this becoming of subjective civic living, one develops 'the skepticism that duty itself is unstable'[78] as well as ethics and law.

Self-Suspensions of Chance

Is it by chance that Agamben invokes – and excludes – the problem of chance as he insists on Kierkegaard's influence on Schmitt? From the earliest pages of the *Sacer* project, exception, Kierkegaard and chance are entangled. '*It is not by chance* that in defining the exception Schmitt refers to the work of . . . Kierkegaard.'[79] Readers are led to believe that any Kierkegaardian exception seems beyond, indifferent to or perhaps even indemnified from chance. It is difficult to reconcile how one might affirm chance[80] after determining an encounter to have been 'not by chance'.

This chance encounter (if it is that) would have something to do with the determinism complicit in exception which Kierkegaard notes in *Repetition*. 'The vigorous and *determined exception* . . ., despite its struggle with the universal, is an offshoot of it.'[81] There is a chance that Agamben's perhaps haphazard non-inclusion of chance, here, is symptomatic of this genealogical method's incapacity to suspend its tacit teleology (as Derrida[82] suspects). When a genealogist excludes chance from a genealogy, does it start slipping a slope into determinist linear history? After its espousal of Weil's understanding of chance, would the writer of *What is Real?* still determine the non-chances between Schmitt and Kierkegaard in *Homo Sacer*?

Chance is a canonical signature at play when philosophy grapples with problems of probability. Probability is at the core of modern decision theory, which, in turn, must be remembered with regard to any power 'who *decides* the exception'.[83] Agamben further develops his earlier *Sacer* critiques of exception through his later genealogical analysis of probability theory, determinism and chance. Although the word 'exception' is unwritten throughout *What is Real?*, it remains suspicious of suspension (which has been indissociable – if not synonymous – with exception in Agamben's earlier texts).[84] This is a key concept for Kierkegaard. *Fear and Trembling* revolves around 'a teleological suspension of the ethical'.[85]

This has been a question of reality for Agamben since his 'commentary' on Paul: '*sovereign autosuspension* . . . in including its outside in the form of exception . . . *coincides with reality* itself.'[86] Glossing Wittgenstein, Agamben suggests, 'probability can therefore never exist, as such, since it is nothing but that very world [that is, in "the world is all that is the case"], a world whose reality is *suspended* in order to govern it and take [or make] decisions about it.'[87]

Improbable Animals of Operational Observance

Agamben is not alone in noting 'the division and articulation within the human being of the human and the animal'.[88] Kierkegaard suggests 'in relation with being a hum[an] being, one recognizes the animal nature . . .'[89] Ever at the thresholds between *bios* and *zoē* (human or subhuman), Agamben addresses that theoretical pet conjured by Schrödinger in the observational position of measuring probability while trying to take into account quantum reality (if there is such a thing). The heaviest canonical analogy of probability-at-work (written by the physicist that 'had arguably the strongest philosophical background') demands that human understanding try to conceive an exceptional nonhuman lifeform in a '"ridiculous case" . . . that we are compelled to suppose is *both alive and dead at the same time*'.[90] Agamben's werewolf[91] metamorphoses into feline form ever unobserved inside boxed time that remains unopened.

Concern with the command of probability attends to the observer's point of view and its intervention onto the observed by observing. His earlier study of monastic rule anticipates this strange performative mystery – *performativum fidei*[92] – 'an *observance* that is rendered *indiscernible from the command*'.[93] *Fear and Trembling* also stresses the limitations of observation: 'the observer's eye views [Agamemnon] with confidence . . . The *observer cannot understand* [Abraham] at all; neither can his eye rest on him with confidence.'[94]

Are we reading Kierkegaard or Schrödinger? As if caught again in uncanny *Repetition*, living by the measures of probability seems 'as difficult as killing a [cat] while letting [it] live'.[95] It becomes difficult to distinguish Heisenberg, quantum physics and probability with Benedict, monastic faith and cenoby.

Biopolitical Operations of Probability

Previous lessons learned from politics now interrupt and intrude upon physics and statistics. Whereas the state of exception is determined to suspend political law, the operativity and calculation of probability is suspected to suspend natural law. Reality now assumes the throne that had heretofore been occupied by sovereign powers in Agamben's previous critiques. Within both physics and politics, governance demands suspension of law, whereby biopolitics deploys itself as *bioprobability*. The crisis of political reality becomes discernible in probabilistic conceptions of reality in general. In 'a certain way, it is *the real* that *suspends its reality* and can thus fall into itself as merely probable'.[96] Such auto-suspension is indissociable with auto-constitution (in both its phenomenological and political valences). Kierkegaard allies himself with Agamben's critique of probability's political incursion:

> P[olitics] consists in this: never venturing more than what is possible at any moment, never beyond human probability . . . Where there is no venturing

beyond the probable, God is absolutely not included, though it does not follow from this that he is present wherever there is venturing beyond the probable.[97]

Politics and probability are found entangled and indissociable. The political demotes the possible to the probable. Politics takes command of humanity as probability feigns control over possibility. In politics as such humanity is perhaps no longer possible. It probabilises the *polis* – as megadata enumerates subhumans – so politics might optimise policing.

Theodicy of Probable Animals

Agamben draws attention to how probability calculus seems reliant upon enumeration. 'If the cause of the rupture with . . . classical physics was the numerical character of the calculation of probabilities', he then wonders along with Simone Weil 'why scientists did not choose to work on the very notion of probability in order to elaborate a model of calculation that is not founded on discontinuity but on continuity – instead of changing the theory of physics from top to bottom'.[98]

Bad faith in raw numbers potentially burgeons into a form of governmental command. This is indicative of Bernoulli's 'law of large numbers, on which every statistical calculation is based'.[99] Kierkegaard shares this suspicion of reality based on vast enumeration.

> How [ironic] that *the law* is this – that everything that *needs numbers* in order to be important . . . *the more numbers it needs, the less important it is*. Everything that can be . . . *realized, only by means of great numbers*, and that men then regard with stupefied admiration, as if it were really important – everything of this kind is unimportant. What is truly important is *quite the reverse, it always needs less and less numbers in order to be realized* . . .[100]

> The reliability of numbers is of course a fraud, they are unreliable; and yet this is what is offered you in *the world, calculated to fool you*, so that *you become part of the numbers* . . . Numbers are used in order to conceal the emptiness of existence, they put you in a state of exaltation, like opium, and so you are *tranquilized* by the *immense* reliability of numbers running into millions . . . *the animal needs no higher certainty than numbers*.[101]

Kierkegaard, the Anti-Bernoulli, transgresses the law by imagining a nonlaw of lesser numbers.[102] Command again is found malforming human life into animality, now, through probability (algorithmically self-optimised by numerical law) rather than sovereignty (administratively auto-constituted by exceptional law). Kierkegaard indicts enumeration as a brute logic of animal survival far less than human living. Numbers 'tranquilise' animals for Kierkegaard (as sovereign power passivises wild werewolves into licking the king's boots).[103] Enumerated lifeforms become more susceptible to such deception. It fools humans into reckoning as animals, for whom unreal numbers are 'realised' as reality itself.

This mechanism fooling folk into 'becom[ing] part of the numbers' is certainly applicable to contemporary information society. Mass datafication by surveillance and platform capitalism[104] tends 'to replace people with data trails, turning them into more effective shoppers or workers . . . the people affected remain every bit as abstract as the numbers dancing across the screen'.[105] Big data is deciphered by parahuman machine-learning 'precisely' by the law of great numbers. The immense algorithmic mining of it – from a 'special perspective'[106] once attributed by providential theodicy to god – is appropriated by governmental command over datafied people, apostate to any *lit*-urgy worthy of the name. Today this virtual gubernation is part of 'The Providential Machine'[107] and due as much solemn attention – which, for Agamben, ever evokes the Dane – as the comedic name Dante attributed to the divine.

Notes

1. Søren Kierkegaard, *Works of Love*, trans. Howard V. Hong and Edna H. Hong (Princeton: Princeton University Press, 1995), p. 409.
2. Giorgio Agamben, *Creation and Anarchy*, trans. Adam Kotsko (Stanford: Stanford University Press, 2019), p. 24.
3. 'There sat all the gods . . . I was granted . . . a wish. "What do you want," asked Mercury. ". . . I choose one thing – that I may always have the laughter on my side." Not one of the gods said a word; instead, all of them began to laugh.' Søren Kierkegaard, *Either/Or*, Part 1, trans. Howard V. Hong and Edna H. Hong (Princeton: Princeton University Press, 1987), pp. 42–3. Cf. Friedrich Nietzsche, *Thus Spoke Zarathustra*, trans. Adrian Del Caro (Cambridge: Cambridge University Press, 2006), p. 146; [Part 3, *On Apostates*, §2].
4. Giorgio Agamben, *The End of the Poem*, trans. Daniel Heller-Roazen (Stanford: Stanford University Press, 1999), pp. 9, 7.
5. Giorgio Agamben, *Remnants of Auschwitz*, trans. David Heller-Roazen (New York: Zone Books, 1999), p. 48.
6. Francis Fukuyama, *Our Posthuman Future* (New York: Farrar, Straus and Giroux, 2002), p. 204 fn.; Cathy O'Neil, *Weapons of Math Destruction* (New York: Crown, 2016), pp. 53, 29.
7. Giorgio Agamben, *The Use of Bodies*, trans. Adam Kotsko (Stanford: Stanford University Press, 2016), pp. 224–33.
8. Cf. Søren Kierkegaard, *The Point of View*, trans. Howard V. Hong and Edna H. Hong (Princeton: Princeton University Press, 1995); Jacques Derrida, *The Gift of Death*, trans. David Wills (Chicago: University of Chicago Press, 1995), p. 58; Gilles Deleuze and Félix Guattari, *What is Philosophy?*, trans. Hugh Tomlinson and Graham Burchell (New York: Columbia University Press, 1994), pp. 61–74.
9. Duchamp's *Mutt* in Agamben, *Creation and Anarchy*, pp. 12–13.
10. Carl Schmitt, *Political Theology*, trans. George Schwab (Chicago: University of

Chicago Press, 2005), p. 15; italics added. Cf. Schmitt, *Politischer Theologie* (Berlin: Duncker & Humbolt, 2004), p. 21

11. Giorgio Agamben, *Homo Sacer*, trans. Daniel Heller-Roazen (Stanford: Stanford University Press, 1998), p. 16.
12. Søren Kierkegaard, *Repetition | Philosophical Crumbs*, trans. M. G. Piety (Oxford: Oxford University Press, 2009), p. 78.
13. Ibid.
14. Jakob Taubes, *Ad Carl Schmitt* (Berlin: Merve, 1987), pp. 55–6.
15. Jakob Taubes, *The Political Theology of Paul*, trans. D. Hollander (Stanford: Stanford University Press, 2003), p. 65.
16. Ibid. p. 66.
17. Ibid. p. 69. Cf. Bartholomew Ryan, *Kierkegaard's Indirect Politics* (New York: Rodopi, 2014).
18. Quoted in Taubes, *The Political Theology of Paul*, p. 69.
19. Ibid. p. 70.
20. Michel Foucault, *The Birth of Biopolitics*, trans. Graham Burchell (New York: Palgrave, 2008), pp. 79–150.
21. Taubes, *The Political Theology of Paul*, p. 108.
22. Ibid.
23. Ibid. p. 77.
24. Jakob Taubes, *Occidental Eschatology*, trans. David Ratmoko (Stanford: Stanford University Press, 2009), p. 191; italics added.
25. Kierkegaard, *Works of Love*, pp. 365–66; Kierkegaard's italics and emphasis.
26. Karl Marx and Friedrich Engels, *The German Ideology*, n.t. (Amherst: Prometheus Books, 1998), p. 183; italics added.
27. Ibid. p. 198; italics added. With my brackets Schmitt and Taubes perform as [Stirner] through which Kierkegaard assumes the gravity of [Hegel] (first as speculative tragedy, then as exceptional farce).
28. Jacques Derrida, *The Beast and the Sovereign*, vol. 1, trans. Geoffrey Bennington (Chicago: University of Chicago Press, 2009), pp. 92, 94.
29. Kierkegaard, *Repetition*, p. 77.
30. Agamben, *The Use of Bodies*, p. 267.
31. Kierkegaard, *Repetition*, p. 78; italics added.
32. Cf. 'to be the first to tell us about the first'. Derrida, *The Beast and the Sovereign*, vol. 1, pp. 330, 92.
33. 'Eros was the god of erotic love but was not himself in love . . . if it did happen to him once, it was an exception . . .'. *Either/Or*, Part 1, p. 63. This first exception is introduced by his first description of the *power of exclusion*: 'precisely because [sensuality] is to be excluded [by spirit or Christianity] it is defined as a principle, as a power . . .', p. 61.
34. Kierkegaard, *Repetition*, p. 77; italics added.
35. Ibid. p. 78; italics added.
36. Agamben, *The Use of Bodies*, p. xix.
37. Thomas Pynchon, *Gravity's Rainbow* (New York: Penguin Classics, Deluxe Edition, 2006), p. 438. Q.v., p. 156, p. 169, p. 233.
38. Agamben, *The Use of Bodies*, pp. xix–xx.
39. Kierkegaard's 'king' that deactivates his sovereignty for love of 'the lowest' 'peasant' in *Philosophical Crumbs* (pp. 102–7) approaches the theo-economics of Agamben's cenoby and impoverished uses beyond ownership in *The Highest Poverty*, trans. Adam Kotsko (Stanford: Stanford University Press, 2013), pp. 122–4, 92–3, 119, as well as the socio-economic justices striven for in the preferential options of Latin American liberation theologies (and those that follow).
40. Agamben, *The Highest Poverty*, p. 139; *The Time That Remains*, trans. Patricia Dailey (Stanford: Stanford University Press, 2005), pp. 23–4.

41. Kierkegaard, *Three Discourses on Imagined Occasions*, trans. Howard V. Hong and Edna H. Hong (Princeton: Princeton University Press, 1993), p. 80. Cf. 'I live as one already dead'. *Either/Or*, Part 1, p. 42.
42. Kierkegaard, *Purity of Heart is to Will One Thing: Spiritual Preparation for the Office of Confession*, trans. Douglas V. Steere (New York: Harper & Brothers, 1948), pp. 91–2; italics added. Q.v., p. 97, p. 191.
43. *Kierkegaard's Journals and Notebooks*, vol. 10, *Journals NB31–NB36*, ed. Niels Jørgen Cappelørn et al. (Princeton: Princeton University Press, 2018), p. 335; italics added; [NB 36:37].
44. *Kierkegaard's Journals and Notebooks*, vol. 10, p. 259 [NB 33:13].
45. Giorgio Agamben, *State of Exception*, trans. Kevin Attell (Chicago: University of Chicago Press, 2005), p. 7.
46. Giorgio Agamben, *Profanations*, trans. Jeff Fort (New York: Zone Books, 2007), p. 85.
47. Jacques Derrida, *Given Time*, trans. Peggy Kamuf (Chicago: University of Chicago Press, 1992), p. 7.
48. Kierkegaard, *Works of Love*, pp. 267–8; Kierkegaard's italics of *mine* and *yours*; all other italics *mine* (if there is such a thing).
49. Consider Agamben's understanding of the Spinozist *conatus*: 'the being that desires and demands, in demanding, modifies, desires, and constitutes itself. "To preserve in its being" means this and nothing else.' *The Use of Bodies*, p. 171. See p. 155 (mode and affection), p. 156 (haecceity and *ecce homo*), p. 167 (between entity and identity with itself).
50. Giorgio Agamben, *What is Real?*, trans. Lorenzo Chiesa (Stanford: Stanford University Press, 2018), pp. 41–3.
51. Agamben, *The Time That Remains*, pp. 18–19, 23.
52. Ibid. p. 109; cf. 2 Thess. 2.
53. Ibid. pp. 106–7.
54. Agamben, *Creation and Anarchy*, p. 10.
55. Kierkegaard, *Philosophical Crumbs*, p. 85.
56. 'The idea of law, of the imperative . . . is thus inscribed in *pragma*; "it must" is inscribed in this doing . . . "it must" weighed from the start on the sense of *pragma*, and of *pragmatic*, in Greek and Lain, in Latin where it was able to follow a very precisely juridical direction, designating sometimes, very strictly, a rule . . . the rule of civil power in ecclesiastical matters.' Jacques Derrida, *Theory and Practice*, trans. David Willis (Chicago: University of Chicago Press, 2019), p. 42.
57. Giorgio Agamben, *Opus Dei*, trans. Adam Kotsko (Stanford: Stanford University Press, 2013), p. 35; *Creation and Anarchy*, p. 9.
58. Agamben, *Opus Dei*, pp. 40–1; Derrida, *Theory and Practice*, pp. 75–7, 83, 90–3, 102, 104, 108.
59. Ibid. p. 27.
60. *If* he is 'a Protestant theologian', Taubes would likely identify Kierkegaard as 'a lay theologian'. *The Political Theology of Paul*, p. 65.
61. Kierkegaard, *Philosophical Crumbs*, p. 85.
62. Ibid.
63. Kierkegaard, *Fear and Trembling*, p. 59. 'We hum[an] beings want to reassure ourselves with the assistance of numbers (and it is quite true that *numbers do impress all relative sovereigns*)'. *Kierkegaard's Journals and Notebooks*, vol. 11.2, Loose Papers 1843–1855, ed. Niels Jørgen Cappelørn et al. (Princeton: Princeton University Press, 2020), p. 352; italics added; [646–7:539]. In this context, Agamemnon as well as any of the angry gods he appeases would represent such relative sovereigns and be numerically impressed as such.
64. Agamben, *The Use of Bodies*, p. 174.
65. Søren Kierkegaard, *The Sickness unto Death*, trans. Howard V. and Edna H. Hong (Princeton: Princeton University Press, 1980), pp. 13–14. One might discern a

meta-conceptual (even if under-conceptualised) articulation of this in the closing paragraphs to the 'Teleology' discussion of the *Greater Logic*: '... such a movement is itself immediately doubled and a first is always also a second. In the concept taken for itself, that is, in its subjectivity, the difference of itself from itself is as an immediate identical totality on its own; but since its determinateness here is indifferent externality, its self-identity is in this externality immediately also self-repulsion again, so that what is determined as external and indifferent to the identity is rather this identity itself, and the identity as identity, as self-reflected, is rather its other'. Georg Wilhelm Friedrich Hegel, *The Science of Logic*, trans. George Di Giovanni (Cambridge: Cambridge University Press, 2010), p. 668.

66. Kierkegaard, *The Sickness unto Death*, p. 14. Cf. 'an exclusively receptive relation' in which one 'simply kept [one]self receptive' and, as such, 'a change occurred in everything [one] received'. Søren Kierkegaard, *Eighteen Upbuilding Discourses*, trans. Howard V. and Edna H. Hong (Princeton: Princeton University Press, 1990), p. 45. Here Kierkegaard perhaps anticipates the subtle but solemn possible differences between (1) self-relation and (2) letting oneself receive relation; *c'est à dire*: between (1) colloquial and autonomously agential apprehensions of auto-affection (aesthetic or ethicist) as merely to affect or '*to feel oneself [se sentir]*' and (2) a far more receptive relation further supplementarily hospitable to an effectual ontology 'in which one *lets oneself be affected* also by a feeling [*se laisser affecter aussi par un sentiment*]' addressed in Jacques Derrida, 'Justices', trans. Peggy Kamuf, *Critical Inquiry* 31.3 (Spring 2005): 689–721, esp. p. 690; italics added; Jacques Derrida, 'Justices', in Appels de Jacques Derrida, ed. by Danielle Cohen-Levinas and Ginette Michaud (Paris: Hermann Éditeurs, 2014), pp. 19–71, esp. p. 21. Such Kierkegaardian receptivity would have something to do with the passivity by which any so-called 'I' of oneself is 'overcome by its own passivity, its ownmost sensibility' in Agamben, *Remnants of Auschwitz*, p. 105.
67. Agamben, *The Use of Bodies*, p. 174.
68. Ibid.
69. Ibid. p. 264.
70. Ibid. p. 170; Agamben's italics.
71. Ibid. p. xix.
72. Ibid. p. xxi.
72. My reading of the Kierkegaardian system (if it is that) inclines to possibilities suggested by Merold Westphal, whereby works of love exceed the religiousnesses (a and b) sketched out within it (and, as such, the system itself). 'Hidden inwardness remains, but it is teleologically suspended in outwardly visible works of love. Here is an interpretation ... that goes beyond Climacus. I call it Religiousness C.' Merold Westphal, *Becoming a Self: A Reading of Kierkegaard's Concluding Unscientific Postscript* (West Lafayette: Purdue University Press, 1996), p. 197.
73. Kierkegaard, *Philosophical Crumbs*, p. 108; italics added.
74. Agamben, *The Use of Bodies*, p. xxi.
75. Agamben, *Opus Dei*, p. 28.
76. Agamben, *The Highest Poverty*, pp. 70, 74, 92–3, 98, 141. Cf. "*Lebensweise*" in Karl Marx and Friedrich Engels, *Die deutsche Ideologie*, *Werke*, vol. 3 (Berlin: Dietz Verlag, 1990), p. 21.
77. Kierkegaard, *Either/Or*, Pt 2, trans. Howard V. Hong and Edna H. Hong (Princeton: Princeton University Press, 1987), p. 263.
78. Ibid.
79. Agamben, *Homo Sacer*, p. 16; italics added.
80. Cf. vicissitudes of chance in 'Nietzsche, Genealogy, History', *The Foucault Reader*, ed. Paul Rabinow (New York: Penguin, 1984), pp. 78, 93; Gilles Deleuze, *Nietzsche and Philosophy*, trans. Hugh Tomlinson (New York: Columbia University Press, 2006), pp. 25–8, 197; John Maynard Keynes, *A Treatise on Probability* (Lexington:

Wildside Press, 2017 [1920]), p. 337. (Keynes might have more in common with Nietzsche, Foucault and Deleuze on such issues than continental theorists are often led to believe, especially if receiving their modes of thinking through Agamben's presentation of them.)
81. Kierkegaard, *Repetition*, p. 78; italics added.
82. Derrida, *The Beast and the Sovereign*, vol. 1, p. 333.
83. Schmitt, *Political Theology*, p. 5; italics added.
84. 'It is important to remember that in the exception . . . the law maintains itself in relation to the exception in the form of its own self-suspension.' Agamben, *The Time That Remains*, p. 104; cf. *The Highest Poverty*, p. 10.
85. Kierkegaard, *Fear and Trembling*, p. 56.
86. Ibid. p. 105; italics added.
87. Agamben, *What is Real?*, pp. 32–3; italics added.
88. Kierkegaard, *The Use of Bodies*, p. 265.
89. *Kierkegaard's Journals and Notebooks*, vol. 10, p. 84. Note this animality within '*To Want to Be First*' alongside Derrida's critique of Agamben (discussed above).
90. Agamben, *What is Real?*, p. 26.
91. Agamben, *Homo Sacer*, pp. 105–9.
92. Agamben, *The Time That Remains*, pp. 134–5.
93. Agamben, *The Highest Poverty*, p. 77; italics added.
94. Kierkegaard, *Fear and Trembling*, pp. 60–1; italics added.
95. Kierkegaard, *Repetition*, p. 78. Science is he that decides the boxception.
96. Agamben, *What is Real?*, p. 33; italics added.
97. *Kierkegaard's Journals and Notebooks*, vol. 10, p. 120.
98. *What is Real?*, p. 23.
99. Ibid. p. 29. 'Bernoulli . . . forms a system with the law of the equality of probabilities and confirms the principle that probability does not concern a real given event but only the tendency to infinity of the number of examined samples', pp. 31–2.
100. Kierkegaard, *The Last Years: Journals 1853–1855*, ed. and trans. Ronald Gregor Smith (New York: Harper & Row, 1965), p. 273; italics added. This critique of what is 'realised' by the numbers is written before the emergence of so-called 'real numbers' after Dedekind or Cantor but would likely still address itself to them. But such real numbers are perhaps no longer numbers at all but rather para-numerical quantities akin to sequences, successions, sections, agglomerations, aggregates, or 'a variety of mathematical entities that may not be numbers' and, as such, elude the critique. Paolo Zellini, *The Mathematics of the Gods and the Algorithms of Men*, trans. Simon Carnell and Erica Segre (London: Allen Lane, 2020), p. 117. Yet Kierkegaard is no doubt influenced by Hegel regarding such numerical problems, whose previous critique arguably anticipates Dedekind and Cantor and would still seem to allege their subsequent quantities of mere approximations of bad infinity by decimal seriality. Georg Wilhelm Friedrich Hegel, *The Science of Logic*, trans. George Di Giovanni (Cambridge: Cambridge University Press, 2010), pp. 192, 202, 210–12, 276.
101. Kierkegaard, *The Last Years: Journals 1853–1855*, pp. 163–4.
102. This radical idea is perhaps still saturated in Kierkegaard's congenital Protestantism and its institution of a *chosen few*. This demands a reboot of the Weberian critique in the present age. However digitally disenchanted, the *populus electus* personally persists in believing itself chosen (as in the 2016 US election) via hyper-personalised algorithmic microtargeting (by entities like Cambridge Analytica). Such targets are prone to constitute themselves silently and secretly elected to personally elect the new elector. Cf. Hobbes: 'I find the KINGDOM OF GOD, to signify . . . a *kingdom properly so named*, constituted *by the votes* of the people of Israel *in peculiar manner*, wherein *they chose God* for their king . . .". *Leviathan* (Oxford: Oxford University Press, 1998), p. 216 [ch. 35, ¶2]; italics mine.

103. *Homo Sacer*, pp. 105–8; [§6]. Cf. the 'exception' to 'large number' of the 'Anti-Darwin' entry in Friedrich Nietzsche, *Twilight of the Idols*, trans. Thomas Common (Mineola: Dover, 2019), p. 44.
104. Consider the 'State of Exception', 'Surveillance Exceptionalism' and 'The New Priesthood' in Susanna Zuboff, *The Age of Surveillance Capitalism* (London: Profile Books, 2019), pp. 71–4, 112–1, 187–90; Nick Srnicek, *Platform Capitalism* (Malden: Polity, 2017), p. 57. See Safiya Umoja Noble, *Algorithms of Oppression* (New York: New York University Press, 2018); Colin Koopman, *How We Became Our Data* (Chicago: University of Chicago Press, 2019).
105. O'Neil, *Weapons of Math Destruction*, p. 48.
106. Agamben, *What is Real?*, p. 35.
107. Giorgio Agamben, *The Kingdom and the Glory*, trans. Lorenzo Chiesa and Matteo Mandarini (Stanford: Stanford University Press, 2011), pp. 109–43; [§5].

Chapter 4

Kierkegaard and the Figure of Form-of-Life

Tom Frost

This chapter offers a corrective to the relationship between Giorgio Agamben and Søren Kierkegaard. My starting point is the literature on Agamben's writings on bare life and the exception, and the thought of Carl Schmitt. After summarising the literature detailing how Schmitt's sovereignty informed Agamben's biopolitics, I consider how Schmitt and Agamben have cited Kierkegaard. Kierkegaard's *Repetition* influenced Schmitt's writings on the exception, and Schmitt read *Repetition* as a model for sovereignty. Kierkegaard's writings informed Agamben's philosophy as well. I read *Repetition* as a model for what Agamben terms 'absolute immanence', or 'form-of-life'. To support this, I explore Agamben's coming politics. This politics eschews relationality and definitions of life based on apparatuses, divisions and caesuras, which produce and sustain bare life. This politics seeks to provide the basis for the figure of form-of-life to live.

Form-of-life is a singularity, conceived of in all its difference from other singularities. It is life lived in a non-relational existence,[1] its own mode of being generated by its manner of being.[2] The ethical subject focuses on *how* it lives its life, through contact with other forms-of-life, and living a life of contemplative use.[3] Contact is separate from relation in Agamben's work. It is true that there is a lack of precision to the difference between the two terms in Agamben, leading to an ambiguity. This is illustrated by the fact that Agamben describes form-of-life as a singularity conceived in all its difference from other singularities. Yet relationality is tied to definitions which are based on difference. Contact is a way of relating to others outside of difference. Form-of-life is not differential or relational. Differential and relational should be understood in a precise way for Agamben. Form-of-life is non-relational in the sense that it is not defined or understood as being held up against other persons or beings and compared and contrasted to that other. Likewise, form-of-life is non-differential in that form-of-life does not depend upon differences between itself and others. Form-of-life is an existential figure, always in the process of repetition, understood in its performative, Kierkegaardian sense. Form-of-life is a new interpretation of Kierkegaard's self. If form-of-life is read existentially, then its construction makes sense. Form-of-life is subject to a continual process of repetition, an existential process that is always-already happening.

Kierkegaard, Schmitt and Agamben

The dominant understanding of life since the eighteenth century has been biological in nature.[4] Yet, as Agamben explains, the concept of 'life' never gets defined as such.[5] What this means is that:

> [T]his thing that remains indeterminate gets articulated and divided time and again through a series of caesurae and oppositions that invest it with a decisive strategic function . . . everything happens as if . . . life were *what cannot be defined, yet, precisely for this reason, must be ceaselessly articulated and divided.*[6]

This ceaseless division finds its most famous enunciation in *Homo Sacer*, where Agamben claims, 'the fundamental activity of sovereign power is the production of bare life as originary political element'.[7] This division has been a theme in Agamben's thought. In *What is an Apparatus?* Agamben explains: 'The event that has produced the human constitutes, for the living being, something like a division . . . This division separates the living being from itself and from its immediate relationship with its environment.'[8] The division of life operates on a number of levels – vegetal and relational, organic and animal, animal and human.[9] These divisions pass as a 'mobile border' within living man, and operate as an apparatus through which the decision of what is and what is not human is possible.[10] The result of this is the creation of a remainder, bare life.

In reading this division of life as central to Agamben's thought, we can understand Schmitt's role in Agamben's oeuvre. In *Homo Sacer*, Agamben sought to focus upon and modify Carl Schmitt's concept of the sovereign decision. For Schmitt, sovereignty was not identifiable through statutes, ordinances or constitutions, but rested on one concrete political fact, namely which individual or body could declare a state of exception and suspend the existing legal order. It was the decision, rather than a preordained power, that decided who was sovereign and determined the law. The exception also applies to the sovereign leader of the state. For

Agamben it was also the sovereign decision that determined who is or is not human, and who is bare life. As a result, Schmitt occupies an important role in Agamben's work. Agamben follows Schmitt in the qualities and nature of the exception, but he seeks to distance himself from Schmitt and found a politics which is not based on this sovereign exception determining who is or is not human.

Schmitt's sovereignty views legal norms as abstractions. These produce political order when they are applied or given force: 'what matters for the reality of legal life is who decides'.[11] The state, in an emergency or state of exception, has the power to decide that it faces an exceptional circumstance, and can suspend the constitution to allow a political struggle to occur to restore order.[12] In a state of exception legal norms are suspended, yet the exception itself remains 'accessible to jurisprudence', as political decisions made by the individual(s) in authority are a part of the law. This leads to a paradox for Agamben: 'the sovereign is, at the same time, inside and outside the juridical order'.[13] The sovereign is outside of the law as it is defined by the suspension of the law; yet the sovereign is inside of the law as the sovereign decision is an aspect of the law. The state of exception simply reveals this 'specifically juridical formal element' in 'absolute purity'.[14] Legal authority survives the suspension of the law. Actions taken outside of the law have a juridical character. The negation of law eventually leads to a new state and a new law – the exception becomes wholly absorbed into the power of the state. The exception undermines the law, but the law requires the exception in order to assert its primacy and to enact its legislative will.[15]

Schmitt argues that the state of extreme emergency proves that the law requires a discretionary sovereign decision that 'emerges from nothingness' when 'looked at normatively'.[16] Schmitt wrote that 'all political concepts are secularized theological notions'.[17] This is why the exception is a miraculous event: 'the exception in jurisprudence is analogous to the miracle in theology'.[18] What makes legality possible is the state's objective capacity to guarantee the continued existence of the law in the face of its enemies. The sovereign exception is the moment in which state authority appears in its purity: a power to enforce the law separated from the norms of law themselves. The capacity to decide on the state of exception, which Schmitt takes to be constitutive of the normal functioning of the legal order, is the 'zenith' of the sovereign's power, who acts as 'God's highest representative on earth'.[19]

In 1933 the Nazis indefinitely suspended the law through their 'Decree for the Protection of the State and People'. For Agamben the Nazis were able to suspend the law because there is no necessary relation between the decision on the state of exception and the fact situation that ostensibly gives rise to it.[20] The Nazi party produced a 'normal' constitutional structure characterised by the profound legal indeterminacy of the emergency situation. For Agamben (and this is part of his move away from Schmitt) that is deeply problematic for Schmitt's account of sovereignty, which depends upon a relatively clear temporal and categorical distinction between the juridical practices of the normal situation (in which the constitution applies) and the emergency situation (in which it is suspended). Once emergency and normality, exception and law, are rendered absolutely undecidable, the sovereign is 'no longer capable of performing the task that *Political Theology* assigned to it':[21] that of distinguishing between exception and law on the basis of a distinction between emergency and normality.

Kierkegaard's *Repetition* catalysed Schmitt's revival of the exception in the early part of the twentieth century. Rebecca Gould makes the point that Schmitt's *Political Theology* is the only serious scholarly reflection on *Repetition*.[22] Nearly every element of Schmitt's deliberations on the exception originates in Kierkegaard. Jacob Taubes made clear that the 'trajectory between [the] Kierkegaardian exception and Schmitt's definition of sovereignty' must be acknowledged.[23] Schmitt acknowledges his debt to Kierkegaard in *Political Theology*. He references Kierkegaard once by vocation, as 'a Protestant theologian who demonstrated the vital intensity possible in theological reflection'.[24] He then quotes approvingly from Kierkegaard to support his focus on the importance of the exception:

> Eventually one grows weary of the incessant chatter about the universal, and the universal repeated to the point of the most boring insipidity. There are exceptions. If they cannot be explained, then the universal cannot be explained, either. Generally, the difficulty is not noticed because one thinks the universal not with passion but with a comfortable superficiality. The exception, however, thinks the universal with intense passion.[25]

Further to this, in a passage where he also explains how his exception differs from Kierkegaard, he argues that the exception:

> [I]s more interesting than the rule. The rule proves nothing; the exception proves everything: It confirms not only the rule but also its existence, which derives only from the exception. In the exception, the power of real life breaks through the crust of a mechanism rendered torpid by repetition.[26]

Schmitt opposes the exception to repetition, seeing repetition as something to be overcome.[27] Schmitt emphasised the unique character of historical events, with historical singularity held up against the idea of repetition in history: 'The big events are unique, irrevocable and unrepeatable. A historical truth is true only once.'[28] It is for this reason that Schmitt's exception is unrepeated and unrepeatable. The seriousness of this miraculous exception is deeper than any generalisations which can be drawn from 'what ordinarily repeats itself'.²⁹ Repetition for Schmitt is related to the norm which stultifies political life and prevents decisions from being made.³⁰ As a result, Schmitt clearly prefers the uniqueness and unrepeatability of historical events over any kind of eternal recurrence.³¹ The human being has:

> [A]n almost irresistible need to eternalise his last great historical experience. Precisely my sense of history guards me from such repetitions. My sense of history especially maintains itself by recalling to memory the unrepeatable uniqueness of all great historical events. A historical truth is true only once. But also the historical call, the challenge which opens a new epoch, is true only once and is correct only once.³²

It is an unrepeatable singularity which marks Schmitt's exception and his sovereign decisionism.

What then is repetition for Kierkegaard? It is true that *Repetition* is a pseudonymous text, written by a fictional narrator, which may not have reflected the views of Kierkegaard himself. My reading of the text could be framed as a reading of that fictional narrator rather than Kierkegaard. Schmitt and Agamben read this text as being of Kierkegaard's view; I follow their approach here. Repetition has an existential repeatable singularity. To Kierkegaard we owe the insightful alignment between the exceptional and the existential, and the notion of exceptionality and repetition as kindred rather than opposed.³³ In *Repetition*, Kierkegaard makes the point that repetition is not recollection.³⁴ Repetition is the antithesis of Platonic recollection, or *anamnesis*.³⁵ Recollection is the source of all knowledge, where learning is a recollection of what we once knew in a pre-existent state before our souls entered our bodies.³⁶ Recollection is the retrieval of an impression of a past actuality: someone who recollects is thinking about the past. Genuine repetition is recollected forwards.³⁷

Kierkegaard's *Repetition* provides the tale of a narrator who moves back to Berlin to relive the life he had there when younger. The narrator, Constantine Constantius, discovered that everything was the same on his return. However, Kierkegaard makes it clear that what Constantius experienced was not repetition but mere recollection. For Kierkegaard 'the only repetition was the impossibility of a repetition'.³⁸ Repetition is a movement of becoming, of coming into existence:

> Repetition means that a past actuality becomes actual once again: someone who repeats is renewing actuality. Recollection and repetition deal with the past in different ways: that which is recollected is complete within itself; it is contemplated as a finished totality, apprehended as an idea. On the other hand, if something is repeated it is re-enacted, actualized; it is not merely represented as an idea but recreated as a reality.³⁹

Both recollection and repetition are movements of truth: the former moves towards a past eternity, and the latter moves towards a future eternity. This illuminates Constantius's remark that 'repetition and recollection are the same movement, only in opposite directions'.[40] Repetition is life that is lived in the moment itself. For Kierkegaard, the one that lives is the one that gives themself to the repetition of life.[41] Life is a succession of repetitions, but such repetitions create something new. Such a position raises the possibility that the very act of repetition opens up to a new sphere of living, a sphere that for Kierkegaard must be embraced. The singular and the irreducible are precisely what is repeatable, which stands in contrast to the sovereign decisionism of Schmitt, which holds that the exception equals the unrepeated and unrepeatable.[42]

In the sections which follow, I wish to read Kierkegaard's 'repetition', the repeatable singularity, as a model for Agamben's 'absolute immanence'. It is true that Kierkegaard wrote that repetition is transcendence. Yet Agamben's immanent life sees Kierkegaard's repetition as a corollary and Schmitt's exception as an antithesis. Agamben's philosophy is driven by a focus upon immanence, understood as the plane of existence *as it is experienced*. This can be contrasted with transcendence as it is usually understood, which is that which goes beyond; in phenomenology the transcendent is that which transcends our own consciousness. For Agamben however, the plane of transcendence extends no further than the plane of immanence, and it is in this sense that his engagement with Kierkegaard should be situated and the repeatable singularity represents absolute immanence.[43]

The exception Agamben is interested in undermines the (Schmittian) law and sovereign decisionism, rather than founds it. This is why in *State of Exception* Agamben wrote that it is necessary to rethink the relation between life and law: 'to show law in its nonrelation to life and life in its nonrelation to law',[44] opens an immanent space for human action. This space, which Agamben calls 'politics', is made after the tie between law and life is severed. The political in Agamben is the existential in Kierkegaard: 'Politics is that which corresponds to the essential inoperability of humankind . . . There is politics because human beings are *argōs* – beings that cannot be defined by any proper operation – that is, beings . . . that no identity or vocation can possibly exhaust.'[45] The next section explores the nature of this immanent life.

Agamben's Existential Life

In 'Absolute Immanence' Agamben provides a close reading of Gilles Deleuze's essay 'Immanence: A Life'.[46] In Deleuze's essay Agamben sees in the term 'life' a capacity to resist force and power.[47] 'A life . . .' marks the radical impossibility of establishing divisions and separations.[48] 'A life . . .' exists on the plane of immanence, and is immanent only to itself.[49] As Deleuze and Guattari explain, immanence must be distinguished from an immanence that is held in relation to the transcendent plane.[50] Immanence has neither a focal point nor a horizon that can orient thought. The only possible point of orientation is the 'vertigo' in which outside and inside, immanence and transcendence, are absolutely indistinguishable.[51] What does this mean for an immanent life? At the end of *What is Philosophy?* life as absolute immediacy is defined as 'pure contemplation without knowledge'.[52] What this means is: 'A life is everywhere, in all the moments that traverse this or that living subjects and that measure lived objects.'[53] This immanent life is 'form-of-life'. Form-of-life is an existential figure, inhabiting a non-relational existence, not lived through forms of identity politics. This figure (under different names) has formed a part of Agamben's thought for many years. Written in 1990, *The Coming Community* opens with a meditation on 'whatever-Being'.[54] This *whatever* (which will be later termed 'form-of-life') is a *radical indifference*: '[T]he coming politics will no longer be a struggle to conquer or to control the state on the part of either new or old social subjects, but rather a struggle between . . . whatever singularities and the state organisation.'[55] Kierkegaard can be read as expressing himself in line with this:

> [T]he established order will not put up with consisting of something as loose as a collection of millions of individuals . . . The established order wants to be a totality that recognises nothing above itself but has every individual under it and judges every individual who subordinates himself to the established order.[56]

Kierkegaard traces the individual's 'collision' with 'the established order', pointing out that the established order would be upset by the fact that the individual wanted to live an immanent life – 'that the single individual wanted to withdraw from his relation to the established order'.[57]

In a way which evokes the operation of repetition, form-of-life is generated by the very act of living.[58] It is a movement of becoming, of coming into existence. This form-of-life (like 'a life') is what Agamben terms a 'monad', signifying itself singular nature. The relationship between monads is complex. The more form-of-life becomes monadic, the more it isolates itself from other monads. However, each monad always-already communicates with the others, by representing them in itself, 'as in a living mirror'.[59] In form-of-life, living and life contract into one another,[60] in a mode of living, a '*how* I am what I am'.[61] Form-of-life is the most idiosyncratic aspect of everyone – their tastes:

> If every body is affected by its form-of-life as by a clinamen or a taste, the ethical subject is that subject that constitutes-itself in relation to this clinamen, the subject who bears witness to its tastes, takes responsibility for the mode in which it is affected by its inclinations. Modal ontology, the ontology of the *how*, coincides with an ethics.[62]

This is not to take the notion of 'tastes' too literally. Tastes – 'the fact [individuals] like coffee granita, the sea at summertime, this certain shape of lips, this certain smell' – are ontological in character.[63] Agamben continues: 'It is not a matter of attributes or properties of a subject who judges but of the mode in which each person, in losing himself as subject, constitutes himself as form-of-life.'[64] This ontology of the 'how' presupposes a doing, a taking responsibility, a capacity for realising this 'how'. The 'how' is repetition, a repeatable singularity which is lived in the moment itself. For Agamben this is where living and life coincide – but what are the limits of this living? To live life as a form indicates that one *must* realise and take responsibility for this condition. Form-of-life must live its own mode of being (as a monad) inseparable from its context (that is to say, a network of relations). However, these relations are non-relational. Form-of-life is in *contact* with its relational context because it has rendered these relations non-relational.[65] 'Contact' means that:

> [F]orm and life . . . dwell in a non-relation. And it is in contact – that is, in a void of representation – and not in a relation that forms-of-life communicate. The 'alone by oneself' that defines the structure of every singular form-of-life also defines its community with others. And it is this . . . contact that the juridical order and politics seeks by all means to capture and represent in a relation . . . forms-of-life are in contact, but this is unrepresentable because it consists . . . in the deactivation and inoperativity of every representation.[66]

Contact occurs when two entities are separated only by their void of representation. 'Representative' politics seeks to capture and represent this void in the form of a relation that will always-already have a negative ground – this capturing will take place through the Schmittian decision.[67] Contrastingly, form-of-life is situated beyond every possible recognition, and beyond the Schmittian exception and decision.[68] In a sense, Agamben is arguing that existence precedes essence:

> Only if I am . . . delivered to a possibility and a power, only if living and intending and apprehending themselves are at stake each time in what I live and intend and apprehend . . . only then can a form of life become, in its own factness and thingness, *form-of-life*, in which it is never possible to isolate something like naked life.[69]

There is a corollary between Agamben's 'living [which] is at stake each time in what I live and intend' and the view from *Repetition* that life is a series of repetitions, and such repetitions create something new. Such a form-of-life cannot be based upon the mutual sharing of properties or the politics of social movements.[70] A community of forms-of-life is not structured by an *absence* of shared properties as a 'negative community'.[71] Forms-of-life are in contact but this consists in the inoperativity of every representation – a non-representable politics.[72]

To summarise – Agamben describes form-of-life as a monad that dwells in non-relational contact with other monads. Therefore, forms-of-life are not in relation, but are in contact. For Agamben, all identities are relational in the sense that every identity is a differential construct. Some people regard these differences as essential (for example, male and female, black and white, Jew and Gentile), while others regard them as arbitrary constructs. The person who regards them as arbitrary constructs lives in 'contact' with others, and focuses on how it lives its life,[73] which involves ways of envisaging an immanent life on the threshold of its political and ethical intensification.[74] The person who regards these differences as ontic realities lives in relation with others, upholding these representational constructs as juridical.

Form-of-life, Repetition, Synthesis, Self

Building upon the previous section, I now wish to extend the connections I am making between Agamben and Kierkegaard. Agamben's claim that the 'subject' is the result of the living being passing through divisions and caesuras (which operates as an apparatus through which the decision of what is and what is not human is possible) is in my argument a new interpretation and concretisation of Kierkegaard's claim that the human being is a synthesis with the possibility of becoming a self. This forms the basis of an existential reading of form-of-life which is subject to a continual process of repetition.

For both Agamben and Kierkegaard, anthropogenesis never stops happening, and first philosophy is the memory and repetition of this event.[75] It is the task of the human being to bring the parts together in their existence, and the human being only manages to be a singular being (form-of-life for Agamben, the self for Kierkegaard) when this happens.

Agamben opens up a new reading of Kierkegaard in a political context. The political is never an end in itself and can never be one except at the cost of the individual. This is shown through Agamben's writings on potentiality (which connect to form-of-life) and Kierkegaard's writings on the self. Agamben argues that if something has the potential-to-be, it must also have the potential-not-to-be. Daniel Heller-Roazen explains:

> The potential not to be (or do) ... is not effaced in the passage into actuality, on the contrary, actuality is itself nothing other than the full realisation of the potential not to be (or do), the point at which, as Aristotle writes, 'there will be nothing impotential' ... Aristotle's definition of potentiality therefore concerns the precise condition in which potentiality realises itself.[76]

Potentiality is more than just unactualised actuality. It is the potential to not-do, the potential not to pass into actuality.[77] The existence of potentiality is the presence of an absence, what Agamben terms a 'faculty'.[78] To be potential is to be capable of im-potentiality.[79] Therefore a thing (for example, a life) is potential when, at its realisation, there is nothing left that is im-potential, nothing able not-to-be.[80] Potentiality thus fulfils itself by letting itself be – by taking away its own potentiality not-to-be.[81]

Every human power is im-potentiality and every human potentiality is always-already held in relation to its own privation.[82] This is both the origin of human power, good and bad, and the root of human freedom.[83] Agamben sees human freedom neither as the power to do an act, nor the power to refuse to do an act – to be free is to be capable of one's own im-potentiality, to be free for both good and evil.[84] Agamben goes on to say in relation to potentiality: '[T]here is in effect something that humans *are and have to be*, but this something is not an essence or properly a thing: it is the simple fact of one's own existence as possibility or potentiality.'[85]

Potentiality is connected to the figure of a form-of-life. 'Letting itself be' – this is a description of how a monad generates its form through its act of living. In other words, a form-of-life is capable of im-potentiality. In turn, im-potential forms-of-life dwell in contact with each other – that is to say, in non-relation with one another. Form-of-life is a philosophical outlook. It is to say that one's identity is a constructed performance. This means that form-of-life is an embodied existential figure, subject to a continual process of repetition, a process that is always-already happening. In a similar vein to Kierkegaard (and explicitly referencing him), Agamben also sees repetition as bringing change:

> What is repetition? There are four great thinkers of repetition in modernity: Kierkegaard, Nietzsche, Heidegger, and Gilles Deleuze. All four have shown that repetition is not the return of the identical; it is not the same as such that returns. The force and the grace of repetition, the novelty it brings us, is the return as the possibility of what was, render it possible anew; it's almost a paradox. To repeat something is to make it possible anew.[86]

For Agamben, repetition restores possibility,[87] which is coterminous to potentiality.[88] Therefore we can say that in living our lives as inseparable from its form, a life which lets itself be, we do so through a series of repeatable singularities which allow us to be capable of im-potentiality.

In a similar fashion to the potential which lets itself be, Kierkegaard begins *The Sickness unto Death* by describing the idea that the human being is a self or has the possibility of becoming one:

> A human being is spirit. But what is spirit? Spirit is the self. But what is the self? The self is a relation that relates itself to itself in the relation; the self is not the relation but is the relation's relating itself to itself. A human being is a synthesis of the infinite and the finite, of the temporal and the eternal, of freedom and necessity, in short, a synthesis. A synthesis is a relation between two. Considered in this way, a human being is still not a self. In the relation between two, the relation is the third as a negative unity.[89]

The human being can be a self when the synthesis, the relation itself, relates itself to itself, or lets itself be. This can be connected to Agamben's potentiality – at a thing's realisation, there is nothing left that is able not-to-be. In both cases, the self is defined without being divided and separated through a decision. Kierkegaard's self (importantly not the human being) does not involve its being held in relation to anything other than itself. It is its own relation to itself. Kierkegaard's description of the self can therefore be favourably compared to Agamben's ontology of potentiality and form-of-life.

Agamben warns against representative politics as a way in which life can continue to be articulated and divided through the repeatable sovereign decision, creating bare life as a remainder. In a similar (although by no means identical) manner, Kierkegaard sees danger in reducing the single human being to a citizen in the state. The individual needs to be kept separate from the masses of society, and not subsumed into the latter. Kierkegaard sees in the state's ethics a modern version of ancient Greece's conception of the relation between the individual and the *polis*, where the task of the individual was to enter into and fulfil their life in the *polis*. Kierkegaard points out this danger in *The Sickness unto Death*:

> If order is to be maintained in existence . . . then the first thing to keep in mind is that every human being is an individual human being and is to become conscious of being an individual human being. If men are first permitted to run together in what Aristotle calls the animal category – the crowd – then this abstraction, instead of being less than nothing, even less than the most insignificant individual human being, comes to be regarded as something – then it does not take long before this abstraction becomes God.[90]

This means that the single individual (as a potentiality) could be subsumed by a collective identity (which represents actuality). A collective identity reduces the human being to the 'animal category', with 'the predominance of the generation over the individual'.[91] In this situation, the individual is deprived of their own significance and becomes 'less than nothing, even less than the most insignificant individual human being'.[92]

Finally, I explore how the self in Kierkegaard is a life that is lived in the moment itself (which is the structure of repetition), and how this repetition models a version of 'contact' between non-relational monads in Kierkegaard. My starting point is Kierkegaard's proposal to 'level' all existence so that the human being becomes the self before God, without appealing to the support of any further authority,[93] removing any transcendent referent for the self to define themselves in relation to. Becoming a self requires that an individual distance themselves from the world of others in the sense of defining themselves through a relation to another. Instead, a self is a non-relational monad, which is held in relation to itself, who is nevertheless in contact with other monads. Here I am arguing that Kierkegaard can be read as opposing the sovereign division of life into citizen and bare life, which involves the production of individual subjects through the actualisation of their potentiality.

For Agamben and Kierkegaard a striving *to other* oneself or others makes no sense. Everybody should take care of themselves in order to become a true self that deserves the name. To secure one's true self no reference to others is necessary. The experience of *being othered* implies for Kierkegaard a dangerous distraction from the true relation of the self to itself – a corollary to Agamben's immanent form-of-life.

For Kierkegaard to be *othered* or to experiencing *othering* means to be threatened by an alteration that seems to make *something* or *someone* out of us. *Othering* produces an *othered self*, imagined as becoming someone or something other *which it is not* and *which it can never become* – a transcendent referent which the self is constantly defined in relation to. For Kierkegaard, if we have undergone an othering we should do our best to undo it and ultimately to rid ourselves of an otherness that threatens us with estrangement from our self.

The Sickness unto Death contends that, once a self is formed, it does *not* stand 'outside' the world, but is immersed in it, as an existential figure. The self gives itself to itself. This means that within the world the self defines its existence not through being defined through its relation to others. True selfhood and true freedom must be an orientation towards oneself as a single individual.[94] Every self must turn towards itself and establish itself before reaching out to others. Giving itself to itself models the structure of repetition which involves living a life in the moment itself. Existentially, there is no possibility of delegating the task of living one's own life. Therefore the figure of the self lives through giving itself to the repetition of life. This opens up a new sphere of living in a movement of becoming. Each moment of becoming is a repetition, a repeatable singularity through which the self lives constantly anew, existing in its own history and own world it shares with others.

The self also relates to others in a non-relational way. Living through repetition the self remains in contact with other selves – living as a non-relational monad avoids the problem of othering. In *Works of Love* Kierkegaard argued that the quality of the human condition is shown through the fact that we all die. This shows that everyone's end is the same and the differences we have in life are mere passing attributes.[95] Death founds an understanding that we are beings for whom living in a world with others matters, and others count in the sphere of our shared existence.[96] However, they count as monadic others who form part of the world in which we live, continuously in contact with them. They are therefore part of the immersed world in which the self lives through a movement of becoming.

This existential approach is evocative of Agamben's form-of-life living its life as a 'how', or a mode of living. Kierkegaard and Agamben focus on a form of life that is brought about by the form itself, as a way of living. Both Agamben and Kierkegaard place the onus on the singular being to live through repeatable singularities. Kierkegaard makes clear: 'The greatness is not to be this or that but to be oneself.'[97] For both philosophers, the space of living is an act of radical self-determination in a world with others.

Conclusion

This chapter has sought to interrogate the relationship of Kierkegaard and Agamben through Kierkegaard's 'repetition' and Agamben's 'form-of-life'. First, I considered how Schmitt and Agamben have cited Kierkegaard, arguing that Kierkegaard's *Repetition* is a model for Agamben's form-of-life. Schmitt's exception is an unrepeatable singularity which founds his sovereign decisionism. In contrast, form-of-life provides the basis of a way of living for forms of life which are able to live their lives as a 'how'. This how is always in the process of repetition in the Kierkegaardian sense. In contrast to Schmitt's unrepeatable singularity of the exception, representative of sovereign decisionism and the division of life, Kierkegaard's self and Agamben's form-of-life posit repeatable singularities which exist as non-relational monads. They do not exist in relation to others but rather in contact with them. Contact is a way of relating to others outside of difference. Form-of-life and the self are non-relational in the sense that they are not defined or understood as being held up against other persons or beings and compared and contrasted to that other. Likewise, they are non-differential in that form-of-life does not depend upon differences between itself and others. This chapter concludes with the argument that form-of-life is an existential figure, always in the process of repetition, understood in its performative, Kierkegaardian sense. If form-of-life is read existentially, then its construction makes sense. Form-of-life is subject to a continual process of repetition, an existential process that is always-already happening.

Notes

1. Giorgio Agamben, *The Use of Bodies*, trans. Adam Kotsko (Stanford: Stanford University Press, 2016), p. 235.
2. Ibid. p. 224.
3. Ibid. p. 231.
4. Gil Anidjar, 'The Meaning of Life', *Critical Inquiry* 37.4 (Summer 2011): 697, 709.
5. Giorgio Agamben, *The Open: Man and Animal*, trans. Kevin Attell (Stanford: Stanford University Press, 2004), p. 13.
6. Ibid.
7. Giorgio Agamben, *Homo Sacer: Sovereign Power and Bare Life*, trans. Daniel Heller-Roazen (Stanford: Stanford University Press, 1998), p. 181.
8. Giorgio Agamben, *What is an Apparatus? and Other Essays*, trans. David Kishik and Stefan Pedatella (Stanford: Stanford University Press, 2009), p. 16.
9. Aristotle, 'On the Soul', in *The Complete Works of Aristotle, Volume One*, ed. Jonathan Barnes (Princeton: Princeton University Press, 1984).
10. Agamben, *The Open*, p. 15.
11. Carl Schmitt, *Political Theology: Four Chapters on the Concept of Sovereignty*, trans. George Schwab (Chicago: University of Chicago Press, 2005), p. 34.
12. Daniel McLoughlin, 'The Fiction of Sovereignty and the Real State of Exception: Giorgio Agamben's Critique of Carl Schmitt', *Law, Culture and the Humanities* 12.3 (2016): 509, 515–16.
13. Agamben, *Homo Sacer*, p. 15.
14. Schmitt, *Political Theology*, p. 13.
15. Rebecca Gould, 'Laws, Exceptions, Norms: Kierkegaard, Schmitt, and Benjamin on the Exception', *Telos* 162 (2013): 77, 85–6.
16. Schmitt, *Political Theology*, pp. 31–2.
17. Ibid. p. 37.
18. Ibid. p. 36.
19. Carl Schmitt, *The Leviathan in the State Theory of Thomas Hobbes*, trans. George Schwab (Chicago: Chicago University Press, 2008), p. 55.
20. Agamben, *Homo Sacer*, p. 170.
21. Ibid. p. 58.
22. Gould, 'Laws, Exceptions, Norms', p. 81.
23. Jacob Taubes, *The Political Theology of Paul*, trans. Aleida Assmann (Stanford: Stanford University Press, 2004), p. 65.
24. Schmitt, *Political Theology*, p. 15.
25. Søren Kierkegaard, 'Repetition: A Venture in Experimenting Psychology', in *Fear and Trembling/Repetition*, trans. Harold V. Hong and Edna H. Hong (Princeton: Princeton University Press, 1983), p. 227.
26. Schmitt, *Political Theology*, p. 22.
27. Gould, 'Laws, Exceptions, Norms', pp. 89–90.

28. Carl Schmitt, *Gespräch über die Macht und den Zugang zum Machthaber/Gespräch über den neuen Raum* (Berlin: Akademie Verlag, 1994), p. 55.
29. Schmitt, *Political Theology*, p. 22.
30. Gould, 'Laws, Exceptions, Norms', p. 90.
31. Matthias Lievens, 'Singularity and Repetition in Carl Schmitt's Vision of History', *Journal of the Philosophy of History* 5.1 (2011): 105, 120–1; Carl Schmitt, 'Die geschichtliche Struktur des heutigen Welt-Gegensatzes von Ost und West. Bemerkungen zu Ernst Jüngers Schrift: "Der Gordische Knoten"', in *Staat, Grossraum, Nomos. Arbeiten aus den Jahren, 1916–1969* (Berlin: Duncker & Humblot, 1995), pp. 544–5.
32. Schmitt, *Gespräch über die Macht*, p. 61.
33. Gould, 'Laws, Exceptions, Norms', p. 93.
34. Kierkegaard, 'Repetition', p. 131.
35. Kierkegaard, 'Repetition', p. 149.
36. Dominic Scott, 'Platonic Recollection and Cambridge Platonism', *Hermathena* 149 (Winter 1990): 73, 74.
37. Kierkegaard, 'Repetition', p. 131.
38. Kierkegaard, 'Repetition', p. 170.
39. Clare Carlisle, 'Kierkegaard's Repetition: The Possibility of Motion', *British Journal for the History of Philosophy* 13.3 (2005): 521, 525.
40. Kierkegaard, 'Repetition', p. 131.
41. Kierkegaard, 'Repetition', pp. 132, 133.
42. Gould, 'Laws, Exceptions, Norms', pp. 83–4.
43. Giorgio Agamben, 'Absolute Immanence', in *Potentialities: Collected Essays in Philosophy*, trans. Daniel Heller-Roazen (Stanford: Stanford University Press, 1999), pp. 226–8.
44. Giorgio Agamben, *State of Exception*, trans. Kevin Attell (Chicago: University of Chicago Press, 2005), p. 88.
45. Giorgio Agamben, *Means without End: Notes on Politics*, trans. Vincenzo Binetti and Cesare Casarino (Minneapolis: University of Minnesota Press, 2000), p. 141.
46. Agamben, 'Absolute Immanence', p. 239; Gilles Deleuze, *Pure Immanence: Essays on A Life*, trans. Anne Boyman (New York: Zone Books, 2001).
47. Agamben, 'Absolute Immanence', p. 220.
48. Ibid. p. 233.
49. Ibid. p. 227.
50. Gilles Deleuze and Félix Guattari, *What is Philosophy?*, trans. Hugh Tomlinson and Graham Burchell (New York: Columbia University Press, 1994), p. 45.
51. Agamben, 'Absolute Immanence', p. 228.
52. Ibid. p. 233.
53. Gilles Deleuze, 'Immanence: A Life . . .', *Theory, Culture, Society* 14.2 (1997): 3, 6.
54. Giorgio Agamben, *The Coming Community*, trans. Michael Hardt (Minneapolis: University of Minnesota Press, 2007), p. 1.
55. Agamben, *Means without End*, p. 88.
56. Søren Kierkegaard, *Practice in Christianity*, trans. Howard V. Hong and Edna H. Hong (Princeton: Princeton University Press, 1991), p. 91.
57. Ibid. p. 93.
58. Agamben, *The Use of Bodies*, p. 221.
59. Ibid. p. 232.
60. Ibid. p. 223.
61. Ibid. p. 231.
62. Ibid.
63. Ibid.
64. Ibid.
65. Ibid. p. 232.

66. Ibid. p. 237.
67. Ibid.
68. Ibid. p. 248.
69. Agamben, *Means without End*, p. 9. The isolation referred to is Schmitt's decision.
70. Agamben, *The Coming Community*, p. 86.
71. Ibid.
72. Agamben, *The Use of Bodies*, p. 237.
73. Ibid. p. 231.
74. Erik Bordeleau, 'Initiating Life: Agamben and the Political Use of Intimacy', *The Journal of Speculative Philosophy* 31.3 (2017): 481, 482.
75. Agamben, *The Use of Bodies*, p. 111.
76. Daniel Heller-Roazen, 'Editor's Introduction: "To Read What Was Never Written"', in *Potentialities: Collected Essays in Philosophy*, trans. Daniel Heller-Roazen (Stanford: Stanford University Press, 1999), p. 17.
77. Aristotle, *Metaphysics*, 1046a, 30–5, in *The Complete Works of Aristotle, Volume Two*, ed. Jonathan Barnes (Princeton: Princeton University Press, 1984); Giorgio Agamben, 'On Potentiality', in *Potentialities*, p. 180.
78. Agamben, 'On Potentiality', p. 179.
79. Ibid. p. 182.
80. Agamben, *Homo Sacer*, p. 45.
81. Ibid. pp. 45–6.
82. Agamben, 'On Potentiality', p. 182.
83. Ibid.
84. Ibid. pp. 182–3.
85. Agamben, *The Coming Community*, p. 43.
86. Giorgio Agamben, 'Difference and Repetition: On Guy Debord's Film', in *Guy Debord and the Situationist International: Texts and Documents*, ed. Tom McDonough (Cambridge, MA: MIT Press, 2004), pp. 313, 315–16.
87. Agamben, 'Difference and Repetition', p. 316.
88. Agamben, *The Coming Community*, p. 43.
89. Søren Kierkegaard, *The Sickness unto Death*, trans. Harold V. Hong and Edna H. Hong (Princeton: Princeton University Press, 1980), p. 15.
90. Kierkegaard, *The Sickness unto Death*, pp. 117–18; cf. Aristotle, *Politics*, Book II, 1281a40-43 in *The Complete Works of Aristotle, Volume Two*, ed. Jonathan Barnes (Princeton: Princeton University Press, 1984).
91. Kierkegaard, *The Sickness unto Death*, p. 118.
92. Ibid.
93. Søren Kierkegaard, *Works of Love*, trans. Howard V. Hong and Edna H. Hong (Princeton: Princeton University Press, 1995), p. 272.
94. Søren Kierkegaard, *Christian Discourses*, trans. Howard V. Hong and Edna H. Hong (Princeton: Princeton University Press, 1997), p. 236.
95. Søren Kierkegaard, *Works of Love*, p. 345.
96. Ibid. p. 353.
97. Søren Kierkegaard, *Either/Or, Part II*, trans. Howard V. Hong and Edna H. Hong (Princeton: Princeton University Press, 1987), p. 177.

II
Agamben and the Death of God

Chapter 5

The Work of Art and the Death of God in Nietzsche and Agamben

Vanessa Lemm

The repercussions of Nietzsche's idea of the death of God were not only felt in the religious sphere, but also in how we think about the meaning and place of creation and creativity in life. Agamben's discussion of creativity as 'inoperativity' is the latest, important contribution to the debate, arguably initiated by existentialism, on how the death of God relates to life as material for artistic creation.[1] In this chapter I situate Agamben's theses on 'inoperativity' in dialogue with motifs drawn from Nietzsche's discussion of the death of God and his conception of the 'work of art without artist'. I argue that Agamben helps us to get beyond the existentialist interpretation of the human subject as creator of its own life (*bios*) by proposing an anarchic conception of giving artistic form to life (*zoē*) that deconstructs the position of mastery over life assigned to modern subjectivity and de-centres the idea of the human agency in the process of creation.[2] However, I also suggest that Agamben's conception of the artistic life downplays or avoids other features of Nietzsche's thinking on the death of God and creation that are tied to animality and the divinity of nature.

In existentialist interpretations of Nietzsche, the motif of the death of God is understood as a liberating event that opens the possibility for the human being to become the sole author of its own life (*bios*) and to assume full responsibility for giving meaning to its life.[3] The realisation of this freedom is the distinguishing feature of our humanity. Julian Young's reading of Nietzsche offers an example of this existentialist approach to the death of God.[4] For him, the death of God does not simply refer to the death of the God of traditional Christianity, but extends to 'anything that performs the meaning-giving function in human life that was once performed by a God'.[5] In line with the tradition of existentialism, Young assumes that meaning is not a given or something we discover but something we make and choose at will. In order to overcome nihilism, namely, the void and meaninglessness which results from the death of God, the individual is called to create her own life story and become the creator of her own life. The heroic self-creation of our life (*bios*) is situated 'beyond good and evil' and hence what counts is not whether we make good or bad choices but whether our life is an authentic expression of our creativity for which we are responsible.

In very broad terms, the problem with this existentialist reading of the death of God is that the human being qua self-creator reoccupies the place left vacant by the Christian God and understands itself as another God (*alter deus*). This Promethean ideal has also been traditionally associated with Nietzsche's teaching on the *Übermensch* as a new type of human being that overcomes the Christian worldview towards greater freedom and creativity. However, Nietzsche never authorises the presumption that the human being qua *Übermensch* can take the place of God. Rather, as Löwith correctly points out, 'the surmounting of Christianity is identical with the human being's surmounting itself'.[6] The existentialist interpretation of the individual qua creator of its own life is overly focused on the 'heroic' task to gain mastery over shaping its life. Thereby, it loses sight of what I shall call the an-archic character of creation, understood as a process that lacks metaphysical foundations and is instead open to chaos and radical contingency. Thus, Nietzsche's call to become 'poets of our life' (*GS*, 299)[7] does not entail a work of (self-)realisation whereby an individual fulfils his or her essence by enacting his or her capacities to create at will, as if who we are and what we become would be a process that is 'mastered' or 'owned' by the individual. For Nietzsche, as I discuss below, the process of creation is never strictly speaking an *individual* (solipsistic) process but is contingent on an 'untimely' relation to its historical situation. Nietzsche speaks of the 'deed' (*TI*, 'Skirmishes', 44)[8] of the artist in quotations suggesting that in fact there is no such thing as a 'deed' and that the word refers to our misunderstanding of the process of creation as if the artist, to use Agamben's words, 'one fine day, . . . decides like the God of the theologians, to put to work [her potential or faculty to create], who knows how or why'.[9] The process of creation in Nietzsche does not occur at will or reflects an existential choice where the latter become elements in the creation of an individual's form of life.

For the existentialist, creation is the expression of a faculty to create at will rather than, to use Agamben's terminology, a complex dialectic between resistance and creation, potential and potential not-to, personal and impersonal dimensions of life. As charged by Heidegger, existentialism remains within the metaphysics of subjectivity.[10] Furthermore, the existentialist account of (self-)creation is a disembodied one; it reinforces the idea that animal life (*zoē*) is accidental, ephemeral, perhaps even detrimental, to the individual's artistic self-realisation (*bios*). The anthropocentrism of the existentialist standpoint ignores the nonhuman dimensions of life (*zoē*) and what this animality means for our 'learning from the artist' to 'become poets of our life' (*GS*, 78, 299).

To appreciate the multiple (human and nonhuman/personal and impersonal) dimensions of Agamben's conception of life and creativity, it is better to follow Foucault's response to the death of God in Nietzsche reflected in his ideas of an 'aesthetics of existence'[11] and his closely related notion of an 'ontology of the present'.[12] Agamben situates his own 'Archaeology of the Work of Art' within this Foucauldian lineage and defines it as an 'investigation of the past [which] is nothing but the shadow cast by an interrogation directed at the present'.[13] Foucault's 'aesthetics of existence' is directly opposed to the Sartrean existentialist ethics of authenticity and its associated conception of creation.[14] Foucault argues that '[w]e should not have to refer the creative activity of somebody to the kind of relation he has to himself but should relate the kind of relation one has to oneself to a creative activity'.[15] Here creativity is not an attribute of the self. Rather, the life (*zoē*) of the individual is a function of a creative activity.[16] Foucault regrets that:

> in our society, art has become something that is related only to objects and not to individuals or to life. That art is something which is specialized or done by experts who are artists. But couldn't everyone's life become a work of art? Why should the lamp or the house be an art object but not our life?[17]

For Foucault, the 'rare art' of 'giving style to our character' (*GS*, 290) is the art of leading a creative life.

In the first section, 'The Work of Art without Artist and the Deactivation of the Artistic Machine', I discuss Agamben's archaeology of the work of art and his thesis that, since the Renaissance, the work of art has been produced through what he calls the 'artistic machine'. I examine his proposal to deactivate this machine by thematising the dimension of human life he calls 'inoperativity', and what this means for his understanding of the process of creation as anthropogenesis. I also raise the question of whether, by deactivating the artistic machine, Agamben may paradoxically be reactivating what he has previously called the 'anthropological machine'.[18] The second section, 'The Death of God and the Death of Man', compares and contrasts the difference between Nietzsche's and Agamben's accounts of anthropogenesis and the relation between animality and divinity. It argues that the death of God as the death of the human being in Nietzsche leads to a naturalistic conception of creativity inspired by Greek and Renaissance art that provides some insights into how to deactivate the 'work-artist-operation machine' without falling into the 'anthropological machine'. This chapter concludes with a third section, 'Contingency, Resistance and Self-Overcoming', on the difference between Nietzsche's and Agamben's conceptions of contingency and resistance in the generation of a form-of-life.[19] For Nietzsche a form of life is generated essentially in and through a process of continuous self-overcoming. In Agamben, a form of life is constituted through a dialectical tension between creation and resistance, the artist's potential (impersonal) and potential not-to (personal). Whereas in Agamben the contingency of creation is located within the action, in Nietzsche creation happens to the activity as an event external to it.

The Work of Art without Artist and the Deactivation of the Artistic Machine

When asked about his vision of the philosophical life, in a 2004 interview, Agamben answered: 'Nietzsche's idea of a work of art without the artist.'[20] Agamben draws this reference from a fragmentary note found in Nietzsche's posthumous writings: 'The work of art, where it appears without an artist, e.g., as body, as organism . . . To what extent the artist is only a preliminary stage. The world as a work of art that gives birth to itself.'[21] This text brings into close relation embodied life and art, the creativity of nature and the work of art, and opens the horizon of a post-humanist approach to creation. The same note also features prominently in Heidegger's essay 'Nietzsches Wort "Gott ist tot"'.[22] Heidegger famously claims that the death of God in Nietzsche announces the 'end' of metaphysics and the rise of nihilism. Yet Heidegger also argues that Nietzsche is the last metaphysician and his conception of the work of art still reflects the metaphysics of subjectivity.[23] As far as I am aware, Agamben does not offer an extended exegesis of Nietzsche's passages on the death of God. However, in *Creation and Anarchy* he builds on the relationship between God, creation and artistic subjectivity that can be found in Heidegger's interpretation of the death of God in Nietzsche. In contrast to Heidegger's reading, Agamben seeks to uncouple creativity from subjectivity and connect it instead with what he calls 'inoperativity', the fact that the essential human activities have no 'work' associated with them.[24] For Agamben inoperativity signals the opening up of a process of creation that overcomes nihilism towards the becoming of 'the work of art without artist'.

In 'Archaeology of the Work of Art' Agamben traces the conception of the work of art from Aristotle's *Metaphysics* and *Ethics*, through the figure of the artist in the Renaissance to the contemporary art of Marcel

Duchamp. Whereas the 'Greeks would privilege the work with respect to the artist (or the artisan)', essentially because according to them 'the *energia*, the true and proper productive activity', does not reside in the artist but in the work,[25] in the Renaissance:

> art has withdrawn from the sphere of activities that have their *energia* outside themselves, in a work, and has been transposed into the circle of those activities that, like knowing or praxis, have their *energia*, their being-at-work, in themselves. The artist ... like the contemplative, [he] now lays claim to the mastery and titulary of his creative activity.[26]

In the Renaissance conception 'art resides not in the work, but in the mind of the artist'.[27] Thus the connection between God and artistic creation, according to Agamben, occurs in the Renaissance: 'It is from this paradigm that there derives the disastrous transposition of the theological vocabulary of creation onto the activity of the artist, which until then no one had dreamed of defining as creative.'[28] Through analogy with God as creator, the artist reflects the human being's nature as one defined by its creative activity. The connection that gets established between work of art, artist and creative activity since the Renaissance conforms what Agamben calls an 'artistic machine'.[29] This machine maintains a continuity with the Christian idea of creation and preserves the idea of God as creator well into modernity. On this view, the Renaissance conception of the work of art secularises the idea of divine creation, elevates the artist to the status of a new God and thereby devalues the work of art as merely contingent and ephemeral.[30] Ever since the Renaissance the artist has become the supreme operator of the artistic machine that 'mechanically' churns works of art.

The theological underpinnings of the modern 'artistic machine' can be found in early twentieth-century 'mysterical' conceptions of religion that identify an analogy between the sacred action of the liturgy and the praxis of the artistic avant-gardes.[31] Agamben understands liturgy and performance as a form of praxis 'in which the action itself claims to present itself as a work'.[32] This performance finds its fullest and perhaps last expression in Duchamp's 'ready-mades' which Agamben takes to be 'existential acts (and not works of art)'[33]: 'I would argue that Duchamp understood that what was blocking art was precisely what I defined as the artistic machine, which in the liturgy of the avant-gardes had reached its critical mass.'[34] Duchamp deactivates the 'work-artist-operation-machine' by introducing any ordinary object into a museum thereby forcing it to present itself as a work of art.[35] It goes without saying that the work is not a work, the operation is not an operation and the artist is not an artist. Duchamp 'does not act as an artist, but at most as philosopher or critic or, as Duchamp loved to say, "as someone who breathes," a simple living being'.[36]

For Agamben, Duchamp exemplifies the Nietzschean idea of the 'work of art without artist'. On this interpretation, Duchamp's ready-mades deactivate the analogy between God as creator and the human being as creator. Here, the death of God entails the death of the artist qua other God. The death of God means that the human being is no longer 'the transcendent title-holders of a capacity to act or produce works'.[37] Instead, Agamben suggests that we need to think of artists as 'living beings who, in the use and only in the use of their members and of the world that surrounds them, gain experience of themselves and constitute themselves as forms of life'.[38] For Agamben, the process of creation after the death of God is situated beyond the paradigm of (self-)mastery that underpins the idea of modern subjectivity. Art becomes 'the way in which the anonymous ones we call artists, by maintaining themselves constantly in relation with a practice, seek to constitute their life as a form of life'.[39] In this process, 'as in every form-of-life, what is in question is nothing less than their happiness'.[40] We are here at the opposite pole of Heidegger's position according to which the death of God signals the hegemony and paroxysm of modern subjectivity. But what does it mean for Agamben that Duchamp 'does not act as an artist' but as 'a simple life being'? Is Agamben suggesting that in Duchamp's ready-mades it is living (*zoē*) that gives itself a form? And what is the relationship between life and creation that Agamben finds exemplified in Duchamp?

After the death of God, the process of creation no longer leads to a work or a product as in the Renaissance conception of the work of art and the artist no longer pursues an ideal of beauty or truth as in the analogy of God's creation. The artistic machine comes to a halt allowing the artist to 'run on idle' and in this way opens new possibilities of life, or what Agamben also refers to as new possibilities of use.[41] The deactivation or inoperativity of the artistic machine becomes the central feature of his understanding of the act of creation after the death of God.

The discussion of inoperativity sheds light on Agamben's thesis on the internal relation between creation and anarchy. Developing Deleuze's insight connecting creativity to resistance, Agamben argues that the act of creation is not simply 'an opposition to an external force'[42] because 'the potential liberated by the act of creation must be a potential that is internal to the act itself, just like the act of resistance must be internal to it'.[43] Agamben identifies an internal principle, a negativity or resistance, that is at work in the act of creation. To make his argument, he returns to Aristotle's *Metaphysics*, according to which 'the one who possesses – or has the habit of – a potential can both put it into action and not put it into action'.[44] On the basis of this Aristotelian assumption, Agamben claims that '[h]uman beings are capable of having mastery of their potential and having access to it only through their impotential; but precisely for this reason, there is in the end no mastery over potential, *and being a poet means being at the mercy of one's own impotential.*'[45] His key hypothesis is that 'the passage to act can take place only by transferring one's own potential-not-to into action'.[46] For Agamben, potential-not-to is another name for the contingency inscribed within the act of creation: '[w]hat stamps the seal of necessity on the work is thus precisely what might not have been or might have been otherwise: its contingency.'[47]

Agamben compares his idea that in creativity there is a transference of one's own potential-not-to into action with Simondon's conception of the nature of the human being as a

> two-stage-being, which results from the relation between a non-individuated and impersonal part and an individual and personal part. The pre-individual is not a chronological past that, at a certain point, is realized and resolved into the individual: it coexists with it and remains irreducible to it.[48]

For Agamben, in the act of creation the impersonal 'precedes and oversteps the individual subject' and the personal 'obstinately resists it'.[49] In this dialectic, the impersonal denotes 'the potential-to exemplified by the artist who drives towards work and expression' and the personal denotes the potential-not-to that 'resist expression and imprints it with its mark'.[50] From this point of view, the work reflects both the impersonal element qua creative potential and the personal element qua resistance in tension with each other.[51]

Agamben's discussion of inoperativity can be understood as a commentary on Nietzsche's conception of the death of God and the becoming 'poets of our lives' (*GS*, 299). Agamben describes potential and impotential as reflected in a tension between style and manner that takes form in the creative life of the poet: 'style is disappropriating appropriation (a sublime negligence, a forgetting oneself in the proper), manner an appropriating disappropriation (a presenting oneself or remembering oneself in the improper).'[52] The model of the poet's life can be extended to 'every speaking human being with respect to their language and in every living thing with respect to its body there is always, in use, a manner that takes its distance from style and a style that is disappropriated in manner.'[53] This tension between 'on the one hand, appropriation and habit; on the other, loss and expropriation' defines what Agamben refers to as 'use'.[54] This idea of use underpins his understanding of the human being as 'the living being without work'.[55] Agamben regrets that 'moderns seem unable to conceive of contemplation, inoperation, and feast otherwise than as rest or the negation of labor'.[56]

Agamben concludes that contemplation and inoperativity are 'the metaphysical operators of anthropogenesis'.[57] The question about 'the work and the absence of work of human beings' is so important for Agamben because on it depends 'the possibility of assigning a nature and proper essence to the human being'.[58] The connection that he establishes between creativity and inoperativity frees the 'human creature from every biological or social destiny and from any predetermined task' and thereby makes the human being available for 'that particular absence of work we are accustomed to call "politics" and "art"'.[59]

Agamben's account of creativity as inoperativity explains how the artist provides a model for what it means to 'constitute' oneself as a 'form of life'. However, Agamben's assumptions that the 'potential-not-to' is internal to the human being, and that her creativity is a function of the personal 'resistance' to the impersonal dimension of life that humans share with non-human life raises the question whether inoperativity as the metaphysical operator of anthropogenesis paradoxically reactivates the 'anthropological machine' he identified in *The Open*. Does inoperativity reconstitute the human through an excluding mechanism by which the animal, life (*zoē*), body, instincts and so on are excluded as 'inhumane'? In the next section, I argue that Nietzsche's conception of creation and creativity provides some insights into how to deactivate the 'work-artist-operation machine' without falling into the 'anthropological machine'.

The Death of God and the Death of Man

In Agamben, inoperativity is a post-metaphysical operator of anthropogenesis. The human being is essentially an 'inoperative' being whose proper humanity is tied to the realisation that it lacks any proper 'work' of its own. In contrast to Agamben, Nietzsche does not understand creation as a process of becoming human.[60] For Nietzsche, the death of God entails the death of the 'human' being. He questions the idea of (anthropo)genesis: 'I do not see why the organic should be thought of as something that has an origin [*entstanden sein muss*]' (KSA, 11:34[50]).[61] According to Löwith, after the death of God, the human being no longer has a fixed place between animality and divinity.[62] As such, the event of the death of God not only leaves the place of God empty, it also leaves the place of the human being empty. Nietzsche notes in a fragment from his posthumous writings: 'Human beings do not exist, for there was no first "human being": thus infer the animals' (KSA, 10:12[1].95). In contrast to Agamben, for whom contemplation is one of the operators of anthropogenesis, the philosophical life is not exempt from Nietzsche's anti-humanism. As Azzam

Abed points out correctly, after the death of God, 'there remains nothing but the animal in the philosopher'.[63]

Some commentators have argued that Nietzsche's radical naturalism means that the human species produces culture or art as if it were carrying out the instructions of its genetic code, like trees growing apples.[64] This would mean that art realises the 'biological destiny' of the human species. But Nietzsche's naturalism is neither atheistic nor positivistic.[65] In fact, Nietzsche saw atheism as symptomatic of the kind of scientific positivism which he rejected (*GS*, 125).[66] In contrast to Agamben, who much like Arendt calls for the need to free the human creature from its 'biological destiny'[67] by moving away from nature, Nietzsche calls for a retranslation of the human being back into nature (*BGE*, 230).[68] From a Nietzschean perspective, the ideas of 'genetic code' or 'biological destiny' are shadows of God that we need to overcome. This is why, to become creative, we must first become '*physicists*': 'we must become discoverers of everything lawful and necessary in the world ... while hitherto all valuations and ideals have been built on ignorance of *physics* and in contradiction to it' (*GS*, 335). Nietzsche's physicists free nature from the idea of God as Creator; they discover that nature herself is creative and artistic. Nietzsche calls for a de-deification of nature: 'When will all these shadows of God no longer darken us? When will we have completely de-deified nature? When may we begin to *naturalize* humanity with a pure, newly discovered, newly redeemed nature?' (*GS*, 109). For Nietzsche this 'newly redeemed nature' reveals that what creates and gives form to life is the animality of the human being, the 'newly discovered' naturalness of the human being. Nietzsche's critique of the traditional conception of culture (which I have referred to as civilisation[69]) unbinds the animal and thereby frees up the possibility of the creation of new forms of life. For Nietzsche, the death of God as the death of the human allows us to recover a new relation between nature and creativity and come to a new understanding of what it means for the human animal to be 'more natural' and creative.

But if the human being is nothing other than an animal, then what does it mean for this animal to create forms of life? From a Nietzschean perspective, the relationship that Agamben establishes between the personal (individual/human) and impersonal (non-individuated/animal) dimension of human life, on the one hand, and the production of works of art whereby the individual resists and leaves a mark on the artistic drive towards expression, on the other hand, remains within a very traditional understanding of creation as a process whereby the human being produces cultural forms by resisting and measuring the expressions of life associated with animality, instincts and drives. Agamben's depiction of the artist as someone who 'drives towards work and expression', who precedes and oversteps the individual subject, echoes the stereotypical characterisation of the artist as an animal whose uninhibited and chaotic expression of impulses and passions – that is, anarchic artistic energies – need to be curbed, controlled and resisted by the individual whereby this resistance 'leaves a mark' and transforms life (*zoē*) into a higher cultural form (*bios*): 'Resistance acts as the critical instance that slows down the blind and immediate thrust of potential towards the act, and, in this way, prevents the potential from being resolved and fully exhausted in the act.'[70]

For Nietzsche, the death of God calls into question the traditional understanding of culture as a production of artefacts that confirm the human being's higher standing or superiority. After the death of God, culture can no longer be conceived as the point of distinction between humans and animals: 'We no longer trace the origin of the human being in the "spirit," in the "divinity," we have placed him among the animals' (*A*, 14).[71] From a Nietzschean perspective, we need to reverse the relationship between creation and resistance posited by Agamben: it is not the human (the personal) that must resist the imposition of the animal (the impersonal) in order to create, but creativity occurs as long as the animal resists the imposition of human form. According to Nietzsche's critique of Christianity, what we need to resist and continuously overcome are cultural forms of domination over life, or what Nietzsche also refers to as 'crimes against life' (*A*, 47). The problem of the Christian worldview is not its adherence to God but the fact that it commits a 'crime against life': 'That we find no God – either in history or in nature or behind nature – is not what differentiates *us*, but that we experience what has been revered as God, not as "godlike," but as a crime *against life*' (*A*, 47). Nietzsche seeks to dispel the prejudice that 'culture' is a distinguishing and ennobling mark of the human species by requiring that we first de-deify nature and 'sound-out' all the idols that hide 'either in history or in nature or behind nature' (*TI*, Preface). But Nietzsche insists that 'this is not what differentiates us' (*A*, 47). What differentiates Nietzsche's naturalism from the more positivistic kind of modern naturalism is an affirmation of life and of the creativity of nature that Nietzsche finds in the Greeks and in the Renaissance.

This point of difference between Agamben and Nietzsche on the relationship between animality and creativity is reflected in their contrasting views on the Renaissance. Whereas Agamben sets up creation as inoperativity against the example of the productivity of the artist in the Renaissance, Nietzsche understands the creativity of the latter as a becoming more natural, more animal, of the human being that overcomes the idea of the human being as a creator modelled after the Christian God towards the creation of a pluriverse of new gods.[72] For Nietzsche, the

Renaissance reflects an overcoming of the God of Christianity rather than his reinstitution in the form of an artistic machine as Agamben suggests in *Creation and Anarchy*. Nietzsche celebrates the Renaissance as an epoch that overcomes the Christian worldview and its associated idea of divine creation by returning to a Greek idea of nature as chaos and creativity: 'The total character of the world is . . . in all eternity chaos – in the sense not of a lack of necessity but of a lack of order, arrangement, form, beauty, wisdom, and whatever other names there are for our aesthetic anthropomorphism' (*GS*, 109). Nietzsche embraces the Renaissance and likewise uses the end of Christianity as the basis for his attempt to overcome the 'mendacity of millennia' through a repetition of the origin of Greek philosophy.[73] From a Nietzschean perspective, the figure of the artist in the Renaissance celebrates the divinisation of (human) nature and exemplifies a 'more natural' naturalness of the human being (*HL*, 10; *BGE*, 239).[74] In contrast to Agamben's anthropogenesis, in Nietzsche the death of God signals a return of and to animal life (*zoē*) as the wellspring of creativity. This immanent relation between animality and creativity in Nietzsche is reflected in the an-archic character of art and creation. Whereas Agamben finds the anarchic dimension of creation in the individual's potential-not-to, Nietzsche finds it in the animality of the human being.

Contingency, Resistance and Self-Overcoming

Nietzsche's and Agamben's different conceptions of the an-archic character of creativity is reflected in their contrasting views on contingency and resistance in the creation of a form-of-life. Whereas Agamben inscribes contingency within the individual's potential-not-to, Nietzsche conceives the contingency of creation as a relation to the outside or exteriority. The work of art reflects an externalisation of the human being that takes the form of an event.

From the perspective of the death of God in Nietzsche, the question rises whether the Aristotelian categories of 'potential to act' and 'potential-no-to act', which Agamben invokes to explain the process of creation, are not examples of the 'inner facts', the 'spiritual causes' that Nietzsche lists among the 'Four Great Errors'. For Nietzsche, the process of creation cannot be explained in terms of a dynamic or state internal to the artist or individual. Instead, Nietzsche understands creation as an event rather than an act. Contingency is for Nietzsche always necessarily the happening of an exteriority, the encounter with a body. To be an artist or to create a form of life means to embrace the contingency of the world and to love it: *amor fati*. The relation between contingency and necessity in Nietzsche culminates in his vision of the eternal recurrence of the same where by affirming life in all its forms 'we stamp the seal of necessity on the work'.[75] Creativity is not being at the mercy of 'what might not have been or might have been otherwise' as in Agamben.[76]

For this reason, Nietzsche maintains that the process of creation is a complex relationship between the artist and her time that gets expressed as 'genius'. Against the background of historical becoming, which Nietzsche conceives as movements of preservation and expenditure, the emergence of genius is radically contingent and culminates in a work that can no longer be ascribed to an artist. Nietzsche describes the untimeliness of creation as an end and turning point, an explosion that disrupts the course of history:

> Great human beings, like great epochs, are explosive material in whom tremendous energy has been accumulated; their prerequisite has always been, historically and physiologically, that a protracted assembling, accumulating, economizing and preserving has preceded them – that there has been no explosion for a long time. If the tension in the mass has grown too great the merest accidental stimulus suffices to call the 'genius,' the 'deed,' the great destiny into the world. (*TI*, 'Skirmishes', 44)

Nietzsche conceives great 'deeds' as events that cannot be traced back to an individual act or cause. They are inseparably entangled with a historical constellation amid which they occur or come into existence. In this historical constellation, the genius is perhaps nothing but an accidental stimulus that calls the 'deed' 'into the world' (*TI*, 'Skirmishes', 44). The idea of creation as an event reflects the historical dimension of contingency in Nietzsche's conception of creativity and results from his rejection of transcendence as a direct consequence of his thinking about the death of God.

However, there is a second dimension of contingency in Nietzsche's idea of creation, which I have referred to as the forgetfulness of the animal.[77] In Nietzsche's naturalism, animal forgetfulness constitutes the link between animality and creativity. Nietzsche finds forgetfulness in strong, full natures in which there is 'an excess of power to form, to mould, to recuperate, and to forget' (*GM*, I, 10). Forgetfulness defines the creativity of the genius of culture who 'uses himself up, who does not spare himself' (*TI*, 'Skirmishes', 44). It is also the source of virtuous one whose 'strength lies in forgetting himself' (*SE*, 4). It belongs to the giver of gifts who Zarathustra loves, 'whose soul is overfull so that it forgets itself' (*Z*, 3, 'Zarathustra's Prologue').[78] Nietzsche describes the process of creation as a natural movement comparable to the movement of a river overflowing its bed. The overflowing of the self in the act of creation is 'involuntary' and 'inevitable' (*TI*, 'Skirmishes', 44; *Z*, 1, 'Prologue'): it cannot be traced back to an intentional subject, a conscious decision, or a wilful act. For

Nietzsche, (animal) forgetfulness is neither a capacity, faculty nor potential but a force of life that is active in the process of creation. The process of creation is contingent on nonhuman form-giving forces of life that cannot be appropriated and yet inherently belongs to us. The artist, for Nietzsche, is someone in whom their animality, their existence as a living being has become creative and productive again.

In Nietzsche, animal forgetfulness stands in an agonistic relationship with memory where forgetfulness undoes given forms and opens to the possibility for the creation of new forms. This movement is comparable to the dynamic tension between style, 'a sublime negligence, a forgetting oneself in the proper', and manner, 'a presenting oneself or remembering oneself in the improper', in Agamben.[79] For Nietzsche creation entails radical expenditure and loss. It is a movement of expropriation whereby the so-called 'hero' suffers a downfall (*Untergang*), abandons herself, overflows and uses herself up. The irruption of accumulated power in the genius's 'deed' is comparable to an act of gift-giving (*Z*, 'The Gift-Giving Virtue'):

> The genius – in his works, in his deeds – is necessarily a prodigal: his greatness lies in the fact he expends himself . . . The instinct of self-preservation is as it were suspended; the overwhelming pressure of the energies which emanate from him forbids him any such care and prudence. One calls this 'sacrifice'; one praises his 'heroism' therein, his indifference to his own interests, his devotion to an idea, a great cause, a fatherland: all misunderstandings . . . (*TI*, 'Skirmishes', 44)

It is by abandoning ourselves that life gives form to us, by destroying a given form, that it re-creates us as a new form. However, whereas in Agamben the tension between style ('loss and appropriation') and manner ('appropriation and habit') settles into a form of 'use' and 'constitutes' a form-of-life,[80] in Nietzsche this tension or struggle cannot be resolved into a final form. Creation is an-archic because, far from persevering an identity or form, Nietzsche conceives (self-)creation as continuous (self-) overcoming.

Nietzsche's conception of self-overcoming that he associates with the overhuman (*Übermensch*) is intimately related to his thinking about the death of God. The overhuman is not a new God. Rather, as mentioned above, 'the surmounting of Christianity is identical with the human being's surmounting itself'.[81] In other words, the death of God in Nietzsche calls for a continuous self-overcoming of the human being. For Nietzsche, there can be no final overcoming of God:

> Christianity, it seems to me, is still needed by most people in old Europe even today; therefore it still finds believers. For this is how man is: An article of faith could be refuted before him a thousand times – if he needed it, he

would consider it 'true' again and again. . . . [It is an] *instinct of weakness* which, to be sure, does not create religions, metaphysical systems, and convictions of all kinds but – conserves them. (*GS*, 347)

God 'remains (*bleibt*)' (*GS*, 125) and continues to 'cast his shadow over Europe' (*GS*, 108). This is why for Nietzsche there also remains the continuous need to overcome God. The freedom of creativity is not a given but always needs to be conquered (*TI*, 'Skirmishes', 39). Hence, we cannot simply abandon the artistic machine to its fate as Agamben suggests.[82] Before we can 'run on idle' like the spiritual artist-philosophers Agamben envisages, there is some work left to do.[83]

Notes

1. Giorgio Agamben, *Creation and Anarchy: The Work of Art and the Religion of Capitalism*, trans. Adam Kotsko (Stanford: Stanford University Press, 2019).
2. I follow Agamben's distinction between *bios* and *zoē*; see Giorgio Agamben, *Homo Sacer: Sovereign Power and Bare Life*, trans. Daniel Heller-Roazen (Stanford: Stanford University Press, 1998).
3. See, for example, Jean-Paul Sartre, *Existentialism and Humanism* (New York: Philosophical Library, 1984).
4. See Julian Young, *The Death of God and the Meaning of Life* (London: Routledge, 2014), pp. 111–25.
5. Ibid. p. 111. See also Gianni Vattimo, who argues that the death of God is the dissolution of absolute values into the plurality of interpretations. Gianni Vattimo, *The End of Modernity: Nihilism and Hermeneutics in Post-Modern Culture*, trans. J. Snyder (Cambridge: Polity Press, 1988), p. 4.
6. Karl Löwith, *From Hegel to Nietzsche: The Revolution in Nineteenth-Century Thought*, trans. David E. Green (New York: Anchor Books, 1967), p. 185.
7. Friedrich Nietzsche, *The Gay Science*, trans. J. Nauckoff (Cambridge: Cambridge University Press, 2001); subsequently abbreviated in the text as *GS* followed by the number of the aphorism.
8. Friedrich Nietzsche, *Twilight of the Idols*, trans, R. J. Hollingdale (London: Penguin, 1990); subsequently abbreviated in the text as *TI* followed by the chapter title and aphorism.
9. Agamben, *Creation and Anarchy*, p. 13.
10. See Martin Heidegger, 'Letter on "Humanism"', in *Pathmarks*, ed. William McNeill, trans. F. A. Capuzzi (Cambridge: Cambridge University Press, 1998).
11. Michel Foucault, *Ethics, Subjectivity and Truth: The Essential Works of Foucault, 1954– 1984*, vol. 1 (New York: The New Press, 1994), p. 255. Foucault acknowledges that his notion of an 'aesthetic of existence' is inspired by the Nietzschean project of giving style to one's character (*GS*, 290). Ibid. p. 262.
12. Michel Foucault, *Dits et Écrits*, vol. 4 (Paris: Gallimard, 1994), p. 687.
13. Agamben, *Creation and Anarchy*, p. 1.
14. See also Marcos Antonio Norris, 'Existential Choice as Repressed Theism: Jean-Paul Sartre and Giorgio Agamben in Conversation', *Religions* 9.106 (2018).
15. Foucault, *Ethics, Subjectivity and Truth*, p. 262.
16. This is a contested point in Foucault scholarship, where some interpreters like Esposito identify the source of resistance to power in the dimension of life linked with animality (*zoē*) whereas others like Judith Revel identify this source in the radical historisa-

tion of the individual's *bios*. See Roberto Esposito, *Bios: Biopolitics and Philosophy* (Minneapolis: University of Minnesota Press, 2008); Judith Revel, 'Identity, Nature, Life: Three Biopolitical Deconstructions', in *The Government of Life: Foucault, Biopolitics, and Neoliberalism*, ed. Vanessa Lemm and Miguel Vatter (New York: Fordham University Press, 2014). On my interpretation, both Nietzsche and Foucault see a closer relation between animality and historicity than either of these two standpoints, as I discuss below.

17. Foucault, *Ethics, Subjectivity and Truth*, p. 261.
18. See Giorgio Agamben, *The Open: Man and Animal* (Stanford: Stanford University Press, 2004).
19. In Agamben's locution of form-of-life, 'life' refers to the lack of a separation and mutual exclusion of *zoē* and *bios*. On Agamben and form-of-life, see Miguel Vatter, 'Law and Life beyond Incorporation: Agamben, Highest Poverty, and the Papal Legal Revolution', in *Agamben and Radical Politics*, ed. Daniel McLoughlin (Edinburgh: Edinburgh University Press, 2016).
20. Ulrich Rauff, 'An Interview with Giorgio Agamben', *German Law Journal* 5.5 (2004): 612–13. On Agamben's continuous and ongoing engagement with Nietzsche's philosophy, see Vanessa Lemm, 'Points of Reference: Friedrich Nietzsche', in *Agamben's Philosophical Lineage*, ed. Adam Kotsko and Carlo Salzani (Edinburgh: Edinburgh University Press, 2017).
21. Giorgio Agamben, *The Man without Content*, trans. Georgia Albert (Stanford: Stanford University Press, 1999), p. 93.
22. Martin Heidegger, in 'Nietzsches Wort, Gott ist tot', in *Holzwege* (Frankfurt am Main: Vittorio Klostermann, 1980), pp. 235–6.
23. Ibid. p. 222.
24. Agamben asks whether there is 'a work proper to man, or whether man as such might perhaps be essentially *argos*, that is, without work, workless [*inoperoso*]'. Giorgio Agamben, *Means without End: Notes on Politics*, trans. Vincenzo Binetti and Cesare Casarino (Minneapolis: University of Minnesota Press, 2000), p. 140.
25. Agamben, *Creation and Anarchy*, p. 5.
26. Ibid. p. 7.
27. Ibid.
28. Ibid. pp. 7–8.
29. Ibid. pp. 8–9.
30. Ibid. p. 8.
31. Ibid. p. 10.
32. Ibid. p. 11.
33. Ibid. p. 12.
34. Ibid.
35. Ibid.
36. Ibid.
37. Ibid. p. 13.
38. Ibid.
39. Ibid.
40. Ibid.
41. Ibid. p. 28.
42. Ibid. p. 16.
43. Ibid. p. 15.
44. Ibid. p. 17. This neo-Aristotelian reading of potentiality is a central theme in Agamben's philosophy; see Giorgio Agamben, *Potentialities: Collected Essays in Philosophy*, trans. Daniel Heller-Roazen (Stanford: Stanford University Press, 1999). See also Leland de la Durantaye, *Giorgio Agamben: A Critical Introduction* (Stanford: Stanford University Press, 2009).
45. Agamben, *Creation and Anarchy*, p. 19; emphasis mine.

46. Ibid.
47. Ibid. p. 20.
48. Ibid. p. 21. Simondon's conception of the human being as a 'two-stage-being' has strong affinities with Nietzsche's idea of the human being as both creature and creator: 'In man, creature and creator are united: in man there is material, fragment, excess, clay, dirt, nonsense, chaos; but in man there is also creator, form-giver, hammer hardness, spectator divinity, and seventh day: do you understand this contrast?'; Friedrich Nietzsche, *Beyond Good and Evil: Prelude to a Philosophy of the Future*, trans. Walter Kaufmann (New York: Vintage Books, 1989), p. 255; subsequent references to this text are abbreviated as *BGE* followed by the number of the aphorism. In Esposito the impersonal is associated with the animal and as such Esposito offers a reading of Simondon which may reconcile the point of difference between Agamben and Nietzsche on creativity and animality. See Roberto Esposito, *Third Person: Politics of Life and Philosophy of the Impersonal*, trans. Z. Hanafi (Boston, MA: Polity, 2012).
49. Agamben, *Creation and Anarchy*, p. 21.
50. Ibid.
51. Ibid.
52. Ibid. p. 45.
53. Ibid.
54. Ibid.
55. Ibid. p. 25.
56. Ibid. p. 26.
57. Ibid. p. 27.
58. Ibid. p. 25.
59. Ibid. p. 27.
60. In Agamben's defense, it should, however, be noted that he distinguishes between two different notions of inoperativity, a potentiality that gives rise to a 'form of life' that further inscribes us into the anthropological machine and a 'pure potentiality' that gives rise to 'form-of-life' which suspends the operation of the anthropological machine. On this difference in Agamben, see Giorgio Agamben, *The Fire and the Tale*, trans. Lorenzo Chies (Stanford: Stanford University Press, 2017), pp. 137–8; and Giorgio Agamben, *The Use of Bodies*, trans. Adam Kotsko (Stanford: Stanford University Press, 2015), pp. 63 and 91. I thank Colby Dickinson for his comments on this point.
61. Friedrich Nietzsche, *Sämtliche Werke: Kritische Studienausgabe in 15 Bänden*, ed. Giorgio Colli and Mazzino Montinari (Berlin: De Gruyter, 1988); subsequently abbreviated as *KSA* with references providing the volume number followed by the relevant fragment number and any relevant aphorism.
62. Karl Löwith, *Nietzsche's Philosophy of the Eternal Recurrence of the Same*, trans. J. Harvey Lomax (Berkeley, Los Angeles and London: University of California Press, 1997), p. 44. See also: 'the whole essence of traditional humanity is no longer relevant for Nietzsche's redefinition of the human being's destiny', Löwith, *From Hegel to Nietzsche*, p. 319.
63. See Azzam Abed, *Nietzsche versus Paul* (New York: Columbia University Press, 2015), pp. 125–6. See Friedrich Nietzsche, *On the Genealogy of Morals*, trans. C. Diethe (Cambridge: Cambridge University Press, 1994), III:7; subsequently abbreviated in the text as *GM* followed by the chapter and aphorism.
64. Brian Leiter, *Nietzsche on Morality* (London: Routledge, 2002), p. 10.
65. On Nietzsche and atheism, see Johann Figl, '"Tod Gottes" und die Möglichkeit "neuer Götter"', *Nietzsche-Studien* 29 (2000) and Richard Schacht, *Nietzsche* (New York: Routledge, 1983), pp. 119–30.
66. On this point, see Carlo Gentili's insightful reading of *GS*, 125. Carlo Gentili, *Nietzsche* (Madrid: Biblioteca Nueva, 2004), p. 273.
67. Agamben, *Creation and Anarchy*, p. 27.

68. On the translation of the human being back to nature, see Vanessa Lemm, *Homo Natura: Nietzsche, Philosophical Anthropology and Biopolitics* (Edinburgh: Edinburgh University Press, 2020).
69. Vanessa Lemm, *Nietzsche's Animal Philosophy: Culture, Politics and the Animality of the Human Being* (New York: Fordham University Press, 2009).
70. Agamben, *Creation and Anarchy*, p. 19.
71. Friedrich Nietzsche, *Antichrist*, trans. R. J. Hollingdale (London: Penguin, 1990); subsequently abbreviated in the text as *A* followed by the aphorism.
72. For Nietzsche, what is divine is that there are many gods, but not the one Christian God. Vattimo therefore maintains that one of the main philosophical outcomes of the death of the metaphysical God is the renewed possibility of religious experience, the rebirth of the sacred in its many forms. Gianni Vattimo, 'The God Who is Dead', in Gianni Vattimo, *After Christianity*, (New York: Columbia University Press, 2002), pp. 16 and 23; see also pp. 11–14. On new gods and a new religion, see Figl, '"Tod Gottes" und die Möglichkeit "neuer Götter"'.
73. Löwith, *From Hegel to Nietzsche*, p. 185.
74. Friedrich Nietzsche, 'Second Untimely Consideration', in Friedrich Nietzsche, *Untimely Meditations*, trans. R. J. Hollingdale (Cambridge: Cambridge University Press, 1997); subsequently abbreviated in the text as *HL* followed by the number of the section.
75. Agamben, *Creation and Anarchy*, p. 20.
76. Ibid.
77. Lemm, *Nietzsche's Animal Philosophy*, 2009.
78. Friedrich Nietzsche, *Thus Spoke Zarathustra*, trans. W. Kaufmann (New York: Modern Library, 1995); subsequently abbreviated in the text as *Z* followed by the chapter and section title.
79. Agamben, *Creation and Anarchy*, p. 45.
80. Ibid.
81. Löwith, *From Hegel to Nietzsche*, p. 185.
82. Agamben, *Creation and Anarchy*, p. 13.
83. Ibid. p. 28.

Chapter 6

Whither the Divine? Nietzsche, Heidegger and the End of Metaphysics in Agamben's Thought

Colby Dickinson

Language and Metaphysics

In 1963, Jean-Paul Sartre published his autobiography, *Les Mots*, a personal meditation on the nature of his writing and the illusions that had sustained it throughout his many productive decades. His reflections on the metaphysical role that words had played in his life, as both author and provocateur, allowed the reader to see how he had sought in his career to establish his own being through words and the sacred aura that they seemingly conjured to guarantee his subjectivity. As he himself would ponder the immensity of his desire for immersion in language as the source of his literary motivations, 'the Universe would rise in tiers at my feet and all things would humbly beg for a name; to name the thing was both to create and take it. Without this fundamental illusion I would never have written.'[1] He would go so far as to consider himself a 'great fetish', one created by his worship of the words that had defined both his private and public sense of self:

> No one can forget or ignore me: I am a great fetish, tractable and terrible. My mind is in bits and pieces. All the better. Other minds take me over. People read *me*, I leap to the eye; they talk to *me*. I'm in everyone's mouth, a universal and individual language; I become a prospective curiosity in millions of gazes; to him who can love me, I step aside and disappear: I exist nowhere, at last I *am*, I'm everywhere. I'm a parasite on mankind, my blessings eat into it and force it to keep reviving my absence.[2]

In the almost mad ramblings both through and within the words that leapt to Sartre's pen, we find a sacrilegious belief in the higher power of words themselves. It is the words that create the space wherein one is invested *by oneself* with meaning. It is the words that allowed Sartre to transgress the religious dimensions of his past, but also to bring about the migration of such dimensions into a secularised linguistic domain where the saint becomes the literary genius. In short, there was a sublimation of his childhood religious beliefs bound up with his inability to let go of the absolute that was once part of a vague belief in God into the role of author, what ultimately really expresses his belief in the sacramental nature of language itself.

Sartre's French Catholic heritage, much as with the writings of Jean Genet, the subject of one of his studies, led him to divinise language itself, the 'words' with which he crafted his own singular existence.[3] As he would continue to frame his narrative, 'I thought I was devoting myself to literature, whereas I was actually taking Holy Orders. The certainty of the humblest believer became, in my case, the proud evidence of my predestination.'[4] As if perceiving directly the way that the religious could actually be preserved within its secularised form, he acknowledges the presence of a sacrality that had not diminished in the least, but had only been transferred into another realm:

> I was taught Sacred History, the Gospel, and the catechism without being given the means for believing. The result was a disorder which became my particular order. There were twists and turns, a considerable transfer; removed from Catholicism, the sacred was deposited in belles-lettres and the penman appeared, an *ersatz* of the Christian that I was unable to be: his sole concern was salvation; the only purpose of his sojourn here below was that he merit posthumous bliss by enduring ordeals in worthy fashion. Decease was reduced to a rite of passage, and earthly immortality was offered as a substitute for eternal life.[5]

The metaphysics of language that Sartre developed as motivation for his writing was nothing new to the period in which he wrote. It was indeed something of the *lingua franca* for the literary artist. As his lifelong companion, Simone de Beauvoir, would suggest on more than one occasion, putting one's life into words was, in part, an effort to give meaning to life itself when viewed through the short lens of death – something which elevated the act of writing to a metaphysical principle. As she put it, 'Though death challenges our existence, it also gives meaning to our lives. It may be the instrument of absolute separation, but it is also the key to all communication.'[6] Her own compulsions to write in a state of frenzy – 'From the moment I began that book I never stopped writing . . .' – had become an attempt to secure meaning against the imposing, encroaching force of a death that threatened to take away whatever could not be transformed into a meaningful articulation. The way in which one's impending death could bring about feelings of loneliness and separation compelled the next exercise in writing and brought about the creation of the author as subject itself.[7] In such activities, she shared with Sartre the belief in a certain metaphysics of language.

It is, of course, nothing new to suggest that such constructs of the author as sovereign self, brought about through an almost mystical though secularised metaphysics, lay at the heart of twentieth-century French existentialist thought. There was for Sartre and Beauvoir, among others, a relentless quest to portray their intimate lives in writing, precisely in order to establish themselves as public and political figures, as literary geniuses and as philosophical giants. Though each would argue in turn for forms of subjectivity that are ultimately divided within in such a way as to seemingly avoid claims to sovereign subjectivity, the secularised metaphysics that underlay their various configurations seems to haunt such claims and yet is something that is often far less analysed and understood for what it is, despite both authors' admittances of such views of their authorial voices.

Giorgio Agamben's emphasis on the sacramental nature of language can be comprehensible today only from the point of view one detects already at work in this existentialist line of thought, though it is certainly not exclusive to existentialism. As I have argued already elsewhere, I believe the same dynamics of establishing the author as sovereign were at work in the subtle but ongoing feud between Agamben and Jacques Derrida as well.[8] A reading of these dynamics that would refuse to posit a distinction between the fetish (Sartre) and the sacrament (Agamben) allows us as well to prioritise the role of language in determining the conditions of material reality and subject formation. Agamben's analysis of the sacrament of language reveals to us a large opening towards comprehending better how the motivations of Sartre and Beauvoir involved a sacralising of language that has permeated Western culture through the lingering influence of a Christian focus on the logos and the individual subject. Though Agamben will ultimately concede that language is in fact no more important than birdsong, God's name in monotheism, he suggests, actually 'names language itself' and involves a 'divinization of the logos' that elevates the role of language within humanity to a metaphysical principle in and of itself.[9] His commentary on the nature of the oath, for example, as a 'consecration of the living human being', hence as a sacrament of power and sacrament of language, illustrates the close bond between language and the human being, as language puts human life in question and the 'oath is situated at their intersection, understood as the anthropogenic operator'.[10] Human beings use the logos to constitute themselves as the 'living being who has language', leaving only humans to 'promise themselves' to the logos in a manner historically understood to be religious, though secularised in the modern period while retaining the same fundamental metaphysical assumptions.

When Agamben thus refers to the oath as one of the first principles of metaphysics, language can be seen as what ushers in the era of metaphysics in the first place – a most significant and revealing claim concerning the role of Western theology in establishing this principle.[11] Though he will go on to link the role of command in sustaining metaphysics in the modern period to Kant's insistence on the categorical imperative, as Agamben himself points out in *Opus Dei*, the bond between language, metaphysics and the construction of the human being becomes an essential critique of Sartre's efforts to have language give him life, while at the same time acknowledging how all of humanity frequently remains caught up in the same game.[12] The real target, then, becomes finding a way past the latent metaphysical presumptions that undergird Sartre's secularised metaphysics. Though Agamben himself will often appear as reticent to engage directly in discussions of the death of God and the end of metaphysics, his philosophy holds dire implications for this trajectory of thought that we must now turn to.

The Decline of the Oath, the Death of God

What Sartre had got caught up within was the often undisclosed metaphysical ground of language itself, something he at once rejected through his blatant atheism, but which he also sought to secretly recover through his use of language, only to reject such efforts at the end of his life (and as recounted in *Les Mots*). In Agamben's parlance, Sartre had tried to secularise the sacred bond between language and humanity, a move that served only to reduplicate the force of the sacred and to conceal the process from the one who was initiating it. Sartre's appeal to the presumed metaphysical basis of language could only be veiled to him because he consciously worked in a philosophical context where the 'death of God' could be taken for granted, though the full implications of this suggestion perhaps continued to remain concealed to him. There is a certain irony in Sartre's secularising of the linguistic dimension of metaphysics in that he was often perceived to be the inheritor of a particular strain of German existentialist thought, especially as embodied in the writings of Nietzsche and Heidegger. The trajectory they carved out concerning the death of God and the end of metaphysics was a powerful course for twentieth-century French existentialism and its embrace of atheism, as well as forms of atheism and nihilism that developed far beyond earlier humanistic impulses.[13]

Heidegger's interpretation of Nietzsche's understanding of nihilism was that Nietzsche was the first thinker to authentically contemplate the nothing that Western metaphysics had consistently perpetuated in its failure to think Being. In Heidegger's words, 'The essence of nihilism is the history in which there is nothing to Being itself.'[14] Nietzsche sought to think Becoming as Being and so to expose this failure of Western thought, not to overcome nihilism but to become further entangled in it.[15] Metaphysics, he would further suggest, has been nihilistic throughout its long history, but has never shown its true face to humanity.[16] Metaphysics has only thought 'the Being of beings as the *a priori*' and so 'merely certifies that metaphysics as such leaves Being unthought'.[17]

> Of course, metaphysics acknowledges that beings are not without Being. But scarcely has it said so when it again transforms Being into a being, whether it be the supreme being in the sense of the first cause, whether it be the distinctive being in the sense of the subject of subjectivity, as the condition of the possibility of all objectivity, or whether, as a consequence of the coherence of both these fundamental conditions of Being in beings, it be the determination of the supreme being as the Absolute in the sense of unconditional subjectivity.[18]

God, even a secularised one locatable within the human subject, is to be found within such a place of identifying Being as the Absolute and as the chance for an unconditional subjectivity, much as Sartre had seemingly only discovered through his autobiographical reflections. It is as such that metaphysics is inherently also always-already theology, just as ontology is also always-already theology.[19]

Nietzsche's thought, Heidegger finds, is a kind of metaphysics, but one that is a particular type of negative theology.[20] It is an ontotheology in which nihilism is 'fulfilled' as the 'death of God', allowing metaphysics to be presented as the course of nihilism unfolding in history.[21] Heidegger's contention on this point is that metaphysics had tried to think Being only as potentially present in beings and so never thought Being itself, never thought it 'as such'.[22] Throughout the history of metaphysics, Being withdrew and so was concealed from view, whereas beings exhibited an unconcealment, or they were shown more prominently than Being.[23] As he will eventually state in this context: 'As history, metaphysics keeps the truth of Being concealed in the unconcealment of the being as such.'[24] This explains why the essence of nihilism is, for Heidegger, the *concealment* of Being, the *nothing* of Being.[25] The essence of Being that can be shown is made manifest in *Dasein* – an ecstatic state of inherence located in one's being-there.[26] As such, Being was misplaced through its content, which is actually nothing, being sealed within values, ones that Nietzsche had himself sought to expose as devalued.[27]

At the same time as he exposes such nihilistic trends in Western thought through his commentary on Nietzsche, Heidegger finds, too, that metaphysics is prohibited from thinking the essence of nihilism, which is grounded in the withdrawal of Being.[28] Yet nihilism, concerned with the essence of the nothing that appears when Being withdraws, is 'thereby of course also a matter of the *essence* of man'.[29] The nothing that humanity fears is actually what lies at its own heart. Rather than perceive nihilism as stereotypically about 'something that disparages and destroys, a decline and downfall', it is rather concerned with

> nothing negative in the form of a destructive element that has its seat in human sentiments and circulates abroad in human activities. The essence of nihilism is not at all the affair of man, but a matter of Being itself, and thereby of course also a matter of the *essence* of man, and only in *that* sequence at the same time a human concern. And presumably not merely one among others.[30]

In ways that foreshadow Agamben's discussions of both Heidegger and the human being in his work *The Open*, Heidegger challenges centuries of Western thought by positing a nothingness at the centre of humanity's essence, elevating the force of nihilism to the key principle of human formation.[31] Nihilism, he will eventually go on to state, involves the essence of Being itself, which is 'that there is nothing to Being itself'.[32] It is for this reason that any attempt to overcome nihilism, which is inextricably connected to the withdrawal of Being, 'appears in a strange light'.[33] Any such effort could only be an attempt to overcome the essence of humanity itself and is therefore flawed from the start. It is intriguing to contemplate the nothing of Being, in this light, as a destruction of all universals in the manner of nominalist thought, a consideration, as we will see in a moment, that leaves some critics perhaps to suggest that Heidegger merely embraces the modern nihilistic currents made available through nominalist thought and that are ultimately and entirely destructive to humanity. Yet Heidegger seems, as well as Agamben, too, to be after something else, something central to existential thought on the whole.

For his part, Heidegger suggests that we live in a time when nihilism only reveals the inauthentic within itself, hence displaying only its negative, destructive features and so is frequently resisted by metaphysicians bent on defending the place of divine being in both society and history.[34] But this struggle between the inauthentic within nihilism and the ruins of metaphysics will yield nothing in the end, he warns, and is only a destructive war being waged by both sides.[35] Wanting to overcome nihilism, as with the desire to overcome metaphysics, is inappropriate to its essence, and to the essence of Being itself, not to mention the essence of humanity as well.[36] It is in this light that we might perceive how Sartre's efforts to secularise (and so possibly overcome) the sacrality of the *logos* only perpetuated such dynamics into the linguistic mediums in which he pursued them. There simply was no way to eradicate what lies at the foundations of our essence.

The situation we find ourselves in, after realising Nietzsche's claims concerning the forms of modern nihilism, is that the absence of the divine is part of the outworking of Being. In Heidegger's estimation,

> The default of the unconcealment of Being as such releases the evanescence of all that is hale in beings. The evanescence of the hale takes the openness of the holy with it and closes it off. The closure of the holy eclipses every illumination of the divine. The deepening dark entrenches and conceals the lack of God.[37]

As such, Being, and the contingency that accompanies it, is a liberating force that frees 'all beings to themselves'. No longer bound to a particular metaphysical construct for the beings that we are, and which is given through a particular being established as the manifestation of Being (and so as necessity), there is only 'the dominion of needlessness entrenched in metaphysics as fulfilled', which is the nihilism that upends whatever highest value has been foisted upon Being and so consequently devalues it. (This point has its precise corollary in Agamben's comments made later regarding the liberating force of contingency and how it frees the human being from its theological signature.)

One could argue that Heidegger's suggestion that needlessness is 'the most extreme need and *is* precisely as if it were not' recalls, too, the Pauline *hos me*, the 'as if not' that allows a being's ontic status to be hollowed out from within by the ontological force of Being which ceaselessly undermines whatever is posited on the level of ontic existence – much as Agamben will argue in his study of Pauline thought.[38] This suggestion is essentially the nature of the ontological difference itself. This dynamic reflects, too, the contingency of all identities at this level, and it is this contingency that, according to Heidegger, must be grasped as what underlies all beings, and what precedes all beings as the force of Being – the force of nothingness – underneath them.

From this angle we can note how Heidegger's assessment of nihilism and the end of certain metaphysical supports for modern secular views overlaps with Agamben's attempts at profanation as an effort to see the end of metaphysics beyond the sacred/secular dichotomy. If the secular merely displaces the sacred, taking it into new, temporal forms, whereas the act of profanation 'neutralizes what it profanes', we can detect within Agamben's thought a Heideggerian impulse that at once responds to Sartre while also undermining the sovereignty of the subject that underpinned a good deal of existentialist claims regarding subjectivity. For Agamben, rather than construct a subject, complete with an almost sacred aura, as that which one can possess – or perhaps achieve literary fame for merely trying to possess – he declares that 'Once profaned, that which was unavailable and separate loses its aura and is returned to use.'[39] Finding a new use for something, whether the subject or some other social identity, is only made possible through rendering the old use inoperative – a point that seems to stem directly from this Nietzschean–Heideggerian line of inquiry.[40] Agamben's task of profaning what appears to us as unprofanable converges with a certain form of nihilism inherent to the Western Christian proclamation that Nietzsche and Heidegger had once sensed and which Gianni Vattimo takes up today in this explicit context.[41] Such insights are reflected as well in Agamben's claims of absolute immanence, indicating how Agamben's work points steadily, if at times indirectly, towards the end of certain metaphysical presumptions behind language and its construction of the human being.

Nevertheless, for all of his indebtedness to Heidegger's reading of nihilism, has Agamben truly escaped the dilemma that Sartre once found himself situated squarely within? Or has he merely reduplicated the same movement as Sartre, though at yet another level of bad faith? Though I will leave these questions ultimately unanswered – as indeed they may be unanswerable for anyone invested in the use of language at some level, as Sartre himself had disclosed – I would argue that what Agamben unveils is a more complex scheme of relations than the simple dichotomy between theism/atheism. He locates a dualistic tension within all normative representations – indeed, within language itself and the metaphysical economies that underpin it – that renders matters more complex and which pits Sartre against Heidegger in an unending tension that cannot itself be effaced.

The bipolar tension between sovereignty and governance that Agamben deftly analyses throughout the *Homo Sacer* series further leads him to a parallel analysis of the religious polarity between deism and pantheism, a tension that is played out repeatedly through history, from ancient to modern times. In his discussion of how the meaning of 'immanent order is nothing other than the relation to the transcendent end', for example, we see how humanity invents various notions of order in an attempt to think a balance between the extremes of pantheism and a Gnostic foreign deity.[42] The signature of order, as he will put it, that keeps together 'substance and relation, ontology and praxis' is intimately related to the manner in which immanence and transcendence refer to each other.[43] Order ceaselessly tries to repair the permanent fracture between these dualistic ends and so resurfaces throughout history at numerous points, including in doctrinal debates on the two natures of Christ and the modern polarity of deism and pantheism.[44] Moving towards a form of absolute immanence as a pure potentiality aligned with contingency means, for Agamben, hinting likewise towards a possible pantheism as the only reasonable option for belief in a divine being in the modern period, though this, too, is a position that he refrains from fully articulating, opting instead only to illustrate how the tension is embedded within all normative orders and how these tensions must themselves be overcome through a logic of *use* rather than *possession*.[45]

What we see in such musings is a continuation of several Heideggerian themes where the tension between theism and atheism is reduplicated in theological debates between Gnosticism and pantheism. Agamben's stress on contingency appears to favour the pantheistic sentiment until one likewise notes that the force of contingency is not intended to simply legitimate another, particular view of divine being, or of the human being for that matter; it is rather a force that works 'all the way down' to the essence of humanity – the nothing, or 'the open', that most truly characterises the human being. Though this position may appear to the theologically minded as tantamount to destroying all metaphysical claims, it is the logical outcome of a particular existentialist strand of thought, from Nietzsche to Heidegger, that Agamben most directly appropriates.

Revisiting the Role of the Will

The intellectual historian Larry Siedentop takes some time towards the end of his intellectual history *Inventing the Individual* to laud the rise of nominalism and the thought of William of Ockham in particular. It was Ockham's insistence upon linking concepts such as contingency, freedom, autonomy and choice that, in Siedentop's analysis, gave rise to scientific thinking, but also paved the way for both modernity and secular liberalism. In his account, Ockham's revolutionary vision gave rise to Christianity's greatest gift to the West: secularism.[46] Siedentop's portrait of the individual, of autonomy and of the migration of sovereignty from an omnipotent deity to the individual certainly accords with the Reformation's attempts to usurp papal and monarchical claims to sovereignty, giving rise, in the meantime, to the sovereign individual, democratic political forms and atheistic beliefs seemingly all at once. It is somewhat of a contrasting vision, however, with Michael Allen Gillespie's attempts to isolate the nominalist's vision of a 'dark God' who remains at the roots of modern nihilistic forces, themselves implicated in permanent revolution, the eradication of authority and tradition, totalitarianism as a political state and terrorism in our world today, though there is certainly cause to disaggregate these possibilities and to further distinguish them, as some forms of permanent revolution – in terms of personal identity, for example – are not entirely negative in their outcome.

In this line of inquiry, Siedentop's suggestion that liberalism itself springs from nominalist thought runs counter to Gillespie's claims that liberalism is at odds with the nominalist strand of thought he identifies with nihilism.[47] From Gillespie's viewpoint, however, it is not terribly difficult to understand why the theologian John Milbank frequently refers to heterodox (liberal) theologies as ultimately indebted to an undisclosed nominalism that gives rise only to a wholly destructive nihilism in the end. In Gillespie's words, nihilism has been repeatedly 'used as an ideological bludgeon to denigrate nearly every intellectual or political movement that someone or other has found objectionable', and we are left to wonder if this is not Milbank's very tactic.[48] But nihilism is perhaps at times, like conservative critiques of postmodern thought would also suggest, one of those 'unwitting agents of perversity'.[49] My concern, however, is that Gillespie paints a broad enough stroke as to implicate all forms of negativity without giving thought to its positive potential nearly as much as its destructive side, something revealed by the fact that he does not provide a positive project for modernity vis-à-vis its 'dark God' at the end of his own analysis.

What Gillespie aims to show is how the omnipotent God of nominalism gave rise to nihilism in its modern forms. Humanity simply replaced God in the scheme of an all-powerful act of willing and introduced a darkness to modern thought that had previously been kept at bay by those realist and analogical speculations that had once tied God's activity to necessity and natural law – something the omnipotent God of nominalist thought was no longer obligated to do. Though Gillespie says nothing about whether or not humanity should, or even could, return to another vision of the divine, or what one is to do when they embrace a secular horizon shorn of the divine (and so leaving humanity as the only ones whose wills matter), there is a sense that one could use his genealogy of nihilism in order to argue for a return to premodern perspectives on the divine. It is quite interesting that Gillespie ends his genealogy of nihilism without any call for a positive project of either retrieving a premodern God or developing a new, more modern vision of the divine, for such a failure seems to echo the very thing he accuses nihilism of doing: destroying the grounds for a particular representation without providing any positive project in its wake. If one wants to remove the God of destruction that lies at the heart of modernity, what might one propose to replace it? The door is subsequently left open for a number of theological views to insert themselves, a position no doubt favourable to many modern theologians, but which misses the larger context of the critique.

From another point of view, however, Ockham's 'dark God' revealed the absurdity of having any conception of an omnipotent deity, and so it was mainly discarded in the modern era in favour of different, self-grounding, autonomous conceptualisations of the human being. What Ockham gave rise to, then, was a theory of sovereignty that saw the individual as entirely self-grounding, autonomous, sovereign of itself – all of which was captured in the idea of an unlimited will and which no doubt undergirded many existential perspectives in the modern period.[50] As Gillespie will frame matters, 'God's will alone determines what is good and evil, and he is not even bound by its own previous determinations.'[51] This what will allow him to eventually conclude that Nietzsche's anti-teleological vision of humanity accords with the nominalist God.[52] It also unities with a vision of God that perceives God *as* nothing, something he attributes explicitly to Ockham's peer, Meister Eckhart, as potentially influential upon Ockham as well.[53] It was only those who took the notion of an omnipotent God seriously who were also able to deploy destructive visions of the predestination and of divine necessity (e.g. Luther and Calvin).[54]

Taking the nominalist revolution in our understanding of the will into account at this point in my analysis of existentialism and Agamben's possible relationship to such trends is paramount for at least three reasons. Firstly, the nominalist theme of focusing on the will and asserting the subject's choice as what grounds their authentic being in the world becomes the platform for existentialist notions of the will, as we see in Heidegger and Sartre especially. Secondly, debates regarding the legacy of nominalism vis-à-vis secularism and the possibility of providing a positive political project after the destruction of previously existing metaphysical grounds are further illuminated as the contested grounds upon which Agamben's work is frequently either received or rejected. Thirdly, it is only after we take this context into account that we can understand why Agamben himself returns to the origins of nominalist thought in his articulation of the will in modern times.

In his discussion of the distinctions between command and demand, for example, Agamben addresses the role of the will in nominalism and, more specifically, Ockham's desire to preserve the 'contingency of decision against an understanding of acting ... that reduces it to pure necessity'.[55] Within this context, Agamben will also discern how absolute power becomes that which allows one to act 'beyond the law and against it' – the very definition of sovereign power as he had taken it up earlier in the *Homo Sacer* series.[56] These reflections lead Agamben eventually towards observing the importance of free will, and the will in Christianity in general, as it attempts to provide a foundation for 'the anarchic sphere of divine praxis'.[57]

The 'metaphysics of the will' in Western philosophy that Heidegger traces through Nietzsche's thought, and which Agamben identifies as a 'will to will' in the figure of the divine, is what Sartre and existentialism in general enshrined within itself as the basis of the subject's self-sovereignty.[58] In words that would almost directly echo Sartre's struggle with words and naming in *Les Mots*, Agamben perceives how '[t]o name, to take a name, is the originary form of the command'.[59] The ontology of command that rests upon a metaphysics of the will and that transforms language into a metaphysical platform for the construction of the sovereign subject is subsequently contrasted by Agamben with an ontology of demand that respects only the singularity of each individual life (as a form-of-life) and which demands to be heard from within the contingency of its own existence. By suggesting this possibility, Agamben at once both continues the legacy of existentialist thought while also dividing it from within, providing an alternative future for consideration of the human being.[60]

The ontology of operativity in Kant's philosophy had become an ontology of command as the ontology of modernity.[61] Hence the role of the will in the West became significantly elevated, as had previously the role of a monotheistic God who 'speaks in the imperative and to whom one speaks in the same verbal mode in worship and prayer'.[62] Agamben's reformulation of the ontological argument rather posits 'that if speech exists, then God exists'.[63] Ontotheology becomes a performance of language itself, leaving metaphysics to coincide with the experience of language.

In terms that resonate with the trajectory of existentialist thought I have been pursuing thus far, the decline in the legitimacy of the oath is what Agamben will call the 'death of God', which is really the death of the *name* of God. The God bound up with this articulation of the will – what nominalism bequeathed to the West – has run its course. A stark contrast is thereby revealed between an ontology of demand that issues forth from a form-of-life lived beyond commands and an ontology of the will that has dominated Western metaphysics, either in traditional theological form or in secularised, existentialist guise for centuries.[64]

The line of critique offered by both Nietzsche and Heidegger concerning the death of God and the end of metaphysics is one that stresses the role of the will in overcoming the sheer contingency of existence. Agamben's discussion of the will, however, potentially opens up a door towards critiques of a particular nominalist strand of thought, Nietzsche's emphasis on the will to power and various forms of nihilism in the modern period alike. Positing an ontology of *command* (established through the will), and as linked to the sovereign decision, in deliberate contrast with an ontology of *demand* (*conatus*) that somehow escapes being simply the dualistic other to the will (as with governance), Agamben develops a modal ontology that could only think the possibility of divine existence – but only the possibility – by pushing beyond the duality of God/no God (as with Being/Nothing in Heidegger) in order to possibly think something like a division of the death of God itself. There is no offer of transcendence in such a wager, however, only the division of immanence itself in order to expose its limitations and introduce what might lie 'beyond' an otherwise totalising account of immanence. Any such state of 'being beyond' is not accompanied by metaphysical claims concerning transcendent states of existence or beings beyond the immanent sphere. Any attempt to consider an alternative to traditional, religious belief in the divine inevitably leads to a position staked beyond the dualistic realm of political-theological (metaphysical) speculation. Only a position that collapses this dualistic thinking founded upon a particular notion of the will as Agamben does (and such also as one finds in Adorno's 'inverted theology' based upon a non-dualistic negative dialectic, as I have suggested elsewhere[65]) might thus be capable of overcoming such an ontotheology.

Conclusion

> The true nihilists are the ones who oppose nihilism with their more and more faded positivities, the ones who are thus conspiring with all extant malice, and eventually with the destructive principle itself. Thought honors itself by defending what is damned as nihilism.
> Theodor W. Adorno, *Negative Dialectics*[66]

Agamben's insistence on the task of profanation only, not the institution of a new political order, echoes Adorno's claim that one must avoid merely presenting 'more and more faded positivities' while decrying what appear as wholly negative efforts. Agamben's work, seen from this light, honours thought precisely through its embrace of such nihilistic forces, though they are ones that need not end with a complete destruction of all that can be seen before us. Though institutions and structures founded upon the 'dark will' and an ontology of command may fade from immediate force, there is yet the possibility of seeing the singular form-of-life lived beyond such inscriptions within the laws and structures that had previously defined (and oppressed) it. This is where Agamben's work functions at its best, as a direct continuation, but also division, of the fundamental positions that had once guided existentialist thought in the modern era.

Notes

1. Jean-Paul Sartre, *The Words*, trans. Bernard Frechtman (New York: George Braziller, 1964), p. 60.
2. Ibid. pp. 194–5.
3. Jean-Paul Sartre, *Saint Genet: Actor and Martyr*, trans. Bernard Frechtman (New York: George Braziller, 1963).
4. Sartre, *The Words*, p. 250.
5. Ibid. p. 249.
6. Simone de Beauvoir, *The Prime of Life*, trans. Peter Green (New York: Penguin, 1965), p. 478.
7. Ibid. p. 479.
8. See the second chapter of my *Between the Canon and the Messiah: The Structure of Faith in Contemporary Continental Thought* (London: Bloomsbury, 2013).
9. Giorgio Agamben, *The Omnibus Homo Sacer* (Stanford: Stanford University Press, 2017), p. 338; all subsequent references to works from the *Homo Sacer* series will be cited from this single volume.
10. Ibid. pp. 351, 353.
11. Ibid. pp. 314–15.
12. Ibid. p. 747.
13. See the broad survey given, for example, in Peter Watson, *The Age of Atheists: How We Have Sought to Live Since the Death of God* (New York: Simon & Schuster, 2014).
14. Martin Heidegger, *Nietzsche*, vol. 4, trans. David Farrell Krell (New York: HarperCollins, 1982), p. 201.
15. Ibid. p. 203.
16. Ibid. p. 205.
17. Ibid. p. 208.
18. Ibid.
19. Ibid. p. 209.
20. Ibid. p. 210.
21. Ibid. p. 211.
22. Ibid. pp. 212–13.
23. Ibid. pp. 214–15.
24. Ibid. p. 239.
25. Ibid. p. 216.
26. Ibid. p. 218.
27. Ibid. p. 219.
28. Ibid. p. 220.
29. Ibid. p. 221.
30. Ibid.
31. See Giorgio Agamben, *The Open: Man and Animal*, trans. Kevin Attell (Stanford: Stanford University Press, 2003).
32. Heidegger, *Nietzsche*, p. 222.
33. Ibid. p. 223.
34. Ibid. p. 239.
35. Ibid. p. 240.
36. Ibid. p. 243.
37. Ibid. p. 248.
38. See Giorgio Agamben, *The Time that Remains: A Commentary on the Letter to the Romans*, trans. Patricia Dailey (Stanford: Stanford University Press, 2005).
39. Giorgio Agamben, 'In Praise of Profanation', *Profanations*, trans. Jeff Fort (New York: Zone, 2007), p. 77.

40. Ibid. p. 86.
41. See, among others, Gianni Vattimo, *The End of Modernity: Nihilism and Hermeneutics in Post-modern Culture*, trans. John R. Snyder (Baltimore: Johns Hopkins University Press, 1988).
42. Agamben, *The Omnibus Homo Sacer*, p. 449.
43. Ibid. p. 451.
44. Ibid. pp. 452, 426.
45. For more on Agamben's potentially pantheistic sentiments, see my *Agamben and Theology* (London: T&T Clark, 2011).
46. Larry Siedentop, *Inventing the Individual: The Origins of Western Liberalism* (Cambridge, MA: Harvard University Press, 2014).
47. Michael Allen Gillespie, *Nihilism Before Nietzsche* (Chicago: University of Chicago Press, 1995), p. xxiii.
48. Ibid. p. vii.
49. Ibid. p. 134.
50. Ibid. pp.14ff.
51. Ibid. p. 22.
52. Ibid. pp. 251–2.
53. Ibid. p. 25.
54. Ibid. p. 26.
55. Agamben, *The Omnibus Homo Sacer*, p. 468.
56. Ibid. p. 469.
57. Ibid. p. 420.
58. Ibid. p. 422.
59. Ibid. p. 349.
60. Agamben's focus on the Franciscan refusal of the will in order to illustrate rather what remains 'inappropriable' as precisely what assisted them in avoiding ever becoming a habit or custom, as the monks do, is crucial to his overall project of achieving a modal ontology. As he registers the distinction between use and possession, 'Use, from this perspective, could have been configured as a *tertium* with respect to law and life, potential and act, and could have defined – not only negatively – the monk's vital practice itself, their form-of-life' (Agamben, *The Omnibus Homo Sacer*, p. 998).
61. Agamben, *The Omnibus Homo Sacer*, p. 744.
62. Ibid. p. 745.
63. Ibid. p. 343.
64. Ibid. p. 1180.
65. See my *Theology and Contemporary Continental Philosophy: The Centrality of a Negative Dialectics* (London: Rowman & Littlefield, 2019).
66. Theodor W. Adorno, *Negative Dialectics*, trans. E. B. Ashton (London: Continuum, 1973), p. 381.

Chapter 7

Sartre and Agamben: Confronting Nothingness and the (Apparent) Death of God

John Gillespie

The Death of God

It would be no exaggeration to say that, since the 1890s, Western culture has been living in the shadow of the Death of God. The concept has influenced a range of thinkers, such as Gide, Malraux, Sartre, Camus and Beckett, who all struggled with the disappearance of the 2,000-year foundation on which Western values have been built and who sought to find a new coherent way of understanding the world. The 'Death of God Movement' even became fashionable in mid-twentieth-century Christian theology, provoking a famous *Time* magazine leading article, asking the question 'Is God Dead?',[1] which replied positively. It is linked to sociological theories propounding religion's inevitable decline and secularisation's inevitable rise, as outlined in Steve Bruce's book *God is Dead: Secularization in the West* (2002).[2] However, the recent religious turn in modern thought, and the New Atheists' compensating vigour, reinforce the view that the Death of God has been much exaggerated.

Having written elsewhere on the Death of God in Sartre,[3] I wish to consider those thoughts in relation to Agamben's work on negativity. Starting with Friedrich Nietzsche's description, I will outline the approaches of Sartre and Agamben in confronting the challenge to coherence when the foundation is shaken by referring to key texts, before comparing them.

Friedrich Nietzsche: The Drama of the Death of God

Nietzsche is one of the most powerful influences on the negativity and nihilism of contemporary thought. Dramatically declaring the Death of God in the 1880s, he intensified the crisis of culture from the late nineteenth century onwards. This concept focused the key ideas of his thought. For Terry Eagleton: 'He has a strong claim to being the first real atheist. Of course there had been unbelievers in abundance before him, but it is Nietzsche above all who confronts the terrifying exhilarating consequences of the Death of God.'[4] Not that this concept, outlined in *The Gay Science* (*Die fröhliche Wissenschaft*) (1882; 1887) and *Thus Spake Zarathustra* (*Also sprach Zarathustra*) (1883–5), was unique to him and cannot be traced back to others.

The Gay Science depicts a madman running around hopelessly looking for God, mocked by unbelieving onlookers. He is filled with guilt and despair: '"Where is God?" he cried; "I'll tell you! *We have killed him – you and I! We are all his murderers* . . . my time is not yet. This tremendous event is still on its way, wandering; it has not yet reached the ears of men."'[5] This message of loss is dramatic, shocking and urgent; all has totally changed. God is dead, killed by a deliberate act. But it will be a long-drawn-out process. Not everyone will want to hear, but that idea must be defeated:

> After Buddha was dead, they still showed his shadow in a cave for centuries – a tremendous, gruesome shadow. God is dead, but given the way people are, there may still for millennia be caves in which they show his shadow. – And we – we must still defeat his shadow as well! (*GS*, 109)

The foundation of everything has gone. How can men cope? 'Is the magnitude of this deed not too great for us? Do we not ourselves have to become gods merely to appear worthy of it?' (*GS*, 120). The tone is one of cheerfulness:

> *How to understand our cheerfulness*
> The greatest recent event – that 'God is dead'; that the belief in the Christian God has become unbelievable – is already beginning to cast its first shadow over Europe . . .

The collapse of Christian faith will be supremely negative:

> for example, our entire European morality. This long, dense succession of demolition, destruction, downfall, upheaval that now stands ahead: who would guess enough of it today to play the teacher and herald of this monstrous logic of horror, the prophet of deep darkness and eclipse of the sun the like of which has probably never before existed on earth? (*GS*, 199)

The mood is positive:

> Indeed, at hearing the news that 'the old god is dead', we philosophers and 'free spirits' feel illuminated by a new dawn; our heart overflows with gratitude, amazement, foreboding, expectation – finally the horizon seems clear again, even if not bright; finally our ships may set out again, set out to face any danger; every daring of the lover of knowledge is allowed again; the sea, *our* sea, lies open again, maybe never has there been such an 'open sea.' (*GS*, 199)

The Death of God is an attack on God, a deliberate destruction of all thinking based on this God. A decadent and enfeebling Christianity (*The Antichrist* [*Der Antichrist*], 1895), and any transcendent source of values, are fiercely rejected. Science, morality and truth are called into question. But this attack is driven by the joyful Promethean freedom of the anti-theistic individual. Nietzsche does not remain in a position of nihilism. The ground is cleared for the free, deified individual, through the will to power, to revaluate all values, to be the Superman. God may be dead, but the desire to live, a belief in the rationality of language and the awareness of a common human condition are retained.

It is against this Nietzschean template of the Death of God – rebellion against God, the confrontation with philosophical coherence, its lengthy process, yet its positive message of individual freedom and the creation of values – that we will consider Sartre and Agamben.

Jean-Paul Sartre, Nothingness and the Death of God

In Sartre, the Death of God is central both to his intellectual context and his thinking. His analysis of Mallarmé's nineteenth-century background emphasises the effects of the Death of God, even before Nietzsche, on the post-revolutionary bourgeoisie.[6] He believed that killing God and the king showed that atheism and the Death of God were integral to revolutionary ideology (*M*, 16), part of an intentional dechristianisation of France, influenced by materialistic scientism, an irreversible process gradually progressing. His description of the ensuing lack of coherence it causes echoes Nietzsche: 'God drags his gravediggers into the tomb that they've been hollowing out for him' (*M*, 17).[7]

The nature of language is affected. Poetry can no longer convey the true, the good and the beautiful since the word is no longer seen as the breath of God. To compensate, poets, such as Baudelaire and Flaubert, install Art as a substitute religion. Mallarmé endures the misery of an epoch in which chance reigns and God cannot provide inspiration. His rebellion exemplifies the new metaphysical ambiguity. A new Prometheus, he reacts, knowing that he will fail, setting out to replace God (*M*, 136). Alongside this anti-theistic unwillingness to accept God, Mallarmé confronts the disappointment of the death of the absolute, condemning poetry to ultimate failure.

Discussing Bataille in 'Le Nouveau Mystique', Sartre takes the Death of God (in the 1940s) as a fact: 'He is dead; he spoke to us and he is silent, all we can touch now is his corpse' (*S* I, 153). God no longer speaks. The God effect is over; just the corpse remains. God is gone, like a soul that has departed. Everyone has survived. No sign of mourning here. However, he recognises the problem: 'these two opposing, unshakeable demands: God is silent, I can't let go of that, everything in me demands God, I cannot forget it' (*S* I, 154). Sartre concedes man's need for God, but maintains that God neither speaks nor exists. The Death of God has led to the absurd in a range of other twentieth-century thinkers: Kafka, Jaspers, Malraux, Camus, Blanchot and Bataille himself. Sartre criticises those who, like Bataille, have yielded, in bad faith, to the temptation of developing transcendent God replacements, unable to live with the absurd.

Sartre's world is that of the Death of God, with consequences for philosophy, poetry, morality and politics, bringing anguish and posing the problem of finding coherence without recourse to transcendence. His default position, outlined in *Les Mots*, since his childhood rejection of God at the age of twelve, is that the question was resolved for him then and there, and that it no longer mattered. The evidence, however, suggests that God remained a preoccupation.

Examining *Being and Nothingness*

In *Being and Nothingness*,[8] Sartre assumes an atheistic position. He starts from himself, the freedom of individual consciousness at the heart of human-reality, *being-for-itself*. The desire of the *for-itself* founds itself in the face of *being-in-itself*, brute being without consciousness. The *for-itself* is constituted through its capacity of negation, *néantisation*, stepping aside from oneself to see what one is not. This gap in this self-understanding is a nothingness. This negation is the foundation of the freedom of the individual and the capacity to choose.

Sartre argues that the fundamental drive of the *for-itself* is to become the *being-in-itself-for-itself*: conscious, yet self-founding and complete. Individual transcendence is towards that goal: 'human-reality is its own surpassing towards what it misses; it surpasses itself towards the particular being it would be if it were not what it is' (*BN*, 142). The *for-itself* sees itself as a failure, being only the foundation of itself as nothingness, so:

'Human-reality is a perpetual surpassing towards a self-coincidence that is never given' (*BN*, 142). Humankind does not seek God, humankind seeks to become God: 'But the being towards which human-reality surpasses itself is not a transcendent God: it lies at its own heart; it is only itself, in the form of a totality' (*BN*, 142). This self-coincidence, the self-founding state of self-deification, is impossible. Sartre suggests that this structure explains why belief in God exists: as a projection of the human desire to be self-founding:

> And if man has a pre-ontological understanding of God's being, it is not bestowed on him by nature's grand spectacles, or the power of society; but God, as the value and supreme goal of transcendence, represents the permanent limit in terms of which man becomes acquainted with what he is. To be a man is to aim to be God; or alternatively, man is fundamentally the desire to be God. (*BN*, 735)

Sartre secularises the idea of God. In desiring to be God, humankind aims to be its own absolute, and failure causes suffering: 'Human-reality . . . is therefore in its nature an unhappy consciousness, without any possibility of surpassing its state of unhappiness' (*BN*, 143). Humankind is condemned to be a free, anguished being, a failed God. The *for-itself*, faced with the absolutes of individual freedom (nothingness) and the world of the *in-itself* (being) will always fail. This fundamental project drives the constant movement of self-transcendence. Sartre's description is really an advocation of a religion of liberty, 'with the project to-be-God that we have taken to be the deep structure of human-reality' (*BN*, 754). His characterisation of the basic drive of the individual seeking to be God is that they must create their own values, and, being a failed God, must constantly remake their moral choices.

Sartre is negative about belief *in* God, but the idea of God is central. His definition of the human project to be God as impossible makes the idea of God impossible. The nature of consciousness is Sartre's key atheological argument. God's existence is defined as logically impossible, incoherent and self-contradictory because, just as humankind cannot be God to themselves, God cannot be conscious and choosing, therefore changing and changeable, and eternal and immutable, at the same time. The *néantisation* of God involved in all consciousness denies the claim that God is the *ens causa sui*. God is contingent (*BN*, 131–2), as is the *for-itself*. Space does not permit discussion of the validity of Sartre's arguments except to say that he rejects a concept of God that is at odds with orthodox Christianity and seems rather to be refuting the 'Dieu des philosophes' rather than the Christian God.

If God is dead, if Sartre has not believed, it is ironic that he places

God at the centre of his description of the free individual while maintaining that God is impossible. Sartre continues to wrestle with the question of God. Surely God is a non-problem and should disappear from his preoccupations? Yet in *Les Mots*, Sartre describes atheism as a cruel, long-distance enterprise, suggesting that the atheist must maintain his disbelief in God against many temptations. He rates the question of God as a very important one. It is clear that, despite the Death of God, the idea of God is paradoxically central to his thought.

Examining *Existentialism is a Humanism*

In his 1945 lecture *Existentialism is a Humanism*,[9] Sartre seeks to spell out the moral consequences of his atheism (*EH*, 33–4). His starting point is Dostoyevsky's dictum: 'If God didn't exist, everything would be permitted' (*EH*, 36). God's absence poses problems: 'the existentialist thinks that it is very annoying that God doesn't exist, for with him disappears all possibility of finding values in an intelligible heaven; there can no longer be any *a priori* good, since there is no infinite consciousness to think it' (*EH*, 35–6).

As for Nietzsche, God is not there to justify human values a priori. There is no absolute figure or principle to provide a coherent system of values, nor a human nature to directs one's choices. We exist, and our existence precedes our essence. We create our own values. He maintains that: 'Existentialism is not the kind of atheism that expends all its energies demonstrating that God doesn't exist. Instead it asserts that, even if God existed, nothing would change' (*EH*, 95). God dead or not, human freedom is absolute.

God is negatively present as Sartre advances his key doctrine of radical human freedom and reinforces his view that each person must make their own values. The nothingness at the heart of being in the consciousness of the individual is the source of the radical freedom. The key consequence is self-deification. So, as in *Being and Nothingness*, Sartre can accommodate an atheistic and an anti-theistic position: his atheistic assertion of freedom can also involve anti-theism, an attack on or refusal of God. In his play *The Flies* (1943), Orestes meets Jupiter, the king of the gods and asserts his discovery of freedom, rejecting him: 'and now there is nothing in the sky, neither good, nor evil and no one to give me orders. . . . I am condemned to have no other law but my own . . . for I am a man, Jupiter, and every man should create his own pathway.'[10]

Examining *Cahiers pour une morale (Notebooks for an Ethics)*

There are no transcendent guidelines. In *Being and Nothingness*, the individual's *being-for-others* potentially led to conflict. In *Existentialism is a Humanism*, Sartre suggests that when choosing, the individual chooses for all people. The *Cahiers*, an unfinished attempt to develop the ethics promised in *Being and Nothingness*, retain the Death of God context, echoing Nietzsche's cheerfulness: '*God's absence* is no longer closure: it is an opening out to the infinite. *God's absence* is greater and more divine than God.'[11] The absence of faith becomes a faith. In the ruined universe, the freedom of the *néant* opens up the terrestrial divinity of humanity. This God-less naturalism becomes a new revelation: 'The great historical change has been the death of God, the replacement of the Eternal by the temporal infinite' (*CM*, 90). God is secularised: 'Today God has fallen into time' (*CM*, 90). Time comes to be seen as an infinite series, an always incomplete totalisation, comprising all the moments of time, and becoming a replacement eternity (*CM*, 90), radically different from a Christian perspective, where all key values are eternal. In this new temporal, never-complete infinite, individual moral choice binds the moral agent for an infinite series of actions. God is no longer there as an 'absolute witness' validating individuals' moral beliefs and choices. By engaging one's understanding in one's time to act historically and fully within it: 'God is still present in history' (*CM*, 92).

Examining God and Creativity

Sartre rejects the dead God as a tranquillising, reassuring myth for moral agents. For the believer, the world is 'déjà vu' (*CM*, 510), so the believer is inessential; all actions, except salvation, are inessential. Humankind has no true moral freedom or responsibility. In the same way, in a God-centred universe, creation is not really creation, but only knowledge, the recreation of the divine creation: but God's Death leads to pure creation (*CM*, 462). For, if the idea of God functions as an alienation of humanity's freedom (*CM*, 485), in reacting to the Death of God and rejecting God, Sartre now suggests that human freedom is no longer an attempt to be 'the being-for itself-in-itself', as argued in *Being and Nothingness*. It is now a 'project of unveiling and creation' (*CM*, 499).

Humanity Assumes the Dead God's Mission

So Sartre connects human freedom closely with the reality of the Death of God: 'thus man finds himself to be the heir to the mission of the dead God: drawing being out of its perpetual collapse in the absolute indistinction of the night: an infinite and impossible mission' (*CM*, 510). Humankind cannot become God. The limited human mission, based on contingency, involves unveiling being: 'Unveiling means creating what is' (*CM*, 501). In other words, the for-itself becomes *Godlike*, creating the world and creating being by surging into the world: 'if the for-itself decides that being has a meaning it will have a meaning for the for-itself, but since the for-itself is an absolute subject, being will, absolutely have a meaning' (*CM*, 502), a joyful discovery (see *CM*, 512).

The Death of God underpins Sartre's doctrine of freedom. It leads to the secularisation of God in the person of the absolute free individual, an incomplete absolute, and opens up the universe for the Godlike mission of creative moral choice, asserting freedom, not trying to become God. Yet Sartre still admits that the temptation to relapse into seeing things from a Godlike perspective is hard to avoid, once he recalls that his hold on being is limited by his finiteness (*CM*, 502). God remains a persistent presence and temptation in his thought.

Examining *The Devil and the Good Lord*

The ethical consequences of the Death of God are also central to *Le Diable et le bon Dieu*, transposed anachronistically to the sixteenth-century Reformation period. The play depicts the warlord Goetz abandoning the absolutes of good and evil to champion a relativistic human morality. The action shows him that doing good and evil amounts to the same. His story is that of someone for whom God dies and is dead. Goetz's discovery of the Death of God is a moment of religious illumination, a conversion to God's non-existence. He is overjoyed at the realisation:

> The silence, that's God. The absence, that's God. God is man's solitude. There was just me; I alone decided what was Evil; I alone invented the Good. I was the one who cheated, who performed miracles, I'm the one who's accusing today; I'm the only one who can absolve me, me, a man. If God exists, man is nothing; if man exists ... God doesn't exist; Joy, tears of Joy! Hallelujah ... No more heaven, no more hell; just the earth.[12]

God's death means liberation for Goetz and for all of humanity. The play celebrates the triumph of the secular, of the earth. Life is truer, more real, more authentic without God, without a witness. It celebrates Sartre's metaphysical liberation. It is yet another attack on the idea of God, illustrating the anti-theistic elements of his thinking. Freedom is set against the Death of God.

However, it is also a call to practical action. It is also evidence of the difficulty he had from this point on in developing values socially and politically, as he sought to come to terms with communism and political action.

Giorgio Agamben, Negativity and the Death of God

Sartre is a key stage on the road to Giorgio Agamben and other atheist theologians. Agamben's involvement is more implicit. Agamben illustrates Nietzsche's view that the working out of the Death of God would be a long, gradual process. He is a contemporary example of the secularised approaches of the Death of God theologians. We will consider Agamben by examining two key early texts: *Language and Death: The Place of Negativity* (1982) and *The Time that Remains: A Commentary on the Letter to the Romans* (2000), both of which illustrate his astonishing erudition and detailed analysis.

Agamben's central theme is the desire to get beyond nihilism and negativity so that a foundation on which ethical and political values for positive human life can be built within an atheological framework. However, as for Sartre, escape from the theological as a source for coherence proves difficult. We will see clear parallels with Sartre. We shall see in Agamben the continued presence of God, rather than outright rejection. This repressed theism has two main characteristics: the unwillingness to accept absolute nihilism (or absolute freedom), and the secularisation of theological values and their application to the political sphere.

Language and Death, Nothingness and Death

The context of *Language and Death* is one in which there is nothing beyond death: the Death of God. Agamben examines the negative foundation of Western philosophy, which has led to the collapse of metaphysics into ethics, and a nihilism whose ungroundedness contemporary thought and politics have not overcome. Beyond this negativity, he wants to find a ground upon which an ethical dwelling place can be built. His thought relates to Sartre's philosophy since it focuses on being and nothingness, although it is Hegel and Heidegger that Agamben references, rather than Sartre.

The faculties of language and death are for Agamben at the root of our being.[13] In approaching being in *Being and Time*, he considers Heidegger's being-for-death, the negativity at the heart of *Dasein*. This negativity is constituted by the concepts of thrownness (*Verworfenheit*), fallenness (*Verfallensein*) and care (*Sorge*). In *Was ist Metaphysik*, Heidegger terms nothingness as 'the metaphysical question par excellence' (*LD*, 3). Death is a constant threat to being there, the key element being the *Da*, the 'there' that discloses the ineluctable negativity of death. There is nothing beyond it.

In Hegel, Agamben shows that 'Any attempt to express sense-certainty signifies, for Hegel, to experience the impossibility of saying what one means' (*LD*, 11); it is 'a dialectical process of negation and mediation' (*LD*, 12). The very meaning of language, as an attempt to grasp meaning in time, the *Diese*, reveals the unspeakable: 'all speech speaks the ineffable. It speaks it; that is, it demonstrates it for what it is: a *Nichtigkeit*, a nothingness' (*LD*, 14). Agamben sees *Da* and *Diese* as the grammatical shifters of language as it takes place. There is a fundamental split at the heart of language going back as far as Aristotle:

> This fracture traverses the whole history of metaphysics, and without knowing it, the ontological problem itself cannot be formulated. Every ontology . . . presupposes the difference between indicating and signifying, and is defined, precisely, as situated at the very limit between those two acts. (*LD*, 18)

Nothingness is revealed in the process of language. Drawing on the history of grammatical analysis, he sees the influence of modern philosophy from Descartes, to Kant to Husserl, as being 'primarily a reflection on the status of the pronoun *I*' (*LD*, 23). The key role of the pronoun in the dilemma underscores the anthropocentric context of this reflection. They are '"empty signs" . . . Their scope is to enact "the conversion of language into discourse" and to permit the passage from *langue* to *parole*' (*LD*, 24). They make utterance happen. Agamben terms this *Deixis* (indication), language referring to its taking place.

> The transcendence of being and of the world . . . is the transcendence of the event of language with respect to that which, in this event, is said and signified; and the shifters, which indicate the pure *instance* of discourse, constitute (as Kant understood perfectly, attributing transcendental status to the I) the originary linguistic structure of transcendence. (*LD*, 26)

So, unlike Sartre, for Agamben the *ontological* dimension, being, corresponds to 'the pure taking place of language as an originary event, while the *ontic* dimension (entities, things) corresponds to that which, in this opening, is said and signified' (*LD*, 26). This ontological move is away from the metaphysical, indeed from God, to a worldview centred on the 'I', where the 'I' speaks language, creates discourse, seeks to take control of things.

Agamben's second Excursus discusses medieval negative theology: 'theological thought is also grammatical thought, and the God of the theologians, is also the God of the grammarians' (*LD*, 27). In discussing language about God, he quotes Alain de Lille that if a pronoun refers to God it falls away from demonstration, and Aquinas, who talks of the path of negation, of corporeal and intellectual attributes: 'so what remains in our intellect is only the fact that God is, and nothing else' (*LD*, 29). Agamben points to Hebrew notions of the secret and unpronounceable name of God: 'As the unnameable name of God, the Gramma is the final and negative dimension of meaning . . . the dimension of meaning is the gramma, of the letter as the ultimate negative foundation of human discourse' (*LD*, 30). In Pascalian terms this discussion focuses on the 'Dieu des philosophes' distant from Christian orthodoxy: a God without attributes, an abstract, Epicurean God, representing a non-incarnational theology, not a God who speaks and who reveals Godself. This description is a reflection of the Death of Himself as creator, as involved with God's people.

Language, the Voice and Negativity

Agamben's history of language uses the concept of the Voice as pure negativity behind all language: 'this Voice . . . enjoys the status of a *no-longer* (voice) and of a *not-yet* (meaning), [it] necessarily constitutes a negative dimension' (*LD*, 35). Utterance and discourse are only possible through the Voice that speaks, not the voice as mere sound. The Voice is the fundamental ontological dimension disclosing the place of language:

> but in such a way that this place is always already captured in negativity, and above all, already consigned to temporality. Inasmuch as it takes place in the Voice . . . language takes place in time. In demonstrating the instance of discourse, the Voice discloses both being and time. It is Chronothetic. (*LD*, 35)

The category of time is born from the use of the present tense, itself marked by negativity. Even Levinas's critique of ontology indicates 'the fundamental negative structure of metaphysics attempting to think the immemorial having-been beyond all being and presence, the *ille* that is before every I and every this, the saying that is beyond every said' (*LD*, 40).

Human language, faced with negativity, is the 'voice of consciousness' (*LD*, 44) and the voice of death. Agamben is concerned that 'Today we live on that extreme fringe of metaphysics where it returns – as nihilism – to its own negative foundation (to its own Ab-grund, its own ungroundedness)' (*LD*, 53). But his overarching argument is that this is not the *Ethos*, the proper dwelling of humanity.

Agamben's analysis of Heidegger's *Dasein* and the problem of language taking place reinforces this negativity. Paradoxically, the *Stimmung* of *Angst* calls in *Dasein* in its loss: 'without a voice in the place of language, Dasein finds *another Voice*, even if this is a Voice that calls only in the mode of silence' (*LD*, 59). *Dasein* is the 'negative foundation of its own negativity' (*LD*, 59), linked as it is to *being-unto-death*: 'Thinking death is simply thinking the Voice' (*LD*, 60). So 'The thought of Being is the thought of the Voice' (*LD*, 61).

God and Silence

Agamben moves to the silence of late-antique Gnostic and Christian mysticism, of God as unspeakable and inexpressible. He contends that the Gnostic Sigé's silence of God as the abysmal silence of the word plays a seminal role in Christian mysticism and philosophy. In a strange sleight of hand, via illustrations from Augustine and Syrian mystical prayer, he states:

> Thus there is no absolute opposition between the Gnostic Sigé and Christian logos, which are never completely separated. Silence is simply the negative foundation of logos, its taking place and its unknown dwelling (according to Johannine theology), in the arche that is the Father. This dwelling of logos in arche (like that of Sigé in Buthos) is an abysmal dwelling – that is ungrounded – and Trinitarian theology never engages to fully emerge from this abysmalness. (*LD*, 65)

Agamben sees this mysticism as showing that Christianity cannot escape this negativity either, fitting it into a template that opposes orthodox Christian doctrine.

Even the consideration of the poetic tradition as language not resting on a negative foundation is undermined by his analysis of the nothingness implicit in the language of love of the medieval troubadours; in poetry, as in philosophy, 'the taking place of language is unspeakable and ungraspable' (*LD*, 77). He concludes that neither poetry nor philosophy can 'grasp the inaccessible place of the word' (*LD*, 78); it is unattainable. But in analysing negativity, Agamben, a complex user of words, always wants to move beyond it; in referring to Leopardi's 'L'Infinito' he points to a place:

'and in the extinguishing of thought, in the exhaustion of the dimension of being, the figure of humanity's *having* emerges for the first time in its simple clarity; *to have always dear* as one's habitual dwelling place, as the *ethos* of humanity' (*LD*, 81).
Agamben's summary is that

> Man is that living being who removes himself and preserves himself at the same time – as unspeakable – in language; negativity is the human means of *having* language . . . The mythogene of the Voice is, thus the original mythogene of metaphysics; but inasmuch as the Voice is also the originary place of negativity, negativity is inseparable from metaphysics. (*LD*, 85)

He thus claims that this split in language permeates the history of philosophy from the Greeks to the present. As far as origins are concerned, the Voice is the beginning for Agamben, not God.

The Voice, 'the mystical foundation for our entire culture' (*LD*, 91), relates specifically to Greek metaphysics and its successors; his discussion in *Language and Death* lies principally outside any serious consideration of Christian theology, even though he suggests it, too, is based on negativity. For him the only hope is to liquidate the mystical, and to think beyond the Voice and its Sigetics 'that dwells, that is, not on an unspeakable foundation, but in the infancy (in-fari) of man' (*LD*, 91). Moving away from this negativity, Agamben talks of being at home in the absolute, of returning to its habitual dwelling place, its ethos 'walking through negativity and absolving it from its demonic scission' (*LD*, 93). A longing for simple humanity.

Agamben, in characterising the persistence of language and death in Western thought, indicates that a negativity equivalent to the Death of God has always been present. Death, in this context, has always been seen as the end; there is no contact with the divine realm or existence and no divine *logos* of revelation. The individual seeks to understand the world through reason, again neglecting the contribution of Christian theology.

His solution is tentative and non-theological: 'And perhaps only beginning with the eclipses of the Voice, with the no longer taking place of language and with the death of the Voice, does it become possible for man to experience an *ethos* that is no longer simply a *sigetics*' (*LD*, 96). 'Its place is the ethos, the infantile dwelling – that is to say without will or Voice – of man in language' (*LD*, 104). As Catherine Mills says:

> the upshot of Agamben's argument throughout *Language and Death* is that any such attempt to understand that which is most 'proper' to man through reference to negative foundation will fail to do justice to the *ethos* – understood in the Greek sense of the proper dwelling place – of humanity.[14]

This ethical dimension is saying yes to language and consenting to its taking place on the grounds of a tentative humanism. For him language becomes the core value that is the foundation of a person's free and speaking being. The anthropocentric roots are clear. The negativity of a person's being without God is rejected, for instance in the violence of the concept and practice of sacrifice, and the existence of a common humanity whose values should be created, served and preserved is asserted. Language becomes a substitute God. As he says in the epilogue 'So, language is our voice, our language. As you now speak, that is ethics' (*LD*, 108). It is a job that still needs to be done.[15]

The 'I' of language as value, as an assertion of humanity, is a statement of anthropocentric rather than theistic faith, an anthropology that is theologically aware, yet without God. It is on this that Agamben bases his involvement in political concerns.

Examining *The Time That Remains: A Commentary on the Letter to the Romans*

Whereas in *Language and Death* an engagement with Christian theology is limited, Agamben's deep respect for Paul and his thought is striking, as is the detailed manner in which he considers the meaning of the letter in *The Time That Remains*. The Letter to the Romans is the most important and theologically detailed of Paul's epistles, and so Agamben's study takes us to the heart of his understanding of Christian theology, the Christian gospel and its implications. This detailed biblical analysis contrasts with the writings of Sartre, which engage neither directly nor extensively with scripture, despite the Christian theological and biblical patterns found in his work.

Agamben comments in detail only on the first ten words (in Greek) of Chapter 1. Agamben's profound knowledge of the letter is clear. His discussion reveals his understanding of the whole epistle and of Paul's theology, seen in the light of intellectual history and a knowledge of language and linguistics. The commentary is based on a seminar which lasted, as in creation, six days along with a further sabbatical day.[16]

The key to Agamben's understanding of Paul is the concept of Jesus as Messiah, a view that has become more widespread in contemporary theological studies.[17] For him the term 'Christ', the Greek translation of the Messiah, has obscured Jesus's messianic role. So Agamben focuses on what it means to live in the Messiah, and in the structure of messianic time.[18] A necessarily brief overview of his arguments will be helpful in showing how they relate to the Death of God.

The key emphasis on calling or vocation (*klesis*) is central to Paul's vision and to the messianic event: the 'messianic vocation is the revocation of every vocation' (*TTR*, 23). The messianic calling changes everything. For Paul this is a call from God, yet here Agamben links it to the secularisation of the concept of vocation. He addresses the question of the secularisation of such concepts, living 'as if' they would truly be realised even though they cannot; 'as if' God, truth and ethics really existed. This is the problem with which Nietzsche grappled (*TTR*, 37) in overcoming nihilism, and confronts readers of Agamben's analysis throughout.

Agamben sees Paul as separated, as part of the remnant produced in the messianic now and an instrument of salvation. Paul describes himself not as a prophet, but an emissary of the Messiah, because in the Messiah prophecy is already fulfilled. Messianic time has already come. Agamben reflects deeply on the nature of messianic time. It is not the eschaton, the end of time, but 'the time of the now' (*TTR*, 61), 'the time that remains between time and its end' (*TTR*, 62). It is a transformation of secular time; it is Gustave Guillaume's 'operational time', not chronological time, but 'the time we need to make time end: *the time that is left us* [*il tempo chi ci resta*]' (*TTR*, 68). The concept of *Kairos*, a seizing of *chronos*, exemplifies salvation for Paul, bringing together the already, but not yet. The time to act.

Agamben emphasises how, through typology, Paul establishes a relation between every past event in biblical history and messianic time: 'messianic time is neither the complete nor the incomplete, neither the past nor the future, but the inversion of both' (*TTR*, 75). Through recapitulation, Paul shows messianic time as a summation of all things past in the present. Messianic time is not oriented solely towards the future (*TTR*, 77), but lives in tension in the present and the past, straining towards the future. That is its particularity.

In considering the *evangelion*, the Gospel, Agamben often mirrors orthodox Christian theology, emphasising it as both announcement and content. Faith in the *evangelion* is powered by *energeia*, by becoming actual. Faith is conviction, an ontological engagement containing a promise: 'Faith consists in being fully persuaded of the necessary unity of promise (*epaggelia*) and realization' (*TTR*, 91). In dealing with the distinction between the law of faith and the law of works, he contends that through faith the law is made inoperative. Messianic power deactivates the law and its works, not by abolishing it, since the Messiah is the *telos* of the law, but by deactivating it and fulfilling it.

Significantly, Agamben sees this process of abolishing and conserving the law as a key element of Hegel's dialectical process, a secularisation of the messianic themes used by him and others in modernity, against Christianity. Agamben himself links his messianic analysis to the operation of secular political power in understanding how 'the law maintains itself in relation to the exception in the form of its own self-suspension' (*TTR*, 104), connecting it to the question of sovereignty. The messianic exception is the paradox of salvation, of the law of faith. 'With regard to this law that applies itself in disapplying itself, a corresponding gesture of faith ensues, applying itself in disapplying itself, rendering law inoperative while carrying it to its fulfilment' (*TTR*, 107). Yet faith, through love of neighbour, recapitulates the commandments.

Faith as both active trust and passive belief Agamben links with *berit*, the pact or covenant in Exodus and Deuteronomy. It is a two-sided thing. It 'is just as much the faith of men as it is the faith of Yahweh' (*TTR*, 118). The pacts with Abraham and his descendants predate this Mosaic law. The theme of grace (*charis*) functions to keep faith and obligation together, enabling the faithful to 'gratuitously carry out good works independently of the law' (*TTR*, 121). For Agamben, the messianic instance goes back towards the Abrahamic promise and provides a space of grace between the covenants of Abraham and Moses. For Paul 'grace entails nothing more than the ability to *use* the sphere of social determinations and services in its totality' (*TTR*, 124), which clearly, for Agamben, has contemporary political applications.

After interpreting these concepts in a relatively orthodox manner, Agamben, influenced by Flüsser, and referencing Lessing, identifies a 'split in faith within Christianity itself' (*TTR*, 124), related to Paul's account.

> The first faith is that *of* Jesus, the religion of the historical Jesus, the faith professed by him in words and actions, and the second faith is the faith *in* Jesus Christ, a faith that fully matured in the Christian community after the crucifixion and coincided with the construction of Christology and the recognition of Jesus as the only-begotten son of God, who was made man and died for the redemption of our sins. (*TTR*, 124)

The first is found in the gospels and the second in the other texts. Agamben insists that 'Paul's faith starts with the resurrection, and he does not know Jesus in the flesh, only Jesus Messiah. The essential content of Pauline faith is not the life of Jesus but Jesus Messiah, crucified and risen' (*TTR*, 126). 'Paul does not believe that Jesus possesses the quality of being the Messiah; he believes in Jesus Messiah, that is all' (*TTR*, 128).

Crucially, Agamben believes the world of faith is not one of

> predicates, of existences and of essences ... In the end it is a world in which I do not believe that Jesus, such-and-such a man, is the Messiah, only-begotten son of God, begotten and not created, consubstantial in the Father. I only believe in Jesus Messiah; I am carried away and enraptured in him, in such a way that "I do not live, but the Messiah lives in me" (Gal. 2:20). (*TTR*, 129)

After outlining the strength of Paul's exegesis and application of the Abrahamic Covenant in the light of Jesus's life, death, resurrection and ascension, and showing the complex interrelation of law and grace in the doctrine of salvation, at this point Agamben's analysis provides evidence of the influence of the Death of God. Space does not permit a detailed theological discussion, but Agamben here effectively secularises Paul's understanding of the Messiah, removing both the historical and transcendent realms in favour of a personal, text-based belief. Jesus's divinity, as son of God, Messiah, as Lord of the New Creation, is rejected, as is his self-awareness as Messiah. Evidence in the gospels that Jesus saw himself as Messiah and was crucified for those claims is ignored (for instance, the Gospel of John is not referenced), and the resurrection is implicitly rejected in favour of the concept of Jesus Messiah. His suggestion that Paul had no concept of the historical Jesus, merely of Jesus Messiah, is scarcely plausible given Paul's Palestinian experience, his association with Jesus's disciples, his knowledge of many witnesses to the resurrection (see 1 Corinthians 15:3–8), and especially his murderous determination, before his conversion, to persecute Christians for claiming, after his crucifixion, that Jesus was indeed the resurrected Messiah. Paul's knowledge and faith are both historical and theological. Furthermore, the division between gospels and letters sets up a false dichotomy, suggesting the absence of the concept of the Bible as divine revelation.

In discussing faith and the word of faith, Agamben draws on J. L. Austin and his theory of the performative utterance to explain that 'only the professing of the mouth accomplishes salvation. Neither a glossolalia deprived of meaning, nor mere denotative word, the word of faith enacts its meaning through its utterance' (*TTR*, 131). The word is not just constative; the performed word takes on a special value, 'the pure event of the word' (*TTR*, 134). The messianic power *of words* is central to Agamben's understanding of Paul's teaching. It is seen in the tension between Paul's concepts of *nomos* and *pistis*. It points

> toward an experience of the word, which – without tying itself denotatively to things, or taking itself as a thing without being infinitely suspended in an openness or fastening itself up in dogma – manifests itself as a pure and common potentiality of saying, open to a free and gratuitous use of time and of the world. (*TTR*, 135–6)

Here Agamben is placing his trust and belief in language as a kind of absolute, a power that is dissociated from the truth and content of what is said, which is not required of it and is linked to the faith in the words believed alone. The difference between this and Christian theistic belief is clear. There is no concept here of the *logos* as God made flesh in Christ (John

1:1–14). This represents a form of linguistic materialism, where the truth comes from the word alone:

> The word of faith manifests itself as the effective experience of a pure power [*potenza*] of saying that, as such, does not coincide with any denotative proposition, or with the performative value of a speech act. Rather it exists as an absolute nearness of the word. (*TTR*, 136)

We are now in full Death of God territory. Having outlined the nature of Paul's doctrine of salvation through grace in relation to the tension between faith and law, and presenting those concepts as focused in the concept of the Messiah and within the seizing of messianic time, Agamben then evacuates the New Testament and Paul's understanding of the factuality and spirituality of the gospel and uses it as a linguistic template to describe the functioning of messianic time. And so Agamben, like Schmitt, provides us with an example of the secularisation of Christian thought forms and doctrines to be applied in a socio-political context. Hence, he goes on to say at the end of Day 6:

> There is no such thing as a content of faith, and to profess the word of faith does not mean formulating true propositions on God and the world. To believe in Jesus Messiah does not mean believing something about him, *legein ti kata tinos*, and the attempt of the Councils to formulate the content of faith in *symbola* can only be taken as a sublime irony. (*TTR*, 136)

In this statement Agamben elevates language and its forms as values, and denies their denotative power. The selective use of Paul is evident. Discussion of the eschaton, the return of the Messiah, is now absent, as is any Trinitarian sense of Father, Son and Holy Spirit, Paul's insistence on the importance of the resurrection and on doctrinal correctness in the churches, and so on. So, language remains, but in a perpetually deconstructed state. As he says regarding the word in its messianic weakness:

> That this potentiality finds its *telos* in weakness means that it does not simply remain suspended in infinite deferral; rather, turning back towards itself, it fulfils and deactivates the very excess of signification over every signified, it extinguishes languages. In this way, it bears witness to what, unexpressed and insignificant, remains in use forever near the word. (*TTR*, 137)

The final section, the Tornada, links the messianic concepts to the political sphere by referencing the image of a dwarf Benjamin borrows from Poe to characterise modern theology:

> The dwarf is in fact theology, who 'today, as we know is wizened and has to keep out of sight' and if historical materialism knows how to put theology to use, it would win this historical battle, thus defeating its fearful adversary. (*TTR*, 138)

Agamben refers to the closeness of Benjamin's philosophy of history to Paul's dialectical understanding of time as being linked to the recapitulation of messianic time: 'in any case this orientation towards the past characteristic of Benjamin's Messianism finds its canonic moment in Paul' (*TTR*, 144). Messianic time is revolutionary time.

Agamben's commentary is conducted within an atheistic worldview, seeing the text within the context of philosophical and intellectual history rather than within the framework of Christian belief. The Death of God context is clearly evident in a text which, paradoxically, treats the biblical data with respect. However, Agamben, while carefully exegeting some elements of Paul's doctrine of messianic salvation accurately, ends up not just detaching the texts from the New Testament data – not only the messianic thought of the gospels and the letters of Paul in particular – but also from their historical context (barely mentioned) and from the early church's understanding and canonisation of his theology. Agamben keeps elements of the messianic form and the concept of messianic time, but secularises Paul's thought, providing a kind of dialectical template of messianic texts for the political concerns of our present age, dissociating from the principal themes of salvation, grace in operation, the doctrine of sin, justification, new creation, the Lordship of Christ, and so on.

This detachment is what one would expect from an age that is wrestling with the problem of the Death of God. Theological concepts are secularised. But why should the historicism implied in messianic time be accepted? Why should this version of Paul's messianic concepts have any authority? Why, by implication, should the activity of a messianic saviour or saviours be accepted? Is messianic time a form of destiny, or just the grabbing of a key moment? Messianism, leaving aside its reference to Paul and the New Testament, can be seen as a process of salvific political restoration and renewal, which fits with Agamben's approach to politics and the public square. Messianism without a Messiah.

Agamben advocates common humanity and justice founded on language because they protect against nihilism, against nothingness and fulfil a strong desire for meaning.[19] They are confronted by an empty heaven. It is the form, the shadow without the substance, and the truth without the reality. There is no divine supernatural intervention by the Messiah and there will be no eschaton, but Agamben's thought implies that we should live 'as if' it all made sense. It is an appropriation and domestication of theology to face up to a world without God. 'The time that remains?'; but what is going to happen, and what will happen afterwards? As Isabelle Chareire so helpfully says: 'unlike Nietzsche, we are not dealing here with a critique of Christianity as such, but rather an instrumental use of Christian symbolism.'[20]

Jean-Paul Sartre, Giorgio Agamben and the (Apparent) Death of God

The coverage of both authors has been necessarily brief, and much has been left unsaid. However, considering them in relation to Nietzsche, it is clear that they are quite different. Like Nietzsche, Sartre is positively anti-theistic and lives in an intellectual context that accepts the Death of God. He is happy to be free and to create his own values. In so far as he retains theological ideas, they are secularised to give structure and coherence to his philosophy. Agamben, of a different intellectual generation, exemplifies the long-drawn-out consequences of the Death of God. In rejecting negativity, his unbelief is indirect but fundamental, and links to his gleanings of intellectual history. More than Sartre, he is motivated by the concept of death. In wanting positivity, rather than being directly anti-theistic, he secularises and undermines orthodox Christian concepts, retaining them but fundamentally changing them to use positively in a world without God. He emphasises language as a key value, rather than freedom.

Both grapple with the split caused by nothingness at the heart of being, since both start by denying a theistic worldview, Sartre by embracing negation in operation of the freedom of action of the individual consciousness and Agamben by putting language in the centre and seeking to overcome the nothingness at its heart.

Neither remains in nihilism. Sartre finds his reality in individual freedom, ultimately struggling to find its expression in a Marxist context, but tending further and further towards humanist belief, as he seeks to find coherence. Agamben finds his value in language, and its expression, and in language as an *ethos*, a dwelling-place of humankind. Both tend towards a form of humanism based on a common humanity. Although neither seems to have discovered a clear coherent foundational belief, both, in texts beyond those we have studied, become involved in the development of political ethics.

All three – Nietzsche, Sartre and Agamben – as one might expect, find it difficult to free themselves from the influence of almost two thousand years of Christian thinking.

Moreover, the presence, in the case of Sartre, of the importance of a person's desire to be God as his basic ontological structure, and his direct rejection of Christian belief, even though he uses Christian themes, and, in the case of Agamben, of his extensive biblical knowledge and focus and his extensive secularised theological engagement suggests that, although the Death of God remains present in our current intellectual context, for both authors God is not as dead as we might expect.

Notes

1. 'Is God Dead?', *Time*, 8 April 1966.
2. Steve Bruce, *God is Dead: Secularization in the West* (Oxford: Blackwell, 2002).
3. See John H. Gillespie, 'Sartre and the Death of God', *Sartre Studies International* 22.1 (2016).
4. Terry Eagleton, *Culture and the Death of God* (New Haven: Yale University Press, 2014).
5. Friedrich Nietzsche, *The Gay Science*, ed. Bernard Williams, trans. Josefine Nauckhoff (Cambridge: Cambridge University Press, 2001), pp. 119–20; all further references are abbreviated in the text as *GS*.
6. See 'L'Engagement de Mallarmé' [Mallarmé's Commitment] and 'Mallarmé (1842–1898)', in Jean-Paul Sartre, *Mallarmé: La lucidité et sa face d'ombre*, ed. Arlette El-Kaïm Sartre (Paris: Gallimard, 1986) (all further textual references are abbreviated in the text as *M*) and his lengthy review of Georges Bataille's *L'Expérience intérieure*, in 'Un nouveau mystique', *Situations* I (Paris: Gallimard, 1947) (all further references are abbreviated in the text as *S* I).
7. All translations of these French texts are mine.
8. Jean-Paul Sartre, *Being and Nothingness*, trans. Sarah Richmond (London: Routledge, 2018); all further references are abbreviated in the text as *BN*.
9. Jean-Paul Sartre, *L'Existentialisme est un humanisme* (Paris: Nagel, 1947); all further references are abbreviated in the text as *EH*. The translations are mine.
10. Jean-Paul Sartre, *Les Mouches*, in *Théâtre complet* (Paris: NRF, Gallimard, Pléiade, 2005), pp. 64–5. The translations are mine.
11. Jean-Paul Sartre, *Cahiers pour une morale*, ed. Arlette El-Kaïm Sartre (Paris: Gallimard, 1983), p. 40; all further references are abbreviated in the text as *CM*.
12. Jean-Paul Sartre, *Le Diable et le bon Dieu*, in *Théâtre complet* (Paris: NRF, Gallimard, Pléiade, 2005), p. 449 (Acte III, Xe tableau, scène iv). The translation is mine.
13. Giorgio Agamben, *Language and Death: The Place of Negativity*, trans. Karen E. Pinkus with Michael Hardt (Minneapolis and London: University of Minnesota Press, 1991 [1982]), p. xii; all further references are abbreviated in the text as *LD*.
14. Catherine Mills, *The Philosophy of Agamben* (Montreal: McGill-Queen's University Press, 2008), p. 27.
15. 'Agamben's analysis focuses on this place of negativity which, by his lights, man occupies in the tradition of Western metaphysics; and he will conclude that if one cannot account for what is proper to man other than through the negative, one will not be able to think the ethical either – and thus remain mired in the disturbing political consequences of that failure.' Martijn Buijs, 'Giorgio Agamben and the Voice of Death', *IXIII*, 8 (accessed 18 May 2020).
16. As I outline Agamben's argument, I will not be tying my exposition to the day on which it is mentioned.
17. See, for instance, N. T. Wright, *Paul and His Recent Interpreters* (London: SPCK, 2013).
18. See Giorgio Agamben, *The Time That Remains: A Commentary on the Letter to the Romans* (2000), trans. Patricia Dailey (Stanford: Stanford University Press, 2005), p. 197; all further references are abbreviated in the text as *TTR*.
19. See Isabelle Chareire, 'Giorgio Agamben et la gloire vide', *Théophylion* 13.2 (2013): 287.
20. '[À] la différence de Nietzsche, nous n'avons pas affaire ici à une critique du Christianisme en tant que tel mais plutôt à un usage instrumental de la symbolique chrétienne.' Chareire, 'Giorgio Agamben et la gloire vide', p. 285. The translation is mine.

III
Existentialist Themes in Agamben

Chapter 8

Death and the Negative in Agamben and Beauvoir

Beatrice Marovich

The powers of death seem to cast a tragic, even catastrophic, shadow in the work of Giorgio Agamben. This is most apparently the case in his *Homo Sacer* series, in which the figure of the *homo sacer* becomes – in Agamben's characterisation – 'a living pledge to his subjection to the powers of death'.[1] The figure of *nuda vita* is laid bare and exposed – made vulnerable – to the powers of death. Benjamin Noys has argued that power for Agamben is, in essence, the power of death itself.[2] Noys argues that if (following Agamben) we have all become a form of *nuda vita*, or bare life, then our lives today are death-driven, as they unfold 'under the constant threat of death'.[3] This might seem to suggest that death is simply a biopolitical problem for Agamben. But in what follows I argue that there are flickers of something a bit more 'death positive' in Agamben's work, as well. Agamben's resistance of death dealing powers is not the wresting of life *from* death, nor the denigration of death so as to produce a form of life that might finally be free from death. Perhaps, instead, it is the creation of a space in which a new use can be found for certain dimensions of death – in which the impotentialities of death might be illuminated. Agamben severs the bonds between death and negativity in order to highlight a natal negativity that releases death for new uses. This is not a conceptual move that belongs to Agamben alone. In interesting ways, it resembles the conceptual death work of existentialist philosopher Simone de Beauvoir, whose natal negativity – which severs the bond between death and the negative – also makes possible other views on death.

Against Heidegger

For both Beauvoir and Agamben, the negative bears what I call a decidedly more natal dimension: the negative harbours something active, resistant, novel and, ultimately, a bit more life directed. While neither makes reference to the work of Hannah Arendt, their gesture to decouple death and the negative highlights their turn against a kind of Heideggerian formulation. What Beauvoir and Agamben share, in their respective critiques of death and the negative, is an intent to raise questions about the intimate relation that Heidegger illuminates between death and negativity.

Heidegger's critique of the metaphysics of presence seems to find, in the existential phenomenon of death (distinct from the biological death of a living body), a potent and lively source of negativity, lack and impossibility. If *Dasein*, for Heidegger, finds its ownmost potentiality-for-being or 'reaches its wholeness' in death,[4] this is far from the annihilation or evisceration of *Dasein*. Rather, this conjunction of death and *Dasein* allows Heidegger to somehow vitiate the 'not-yet' or the 'lack of totality' in *Dasein*, which prevents it from becoming fully present to our experience.[5] *Dasein* finds its 'end' in death, Heidegger suggests. But he also argues that this 'end' should not be understood as an ending within actuality – as something that simply stops, or only becomes accessible when the end arrives.[6] The ontology of life, Heidegger suggests, is subordinate to the ontology of *Dasein*, as is the existential analysis of death.[7] Therefore, while death may allow him to express a particular dimension of *Dasein* (its negative qualities; what we perceive as its state of lack), and while this may be an 'end' for *Dasein* in the sense that it allows *Dasein* to access a potential that is impossible within actuality, death is not where *Dasein* falls into a state of inactivity, or becomes nothing. In death, *Dasein* finds not perishing or extermination but a form of actualisation that it is, in actuality, impossible. Death is, for *Dasein*, 'the possibility of no longer being-able-to-be-there' or, to put it otherwise, 'death is the possibility of the absolute impossibility of Dasein'.[8] So it is that being-toward-death, for Heidegger, is also 'being towards a possibility'.[9] Death is a potentiality.

Beauvoir's most explicit conversation with Heidegger on death might be in her early essay 'Pyrrhus and Cineas'. Here Beauvoir reflects on what she calls the 'gratuitous', or directionless, dimension of existence. We are, Beauvoir argues, nothing but the sum of our actions – we are what we do in the face of what is thrown in front of us, or what we are thrown into. The life of each human is 'absolutely gratuitous at every instant'.[10] Beauvoir is not focused on the gift quality of this gratuitousness (which might require gratitude towards a life-giver). Rather, it is the purposelessness that she emphasises. Human life, she says, is 'without reason' and 'without end'.[11] Beauvoir argues that this frees us to focus on action – what we do now, not where we are going. Our life, then, is a sum of 'projects towards singular ends'.[12] What matters is not some alienated ultimate aim, or universal purpose. Instead, every singular action matters because living is a shifting and aimless assemblage of singular acts and projects.

Beauvoir takes aim at Heidegger because, she suggests, the notion of being-towards-death imports too much direction and purposiveness into life. One must not suggest, as she believes Heidegger does, that the 'authentic project' of human life is 'being for death [*être pour mourir*]'. Beauvoir calls this an argument that death is 'our essential end' or that the human being is '*for* death' – designed for, aimed towards, or living for, its death.[13] Beauvoir argues, instead, that the human is '*for* nothing'.[14] Human life is a being towards nothing, rather than a being towards death. Beauvoir claims that 'the nothingness that anguish reveals to me is not the nothingness of my death', rather 'it is the negativity at the heart of my life'.[15] Human life is a series of singular projects 'toward singular ends' rather than 'projects toward death'.[16] Rather than locate the directionless contingency of human life in its finitude, mortality and death, Beauvoir chooses to root it in an experience of nothingness in which she sees a form of freedom. The removal of death, as the horizon of human life, allows her to import a more infinite dimension into the finitude of a life.

Beauvoir found the conflation of death and nothingness to be nihilistic, and she was intent to underscore that she was not a nihilist. In nihilism, said Beauvoir, life itself appears to be nothing more than death in disguise. Death becomes the ultimate, for the nihilist, so life disintegrates in a unified field of nothingness and death.[17] So Beauvoir argued that nihilism – especially the equivocation of death and nothingness – was to be rejected. Beauvoir believed her claim – that nothingness was 'the negativity at the heart of my life'[18] – to be anti-nihilistic. Death, for Beauvoir, was the end of life in a body. But nothingness was the pulsing, creative, life-giving negativity at the heart of the body. Nothingness fed into, and created the conditions for, being.

Given Heidegger's own attempt to emphasise that *Dasein*'s being-towards-death does not end with death, and that the ontology of *Dasein* contains both the ontology of life and the ontology of death within it, it is certainly possible to argue that Beauvoir has subjected Heidegger's work to a misreading. There is, perhaps, more resonance between the endlessness of *Dasein* (even as it is directed towards death) and the gratuitous directionlessness of life that Beauvoir wants to emphasise. But the fidelity of Beauvoir's reading is beside the point. Instead, I am interested in the fact that Beauvoir wants to cut the connections between death and nothingness. Heidegger serves as a useful figure for her to critique in this enterprise. By critiquing Heidegger's co-implication of death and the negative, Beauvoir illustrates clearly her own decoupling. Death, it would seem, serves as too high a wall or too sharp a limit on life. It is too deterministic, leaving too little room open for the infinite dimensions of the finite. Nothingness, on the other hand, seems to hold a riper set of potentialities. It is emptier, so also more potent, than death. Nothingness can be more infinite, more life-oriented, than death.

Agamben's reading of Heidegger's being-towards-death differs greatly from Beauvoir's. Agamben would likely critique Beauvoir's readiness to find possibility in the negative. In *Language and Death*, Agamben offers a critique of nihilism that is more comprehensive and exacting than Beauvoir's, and would also seem to apply to Beauvoir's philosophy. And yet I think it is worthwhile to reflect on the resonance between Beauvoir's and Agamben's decoupling of death and the negative. In crucial ways, Beauvoir's thought offers us the image of a simple cut that can help us to discern what might not otherwise look like a clear cut in Agamben's thought. While Beauvoir believed that it was possible to find, in nothingness, a dimension of potentiality beyond nihilism, Agamben reads philosophies of nothingness (like Beauvoir's) as part of a longer metaphysical history that sources the negative as the ungrounded, mystical foundation of metaphysics itself. Agamben suggests that the collapse of metaphysics has not resulted in the disappearance of metaphysics but has arrived instead at nihilism – the negative mystical foundations of the metaphysical enterprise.[19] The task Agamben sets for himself, in *Language and Death*, is to push beyond such philosophies of death and negativity in order to locate a form of thinking that does not become entrapped, yet again, in this foundational nihilism.

Agamben argues that the link between language and negativity, in Western thought, is deep and ancient. Agamben gestures towards a long history that links the negative to ontotheology, and in which the negative (in its many guises) serves as the ungrounded ground of metaphysics.[20] The roots of this negative foundation are continuously watered and given nutrition through language. When the name of God is limned with the power of the negative, or when the 'silent voice' serves as the negative mystical foundations of the *logos*, the links between metaphysics and the negative are strengthened and affirmed. It is in the work of Hegel, however, that Agamben finds the clearest link between language (in all its ancient negativity) and *death*. Focusing largely on the manuscripts of lectures that Hegel presented in Jena, Agamben targets Hegel's theory that in human language (or Voice) there is the 'memory' of 'the animal's death'. Through language a distinction is drawn between the human and the animal, and this puts to death the line of connection between human and animal – it puts the animal within the human to death. The human Voice puts the animal voice to death. And so it is Voice – human language – that 'preserves and recalls the living as dead', at least to the extent that language harbours the 'trace of memory and death' or a trace of 'pure negativity'.[21] If, as Agamben puts it, 'the death of the animal is the becoming of consciousness'[22] and of language, then language always bears the traces of animal death. If language harbours the trace of animal death, then it 'dwells in the realm of death'.[23] The mystical negativity of language is pulled in the direction of nothingness, nihilism and ultimately death. To live within this living death, Agamben suggests, is to be pulled, constantly, back towards nihilism. He poses that, moving beyond this conflation of language, negativity and death will mean finding 'an experience of speech' that 'no longer presupposes any negative foundation'.[24]

Agamben acknowledges that Heidegger sought out a philosophy of the negative precisely in order to move beyond metaphysics. But Agamben argues that Heidegger's death-oriented philosophy merely pulled him back into the negative foundations of metaphysics. On the surface, it would appear that Heidegger is aware of the complicity between Hegel's Voice and metaphysics. For Heidegger, Agamben notes, every characterisation of language that begins with voice is 'in sympathy with metaphysics'.[25] For this reason Heidegger speaks not of voice but instead of *silence* – a form of language that seems to lack any trace of a voice.[26] Silence is the negative dimension of language. But Agamben suggests that this silent voice is still pulled in the same direction as Hegel's Voice. For Hegel, the human Voice finds itself through death and negativity – Voice emerges out of the violent death of the animal dimensions of voice. And so, in Voice, there is a 'magic power' of negativity and death that facilitates the emergence of Voice. While Heidegger resists the presence-oriented Voice, the *silent voice* of *Dasein* remains a being-towards-death. In this sense, death and negativity continue to provide a 'magic power' that inverts the negative into being. This is as much the case for Heidegger as it was for Hegel, Agamben suggests.[27]

Agamben ultimately implies that critiques of metaphysics such as Heidegger's – hoping to 'surpass' the horizon of metaphysics by 'radicalizing the problem of negativity' – are destined to lead to a repetition of metaphysics, because they are drawn back into ontotheology's negative foundations.[28] This is, Agamben suggests, a problem that lends to a tragic view of human life; as if the best and most proper activity of human life is to 'return as soon as possible' from whence we came, 'to ascend beyond [our] birth' towards 'the silent experience of death'.[29] This is the nihilistic, negative, pull of Western philosophy at work. Agamben's critique of a philosophical tradition that leaves human life irrevocably exposed to death and negativity implicitly evokes the figure of *nuda vita*, or bare life, unconditionally exposed and subjected to the powers of death. The figure of bare life is a living dead figure – a testimony to the death-oriented legacies of the Western metaphysical tradition and the politics that emerges in its wake.

Agamben suggests that the only way to experience a language *not* marked, as the Western tradition has been, by negativity and death is to dwell not in the negative foundations of the mystical but instead in the 'infancy (*in-fari*) of man'.[30] We need, to use terms that Agamben does not, a more natal orientation. This is not, however, a commendation to turn away from negativity in order to find a 'positive' orientation. Agamben is exhaustively sceptical of easy reversals. And, despite his critique of negativity, in *Language and Death* Agamben does not counteract the negative with a normatively positive or vital force. As Yoni Molad has argued, while Agamben offers a clear critique of nihilism in this text, there remains a 'redemptive potentiality' within the nihilistic that can be profaned, or put to new use.[31] The task for thinking, then, is not to evade negativity and death by turning towards a force that obliterates nihilism. Instead, Agamben finds a kind of impotentiality in the infancy that resists dwelling in death. As an act of impotentiality, the infancy that resists dwelling in death plays – in its own novel way – with the functions of the negative and acts of negation.

Agamben does not develop, at length, what such an infancy would look like, in its resistance of death and the negative. It is, perhaps most simply, the experience of language 'not marked by negativity and death'.[32] Catherine Mills explicates this infancy by, first, distinguishing it from the neonatal developmental stage in human biology. This infancy is something more prosaic, she suggests. Infancy is not the biological condition of being a neonatal. Instead, it is a condition of emergence from within a speechless place. It is not a moment in time to which we cannot return but, rather, something from which we are always emerging. Infancy is 'the originally speechless moment that continues to persist in any present moment of utterance'.[33] Infancy, in its speechlessness, is the impotentiality of language or speech – the resistance of it. Resisting the negativity of Western thought, which dwells always in death, is not the turn towards a positive force that would obliterate this negativity. It is, instead, a domain of impotentiality within this negativity. This impotentiality is not 'positive' (like Beauvoir's nothingness). But it is resistant. In that sense, both Agamben and Beauvoir wrest from their critique of Heidegger a form of negativity that resists a co-implication with death.

Natal Negativity

Agamben is in conversation with the work of Hannah Arendt in other projects. But his notion of infancy, in *Language and Death*, does not make any explicit reference to the work of Arendt or her philosophical concept of natality. Beauvoir's work, too, is unrelated to Arendt's in any explicit way. And her intimation that there is a kind of freedom in the experience of the negative – when it is not directed towards death – is not a reference to Arendt's natality. Nevertheless, I suggest that in Beauvoir's and Agamben's critiques of Heidegger's being-towards-death, negativity itself is cast in a different light: Beauvoir and Agamben illuminate a natal negativity.

While the philosophical concept of natality cannot be reduced to the work of Hannah Arendt, her name is the one most frequently connected to the term. She is, in other words, the most common reference point for thinking natality. Her own philosophy of natality appeared as a counterpoint to Heidegger's being-towards-death – a contestation against the claim that mortality and finitude determine who we are and how we live. Arendt finds meaning, instead, in the phenomenon of human birth. There is, then, something like a counter-Heideggerian impetus in the philosophy of natality – one that invokes traces of Heidegger[34] while also subjecting his thought to critique. In Beauvoir's and Agamben's counter-Heideggerian impulses, something natal emerges. This natality infuses their negativity with a power other than death.

Natality expressed, for Arendt, 'the new beginning inherent in birth'.[35] Instead of the biological birth of human bodies, natality was meant to gesture towards the ontological roots of the 'faculty of action'.[36] Natality was meant to describe the way that we 'insert ourselves into the human world' through 'word and deed'. It was meant to describe a kind of 'second birth', which was the beginning of our political lives:[37] our self-creation as political creatures in a communal world.

Arendt's dissertation, on the work of Augustine of Hippo, did not originally reference natality. But some thirty years after its completion Arendt added the term during revisions to the text. In her dissertation Arendt was intent to analyse the role that death played in Augustine's philosophy. Ultimately, Arendt suggested, Augustine (like other Western philosophers, both before and after him) envisioned the future of earthly life to be nothing other than death. This meant that life for thinkers like Augustine was 'determined by death' and might even 'more properly be called death'.[38] In *Life of the Mind*, Arendt argued that had Augustine only realised the consequences of his own notion that 'every man, being created in the singular, is a new beginning by virtue of his birth' then he would have understood (as she believed the Greeks once did) that we are not *mortals* but instead *natals*. Arendt believed this realisation revealed a dimension of freedom in human existence that the fixation on death was unable to reveal.[39] Natality was a condition for freedom because, Arendt argued, freedom itself was the capacity to begin and begin again. As she put it in her essay 'What is Freedom?': 'because he is a beginning, man can begin; to be human and to be free are one and the same'.[40] Or, put a bit less optimistically, 'we are doomed to be free by virtue of being born'.[41] It was, perhaps, the freedom inherent in natality that rendered it a political (rather than a biological or metaphysical) concept, for Arendt. As Patricia Bowen-Moore has put it, birth brings the principle of freedom into the world – the birth of a human is the birth of a freedom. Because of this, 'the actor can make his birth politically relevant'. Bowen-Moore suggests that this link between freedom and natality is the primary reason why Arendt believed that natality (rather than mortality) could be considered 'the central category of political as distinguished from metaphysical thought'.[42] Arendt understood the inherent and unbreakable link between natality and freedom to be a politicisation of the concept, and she believed that the political utility of natality prevented it from spinning off into metaphysics. Action, for Arendt, was 'the political activity par excellence' and the active dynamism of the natal seemed to protect it from the speculative shadows of metaphysics.[43] Philosophies directed towards our mortality, which kept death at the forefront of our thought, were inherently inactive because Arendt argued that death is always a 'not yet', something that is on the outside or in the future. Moreover, this is a future of fear and of threat. So it is, Arendt argued, that living towards death was a state of earth-bound frustration in which the only thing to be loved is nothingness – and nothing is to be desired 'except freedom from fear'.[44]

Both Beauvoir and Arendt were fixated on the power and centrality of freedom. More, as Sonia Kruks has pointed out, both Beauvoir and Arendt understood freedom as relational. That is to say, freedom was not the actualisation of individual autonomy or sovereign individuality. Rather, both insisted that 'freedom is possible only through our being in the world with others'.[45] Perhaps because freedom is both contingent upon and actualised within our relations with others, both Beauvoir and Arendt also seem to stress the link between birth and freedom – freedom is inherent within us, like a genetic inheritance, yet also outside of our control. Beauvoir, like Arendt, stressed that freedom is linked to 'the original upsurge of our existence'. Not our physical birth, perhaps, but another creative impulse. The human, Beauvoir argued, is 'originally free' in the sense that 'he spontaneously casts himself into the world'.[46] For Arendt, natality is political freedom (as well as freedom from metaphysics). And freedom was an inherently active principle. Beauvoir, too, understood freedom to be a 'principle of action'.[47]

Unlike Arendt, however, Beauvoir emphasised the links between freedom and the negative. The freedom inherent in natality was, for Arendt, creative in the sense that it was the birth or beginning of our lives as human political actors. For Beauvoir, being cast into the world was a form of self-erasure – it called us back to the nothingness that we are, most elementally. Being 'cast into the world', Beauvoir argued, was a reminder that human life is a condition of 'pure contingency'.[48] She argued that human beings realise their freedom by accepting the fact of their pure contingency – by acknowledging their inherent nothingness, their state of lack. Beauvoir suggested that the act of casting ourselves into the world began by making ourselves into 'a lack of being'. She suggested that in this outcast moment – steeped in the negative – it was possible to 'feel the joy of existing'.[49] Existence, for Beauvoir, was not obliterated with nothingness but constituted by it. 'To exist is to *make oneself* a lack of being; it is to *cast* oneself into the world.'[50] For Beauvoir, then, freedom bears natal dimensions. But, for her, freedom and natality are also part of the negative: they are movements towards nothingness.

The links between Agamben and Arendt are, on one level, more explicit. Agamben engages Arendt in extensive conversation in his *Homo Sacer* project. It is through the work of Arendt that Agamben rethinks the notion of life, which helps him to build his critique of Western biopolitics. Because Arendt's work helps Agamben to rethink the concept of life, it is hardly surprising that her philosophy might also help him critique what he saw as the nihilistic Western philosophical fixation on death. And yet, in *Language and Death*, when Agamben's thought offers a flicker of natality through the notion of infancy, Arendt's ideas are not explicitly present.[51]

For Arendt, natality was a 'second birth' that was not intended to be biological but could still emphasise an inherent dimension of (collective, rather than individual) power and freedom within a human who has been born. Agamben's evocation of the infancy of the human figures a neonatal dimension of the human that is not intended to focus on our biological birth. Rather, infancy offers Agamben a form of potentiality that resists the death drive of Western philosophy. To live towards death, Agamben suggests, is to exist (like the bare life of the *homo sacer*) as a 'living pledge' to our 'subjection to the power of death'.[52] This pulls us perpetually back towards the negative foundations of metaphysics. For Arendt, the focus on death and the attempt to find a space of peace that can turn against the future threat of death results in a craving for eternity. In both cases, then, death pulls us back to the negative foundations of metaphysics.

For Arendt, natality is an inherently political, rather than a metaphysical, concept. It is action-oriented, and it resists the death drives of Western metaphysics. For Agamben, infancy serves as an active negation of, or a resistance to, the deep links between death and the negative in the Western metaphysical tradition. In this sense, infancy arguably puts negativity to a new use (illuminating the impotential of this Western nihilism), and in its active negation it also arguably becomes more of a political concept than a metaphysical one. For these reasons, Agamben's critique of the collapse of death and the negative – and the new use to which he puts the negative – bears a natal dimension. Cutting the cords that link death and the negative facilitates a form of the negative that is not death driven, and does not find its centre of gravity in the negative foundations of metaphysics.

Without Denigrating Death

While both Agamben and Beauvoir are critical of the collapse between death and the negative, and while both suggest that the negative seems to bear a more natal dimension, both also clear a space for death within thought. Both Agamben and Beauvoir seem to suggest that there is a form of danger in the denigration of death. The decoupling of death and the negative is not an attempt to transcend, or be done with, death. Instead, perhaps, it illuminates dimensions of death that are obscured when it is simplistically coupled with negativity.

Beauvoir did not love, or embrace, death. In *A Very Easy Death* – Beauvoir's experience of her own mother's death – Beauvoir noted a similarity between herself and her mother. 'Maman loved life as I love it,' she wrote. 'And in the face of death she had the same feeling of rebellion that I have.'[53] Beauvoir also argues, in this memoir, that there is no such thing as a 'natural' death. Every death has a cause, she says, and 'nothing that happens to a man is ever natural'. She accepts the fact of human mortality: 'All men must die.' But 'for every man his death is an accident and, even if he knows it and consents to it, an unjustifiable violation'.[54] Beauvoir openly acknowledges her own rebellion against death. And yet she does not see death as something to deny, denigrate, erase or eviscerate. For Beauvoir death is simply one of the factors (perhaps the key factor) that renders life ambiguous.

Beauvoir admits that the ambiguities of life on earth bear tragic dimensions.[55] The life–death relation is strange, unsettling and ultimately ambiguous. This has led, over and over again, to the creation of a dualism in which life and death do battle against one another. But Beauvoir cautions against choosing sides. For one thing, this establishes a hierarchy between body and soul. Should we choose the ultimate triumph of life, this would require the belief that our soul can outlast our bodies in a dimension of metaphysical immortality. This leads, then, to an elimination of life's ambiguity by 'making oneself pure inwardness' – a pure soul that can escape from the sensual world. To choose the triumph of death, on the other hand, was a nihilistic denial of life, turning life into 'a veil of illusion'. Life becomes the lie that masks the truth of death. Instead of creating such a dualism, Beauvoir argued that we should 'assume our fundamental ambiguity' and 'draw strength' from it.[56] This ultimately demands that we acknowledge the complex ambiguities of the life–death relation – making spaces within life for death, and spaces within death for life.

Beauvoir – echoing a host of other twentieth-century thinkers – argued that Western technological modernity had created a form of malaise through its denial of death. The denial of death had become a distraction, an obsession, perhaps even a perversion. She saw, in this, a denial of limit conditions or a denial of our finitude.[57] Death has its own necessity, she noted. 'The present must die so that it may live; existence must not deny this death which it carries in its heart.'[58] And yet, Beauvoir did not seem to believe that an acknowledgement of our finitude required a *love* or an *embrace* of death. Indeed, she even argued for a kind of paradoxical and perhaps even nonsensical inhabitation of finitude that would seek to reflect or reveal some dimension of the infinite within it.[59] This would not be the revelation of an immortal soul within a finite body, but perhaps better put, a kind of stubborn rebellion, a defiant act of the body's will.

Beauvoir was also deeply critical of the misogynistic sentiments at work in the denial of death. She deemed both old and young age death to be 'ferments' that give life a particular sort of funk.[60] But, of course, the fermentation process can also be described as cultivated decay. While some crave the tang of a ferment, others find the mere smell to be disgusting. Over the course of modernity, through processes of refrigeration and chemical advances in food preservation, fermentation practices fell out of practice. Beauvoir argued that symbols of fermentation, germination, death and decay had become icons of contempt and disgust in modernity. And, she argued, women were blamed for this because the bodies of women were seen as the locus from which both natality and mortality were generated. The foetus, Beauvoir argued, captured the inextricable entanglement of birth and death. It was a sign of fragile, mortal, vulnerable dependence as well as a sign of emergence. The foetus was a reminder that 'to have been conceived and born as an infant is the curse that hangs over [man's] destiny, the impurity that contaminates his being'. The foetus is a reminder that the human is not immortal and is, instead, small, dependent and helpless.[61] And so it is that, symbolically, the mother (whose body births) is also understood to be she who 'dooms [men] to death. The quivering jelly which is elaborated in the womb (the womb, secret and sealed like the tomb) evokes' the 'soft viscosity of carrion' and men 'turn shuddering away'.[62] For Beauvoir, then, the fear of death is also a fear of birth and of women – a fear of the mother's birthing, mortalising body. These are fears about finitude, mortality and carnality. And so, in the denial of death, there is also a denial of carnality and an abjection of women and mothering.

In *Remnants of Auschwitz*, Agamben reflects on the figure of the *Muselmann* – a term that literally means 'the Muslim' and was used in concentration camps to refer to a person whose suffering, starvation and exhaustion had left them hovering at the border of life and death. Agamben's own use of the term is problematic.[63] But what I want to look at, for the moment, is the way that this figure serves – in *Remnants of Auschwitz* – as a 'living dead' figure that can expose something about Agamben's thoughts on the life–death relation. While Agamben notes that the figure of the *Muselmann* was sometimes deemed a 'walking corpse', it would be inappropriate to call such a person a 'corpse'. This is not, for Agamben, because this is a person who is still alive. Rather, he argues that in the camps 'death cannot be called death' and so 'corpses cannot be called corpses'. What appeared in concentration camps, Agamben argues, was not only or simply 'the negation of life'. More, the camps also violated the dignity of death.[64] What humans were subjected to in the camps, Agamben argued, 'was not death', but instead 'something more appalling'.[65] The camps were a 'degradation of death'.[66] Instead, bodies were 'eliminated'.[67] The key distinction, for Agamben, seems to be that there was no ritual respect for the bodies of those who died. There were no funeral rites. There was no space opened up for death that could allow for the effective transition between zones. Instead, bodies were caught in a zone of indeterminacy. The camps were a violation of both life and death – a *degradation* of both life and death. They produced a form of bare life that was neither alive nor dead but hovered indeterminately between the zones – a living dead figure. Bare life, for Agamben, is subjected to the powers of death. But the powers of death, wielded politically, may not exhaustively describe the life of death.

Living dead figures such as the *Muselmann* or the *homo sacer* are fixtures in Agamben's thought. Such living dead figures, for Agamben, are not only half-dead but are also still inscribed with a marginal upsurge of power that more closely aligns with life. In his essay 'In Playland: Reflections on History and Play', Agamben creates a parallel between ghosts and babies. Death can produce the 'unstable signifier' of the ghost, if there is no ritual transformation of the dead into an ancestor. But birth, too, can produce unstable signifiers. Death does not immediately produce ancestors, he suggests, just as birth does not immediately produce men and women. Instead it produces babies, which are given a special status in human societies. 'If the ghost is the living-dead or half-dead person,' he writes, 'the baby is a dead-living or a half-alive person.'[68] If the foetus was an icon for the ambiguous entanglement of life and death, for Beauvoir, perhaps babies and ghosts serve as similar figures for Agamben. They are ambiguous and contingent figures, hovering in a zone of indeterminacy between life and death. But this indeterminacy may not necessarily be the result of a political violence or violation. Instead, perhaps, the living-dead status of a baby highlights a kind of resistant impotential within such indeterminate figures.

Perhaps the problem, for Agamben, is not death itself or even the indeterminate nature of the life–death relation. Perhaps, instead, it is the use to which the life–death relation is put. The life–death relation becomes politically problematic when it becomes a mode of political capture – a relation of sovereign exception that produces and reproduces the living death of bare lives. But a rejection of, or resistance of, this death-dealing power is not the wresting of life *from* death, nor the denigration of death so as to produce a form of life that might finally be free from death. Perhaps, instead, it would be the creation of a space in which a new use can be found for certain dimensions of death – in which the impotentialities of death might be illuminated.

Both Agamben and Beauvoir critique the conflation of death and negativity, arguing (in very different ways) against a Heideggerian being-towards-death. Instead, Agamben and Beauvoir illuminate a natal dimension within the negative that casts negativity in a different light. Despite the fact that both thinkers seem to find something more life-affirming in the negative, neither of these thinkers ultimately denigrate death. Indeed, I have suggested that for both Agamben and Beauvoir there are the flickers of something decidedly more 'death positive'. This is not to say that either of them are figuring death as beloved or desirable. As Beauvoir makes especially clear, death is something to be resisted and can even be thought of as 'horrible'. To say that they offer a suggestively death-positive view is not to say that they think of death as *a good thing*. Rather, it is to say that they seem to respect the fact that life and death are entangled, or integrally related. In decoupling death from the negative, perhaps, they have wrested the figure of death from a co-implication with any pure form of the negative. Death, apart from the negative, appears in a range of different guises. Some of these might be violent. Yet death need not always be seen as violent. It is also a reminder of the mortal fragilities and vulnerabilities that keep us open, and attentive, as we seek to protect one another from violence.

Notes

1. Giorgio Agamben, *Homo Sacer: Sovereign Power and Bare Life*, trans. Daniel Heller-Roazen (Stanford: Stanford University Press, 1998), p. 99.
2. Benjamin Noys, *The Culture of Death* (Oxford and New York: Berg, 2005), p. 32.
3. Ibid. p. 19.
4. Martin Heidegger, *Being and Time*, trans. John Macquarrie and Edward Robinson (New York: Harper Perennial, 1962, 2008), p. 281.
5. Ibid. p. 286.
6. Ibid. pp. 287–9.
7. Ibid. p. 291.
8. Ibid. p. 294.
9. Ibid. p. 305.
10. Simone de Beauvoir, 'Pyrrhus and Cineas', trans. Marybeth Timmermann, in *Simone de Beauvoir: Philosophical Writings*, ed. Margaret A. Simons (Urbana and Chicago: University of Illinois Press, 2004), Ebook, Loc 2275 of 7355.
11. Ibid. Loc 2369 of 7355.
12. Ibid.
13. Ibid. Loc 2349 of 7355.
14. Ibid.
15. Ibid. Loc 2359 of 7355.
16. Ibid. Loc 2369 of 7355.
17. This is, in fact, part of her critique of nihilism in *The Ethics of Ambiguity*. Here she writes, 'The nihilist is right in thinking that the world *possesses* no justification and that he himself *is* nothing. But he forgets that it is up to him to justify the world and to make himself exist validly. Instead of integrating death into life, he sees in it the only truth of the life which appears to him as disguised death. However, there is life, and the nihilist knows that he is alive. That's where his failure likes. He rejects existence without managing to eliminate it.' Simone de Beauvoir, *The Ethics of Ambiguity*, trans. Bernard Frechtman (New York: Citadel Press, 1948, 1976), p. 57.
18. Beauvoir, 'Pyrrhus and Cineas', Loc 2349 of 7355.
19. See, for instance, Agamben's discussion of nothingness and metaphysics in *Language and Death: The Place of Negativity*, trans. Karen E. Pinkus and Michael Hardt (Minneapolis: University of Minnesota Press, 1991), p. xiii.
20. Agamben is certainly not the only thinker to make this argument. For a sustained argument that affirms these links between theology and the negative, but which remains deeply theological (affirming the nothingness of God), see Ray L. Hart, *God Being Nothing: Towards a Theogony* (Chicago & London: University of Chicago Press, 2016).
21. Agamben, *Language and Death*, p. 45.
22. Ibid. p. 47.
23. Ibid. p. 46.
24. Ibid. p. 53.
25. Ibid. p. 55.
26. Ibid. p. 57.
27. Ibid. p. 60.
28. Ibid. p. 85.
29. Ibid. p. 90.
30. Ibid. p. 91.
31. Yoni Molad, 'Nihilism', in *The Agamben Dictionary*, ed. Alex Murray and Jessica Whyte (Edinburgh: Edinburgh University Press, 2011), p. 138.
32. Agamben, *Language and Death*, p. 95.

33. Catherine Mills, *The Philosophy of Agamben* (Abingdon, Oxon and New York: Routledge, 2008), p. 26.
34. Hauke Brunkhorst, for instance, illuminates the contribution that Heidegger's idea of thrownness (*Geworfenheit*) makes to Arendt's thinking about natality. Natality might be read as a kind of thrownness without death. See Hauke Brunkhorst, 'Equality and Elitism in Arendt', in *The Cambridge Companion to Hannah Arendt*, ed. Dana Villa (Cambridge and New York: Cambridge University Press, 2000), p. 188.
35. Hannah Arendt, *The Human Condition* (Chicago and London: University of Chicago Press, 1958), p. 9.
36. Ibid. p. 247.
37. Ibid. p. 176.
38. Hannah Arendt, *Love and Saint Augustine*, ed. Joanna Vecchiarelli Scott and Judith Chelius Stark (Chicago and London: University of Chicago Press, 1996), p. 11.
39. Hannah Arendt, *The Life of the Mind* (San Diego, New York and London: Harcourt, Inc., 1971, 1978, 1977), p. 109.
40. As cited by Chelius and Scott in Arendt, *Love and Saint Augustine*.
41. Citation from her dissertation in Chelius and Scott's introduction, *Love and Saint Augustine*, p. 148.
42. Arendt cited in Patricia Bowen-Moore, *Hannah Arendt's Philosophy of Natality* (London: The MacMillan Press, 1989), p. 57.
43. Arendt, *Human Condition*, p. 9.
44. Arendt, *Love and Augustine*, p. 13.
45. Sonia Kruks, *Simone de Beauvoir and the Politics of Ambiguity* (Oxford and New York: Oxford University Press, 2012), p. 128.
46. Simone de Beauvoir, *The Ethics of Ambiguity*, trans. Bernard Frechtman (New York: Citadel Press, 1976 [1948]), p. 25.
47. Ibid. p. 23.
48. Ibid. p. 25.
49. Ibid. p. 41.
50. Ibid. p. 42.
51. As Leland de la Durantaye points out, Agamben was reading Arendt as early as 1968, so her influence on *Language and Death*, while not acknowledged, is certainly not unthinkable. See Leland de la Durantaye, *Giorgio Agamben: A Critical Introduction* (Stanford: Stanford University Press, 2009), p. 207.
52. Agamben, *Language and Death*, p. 99.
53. Simone de Beauvoir, *A Very Easy Death*, trans. Patrick O' Brian (New York: Pantheon Books, 1965), p. 91.
54. Ibid. p. 106.
55. Beauvoir, *Ethics of Ambiguity*, p. 7.
56. Ibid. p. 9.
57. Ibid. p. 121.
58. Ibid. p. 127.
59. Ibid. p. 130.
60. Simone de Beauvoir, *The Second Sex*, trans. Constance Borde and Sheila Malovany-Chevallier (New York: Vintage Books, 2009, 2010, 2011 [1949]), Ebook, Loc 612 of 2521.
61. Simone de Beauvoir, *The Second Sex*, trans. H. M. Parshley (New York: Alfred A. Knopf, 1953), p. 146.
62. Ibid. p. 148.
63. He does not, for instance, interrogate the anti-Islamic use of the term despite the fact that he also uses this term constructively.
64. Giorgio Agamben, *Remnants of Auschwitz: The Witness and the Archive*, trans. Daniel Heller-Roazen (New York: Zone Books, 1999), p. 70.

65. Ibid. p. 71.
66. Ibid. p. 72.
67. Ibid. p. 74.
68. Agamben, *Infancy and History*, p. 83.

Chapter 9

Endless Ontology: Agamben and Sartre on Death

Andrew Welch

Between *Infancy and History* (1978) and *Language and Death* (1982), Agamben outlines a paradox in the understanding of death. At first glance, death seems to dissolve form. Time's horizon closes, experience ceases to renew itself, and the body decomposes. Yet death also turns out to be the limit that gives life its shape. In *Infancy and History*'s reading of Montaigne, life can achieve narrative closure only through death, which shapes what has been into a previously imperceptible coherence. When life is read as narrative, the form of one's death retroactively determines that life's meaning: as the dictum attributed to Solon declared, 'Call no man happy until he is dead.' Life can be constructed only through the anticipation of its end. By turn, *Language and Death* develops a reading of Heidegger that tries to disengage from this narrative logic, and instead considers death as the *telos* that grounds the possibility of meaning. Our confrontation with finitude becomes the source of all significance, since finitude is what gives decision its consequence. Yet at the same time that Heidegger relinquishes the narrative function of death, he also sets death at the ontological centre of life, definitive of the beings that we are. The result amplifies death's teleological force, since it is only within death's horizon that our understanding of being can emerge.

Both of these views, death as narrative and death as *telos*, draw the intelligibility of life from its end. Especially in *Language and Death*, Agamben will veer away from this line of thinking. Instead, he tests an understanding of death that abandons any sense of *telos*, whether narratological or ontological. This rethinking of death will prove crucial to the development of a substantial concept of life as potentiality – a project that runs through much of his more recent writing, including the nine volume *Homo Sacer* project (1995–2014). That exacting sense of life as potentiality cannot be reconciled with any external end, and in fact, potentiality may be understood as the suspension of all *telos*. Potentiality conceives of death without end, and, I will argue, reimagines death as a site of beginning.

Agamben's rethinking of death finds strategic precedent in Sartre's *The Transcendence of the Ego* (1936), which endeavours to strip phenomenology of the self, or *I*, as the seat of consciousness. In place of the self, Sartre will offer nothing other than the movement of consciousness, insisting that the *I* arises only as a by-product of consciousness reflecting on experience. Agamben appropriates this strategy in order to reroute thought away from *telos*. Thought as potentiality follows a vertiginous reflexive movement that turns back into itself, thereby never arriving at the end. I will close by suggesting that by using reflexivity to undo teleology, both figures gesture towards an ontology of endlessness.

Life as Potentiality

The concept of life as potentiality guides Agamben's analysis of biopolitics throughout the *Homo Sacer* project. Life and death, Agamben insists, 'are not properly scientific concepts but rather political concepts, which as such acquire a political meaning precisely only through a decision'.[1] Sovereignty is the force that decides their meaning, and it enacts this decision in excess of any logic or law, since any such apparatus would itself be the product of a prior decision, rather than its foundation. Once sovereignty's law has decided upon life, life falls subject to the biopolitical management that determines its value and defines its ends. Life is actualised to exhaustion, with nothing left in reserve. Under biopolitics, life is already at its end – already, in a sense, dead: 'A law that seeks to decide on life is embodied in a life that coincides with death.'[2] An important current of the *Homo Sacer* project attempts to deactivate the *telos* of life and death, detaching life from the medicalised body and carrying death past the mere exhaustion of life.

What is lost when 'we are all virtually *homines sacri*' is potentiality.[3] Any sense of life as a qualitative practice disappears, diminished to a medical question whose status is ultimately determined by legal dispute. Under this regime, life's potentiality is absorbed by technocratic prescription. The living being, *zoē*, is divided from *bios*, its socio-political form as 'law-abiding', as 'citizen', as 'human', as whatever sovereignty appropriates as the sacred object whose maintenance justifies its groundless exercise of power. The division of life from itself strips life of form, which Agamben defines through the capacity to refrain from a given end. Potentiality is shaped by an 'internal resistance' to its own actualisation.[4] If potential were defined by its actualisation, it would cease to be potential. Agamben builds this claim through Aristotle: is a kithara player still a kithara player even when not playing? Since we must conclude that the answer is *yes*, the potentiality intrinsic to the performance of music is in fact defined by 'the possibility of its non-exercise'.[5] Any possibility that cannot be averted is not in fact possible, but rather necessary and actual, which is to say that it is *im*possible. Potential, then, must be understood as 'the suspension of the act'.[6] 'The "potential not to"', Agamben writes, 'is the cardinal secret of the Aristotelian doctrine of potentiality, which transforms every potentiality in itself into an impotentiality.'[7] This arc of thought guides the profound inversion in Agamben's reading of biopolitics: life's capacity for form lies in the withholding of potential, while 'bare life' is conceived as a state of extreme actualisation that leaves nothing unfulfilled.

At the core of Agamben's reworking of potentiality is the suspension of any fixed outcome, product or end. The suspension of the end relies on the internal resistance of the 'potential-not-to', preserving potentiality 'as a field of forces stretched between potential and impotential, being-able-to and being-able-not-to, acting and resisting'.[8] The internal resistance that sustains potentiality becomes perceptible in forms of self-reference, which leave behind an 'inoperative remainder' that turns the movement of potentiality away from actualisation and back in on itself.[9] For example, poetry not only indicates a field of semantic reference as its content, but also exhibits its own medium of language, exposing how the potentiality of language as such exceeds the particular configuration that makes up the poem.[10] Self-reference thus 'implies a constitutive excess of potential over any realization in the act'.[11] The true referent of poetry is poetry itself, not as a finished work but as a potential that through the suspension of its *telos* unworks any possible realisation. Through self-reference, potentiality averts any teleology and any external end. It is end-less.

Death as Narrative: *Infancy and History*

The potentiality exhibited in self-reference will ultimately provide Agamben with the resources to withdraw from the teleology of death. This process begins in *Infancy and History*. *Infancy and History* follows the transformation of experience under the scientific revolution, which sought to merge experience into knowledge – concepts that Agamben argues were theretofore distinct. This conflation resulted in the 'destruction' of the singularity of experience, which was subsequently folded into and governed by objective knowledge. In the model of 'traditional experience' represented by Montaigne's *Essays*, knowledge was the possession of the divine intellect, while experience was a human phenomenon, generating local forms of common sense that could be captured by maxim, proverb or story. Experience and knowledge are united only in death, since death is the process through which the particular texture of lived experience merges with its universal source in the divine intellect. Agamben proposes that 'nearing to death' is the 'ultimate goal' of this classical conception of experience, since, while death is the passage to knowledge, one's death can never be grasped as experience.[12] In this respect Montaigne can declare, following Plato in the *Phaedo*, 'That to philosophize is to learn to die.'[13] The anticipation of death comes to define an ethical and aesthetic outlook stretched across multiple interwoven temporalities. Looking ahead, death offers a glimpse of the totality that lies beyond the limits of human understanding. Looking behind, the prospect of death reveals a life's previously indiscernible structure. What could seem a heterogeneous series of unrelated events takes on coherence and significance in the final retrospect. Death's transcendence thus provides a retroactive foundation to an otherwise groundless life. In short, death forms life.

This conception of death suffuses Montaigne's classical inheritance, running from Sophocles, Solon and Plato through to Seneca's formulation: 'What you have done in the past will be manifest only at the time when you draw your last breath.'[14] If life can be interpreted only from the threshold of death, then death functions as a narratological principle. Indeed, this logic runs parallel to the narrative theory of Peter Brooks, who holds that the ontological origin of narrative is in fact the ending, since 'only the end can finally determine meaning'.[15] In so far as '[t]he end writes the beginning and shapes the middle', the structure of narrative must be understood in reverse.[16] For Montaigne, and for his thanatological ancestry stretching back to Socrates, the disorder of experience becomes an intelligible narrative only under the governance of its end. While this future-retrospective narrative movement was meant to provide a sense of urgency to the practice of living, it also entailed apprehending one's ongoing life as a finished product – or, more precisely, a text. 'Traditional experience' not only anticipates death but also textualises it, a process that would reach its apex in the neoclassical theatricality of the 'good death'.[17] In order for life to read properly in retrospect, the death to come must construct the narrative of who one will have been. Treating death as a vocation in this radically narrative manner thus undermines the presence of experience, since in 'nearing to death' experience is accessed only by looking back on the present from an anticipated end. When read in the *will have been* of the future perfect tense, the book of life's ink is already dry.

Infancy and History invokes Montaigne's sense of death in order to develop a historical contrast to experience under modernity. Yet there is a tension between the generative teleologies of Montaigne's figures of life writ unto death[18] and Agamben's later elaboration of potentiality. The crucial image, which recurs throughout Agamben's work, pictures thought as a blank space of inscription: 'the *nous* ["the intellect or potential thought"] is like a writing tablet on which nothing is written.'[19] The image of the blank writing tablet, drawn from Aristotle, sits uncomfortably alongside Montaigne's book of life. While the latter is thought expressed and inscribed, the blank tablet is thought held in reserve, unactualised. This is a difficult image of potentiality, since Aristotle will admit that, if thought is in fact thought, it cannot simply withhold itself and remain suspended in the potential to think without ever thinking. This would be a potential to think that loses its very essence in its exercise – that is, a thought that could have no contact with actual thinking. Agamben seconds this point: we cannot think potentiality as 'idleness or inertia'.[20] At the same time, there is no object of thought that could adequately define thought's activity, because any object that thought might take would trivialise thought. No longer thought as such, it would be mere thought of something. What resolves this problem is self-reference, as Aristotle is led to conclude, 'thought is the thinking of thinking'.[21] In Agamben's gloss: '[Thought] thinks a pure potentiality (to think and not to think).'[22] This thought thinks without actualising itself by circulating its activity back into the wellspring of its own potential. The blank tablet is an incipient writing that experiences its own capacity to refrain. It 'writes its own passivity'.[23]

Death as *Telos*

As a potentiality that resists the actual, the thought of thought refuses every external teleology. Accordingly, Agamben's potentiality cannot reconcile itself to the death established by Montaigne's tradition,[24] beaconing towards a pre-inscribed conclusion from which thought would retrospectively derive its meaning. Understood in this sense, death is potentiality's end. *Language and Death* intervenes in this dilemma by attempting to think potentiality from within the necessity of death. Agamben launches this project through a revision of Heidegger's analysis of being-towards-death in Division II of *Being and Time*. Being-towards-death runs alongside of (and ultimately beyond) the classical notion of 'nearing to death' that Agamben had extracted from Montaigne. In Heidegger's hands, death will become a fundamental ontological mode rather than a psychological or narrative condition. Heidegger begins with the notion that the narrative totality of one's existence can never be present to oneself, since existence is always incomplete up until the moment of death. However, while Montaigne conceives of an ambivalently eschatological and textual afterlife, Heidegger will reject the posthumous, pushing past the notion that life can be grasped only by the impossible vantage of death as 'merely formal'.[25] For Heidegger, death is not biological cessation, nor dénouement, but rather our 'ownmost possibility'.[26]

While all other possibilities concern some particular object or content, death is the possibility that ends possibility as such.[27] It is the very horizon in which possibility unfolds. And while the conditions of one's death are unknowable, death's eventuality is absolutely certain. Nothing is more possible than death. All experience of possibility is thus shaped by the inevitable possibility of death. Heidegger's *Dasein*, 'being-there', the unique historical being that poses its own being as a question, dwells in the experience of possibility. Its seminal possibility is death. In Heidegger's words, 'Being-towards-death, as anticipation of possibility, is what first *makes* this possibility *possible*, and sets it free as possibility.'[28] Accordingly, Heidegger insists on 'the problem of the finitude in man as the decisive element which makes the understanding of being possible'.[29] *Dasein* lives within the self-conscious sense of ending that Heidegger calls being-towards-death, and it is *Dasein*'s awareness of this end that discloses the nature of being. 'Death', Heidegger writes, 'is a way to be, which Dasein takes over as soon as it is.'[30] Or, as Agamben will later put it in *Remnants of Auschwitz*, being-towards-death means 'creating the possible through the experience of the impossible' – that is, the experience of death.[31]

Being-towards-death emerges from Heidegger's account of time. Heidegger finds *Dasein* standing outside of itself in an 'ecstatic' temporality, phasing through recall and anticipation. This capacity for historical and futural projection, existing 'ahead-of-itself' and 'letting-itself-*come-towards*-itself' ultimately gestures towards *Dasein*'s end.[32] Every thought and every act draws on a limited (yet unknowable) reserve of time. Existence takes place in a time that is always oriented by finitude. This relation to time creates both the opening in which *Dasein* unfolds and the limit that shapes its possibility. Since any decision can become meaningful only within the temporal horizon traced by death, we can say that finitude generates the very possibility of significance. In turn, exposure to the necessity of death opens the possibility of 'authentic decision'. Heideggerian authenticity consists of a standing 'resolute' before the end. Death, then, is *Dasein*'s *telos*, and ending is *Dasein*'s ontology. Tasked with bearing death as the limit that opens the possibility of meaning, *Dasein* lives a continuous dying until the moment of its bodily demise.

Being-towards-death focuses the singular texture of life in its very impermanence. The temporal ecstasy that draws *Dasein* 'ahead-of-itself' towards finitude in turn urges *Dasein* towards 'resoluteness'.[33] Life is redeemed not in spite of death, but through it. Rather than perceiving experience backwards from an anticipated end beyond the present, being-towards-death is meant to attend to the possibility of the very moment of existing, since the passage of time achieves significance only because of life's finitude.[34] In fact, Heidegger's project in *Being and Time* could be understood as an attempt to establish the fundamental nature of *Dasein*'s potentiality, and thereby unveil its vastness.[35] While both Heidegger and Montaigne find an ethical orientation in thinking death as *telos*, the teleological current of Heidegger's thought unworks any preformed retrospective, since it is not the ending itself but rather the movement towards the end that opens the space for any authentic decision whatsoever. Potentiality is thus tightly linked to authenticity, which is possible only under the shadow of death. From this shadow *Dasein* draws its essence, as the special kind of being engaged in possibility by way of its own finitude. As Heidegger writes, 'Death, as possibility, gives Dasein nothing to be "actualized," nothing which Dasein, as actual, could itself *be*.'[36] For Heidegger, the appropriation of life's end as *telos* is the fundamental condition of possibility. Living means living one's death. Being-towards-death emerges as the most radical of teleologies.

Death without End: *Language and Death*

In this section, I will read *Language and Death* as an attempt to reground *Dasein* in light of the full ramifications of the relationship between being and language, which will mean dissolving the notion of death as *Dasein*'s end.[37] Agamben begins this process by focusing on the deictic work of the shifter *Da* present in *Dasein* – traditionally translated 'being-there', but rendered for emphasis in *Language and Death* as 'being-the-*there*'.[38] Because shifters refer solely to their context, they are tasked with bridging the gap between language and discourse – the system of signs at large and the specific articulatory event in which this system is invoked. Shifters are uniquely capable of activating the sign system because they are signs whose signifieds are, in turn, acts of indication. In other words, the signifieds of *this*, *here* and *now* are nothing other than the space-time of their enunciation. To develop this point, Agamben draws on Émile Benveniste's discussion of the *utterance*, which channels language into the event: the utterance 'includes that which, in every speech act, refers exclusively to its taking place . . . independently and prior to what is said and meant in it'.[39] Pronouns perform the utterance in so far as they are '"empty signs," which become "full" as soon as the speaker assumes them in an instance of discourse'.⁴⁰ For example, 'the form of *I* has no linguistic existence except in the act of speaking in which it is uttered'.⁴¹ Because *I* can refer only to its speaker, and only for the duration of the utterance, it is 'unique by definition and has validity only in its uniqueness'.⁴² Accordingly, 'before they designate real objects, [pronouns] indicate precisely that *language takes place*'.⁴³ The pronoun thus reflexively envelops the relationship between language and discourse. Seizing this point, Agamben insists that to understand *Dasein* as the being that stands outside of itself, we must follow the itinerary of its shifter – we must pass through *there*. It is *there*, in the utterance, that *Dasein* experiences the system of language as a living event. Having reworked *Dasein* into being-the-*there*, Agamben again revises *Dasein* as 'to be the taking place of language'.⁴⁴ Drawing this argument forward towards Agamben's analysis of potentiality, we might revise yet again: *Dasein* is language speaking itself.

Through Benveniste, Agamben will rework *Dasein*'s relationship to time, and therefore to death. Heidegger derives death from temporality, the 'horizon for all understanding of being',⁴⁵ but Agamben notes that the experience of time is itself a product of language. Benveniste argues that it is only 'the insertion of discourse into the world' that produces a notion of presence from which time can flow: '*here* and *now* delimit the spatial and temporal instance coextensive and contemporary with the present instance of discourse containing *I*.'⁴⁶ This grammatical present invokes a moment of utterance that is 'renewed with each production of discourse', such that 'the feeling of a continuity emerges' between discursive events.⁴⁷ This feeling of continuity, linking utterance to utterance, is none other than time, and from it, past and future are derived.⁴⁸

Dasein unfolds in a horizon of time that is revealed in the utterance *there*, as the shifter that '*indicate*[*s*] the instance of discourse'.⁴⁹ But how can we apprehend the event of language from within language? How can we possibly understand the very medium of understanding? As Agamben will later frame the problem, 'what is unnameable is that there are names'.⁵⁰ In *Language and Death*, Agamben will address the impossibility of our being in language through the figure of the Voice. Agamben first follows Heidegger's sense that in order to use a human language, one must appropriate a pre-existent system of signification that displaces an immediate relation to the living animal voice. To clarify *Dasein*'s unique relation to language, Agamben alludes to Callimachus' evocation of the braying of the ass and the chirping of the cicada⁵¹ – beings of pure language, whose modes of expression inhere in their nature. Humans have such a voice, too, until we enter the system of conventional language. Then this voice ceases. The intimate voice of our living being must fall silent – or die – for human language to emerge, such that, as Agamben will later write, 'subjectification and desubjectification coincide at every point'.[52] Thus, in Daniel McLoughlin's reading of Agamben's treatment of the Voice, an 'experience of incapacity inheres within every act of speech, from the most profound to the most quotidian'.[53] The 'Voice' that is bound for signification (differentiated from the living voice with a capital) thus negotiates between the voice's unmediated language and the learned semiotic system to which it must be reconciled. This Voice 'is no longer a natural sign and not yet meaningful discourse'.[54] We can understand this Voice as the negative space between echolalia and the sign, between which Agamben insists 'there is no link, not even a negative one'.[55] That is, it is not that the lost voice of our sonorous animality serves as a foundation for the emergence of language. Instead, language arises out of the impassable abyss between vocalisation and conventional signification. The event of language takes place in the void of the Voice, which is neither sound nor meaning but the impossibility of their relation. The event of language is an act of groundless and incomplete self-reference, leading Agamben to characterise the Voice as the 'supreme shifter'.[56] In turn, 'every shifter is structured like a Voice'.[57] As the shifter announces the taking place of language yet must do so from within language, so the Voice must perform our coming into language through its own death. Accordingly, to experience the end of the Voice through its absorption into the sign is to begin to die. If we did not lose our living animal voice, then we would remain within an immediate relationship to language. Being is disclosed to us only because we enter the system of conventional signs. Our alienation from this system – which is not native to us, and which we inhabit with the self-consciousness of a second tongue – sets us apart from being and thereby makes being perceptible to us. *Dasein* is revealed through the mediation of its alienated language. 'Negativity', Agamben concludes, 'is the human means of having language.'[58]

To summarise this account: the death of the living voice ushers us into language, our entry into language opens the horizon of time, and the horizon of time is bounded by death. While Heidegger sees *Dasein* oriented towards death as its constitutive end, Agamben moves *Dasein* into the space of language, a space cleared by the death of the voice. Death is no longer *telos* but inception. Here Agamben confronts the central project of *Language and Death*, which is to connect 'the "faculty" for language and the "faculty" for death'.[59] Being-towards-death is a repetition of the death of the voice: '*Death and Voice have the same negative structure and they are metaphysically inseparable.*'[60] Death empties the Voice so that language can take place within it. Death is how language comprehends its own unspeakable beginning.

Through the figure of the Voice, Agamben establishes *Dasein*'s *there* as an event of language. Being-the-*there* no longer requires any further supposition beyond what is granted by the force of its own utterance. This reflexive movement of the Voice is the source of *Dasein*'s potentiality. We recall that Agamben will later picture potentiality in the image of the writing tablet on which nothing is written – the thought that thinks nothing but itself. In Agamben's later formulation, 'internal resistance' prevents potentiality from exhausting itself.[61] This internal resistance is supplied by the Voice, as neither sound nor semantic meaning but what remains stranded between them. The elements of language are thus disjoined from the moment of their emergence out of the non-place of the Voice, and their irresolvable disjunction sets *Dasein* apart from its own taking place in language. The reflexivity of the Voice reorients *Dasein*'s relation to death: death is no longer a formative end but rather the site of *Dasein*'s irretrievable beginning. Instead of establishing death as the *telos* that bounds *Dasein*'s world, Agamben finds in death the inception of the Voice. From the void of the Voice, *Dasein*'s potentiality emerges.

Consciousness, Reflexivity and the Problem of Narrative

I have argued that Agamben's ambivalent engagements with Montaigne and Heidegger outline a unique conception of death without end. Agamben follows Montaigne's sense of death as narrative and Heidegger's sense of being-towards-death only up to the point where teleology threatens to supplant potentiality. He then reconstructs each logic through a reflexive turn that allows the mode of being in question – experience, language, thought – to constitute itself, rather than find itself directed towards an external end that would define its activity. Death remains, but emptied of *telos*. I will now suggest that this strategy shares its choreography with Jean-Paul Sartre's approach to the relationship between narrative and consciousness, especially in *The Transcendence of the Ego*. This convergence guides Agamben's rethinking of death along an existentialist trajectory.

Sartre's thought has a troubled relationship to narrative. In his *War Diaries*, he recalls experiencing his own life as an integral 'oeuvre', a 'series of works related to each other by common themes and all reflecting my personality':

> A life: in other words, a tapestry-frame to be filled, with (already) a throng of rough-tacked outlines still needing to be embroidered. A life: in other words, a whole existing before its parts and being realized through its parts. To me, an instant did not appear like some vague unit aggregated to other units of the same kind; it was a moment that rose against a background of life. That

life was a rosette-like composition wherein beginning and end coincided: maturity and old age gave meaning to childhood and adolescence.⁶²

Sartre discovers that he has learned to interpret his experience in this projective-retrospective fashion through the pre-eminent commodity of narrative retrospection – the book:

> I envisaged each present moment from the point of view of an accomplished life – or, to be precise, I should say: from the point of view of a biography. And I considered myself bound to account for that moment to this biography: I felt its full meaning could be deciphered only by placing oneself in the future, and I always sketched out for myself a vague future that would allow me to make my present yield up its whole significance.⁶³

Yet he comes to realise that this pre-emptively posthumous existence was inherited from Romantic mythology: 'Shelley, Byron, Wagner'.⁶⁴ His life had been modelled on a 'biographical illusion, which consists in believing that a lived life can resemble a recounted life'.⁶⁵ At stake in this profoundly textual teleology is the relationship between experience and narrative. The present is rendered incomplete, dependent on a future that will 'yield up its whole significance'. Awaiting the future that will transform the cacophony of experience into coherent narrative, young Sartre is an unwitting practitioner of the *ars moriendi* championed by Montaigne.

In *Being and Nothingness*, dissolving the present for future redemption reads as a form of bad faith, ensuring that the spontaneity of consciousness is governed by the *telos* of biography. Our consciousness, as nothing in itself, 'can have being only as we do not see it'; it is 'the being which determines itself to exist inasmuch as it cannot coincide with itself'.⁶⁶ Consciousness is self-negation. However, Sartre also holds that our personhood is oriented around a 'fundamental project', through which we choose our mode of being, and through which all of our activity must be understood. This concept shares a retroactive textual logic with the youthful extravagance of life as biography – 'a whole existing before its parts and being realized through its parts' – as well as with the heritage of Montaigne's thanatology. This link is strengthened by Sartre's recurring reference to Malraux's aphorism, 'The terrible thing about Death is that it transforms life into Destiny.'⁶⁷ Death is thus 'the final arrest of Temporality by the making-past of the whole system'.⁶⁸ What is 'terrible' about death is that it reifies life into narrative. The dead are doomed to exist only as 'biographical illusions' in the perceptions of others.

Any purposeful intervention in a given state of affairs seems to depend on narrative. Narrative is the means by which one authentically transforms one's facticity. Yet even in its authentic mode, narrative threatens to harden into an ends-directed project. Commitment to the *telos* of the project inevitably straitens the spontaneity of consciousness, which is the source of our freedom. The problem of *telos* persists throughout Sartre's writing: can radical spontaneity reconcile itself to any end? Ethical and political imperatives demand recourse to narrative, harnessing the force of consciousness for the sake of productivity. However, *The Transcendence of the Ego* pre-empts the ethical and political questions to which Sartre harnesses the question of consciousness in later writing. Instead, this early text theorises a consciousness that refuses all external dependence, emerging out of its own activity for its own sake. Sartre thus approaches a conception of thought as, in Agamben's idiom, 'the thinking of thinking'.

The Transcendence of the Ego is written as a direct response to the development of the transcendental ego in Husserl's phenomenology – the *I* to which perceptions and experiences are attached. Sartre's conclusion is stark: consciousness is not grounded in any self, ego or *I*. In its most fundamental aspect, consciousness is radically prior to any personal, psychological or historical attributes. Consciousness cannot be defined by its objects or content – only by its own movement. To draw out the consequences of these claims, we need to address Husserl's original rationale. In the *Cartesian Meditations*, Husserl had posited a transcendental *I* in order to unify and individuate each distinct consciousness. I am able to link the entire chain of my perceptions together as mine because there is some primordial *I* that operates through the act of perception, even if only to log and retain the intentional objects of perception as belonging to me and not you. That operation of intending and retaining distinguishes my consciousness from yours only in so far as there is some sense of self to which this distinct set of perceptions can be attached. Husserl initially works to distinguish the transcendental *I* from the psychological and biographical self, but the *I* eventually acquires a 'substrate of habitualities' characterised by specific 'properties' – the tendencies, capacities and 'abiding style' that lead Husserl to conclude that the ego bears a 'personal character'.[69] At this point Husserl recognises the need for a 'genetic phenomenology' that promises to go beyond the fundamental constituents of conscious experience.[70] Consciousness is gradually overwritten by the teleological machinery of narrative.

For Sartre, all of this threatens to constrain the autonomy of consciousness. He insists that consciousness does not require an 'I think' or 'I perceive' attached to it. Perceptions do not belong to a subject, and while they may in a formal sense be understood to come from a specific point of view, this perspective does not entail any psychological substance. It is not *I* that perceives, but rather a pure consciousness prior to any sense of self. Sartre argues that while we may think of our experiencing being as rooted in the psychological unity of a self, in fact, that very notion of selfhood is a mirage generated by the consciousness that precedes it.

Sartre believes that, if we follow Husserl, then the self becomes the end of consciousness, such that the persistence of consciousness becomes inextricable from the self. All experience would be reduced to the reproduction of the self, and all objects of consciousness would be crowded out by the overbearing presence of the *I*. Thought never escapes the self at its centre, constructing every idea and every object in its own image. Sartre figures this usurpation with a startling violence: the transcendental *I* 'would violently separate consciousness from itself, it would divide it, slicing through each consciousness like an opaque blade'.[71] Experience would be suffocated by its source, leading to a dramatic conclusion: 'The transcendental *I* is the death of consciousness.'[72] The *telos* of the *I* is the death of consciousness because consciousness can have no end. Any source or destination would consign the radical openness of consciousness to the limitations of psychology. In other words, Sartre postulates that the self is the end of thought – it is thought's death.

In order to eliminate the transcendental *I*, Sartre must develop an alternative explanation of the unity of consciousness. Our experience seems to unfold in a connected sequence. How can we explain this if there is no self to bind this duration together? Moreover, without this self, how can we explain the fact that we can access only our own experiences, and not each other's? Sartre begins by noting that we routinely perceive without centring ourselves in our perceptions. In fact, many perceptions may not include any sense of self at all. Sartre calls this purely intentional form of perception 'pre-reflective consciousness'. However, when consciousness reflects on experience, it can take its own pre-reflective experience as an object. I may experience *walking* without any awareness of my self, and then I may on subsequent reflection perceive that *I was walking*. Reflection attaches a self to the event *walking*, even though there was no sense of self present in the initial experience. Further, reflection does not simply retroject the self into my experience – it makes that retrojection the very source of that experience. Reflection imposes a subject–predicate structure on what had been an immersive flux. By reflecting on perception, consciousness generates the *I* as the subject of experience. The *I* now appears where it never existed, claiming responsibility for the very experience to which it was superfluous.

The Thinking of Thinking as Endless Ontology

At this point let us recall Agamben's conception of the potentiality of thought as 'the thinking of thinking'.[73] This reflexivity prevents thought from realising itself in any particular object or content, at which point it would become actual and thereby dissolve its potentiality. Instead, in thinking itself, thought never finds an end. Reflexivity is the technique that sustains potentiality. Its representative image is the blank writing tablet, neither active nor idle, that paradoxically 'writes its own passivity'.[74] With this image in mind, we can see that for Sartre, Husserl's transcendental *I* begins as the thinking of thinking, but soon demands actualisation in an ego. Thought thus thinks into being its own source, an *I*. And in this source, it finds an object, and a resting place, and its death.

This process is an instance of what Sartre will come to call bad faith, which we might in turn call frozen reflexivity. It posits the self as the illusive origin and specious end of consciousness, denying its own spontaneity in the name of identity. This self is the place where consciousness freezes its reflexive movement into an object that it misinterprets as a subject, and thereby collapses the potentiality of thought into an actual entity. Thought is conflated with its psychological location, and, by extension, with the subjectivity of the thinking being. For Sartre, this misidentification is ruthlessly constricting. His most fundamental thesis is that the possibility of consciousness vertiginously exceeds the self, and yet the self routes all consciousness through itself and thus delimits the horizon of thought.

What Sartre discovers is that the spontaneity of consciousness cannot be sustained by expanding its objects. Instead, he proposes that consciousness cannot find closure in the self – it must continue past the point where the self emerges without settling into an *I*: '[T]ranscendental consciousness is an impersonal spontaneity. It determines itself to exist at every instant, without us being able to conceive of anything *before* it. Thus every instant of our conscious lives reveals to us a creation *ex nihilo*.'[75] Continuously creating itself anew, this sense of consciousness is a model of Agamben's sense of thought as the thinking of thinking. Both figures suggest that only a self-determining thought can evade the problem of *telos*. Agamben remarkably conceives thought as impotentiality – creating itself '*ex nihilo*' only to withdraw back into itself, unactualised. Even as Agamben traces its lineage back to Aristotle, this procedure finds a significant and rigorous precursor in Sartre.

Agamben himself comments only briefly and ambivalently on Sartre's argument. He notes that Gilles Deleuze found in Sartre's text a conception of 'an impersonal transcendental field, not having the form of a synthetic personal consciousness of a subjective identity'.[76] At stake for Deleuze is a move beyond what Agamben calls 'the tradition of consciousness in modern philosophy'.[77] This 'irrevocable step' allows to Deleuze to formulate the radically impersonal concept of the singularity, which altogether dispenses with consciousness as a site of analysis. Agamben by turn will not refer thought back to any agent – not mind, not subject and not consciousness. Crucially, thought 'thinks itself', and in thinking itself it refrains from realising itself. For Agamben, Sartre's emphasis on consciousness is still too psychological, too humanistic and too beholden to a Cartesian legacy that he displaces in favour of classical and scholastic resources.[78]

Yet, while Agamben pointedly departs from Sartre's emphasis on consciousness as the site of thought, Sartre's resistance to the objectification of thought resonates across Agamben's writing. Even more crucial is their shared motivation: both work to suspend teleological analysis. While Heidegger's *Dasein* lives in a world of being-towards-death, we saw that Agamben repositions death as *Dasein*'s beginning, rather than its end. Agamben uses this gesture to disaggregate death, closure and *telos* – terms that no longer operate as synonyms, but instead must be conceived and addressed according to their own distinctive logics. This project of differentiation grounds the analysis of the relationship between life and death at the centre of the *Homo Sacer* series, allowing Agamben to recognise the catastrophe of 'bare life' as a life reduced to *telos*, determined in advanced. In Sartre's account of consciousness, consciousness travels from spontaneity to teleology by generating and then identifying with the self. The self becomes the beginning and end of consciousness even as consciousness remains, in itself, nothing. This void within consciousness defines existence as a struggle against premature closure. Both thinkers pass through a moment of radically aimless reflexivity that unravels all *telos*. This moment, as potentiality or as spontaneity, is what their projects share. The question of life can thus be understood as the maintenance of a reflexivity that may not last indefinitely, but is never destined to end. What they share, then, is a philosophical orientation: an endless ontology.

Notes

1. Giorgio Agamben, *The Omnibus Homo Sacer* (Stanford: Stanford University Press, 2017), p. 135.
2. Ibid, p. 152.
3. Ibid, p. 96.
4. Giorgio Agamben, *Creation and Anarchy: The Work of Art and the Religion of Capitalism*, trans. Adam Kotsko (Stanford: Stanford University Press, 2019), pp. 16–17.
5. Ibid. p. 17. Agamben offers two recurring models of potentiality. The first is Herman Melville's Bartleby, the scrivener who responds to all requests by simply stating, 'I would prefer not to', and the second is Glenn Gould, the pianist who was known to 'practise' without playing and famously ceased to perform at the age of thirty-one: 'Even though every pianist necessarily has the potential to play and the potential to not-play, Glenn Gould is, however, the only one who can not not-play, and, directing his potentiality not only to the act but to his own impotence, he plays, so to speak, with his potential to not-play' (Giorgio Agamben, *The Coming Community*, trans. Michael Hardt (Minneapolis: University of Minnesota Press, 1993), p. 35; see also Agamben, *Creation and Anarchy*, p. 19). Agamben goes on to distinguish ability, which

'negates and abandons his potential to not-play', from Gould's mastery, which 'conserves and exercises in the act . . . his potential to not-play' (*The Coming Community*, p. 35). Tyson Edward Lewis finds in Agamben's Gould a '*positive expression of an impotence, a lack of will*' ('On Study: Giorgio Agamben and Educational Potentiality', *Educational Philosophy and Theory* 46.4 (2014): 345).
6. Agamben, *Creation and Anarchy*, p. 17.
7. Giorgio Agamben, *Potentialities: Collected Essays in Philosophy*, ed. and trans. Daniel Heller-Roazen (Stanford: Stanford University Press, 1999), p. 245.
8. Agamben, *Creation and Anarchy*, p. 19.
9. Ibid. p. 24.
10. Agamben reads poetry as the discourse that stages a tension 'between sound and sense, between the semiotic and the semantic sphere' in which medium of communication interrupts its own communicative function (*The End of the Poem: Studies in Poetics*, trans. Daniel Heller-Roazen (Stanford: Stanford University Press, 1999), p. 109). Rhyme, caesura and enjambment are 'limits and endings' that in different ways drive a 'schism [between] sound and sense' (*The End of the Poem*, p. 110). This inexpressible differential is ultimately rendered 'indifferent' or 'inoperative' through the work of the poem, collapsing word and world. William Watkin terms this phenomenon 'logopoiesis', positioning poetry as definitive of Agamben's understanding of potentiality. See *The Literary Agamben: Adventures in Logopoiesis* (London: Continuum, 2010).
11. Agamben, *Creation and Anarchy*, p. 24.
12. Agamben, *Infancy and History*, p. 19.
13. In a recent editorial criticising the 'social distancing' measures enacted to mitigate COVID-19, Agamben ('Distanziamento sociale', *Quodlibet*, 6 April 2020, https://www.quodlibet.it/giorgio-agamben-distanziamento-sociale) takes his epigraph from the essay of this title: 'It is uncertain where death awaits us; let us await it everywhere. Premeditation of death is premeditation of freedom. He who has learned how to die has unlearned how to be a slave. Knowing how to die frees us from all subjection and constraint' (Michel de Montaigne, *The Complete Essays of Montaigne*, trans. Donald M. Frame (Stanford: Stanford University Press, 1957), p. 60).
14. Seneca, *Epistles*, 3 vols, trans. Richard M. Gummere (Cambridge, MA: Harvard University Press, 1917), 1: p. 191.
15. Peter Brooks, *Reading for the Plot: Design and Intention in Narrative* (New York: Knopf, 1984), p. 22.
16. Ibid.
17. In the pages of *The Spectator*, Joseph Addison developed the most self-conscious interpretation of death via the *logos* of the theatre: 'The End of a Man's Life is often compared to the winding up of a well-written Play, where the principal Persons still act in Character, whatever the Fate is which they undergo' (Joseph Addison and Richard Steele, *The Spectator*, 5 vols, ed. Donald F. Bond (Oxford: Clarendon Press, 1965), 3: p. 299).
18. The *Essays*' preface 'To the Reader' famously declares, 'I am myself the matter of my book' (Montaigne, *The Complete Essays*, p. 2).
19. Quoted in Agamben, *Potentialities*, p. 244; see also Agamben, *The Coming Community*, pp. 35–6 and Agamben, *Creation and Anarchy*, pp. 23–4.
20. Agamben, *Creation and Anarchy*, p. 266.
21. Quoted in Agamben, *Potentialities*, p. 250.
22. Agamben, *Potentialities*, p. 251; see also Agamben, *Creation and Anarchy*, pp. 23–4.
23. Agamben, *The Coming Community*, p. 36.
24. However, there is a strong current of classical dissent from what Herbert Marcuse called 'the ideology of death'. Diogenes notably rejected his peers' valorisation of death, instructing that his corpse be thrown outside the city walls so it could be eaten by wild animals (Thomas Laqueur, *The Work of the Dead: A Cultural History of Mortal Remains* (Princeton: Princeton University Press, 2015), pp. 35–7). Laqueur's

The Work of the Dead explores how an ostensibly secularising age has almost universally resisted Diogenes' radical example.
25. 'Has not the impossibility of getting the whole of Dasein into our grasp been inferred by an argument which is merely formal?' (Martin Heidegger, *Being and Time*, trans. John Macquarrie and Edward Robinson (New York: Harper & Row, 1962), p. 280).
26. Heidegger, *Being and Time*, p. 295.
27. In Heidegger's formula, death is '*the possibility of the impossibility of any existence at all*' (Ibid. p. 307).
28. Ibid. p. 307.
29. Martin Heidegger, *Kant and the Problem of Metaphysics*, trans. Richard Taft (Bloomington: Indiana University Press, 1997), p. 240.
30. Heidegger, *Being and Time*, p. 289.
31. Giorgio Agamben, *The Omnibus Homo Sacer* (Stanford: Stanford University Press, 2017), p. 812.
32. Heidegger, *Being and Time*, pp. 236, 372.
33. Ibid. pp. 279, 344.
34. Agamben's reading of death centres on *Being and Time*, which focuses on the phenomenological experience of individual beings. However, in *Time and Death: Heidegger's Analysis of Finitude* (Farnham: Ashgate, 2005), Carol White argues that Heidegger's late work rethinks death as an epochal phenomenon addressed at the level of whole civilisations, thus entirely relinquishing the dimension of individual experience that is the focus here. Accordingly, while this analysis of death is Agamben's point of departure, it does not reflect the full trajectory of Heidegger's engagements with death.
35. Leland de la Durantaye, *Giorgio Agamben: A Critical Introduction* (Stanford: Stanford University Press, 2009), pp. 24–5.
36. Heidegger, *Being and Time*, p. 307. However, *Being and Time*'s insistence on the fundamental openness of *Dasein* is often folded into pronouncements of the historical task of the *Volk*. Matthew Abbot, in *The Figure of This World: Agamben and the Question of Political Ontology* (Edinburgh: Edinburgh University Press, 2014), notes that Agamben consistently averts this dimension of Heidegger's thought: 'what he wants to take from Heidegger's philosophy of the history of being is something that could never be set to *work* in the becoming of a historical people' (p. 74). Agamben, as we will see, develops a conception of *Dasein* in the absence of any task, whether individual or collective, ontological or historical.
37. While this account will position *Language and Death* as a reorientation of Heidegger's project in *Being and Time*, Frances Restuccia has forcefully distinguished Agamben's thought from Heidegger on a number of interrelated issues, two of which are especially relevant here: (1) Heidegger grounds being on negativity; Agamben endeavours to negate negation; (2) Heidegger thinks being as unveiling, disclosure, *aletheia*; Agamben develops what Restuccia calls an 'ontology of nudity' defined by a 'lack of lack', apprehending what is already present ('Agamben's Post-Metaphysical Metapolitics: Departing from Heidegger', *Theory and Event* 21.3 (2018): pp. 677, 678).
38. Giorgio Agamben, *Language and Death: The Place of Negativity*, trans. Karen E. Pinkus with Michael Hardt (Minneapolis: University of Minnesota Press, 1991), p. 5.
39. Ibid. p. 25.
40. Ibid. p. 24.
41. Émile Benveniste, *Problems in General Linguistics*, trans. Mary Elizabeth Meek (Miami: University of Miami Press, 1971), p. 218.
42. Ibid.
43. Agamben, *Language and Death*, p. 25.
44. Ibid. p. 31.
45. Heidegger, *Being and Time*, p. 39.
46. Benveniste, *Problems in General Linguistics*, p. 219.

47. Quoted in Agamben, *Language and Death*, p. 36.
48. *Remnants of Auschwitz* returns to Benveniste's claim that the discursive *I* generates 'a unitary center to which one can refer lived experiences and acts, a firm point outside the oceans of sensations and psychic states' (Agamben, *The Omnibus Homo Sacer*, p. 842). Here Agamben concludes that 'Subjectivity and consciousness, in which our culture believed itself to have found its firmest foundation, rest on what is most precarious and fragile in the world: the event of speech' (p. 843).
49. Agamben, *Language and Death*, p. 39.
50. Agamben, *Potentialities*, p. 211.
51. Ibid. pp. 84, 107.
52. Agamben, *The Omnibus Homo Sacer*, p. 839.
53. Daniel McLoughlin, 'From Voice to Infancy: Giorgio Agamben on the Existence of Language', *Angelaki: Journal of the Theoretical Humanities* 18.4 (2013): 156.
54. Agamben, *Language and Death*, p. 33.
55. Ibid. p. 57.
56. Ibid. pp. 36, 61.
57. Ibid. p. 84.
58. Ibid. p. 85.
59. Ibid. p. xii.
60. Ibid. p. 86.
61. Agamben, *Creation and Anarchy*, pp. 16–17.
62. Jean-Paul Sartre, *War Diaries: Notebooks from a Phoney War, November 1939–March 1940*, trans. Quintin Hoare (New York: Verso, 1999), p. 79.
63. Ibid. p. 80.
64. Ibid.
65. Ibid. p. 81. These passages are discussed by Lior Levy, who defends a notion of self or ego as an imaginative construct that provides real significance to human life ('Reflection, Memory, and Selfhood in Jean-Paul Sartre's Early Philosophy', *Sartre Studies International* 19.2 (2013): 90–1). Further discussion of the ethical and political value of Sartre's conception of the ego can be found in Christian Gillam, 'Sartre as a Thinker of (Deleuzian) Immanence: Prefiguring and Complementing the Micropolitical', *Contemporary Political Theory* 15.4 (2016): 374–5. I do not attempt any such evaluation here. My interest is in the resonance between Sartre's critique of the ego and Agamben's model of potentiality as reflexive thought.
66. Jean-Paul Sartre, *Being and Nothingness: A Phenomenological Essay on Ontology*, trans. Hazel E. Barnes (New York: Washington Square Press, 1956), p. 78.
67. Ibid. pp. 171, 174, 596.
68. Ibid. p. 147.
69. Jean-Paul Sartre, *The Transcendence of the Ego: A Sketch for a Phenomenological Description*, trans. Andrew Brown (New York: Routledge. 2004), pp. 67–8.
70. Ibid. p. 69. David Carr elaborates the difficulty of distinguishing the transcendental ego from the empirical ego, since Husserl's argument seems to blur the former into the latter ('Kant, Husserl, and the Nonempirical Ego', *The Journal of Philosophy* 74.11 (1977): 685–6).
71. Sartre, *The Transcendence of the Ego*, p. 7.
72. Ibid.
73. Agamben, *Potentialities*, p. 250.
74. Agamben, *Infancy and History*, p. 36.
75. Sartre, *The Transcendence of the Ego*, p. 27.
76. Quoted in Agamben, *Potentialities*, pp. 224–5. Agamben's text slightly misquotes Deleuze. The original reads: 'an impersonal transcendental field, not having the form of a synthetic personal consciousness *or* a subjective identity' (Gilles Deleuze, *The Logic of Sense*, trans. Mark Lester with Charles Stivale, ed. Constantin V. Boundas (New York: Columbia University Press, 1990), p. 98; my emphasis).

77. Agamben, *Potentialities*, p. 225.
78. Agamben suggests that, despite the 'impersonal spontaneity' of his conception of experience (Sartre, *The Transcendence of the Ego*, p. 27), Sartre 'does not fully succeed in liberating [thought] from the plane of consciousness' (Agamben, *Potentialities*, p. 225).

Chapter 10

Destituent Potential and Camus's Politics of Rebellion

Tim Christiaens

> Salvation's too big a word for me. I don't aim so high. I'm concerned with man's health; and for me his health comes first.
>
> Albert Camus[1]

Reform or revolution? – the perennial question of political action. When people find a legal order unjust they can either change the system from within or overhaul it completely and start anew. Giorgio Agamben, however, believes both options remain caught in the logic of sovereignty. For him, the opposition between reform and revolution is stuck in an 'unceasing, unwinnable, desolate dialectic between constituent and constituted power, between the violence that puts the juridical in place and violence that preserves it'.[2] Whereas constituent power is the revolutionary force that founds a legal system, constituted power is the force that preserves it once it is established. Both, however, keep human beings submitted to the law, the difference being only whether it is an old or a new legal order. Agamben proposes to add a third option, 'destituent potential',[3] to avoid the choice between reforming a constituted power or mobilising constituent power. Whereas legal orders build communities by interpellating people to a common identity and vocation, the so-called 'coming community' generated by destituent potential arises when people refuse to accept these vocations without creating new vocations of their own. The question lingers, however, whether this attitude of detachment vis-à-vis one's juridical or social identity is politically satisfactory. Is Agamben's destituent potential really preferable to reform and revolution?

I first outline Agamben's critique of constituent and constituted power to see why he dismisses the dual options of reform and revolution. Afterwards I explain his account of destituent potential and why it disappoints on three fronts. It is firstly crypto-Gnostic by depreciating this actual world in favour of a messianic exodus from actuality. Agamben, secondly, presents his readers with a perfectionist all-or-nothing choice. It is either total redemption through destituent potential or eternal damnation in the endless cycle of law-making and law-preserving violence. This puts unrealistic demands on concrete political struggles and hinders the comparison between better and worse constituted orders. Agamben, lastly, presents destituent potential primarily in negative terms, which renders the positive outcome of his redeemed community underdetermined. Because he mainly discusses how redemption is *not* like any previous form of life, he fails to specify how purportedly redeemed human beings would interact with each other. I, thirdly, use Albert Camus's politics of rebellion as an alternative escape from the dilemma between reform and revolution. By starting from the experience of rebellion against injustice and the sense of solidarity that flows from it, Camus develops a politics that dissolves the relation of subordination to the law through the affirmation of a common human nature that evades the law. This does not lead to a politics of destituent potential, however, but to a continuous struggle against the concrete injustices that have caused the experience of rebellion. This struggle leads to reforms or revolutions depending on which strategy works best in a given political conjecture. Camus's politics hence leaves the possibilities for reform and revolution open, but does not reduce either to subjecting people to a legal system. Both reform and revolution are born in an experience of rebellion that escapes the law and to which they are to remain faithful.

Agamben's Critique of Reformist and Revolutionary Politics

Agamben launches his *Homo Sacer* project with an attack on the law's dependence on sovereign power to regulate forms of life.[4] In a nutshell, the hierarchy of powers in a constituted legal order depends for its stability on the presence of a highest authority, the sovereign. The latter is responsible for guaranteeing the applicability of the law to real living beings, but it can suspend this application in emergency situations. Whenever society is in disarray, the sovereign declares the state of exception and re-establishes the dominant form of life by force. In those instances, people are reduced to bare life, stripped of social qualities and relations until nothing is left but their exposure to the sovereign's decision over life and death. Reformism is hence futile for Agamben. It changes specific parts of the legal system, but keeps the lurking violence of sovereign power in place. Notwithstanding this scathing critique of the law, Agamben equally dismisses revolutionary philosophies like Antonio Negri's.[5] According to Negri, constituted power is indeed tainted by the logic of sovereignty, but constituent power provides a viable alternative.[6] One usually frames constituent power as the people's extra-legal power to found a state and its legal order, whereas sovereignty is the law's highest authority tasked with preserving the legal order. For Negri, an emancipatory politics should affirm the continuously creative force of the people's non-juridical constituent power against the constituted powers that try to fix human conduct according to pre-established legal standards. Agamben, however, has two reasons to suspect that the distinction between constituent power and sovereignty tends towards indistinction.

First, Agamben observes that the reference to 'the people's constituent power' is usually a story constituted powers tell the populace to legitimate themselves rather than an actual historical event. The legal order invokes a pure origin outside the law in 'the people' to grant itself the authority to exercise power over this same people. 'Constituent power is what constituted power must presuppose to give itself a foundation and legitimate itself.'[7] Agamben, however, suspects that it is all façade and no content.[8] 'The people' never appears in its pristine purity; there are only political factions claiming to talk in the name of 'the people'. The latter never really existed, but is retroactively invented *as if* it were the source of legitimate power. Negri is hence chasing ghosts if he wants to put constituent power in the centre of politics. 'Constituent power' is no pure extra-legal force, but a legal invention to justify constituted powers.

Second, revolutions, of course, do occur. Legal orders perish and new ones emerge all the time. Even if these events do not originate in 'the people', revolutions still establish new constituted powers. According to Agamben, however, they fail to escape the logic of sovereignty.[9] On the one hand, constituent power can quickly dissolve into nothing more than a new constituted power. Once the revolutionary faction takes over the state apparatus and crowns itself the new sovereign, the constituent moment dissipates. A new sovereign is established to enforce a new form of life, but the logic of sovereignty itself remains unaffected. On the other hand, the revolutionary group could refuse to transition to a constituted power in the name of some permanent revolution. Agamben uses Hannah Arendt's study of revolutionary movements in *The Origins of Totalitarianism* to argue that this choice creates an unstable tension in the state apparatus where the constituent power itself takes on the violent characteristics previously ascribed to the sovereign.[10] The revolutionary movement progressively resembles the sovereign power it seeks to dethrone. Arendt observed that, once revolutionary movements like the Nazis in Germany or the communists in Russia took power, they left the old state apparatus intact, but supplemented it with a proliferation of new institutions that destabilised the constituted order. In the USSR, for instance, the Tsarist state apparatus remained, but a chaotic flux of party organisations repeatedly undermined the state's operations and replaced them with new regulations until, a few months later, those new rules would again be superseded.[11] Eventually the population was exposed to a perpetually transforming amalgam of institutions and laws that were just as violent, if not more so, as the Tsarist regime. The permanent revolution of constituent power is, for Agamben, ultimately a frantic lawmaking machine that produces ever new rules until nobody knows which rules to follow and whose orders to obey. Any mistake could, however, prove deadly. To promote the continued existence of the revolution, the movement has to keep resetting the rules and enforcing them with violence if need be, a situation worryingly similar to the sovereign's state of exception. In this 'permanent state of lawlessness',[12] nobody knows which laws to observe because it is ultimately the revolutionary movement that decides *post factum*. The irony here is that, in order to fight sovereign power, revolutionary movements are ultimately obliged to declare their own permanent state of exception and wield the power over life and death themselves.

Agamben's Politics of Destituent Potential

Given the limitations of revolution and reform, Agamben aims not to amend or replace the law, but to undermine the logic of sovereignty itself.[13] He wishes to dissolve the relation of subordination between life and the law by deposing sovereignty's hold over the life and death of its populace. According to Agamben, the central problem is that political communities have until now mainly been legal constructions. The Italian people, for instance, comes into being through the equal subjection to the Italian legal system and hence to a sovereign who guarantees the application of that system. Agamben's 'destituent potential' looks for a way to construct political communities on a non-juridical basis. It does not directly build a new form of life with its own legal order, but breaks the bond between life and law, so that life can find its own form beyond the law. Agamben's hope is by deactivating the law's applicability to life, the latter can be liberated from sovereign power.[14]

Agamben finds this possibility by metaphysically subverting the notion of 'form of life'. He argues that a form of life results from human beings collectively submitting to a legal order under a sovereign's authority. The laws of these forms of life regulate the community by interpellating human subjects to particular identities, such as 'Italian citizen', 'Muslim', 'woman' and so on. A form of life distributes a series of social roles or vocations – Agamben also calls them 'works' (*opere*) – and expects human beings to enact them. The more people fulfil their vocations, the better they are members of their community. A Muslim, for instance, becomes a better Muslim by actualising the kinds of behaviours prescribed in the Qur'an. Agamben, however, argues that what makes humankind unique is its potentiality *not to* perform one's designated identity. 'Other living beings are capable only of their specific potentiality; they can only do this or that. But human beings are the animals who are capable of their own impotentiality.'[15] A lion cannot but act as a lion, but a Muslim cannot act as a Muslim. There is no inner necessity to the social roles human beings perform. They could always have acted differently. Agamben concludes that humankind's vocation lies not in actualising some particular, pre-established identity or form of life, but in deactivating all possible vocations.[16]

> What is at issue is the very nature of man [*sic*], who appears as the living being that has no work, that is, the living being that has no specific nature or vocation. If he were to lack an *ergon* of his own, man would not even have an *energeia*, a being in act that could define his essence: he would be, that is, a being of pure potentiality, which no identity and no work could exhaust.[17]

There is purportedly no form of life with which human beings could completely coincide due to humankind's essential 'inoperativity' (*inoperosità*). The way out of the law's aporias lies hence not in enforcing a form of life or constructing a new one, but in distancing oneself from any form of life that would claim to exhaust human potentiality. Constituent power establishes a form of life, constituted power enforces it, but destituent potential affirms human inoperativity to show the gap between human beings and the forms of life they inhabit.

One of Agamben's key paradigms is Bartleby from Melville's short story 'Bartleby, the Scrivener: A Story of Wall Street'.[18] Bartleby works as a scribe in a New York law office, when he suddenly withdraws from his role. The office's boss imposes on Bartleby the identity of a clerk by issuing commands, but by insisting that 'he would prefer not to', Bartleby subverts the power-relation. He refuses to be identified as a scribe, but he does not establish a new identity. The subversive gesture only detaches Bartleby from his social role. By enacting his potentiality not to do what his boss demands, Bartleby deposes the latter's authority without submitting to a new authority, like a revolutionary movement or a trade union, for example. He merely cultivates his lack of vocation. For Agamben, this method of self-subtraction leads to a lifestyle not subjected to a legal order.

In his commentary on the letters of Paul, Agamben calls this a life 'as if not' (*hos me*).[19] For Paul's messianic message, it does not matter whether one is a slave or a master, married or unmarried, in mourning or happy. The crux of the matter is rather one's identification with one's form of life. One should mentally detach oneself from one's current mode of existence, as if one did not possess it. Whatever activity one actually performs is just one among many potential modes of conduct one could enact. One could always have acted differently. Whereas for Bartleby this leads to inaction, people can, for Paul, still perform the activities that belong to a specific form of life, but without identifying with them: weep as if you were not sad, act like a woman as if you were not a woman, be an Italian citizen as if you were not, and so on. When Bartleby distances himself from his vocation as a scribe he gradually becomes inactive, but for Agamben it is more important that one repeats Bartleby's mental disidentification with one's identity rather than actually becoming inactive.

According to Agamben, cultivating inoperativity discloses a coming community beyond the political communities constituted as forms of life. Whereas the latter require legally enforced vocations and shared identities, the life *hos me* finds common ground in humankind's shared impotentiality, the common capacity to subtract oneself from one's social role. Since inoperativity belongs to human nature, there is an 'inessential commonality'[20] among human beings with regard to their capacity to detach themselves from legally regulated social identities. What remains of life after it has subtracted itself from the forms the law has imposed upon it, is the bare potential to enact all kinds of different identities. Once Bartleby conducts his life *as if* he were *not* a scribe, there is no limit to what he could be. What Bartleby ultimately reveals is humankind's omnipotentiality in so far as the mere fact of its existence in no way determines the form this existence can subsequently take. The being of humanity is constitutively open. According to Agamben, in this conception of human community,

> such-and-such being is reclaimed from its having this or that property, which identifies it as belonging to this or that set, to this or that class (the reds, the French, the Muslims) – and it is reclaimed not for another class nor for the simple generic absence of any belonging, but for its being-such, for belonging itself.[21]

Human beings do not form a community by subjecting to a common form of life guarded by sovereign power, but by collectively subtracting themselves from their social roles and cultivating their inoperativity in a 'community without identity'.[22]

With regard to its political implications, Agamben's metaphysical approach has given rise to a lot of speculation. The divergent interpretations usually reveal more about the interpreters than about Agamben. The anarchist Newman associates the coming community with Stirner's union of egoists, the radical democrat Prozorov aligns it with Lefort's agonistic democracy and the neo-Marxist Smith with Virno's post-workerist exodus.[23] Agamben himself affirms none of these options explicitly. He calls the anarchist project a failure,[24] links the modern democracy Lefort defends with the dispositifs of *oikonomia* and the Debordian spectacle[25] and repeatedly signals his unease with the post-workerist tradition.[26] In my view, this variety of interpretations points towards shortcomings in Agamben's own philosophy. Agamben might just not have a viable politics to endorse. Three problems are worth mentioning.

First, Agamben's depreciation of actual forms of life in favour of an ethic of self-withdrawal into inoperativity betrays a crypto-Gnostic separation between the created world and redemption.[27] Gnosticism was an early Christian heretical movement that radically rejected the material world in favour of spiritual redemption. By withdrawing oneself from the actual material world, the soul could purportedly achieve salvation. Agamben advises his readers to detach themselves from their actual identities, like Bartleby, but this leaves them no incentive to change their form of life. His politics primarily undermines the apparent necessity or essentiality attached to particular human vocations. Agamben shows that, whatever vocation we have received in a given form of life, there is nothing that ontologically forces us to conform to this standard. One can always prefer not to. When discussing redemption, however, Agamben likes to quote Benjamin, stating that 'everything will be as it is now, just a little different'.[28] Such a message might suffice for Agamben, but it does not for the many people who suffer right now in the actual world. They need a world that is more than 'just a little different'. We should not forget that, after his act of defiance, Bartleby, rather than provoking change, 'dies alone in prison as the world goes on around him'.[29] That Agamben omits this outcome reveals just how unimportant Bartleby's actual state of being is for the life *hos me*. Agamben's kingdom seems not to be of this world. Agamben locates redemption in humankind's self-subtraction from this actual world into an abstract realm of potentiality where things could always have been different. This argument informs us little about the values that could induce us to enact actual change *hic et nunc*. Why would anyone still bother with improving the actual world if salvation lies in merely a different, post-essentialist attitude towards this world?

Second, Agamben mobilises a particular strand of utopian messianism that reduces politics to all-or-nothing decisions: either one opts for destituent potential or one gets caught in the cycle of constituent and constituted power.[30] This obscures the possibility of comparing and evaluating different constituted legal orders. Despite the reality of sovereign violence, one would still prefer to live in a liberal democracy than in a totalitarian dictatorship. For Agamben, however, both are equally tainted by the logic of sovereignty, the latter just more explicitly. Without these comparative differences, it is unclear from Agamben's perspective why one would struggle for democratic rights or political emancipation. Rebecca Solnit rightly points out that messianism can have a paralysing effect on political action.[31] In most instances, ultimate salvation is not a realistic outcome, but that does not render all improvements impossible or undesirable. Everyday concrete struggles for a minimum wage, for example, might not deliver us from evil, but it at least makes the world a little less evil for the poor. By emphasising redemption rather than small-scale improvements, Agamben falls prey to utopian perfectionism. This leads to 'the grumpiness of perfectionists who hold that anything less than total victory is a failure, a premise that makes it easy to give up at the start or to disparage victories that are possible'.[32] If only complete redemption will do, most concrete advances in political emancipation are bound to disappoint.

Third, Agamben's emphasis on negations obscures the view of what a coming community would concretely look like. One subtracts oneself from one's form of life by cultivating 'im-potentiality', 'in-operativity', 'a life as if not'. That does not, however, specify how a society of Bartlebys or a Pauline community would actually function. Agamben presumes that out of a series of negatives something positive will miraculously appear. As Negri writes, 'missing in Agamben is a value that might distinguish between the anarchic lure of the void and the loving construction of the social'.[33] Being in a community entails more than either adhering to a particular collective identity or sharing in human inoperativity. It means involving oneself in some form of intersubjective praxis. Ultimately, Agamben argues for nothing more than that everyone is always already in community thanks to the universal absolute potentiality to belong to a community. This might be true, but it says nothing about how people interact. How do people in a coming community talk to each other, care for the sick or make love? Agamben's ontologising notion of the coming community is too thin to answer these questions. It eclipses the messy reality of human togetherness.

Camus's Politics of Rebellion

Agamben poses the challenge of escaping the logic of sovereignty. Until now, legal orders have relied on sovereign violence to enforce forms of life. Agamben, however, rejects the usual solutions, reformism and revolutionary insurrection. He proposes a 'destituent potential' that annuls the law's hold on life without constituting a new legal order. He argues for a dissolution of life's submission to sovereignty rather than a revised or renewed legal system. By subtracting oneself from one's actual form of life in a life as if not, one supposedly escapes the grasp of sovereignty. The problem with this approach is that it is crypto-Gnostic, perfectionist and too abstract. One should hence look for an alternative escape that (1) affirms this actual world, (2) values small-scale improvements and (3) gives concrete guidelines for collective conduct. I propose these qualities can be discovered in an unlikely source, namely Albert Camus, an author Agamben mentions only once in his entire oeuvre.[34]

Camus's work shows surprising affinities with Agamben's. Camus, firstly, highlights the violence of the state of exception and totalitarianism in pieces like *The Plague* and *The State of Siege*, where he depicts social crises through the prism of capital punishment as if the plague were a sovereign that decides over whose lives are worthy of being lived.[35] More importantly, however, Camus elaborates a critique of revolutionary politics in *The Rebel* remarkably similar to Agamben's worries about the persistence of constituent power.[36] He argues that, by promising heaven on earth, communists condemn society and themselves to a permanent revolution where the ends always justify the means. No sacrifice is supposedly too great if the reward will be the end of history. Since human beings, however, persistently fail to completely conform to any pre-established notion of paradise on earth, revolutionary institutions must permanently suspend the rule of law to violently enforce their will.[37] Humankind is not infinitely malleable according to a preconceived ideal form of life, so there are always 'fissures in the totality'[38] that supposedly have to be suppressed. When it comes to political action and community, however, Camus deviates sharply from Agamben. His position is decidedly unmessianic: he rejects all notions of salvation and chooses to remain faithful to the earth.[39] Instead of depreciating this world for an attitude of detachment, Camus calls for a deeper involvement in this world to improve it. Rather than seeking ultimate redemption in withdrawing from actuality and intersubjective praxis, Camus pleads for a collective rebellion against concrete injustices in this world. Allow me to first explain Camus's notion of rebellion, afterwards how it evades the logic of sovereignty, and thirdly how it counters the problems Agamben faces.

Camus's paradigm for rebellion is slaves' defiance of their master's orders.[40] Slaves are juridically pieces of property the master can command at will. Yet, in contrast to other properties, slaves can rise up against their subordination when the master denies them a humane treatment. In their defiance, they stress their value as human beings in opposition to power.

In contrast to Agamben's Bartleby, however, who only withdraws from his relation of subordination by negating his boss's orders, the slaves also affirm something about themselves beyond their potentiality not to. They affirm that their humanity entitles them to a better treatment *hic et nunc*. They press for change in this world by affirming what Camus provocatively calls their 'human nature'.[41] Camus is, however, not an essentialist trying to fix the human form of life. He does not identify a human nature to subsequently interpellate people to enact this nature as their vocation. He, on the contrary, argues that this human nature is 'an obscure existence'[42] that only reveals itself negatively in the experience of rebellion. For Camus the absurdist, our vocation in life cannot be positively defined. The universe is ultimately indifferent to human desires for meaning in life, so there is no ontological foundation on which to build our form of life.[43] We *can*, however, experience which situations conflict with our desire for meaning. The rebellious slave working ungodly hours might not know what his human nature or ultimate vocation in life is, but he can be certain that his current condition does *not* constitute his purpose in life. The reality of his suffering radically contradicts his appeal for a meaningful life.

> The first and only evidence that is supplied to me, within the terms of the absurdist experience, is rebellion. . . . Rebellion is born of the spectacle of irrationality, confronted with an unjust and incomprehensible condition. . . . It insists that the outrage be brought to an end.[44]

In the negation of a power relation, the rebel affirms an obscure yet real limit that ought to be respected. Camus gives, in other words, a phenomenological argument for how an experience of rebellion against meaningless suffering gives birth to a moral claim for this suffering to end.

Camus's politics of rebellion evades the logic of sovereignty, though not in the same way or to the same extent as Agamben's destituent potential. For Agamben, the oppressed escape the law by disidentifying with the vocations the law has imposed on them. Camus's rebel also refuses his vocation as a slave but simultaneously demands recognition for a common human nature beyond the law.[45] Legally, the slave might be nothing but property, but in the moment of rebellion he experiences himself as more and desires others to do so as well. Though he cannot fully articulate what this surplus is, he knows that it is not exhausted by the social role the law grants him now. By affirming this excess, the slave escapes his subordination to the law and its representative, the master. He identifies not with his socio-juridical identity but with this indeterminate surplus 'human nature' beyond the law. In contrast to Agamben's Bartleby, where the negation of his actual condition leads to an affirmation of his omnipotentiality *without* relating it back to actuality, the slave's defiance demands recognition *in* the actual world. The slave's preference not to follow the master's orders moves beyond Bartleby's in so far as it calls for a change in his current, actual condition, not just a change of attitude.

There is, however, a tragic element implied in Camus's version of rebellion absent from Agamben's philosophy. Since the basis of political action lies in a surplus of humanity that can never find adequate expression in a given form of life, any subsequent recognition the rebel receives will fall short. It is constitutively impossible to definitively institute a fully human order that does not give rise to further rebellions. Agamben's life as if not, on the contrary, holds the promise of a conclusive solution to the incessant cycle of constituent and constituted power. For Agamben, figures like Bartleby definitively escape the grip of the law. Camus's politics of rebellion cannot deliver such a decisive break with the law, only momentary ruptures of rebellion against the law. This politics ultimately entails a Sisyphean labour whereby each victory leads to new political forms that instigate the battle all over again. Human rights can, for instance, constitute an effective solution to some forms of oppression, but even they can never encapsulate the surplus of humanity denied in the legal form.[46] Still, Camus's politics cannot be reduced to (1) revolutionary or (2) reformist programmes.

(1) Although the rebellion rejects a given constituted order that allots the identity of slaves to some and of masters to others, the rebel does not simply produce a new, constituent power. No determinate political programme flows from the concrete experience of rebellion. The latter only contests the injustices of a constituted order and attempts to correct them. From human nature experienced in rebellion no conclusions can be drawn about an alternative form of life that would supposedly settle all our discontents. The slave only knows that his current form of life is unjust, not which form of life would bring him everlasting happiness. The risk of revolutions remains that they 'suppress in the world and in man everything that escapes the Empire, everything that does not come under the reign of quantity'.[47] Camus hence vehemently opposes all attempts to definitively fix an ideal form of society.

(2) This emphasis on correcting wrongs, however, does not make Camus a reformist either, even though his sympathies lie more on that side of the dilemma. He, for example, supports syndicalist wage struggles against communist revolutions.[48] According to Camus, syndicalists focus on the negative task of combatting workers' submission to the capitalist class rather than building a new form of life. They might never reach a state of everlasting justice, but they are continuously vigilant for abuses of power. Instead of imagining and implementing a utopia, the syndicalist rebel corrects specific wrongs one at a time. From this perspective, it is

even possible to mobilise constituent power and support a revolution, but only in so far as the activists emphasise adjusting wrongs rather than shaping society according to some pre-established programme. Whether rebels wage revolutions or call for reforms is of lesser importance to Camus as long as they remain faithful to the original experience of rebellion and the surplus of human nature revealed in that event.

Allow me to return to my three objections to Agamben's concept of destituent potential to reiterate exactly how Camus evades them. My first objection is that Agamben's destituent potential is crypto-Gnostic because it locates redemption in a withdrawal from actuality into potentiality. On first sight, Camus also stresses the negation of actuality. When, in *The Plague*, the protagonist Rieux has just witnessed a young boy's painful death, he protests: 'Until my dying day I shall refuse to love a scheme of things in which children are put to torture.'[49] In his rebellion, Rieux rejects a world that could tolerate such suffering, but this negation does not lead him to withdraw from actuality. Rieux rebels against the actual world in order to change it. His efforts are directed to improving *this* world, not to escaping its horrors in a life *hos me*.

My second objection, again, is that Agamben forces his readers into a stark opposition between messianic perfection or damnation while neglecting opportunities for small improvements. This leaves Agamben with little standards to prefer one actual form of life over another. Camus's rebellions, on the contrary, focus on correcting concrete wrongs, not on establishing some final salvation. From the experience of rebellion, the rebel derives standards for evaluating different forms of life. Camus himself was, for example, deeply moved by the fate of prisoners sentenced to death.[50] It convinced him that a world without capital punishment is better and worth fighting for. By overcoming such injustices, humanity establishes a better future. It is, for Camus, of lesser importance that rebellions acquire only temporary and limited victories, as long as real improvements are made. After the abolition of capital punishment, new injustices will appear and old power imbalances might return, but prisoners will at least temporarily have found a more dignified existence. For Camus, the experience of rebellion thus saddles human beings with the tragic never-ending task of responding to injustices, only to start all over again once new wrongs emerge.

My third objection: Agamben's coming community is too abstract as a concept to capture the intersubjective praxis that comes with human togetherness. It subsequently fails to provide any guidelines for how to live a dignified life. By grounding rebellion in an individual's experience, Camus seems to render it a solitary affair. He, however, notices that rebels are willing to die even for the suffering of others.

> If the individual, in fact, accepts death and happens to die as a consequence of his act of rebellion, he demonstrates by doing so that he is willing to sacrifice himself for the sake of a common good which he considers more important than his own destiny. . . . Therefore he is acting in the name of certain values which are still indeterminate but which he feels are common to himself and to all men. We see that the affirmation implicit in every act of rebellion is extended to something that transcends the individual in so far as it withdraws him from his supposed solitude and provides him with a reason to act.[51]

That individuals accept death for a higher purpose, even if that purpose cannot be grounded in some ultimate meaning of life, suggests a communal dimension. It reveals a love and sense of responsibility for those who suffer. 'This love finding no outlet and God being denied, it is then decided to lavish it on human beings as a generous act of complicity.'[52] This love comes from the insight that if I or the suffering other deserve to be treated more respectfully, then everyone ought to be treated that way – even our oppressors. This lays the basis for an immanent human solidarity that Camus summarises with the phrase 'I rebel, therefore we are.'[53] The indignation towards suffering that someone experienced in a concrete instance reveals that *no one* should be treated in this way and thus that *everyone* deserves better. Rebellion does not posit a universal vocation for humanity, but a universal negation of our present, actual vocations in the name of an unnamable surplus. What all human beings share is the fact that they are more than the vocation any concrete form of life assigns them. This 'more' is revealed in the experience of rebellion, but it will never fit in any alternative form of life.

Contrary to Agamben's approach, Camus's sense of community through rebellious solidarity gives more concrete instructions into how to conduct oneself. For Camus, community emerges through a collective fidelity to one's determination to end a concrete wrong that provides guidance to one's conduct. One should live one's life in such a way that no one should have to relive the pains that instigated the rebellion. In *The Plague*, for instance, it is the experience of suffering around them that encourages Rieux and the other characters to band together and fight the epidemic as a collective.

> Many fledgeling [sic] moralists in those days were going about our town proclaiming there was nothing to be done about it and we should bow to the inevitable. And Tarrou, Rieux, and their friends might give one answer or another, but its conclusion was always the same, their certitude that a fight must be put up, in this way or that, and there must be no bowing down. The essential thing was to save the greatest possible number of persons from dying and being doomed to unending separation. And to do this there was only one resource: to fight the plague.[54]

The experience of rebellion discloses a human solidarity in perpetual struggle against the evil absurdity of the world. Leading a good life means here living up to the call to diminish suffering in the world.

Conclusion

One of the central questions of political action concerns the choice between reform or revolution. Agamben rejects both trajectories because they operate within the same logic of sovereignty. They either amend or establish a legal order without questioning the sovereign power required to render the law applicable to living beings. He employs the concept 'destituent potential' to imagine a life beyond the law: by affirming human inoperativity instead of a legally imposed vocation, human beings can form a coming community beyond enforced legal identities. This entails conducting a life *hos me* where one disidentifies with one's given form of life to cultivate one's potential to enact many different potentialities instead. I have argued that this option is crypto-Gnostic, perfectionist and too abstract. It turns attention away from the actual world and emphasises ultimate redemption. This hinders our capacity to compare actual forms of life and to struggle for concrete improvements. Agamben's notion of coming community also remains overly abstract by conceptualising community without the intersubjective dimension of human praxis.

I have proposed to return to Camus's notion of rebellion for a more promising course of action. Camus starts from the individual's experience of injustice as an infraction upon human nature. Instead of fixing this 'human nature' and calling for another form of life on this foundation, Camus argues human nature can be defined only as a surplus of humanity denied in a concrete social order. The rebel contests this order by struggling for the recognition of this excess. This struggle can take the form of revolution or reform as long as it remains loyal to the original experience of injustice and the task to amend this concrete wrong. Whether it is reform or revolution that succeeds in diminishing human suffering is of lesser importance. Compared to Agamben's destituent potential, the downside of Camus's politics of rebellion is that it renders any conclusive solutions impossible. There are only temporary responses to the clash between surplus humanity and the oppressive forms of life in which it is caught. There is, however, no final reconciliation between life and its form. On the upside, Camus's notion of rebellion affirms this actual world, values concrete improvements and gives concrete guidelines for collective praxis. The rebel affirms a surplus of humanity revealed in the experience of injustice and primarily combats the power-relation that has denied this surplus. He consequently does not seek ultimate redemption, but less evil in the world. Through this rebellion, a human community emerges in the struggle against evil. Its main guideline is that it fights for a world where people would no longer have to suffer from the injustices that have given rise to the rebellion.

Notes

1. Albert Camus, *The Plague* (London: Penguin Books, 2010), p. 209.
2. Giorgio Agamben, *The Use of Bodies* (Stanford: Stanford University Press, 2016), p. 266.
3. Some scholars translate *potenza destituente* as 'destituent power' to highlight the contrast with 'constituent power', but I opt for Kotsko's translation to not conflate potentiality (*potenza*) with power (*potere*). Since Agamben stresses his re-examination of the concept of potentiality (see *Homo Sacer: Sovereign Power and Bare Life* (Stanford: Stanford University Press 1998), pp. 43–8), it is crucial to see the distinction between the 'powers' that subordinate life to the law and the 'potential' that can liberate life from the law.
4. Agamben, *Homo Sacer*, pp. 1–12.
5. Ibid. pp. 43–4.
6. Antonio Negri, *Insurgencies: Constituent Power and the Modern State* (Minneapolis: University of Minnesota Press, 1999).
7. Agamben, *Use of Bodies* p. 267.
8. Agamben links this to his critique of *auctoritas* and *potestas* (Ibid. pp. 264–5). According to Agamben, legal orders have repeatedly captured humankind's destituent potential and inoperativity by incorporating it at the heart of political power as *auctoritas*. In order to exercise political power (*potestas*) over the population, legal institutions have invoked transcendent authorities like 'God', 'the emperor' or 'the people' to justify their actions. These entities are themselves inoperative, but authorise the actions of their supposedly inferior agents. Whatever a national government does, is, for instance, justified thanks to the mandate it received from 'the people' during the previous elections. 'The people' never acts independently, but it gives a legitimation by fiat for everything the government decides.
9. I will here not discuss the way Agamben links these two outcomes to misconceptions in the ontology of potentiality. See Leland de la Durantaye, *Giorgio Agamben: A Critical Introduction* (Stanford: Stanford University Press 2009), pp. 228–34; Sergei Prozorov, *Agamben and Politics: A Critical Introduction* (Edinburgh: Edinburgh University Press, 2014), pp. 116–20.
10. Agamben, *Homo Sacer*, pp. 41–2.
11. Hannah Arendt, *The Origins of Totalitarianism* (New York: Harcourt, 1976), p. 399.
12. Ibid. p. 394.
13. Agamben, *Use of Bodies*, p. 268.
14. Ibid. pp. 272–3.
15. Giorgio Agamben, 'On Potentiality', in Giorgio Agamben, *Potentialities* (Stanford: Stanford University Press, 1999), p. 182.
16. Agamben, *Use of Bodies*, p. 273.
17. Giorgio Agamben, 'The Work of Man', in *Giorgio Agamben: Sovereignty & Life*, ed. Matthew Calarco and Carlo Salzani (Stanford: Stanford University Press, 2007), p. 2.
18. Giorgio Agamben, 'Bartleby, or on Contingency', in Giorgio Agamben, *Potentialities* (Stanford: Stanford University Press, 1999).
19. Giorgio Agamben, *The Time That Remains* (Stanford: Stanford University Press, 2005), pp. 23–6.

20. Giorgio Agamben, *The Coming Community* (Minneapolis: University of Minnesota Press, 1992), p. 18.
21. Ibid. pp. 1–2.
22. Ibid. p. 86.
23. Saul Newman, 'What is an Insurrection? Destituent Power in Agamben and Stirner', *Political Studies* 65.2 (2017); Sergei Prozorov, 'Living *à la mode*: Form-of-life and Democratic Biopolitics in Giorgio Agamben's *The Use of Bodies*', *Philosophy and Social Criticism* 43.2 (2017); Jason Smith, 'Form-of-Life and Antagonism: On *Homo Sacer* and *Operaismo*', in *Agamben and Radical Politics*, ed. Daniel McLoughlin (Edinburgh: Edinburgh University Press, 2016).
24. Agamben, *Use of Bodies*, pp. 274–5.
25. Giorgio Agamben, *The Kingdom and the Glory* (Stanford: Stanford University Press, 2011), pp. 142, 259.
26. Giorgio Agamben and Adriano Sofri, 'Un'idea di Giorgio Agamben', *Reporter*, 9–10 November 1985, pp. 32–3.
27. See Simon Critchley, *Faith of the Faithless: Experiments in Political Theology* (London: Verso Books, 2012), pp. 195–203.
28. Agamben, *Coming Community*, p. 53.
29. Jessica Whyte, *Catastrophe and Redemption* (Albany: SUNY Press, 2013), p. 120.
30. Saul Newman and John Lechte, *Agamben and the Politics of Human Rights* (Edinburgh: Edinburgh University Press, 2015), p. 112.
31. Rebecca Solnit, *Hope in the Dark: Untold Histories, Wild Possibilities* (Edinburgh: Canongate Books, 2016), pp. 77–82.
32. Ibid. p. 77.
33. Antonio Negri, *The Porcelain Workshop: For a New Grammar of Politics* (Los Angeles: Semiotext(e), 2008), p. 88.
34. Giorgio Agamben, *The Idea of Prose* (New York: State University of New York Press, 1995), p. 89.
35. Camus, *The Plague*, p. 185. I will here not discuss Camus's choice to allegorise sovereign violence and the Nazi occupation with a state of emergency caused by a disease. Like Sartre and Barthes have noted, Nazis can be held responsible for their crimes whereas pestilent bacteria are a mere force of nature. I agree with Ricœur that Camus's choice betrays that Camus is ultimately more interested in the metaphysical rebellion against God and the human condition than in actual political struggles. That should not, however, prevent us from reading him as a political thinker. See Jean-Paul Sartre, 'Réponse à Albert Camus', in Jean-Paul Sartre, *Situations IV* (Paris: Gallimard, 1964); Paul Ricœur, 'L'Homme révolté', in Paul Ricœur, *Lectures II: La Contrée des philosophes* (Paris: Seuil, 1992); Roland Barthes, 'La Peste: Annales d'une epidémie ou roman de la solitude?', in Roland Barthes, *Œuvres complètes I: 1942–1965* (Paris: Seuil, 1993).
36. Albert Camus, *The Rebel: An Essay on Man in Revolt* (New York: Vintage Books, 1991), pp. 188–252.
37. Ibid. p. 240.
38. Ibid. p. 238.
39. Ibid. p. 306.
40. Ibid. pp. 13–22.
41. Ibid. p. 237.
42. Ibid. p. 252. See also Arnaud Corbic, *Camus et l'homme sans Dieu* (Paris: Cerf, 2007), pp. 76–80.
43. See Albert Camus, *The Myth of Sisyphus* (New York: Vintage Books, 2018).
44. Camus, *The Rebel*, p. 10.
45. Ibid. p. 283.
46. Agamben (*Homo Sacer*, pp. 126–35) is more sceptical of human rights on the basis of two arguments. They, firstly, render individuals dependent on the political institutions

implementing or suspending these rights. From the moment one recognises a particular moral claim as a 'human right', one captures it within the legal order that relies on the sovereign's willingness to apply the law. The prevalence of the state of exception suggests that this will is less available than one would expect. Human rights, secondly, render modern politics unstable because they emphasise the question of who belongs to the 'human'. One is granted 'human rights' on the basis of one's belonging to humankind, but this entails that when an institution wishes to exclude a group from enjoying those rights, they have to exclude them from humanity as such.

47. Camus, *The Rebel*, p. 234.
48. Ibid. pp. 297–8.
49. Camus, *The Plague*, p. 208.
50. Albert Camus, 'Reflections on the Guillotine', in Albert Camus, *Resistance, Rebellion, and Death* (New York: Vintage Books, 2012).
51. Camus, *The Rebel*, pp. 15–16.
52. Ibid. p. 19.
53. Ibid. p. 22; translation modified.
54. Camus, *The Plague*, pp. 128–9.

Chapter 11

A Politics Like No Other: Agamben, Fanon and the Colonial Fracture

Susan Dianne Brophy

Fundamental to existentialist inquiry is the challenge of devising a meaningful politics based on the philosophical analysis of specific experiences.[1] While Giorgio Agamben wavers in the face of this challenge, Frantz Fanon does not, and the reason for this stems from how 'the other' and 'othering' configures each thinker's views on being and praxis. Agamben and Fanon deploy divergent existentialist frameworks – anti-humanist and humanist, respectively – which not only leads to differences in how they view the agency of the self in relation to the other, but also sheds light on why Fanon succeeds in the formulation of a far-reaching politics while Agamben falters.[2]

The aporia between 'being and acting, substance and praxis' appears often in Agamben's writings.[3] He comments that the total identification of being and praxis is the 'cosmos' of the divine absolute,[4] noting that when being is defined by praxis and praxis defined by being, the two become indistinguishable.[5] Beyond a metaphysical questioning of what it means to be and do, this indistinguishability obliges a deeper existentialist questioning of what can be done when the individual is made to live in estrangement to the self. As he grapples with this predicament across the nine volumes of *Homo Sacer*, the nimbleness of his philosophical mind is on display, but so, too, is a persistent blind spot. Despite the eclecticism of historical periods, interlocutors and allegories, the permutations of his existentialist inquiry amount to a repeated negation of the other that harbours a certain colonial logic.

As Agamben deconstructs the Western philosophical tradition, he acknowledges in a quintessentially existentialist tenor that 'what is at stake between [being and praxis] is the idea of freedom'.[6] The hyper-alienated figure of *homo sacer* is emblematic in this regard. Both internal to the self and between the self and institutional repositories of sovereign power (that is, state, city and church), what defines *homo sacer* is an individuated experience of the indistinguishability between being and praxis. The conceptual rendering of this phenomenon relies on an idiosyncratic Westernism, which allows Agamben to hoist atop the universalised 'Greco-Latin pedestal'[7] the meticulously conceived yet unexceptional experience of *homo sacer*.[8] With this, the *Homo Sacer* series ultimately accomplishes a meta performance of inclusive exclusion, which entails internalising or allegorising (that is, including) and ignoring or diagnosing (that is, excluding) the other. Because Agamben's existentialist treatment of being and praxis entails such othering, it endorses the thinnest conception of the human and leads to a limited politics.

To grasp the political limits of Agamben's anti-humanist existentialism, I turn to Fanon, which brings humanism into contact with the study of being and praxis.[9] Renowned for his contributions to psychoanalysis and his involvement in the Algerian War of Independence, it is Fanon's political philosophy that interests me here. His driving force was revolutionary anticolonialism; as such, there is an existential and not merely existentialist urgency to his writing. In *Black Skin, White Masks*, Fanon queries the colonised-other's dehumanising aspiration to be the coloniser-self, and in *The Wretched of the Earth*, he pens a treatise on the revolutionary praxis of becoming a human self – one that calls for collective struggle and a radical, universalist rethinking of what it means to be human. More than a polemical pose, Fanon's work exposes the fraudulence of the Western philosophical tradition by targeting those decadent ideas of self that trade (intentionally or not) on the vulgarity of othering. His account of the contextually specific experiences of racialised, colonised individuals indicts the praxis of othering that constrains being, which leads him to a comprehensive politics: an ethical universalism that emanates from differentiated human experiences, has a vision of human solidarity and strives for rehumanising praxis writ large.[10]

To support these claims, I trace Agamben's existentialist treatment of being and praxis across the *Homo Sacer* series, highlighting the import of the realm of non-relation and stressing its provenance as a fascistic ontology.[11] From there, I examine similar themes in Fanon's work, which involves an assessment of his existentialist proclivities to arrive at a notion of radical relationality. Finally, through a mix of comparative analysis and immanent critique, I conclude that, while Fanon defies the Manichaean fracture that separates the human from humanity, Agamben internalises it as a transcendental yet individuated phenomenon as the basis of his anti-humanist politics. Although he calls for a principled reimagining of non-relation as the basis of a radical politics, I show that non-relationality both underpins and connects fascism and colonialism; on this basis, I argue that there is reason to be doubtful about the type of anti-humanist politics that can emanate from a recuperation of non-relationality that neither acknowledges this connection nor addresses its specific challenges. In view of what results from these divergent frameworks, therefore, readers of Agamben interested in applying his politics more broadly to decoloniality may consider treading carefully.

Non-Relation as Potentiality

In his multivolume existentialist commentary on being as the vanishing ground of praxis and praxis as the vanishing ground of being, Agamben investigates different pathways to arrive at the potentiality of the truly political act. Methodologically speaking, he relies on a triadic formulation that involves variations of the same three manoeuvres: discovery of an originary fracture; identification of a threshold experience in the midst of said fracture; and a commentary on the violence that results from attempts to close this fracture. To disrupt the fracture–threshold–violence triad, he advocates pausing at the threshold – what he refers to as stasis, idleness, deactivation or inoperativity – in order to resist the violent collapse of being and praxis and to keep intact the realm of non-relation as potentiality.

Non-relation, as a liminal or threshold experience, proves central to how Agamben wrests ethics and politics from the perverse fate of being and praxis. To explain the significance of the non-relation, I proceed not according to the year of publication, but according to the post hoc ordering of the *Homo Sacer* series. This linearity does not reflect the actual evolution of the concepts in question, but it speaks best to Agamben's curatorial intent as he examines the potentiality of the liminal. Across varied iterations of being and praxis (that is, being, existence, facticity, life and praxis, act, practice, habit, use), each imperfect synonym adds another layer to his study. None ever finds its equivalent, and that is the point. It is not a matter of understanding the irreducibility of each concept in so far as being is irreducible to existence or that praxis irreducible to action, but to comprehend the aporia between being and praxis as a generative realm of non-relation.

In the first volume, Agamben explores the *zoē/bios* fracture.[12] The beingness of *zoē* is suspended to produce the citizen as *bios*, an instance of abandonment that both entails the realisation of *zoē* as potentiality and makes possible that prototypically 'modern' species of sovereign power, namely biopolitics.[13] The formative idea in this architecture of sovereignty, most evident at its fascistic extremes, is the non-relation. Variably referred to as the 'ban' or 'suspension',[14] non-relation is the backdrop for the constitutive void – that aporetic realm where cause and consequence become indistinguishable. In this 'zone of indistinction in which *zoē* and *bios* constitute each other in including and excluding each other',[15] sovereign praxis reaches its most violent ends. This is because the realm of non-relation is also the realm of pure immediacy – a 'reactionary decisionist model of sovereignty'[16] that Agamben identifies as the ontological root of fascism. Consider that value (as the qualified expression of worth, moral or otherwise) is conditional on the experience of a relation, but in the non-relational realm there is no such condition, and accordingly, no basis upon which one can ascertain the value of anything, not even life. When 'the experience of facticity' is 'immediately political', the body is indistinguishable from politics, and the concentration camp 'becomes the absolute political space' wherein the value of life is immediately non-value.[17] If sovereign praxis in the realm of non-relation produces the camp, what can be done? The immediacy of the absolute decision as negation must itself be negated (that is, double negation)[18] and turned into pure undecidability. This appeal to undecidability is a safeguard against the decisionism that equates life and non-value.

In *The State of Exception*, non-relation as the fount of sovereign praxis finds expression as inclusive exclusion, which he describes as '[b]eing-outside, and yet belonging'.[19] For law to have force, the norms that validate law are suspended to create a 'double paradigm, which marks the field of law with an essential ambiguity'.[20] This is accompanied by the threshold experience of life, that is, life suspended as fact to create the grounds for the realisation of law. Law's suspension of life is a relation of 'pure inclusion',[21] the consequence of which (for state and self alike) is the fracture between 'concrete praxis' and the 'immediate reference to the real'.[22] This fracture Agamben sees as also generative in a political sense, as long as it remains as potentiality and not activated toward specific ends.[23] Such praxis must be unbounded and non-prohibitive, a realisation of idleness born from non-relation, which is typified by the title of the third instalment, *Stasis*. While analysing the relation between sovereign power and political membership, Agamben again deploys the diagnostic triad: fracture–threshold–violence. Here the exclusion of the family/*oikos* from the city/*polis* makes possible stasis as 'a threshold of indifference'.[24] Once the socio-political unit of citizen emerges, so, too, does 'the people' as an undifferentiated mass that forms the body of the state (or Leviathan).[25] Of particular interest for Agamben are the 'theological roots'[26] of this fracture, which he explores across the three subsequent volumes.

At first in *The Sacrament of Language*, God (unlike the state later on) is pure identification of authority and action, of the word and praxis 'in which essence and existence coincide',[27] whereas man is fractured as 'living being' and 'speaking being', a liminality between life and politics.[28] Later, in *The Kingdom and the Glory*, what was once united in God is split in theology to produce a 'fracture between being and praxis', the result of which is anarchic power wherein 'praxis does not have any foundation in being'.[29] The 'machine of government' finds its purpose in this fracture[30] as it strives for a 'functional correlation' between the absolute and the contingent.[31] This correlation closure houses the anarchic roots of fascist praxis; non-relational in a manner akin to the unitary notion of God, its totalising power operates most violently because it is praxis 'without foundation'.[32] The consequences of this correlation are the subject of *Opus Dei*. Agamben explains that when effect alone is taken as 'real', being and praxis become indistinguishable:[33] 'being is resolved into praxis and praxis is substantiated into being'.[34] In this morass of disempowerment he recognises the appeal of free will as a calling in modern political philosophy, but he mourns its conscription by Kant, whose content-free self exercises will as a compulsive 'duty-to-be',[35] and, as such, portends the foundationless 'functional correlation' characteristic of the state of exception.[36]

The shift in *Remnants of Auschwitz* from the divine to the human allows Agamben to ground this suspicion of the compulsive 'duty-to-be' in the context of the camp, a site where the anarchic, non-relation attains extreme effectiveness as 'pure praxis'.[37] In this instalment he conveys the depths of the dehumanising experience of pure praxis that emanates from the non-relational. *Muselmann* is the pure effect of anarchic power, a non-value wrought by totalising operativity that brings into reality the non-human,[38] that is, 'the Being of death'.[39] Enclosed in the circular dissolution of being and praxis is 'Being of death', but it is in this fracture between the living and speaking, or 'the inhuman and the human', that Agamben locates the potentiality of human being once again.[40] This is manifest in his identification of the witness as the exemplary political subject. As the remnant in-betweenness of the human and inhuman, the witness is the 'pure existence' of the possibility of 'enunciation', which exists when the compulsive 'duty-to-be' is negated.[41] Notably, however, the witness is an individuated self-witness, which hints at why Agamben concludes that 'subjectivity' is the battlefield of dehumanising biopolitical praxis.[42] This subjectivity experiences otherness as the threshold experience of the self as non-being, and to dwell as a pure self-referent other is to keep intact the potentiality of the non-relation.

From the exercise of sovereign praxis as the absolute dissolution of being in the context of the camp, Agamben switches focus in the penultimate volume of the series. When he analyses the lifeworld of Franciscan monks in *The Highest Poverty*, he locates a new outcome for the aporia between being and praxis, namely the possibility of 'form-of-life'. Instead of sovereign praxis and the compulsive 'duty-to-be' operating as the vanishing ground of being, there is a 'neutralization and transformation' of life and rule into 'form-of-life'.[43] He explains how the friars are not compelled by the 'normal' force of law, and, as such, can reverse the fated collapse of being and praxis commonly experienced by those in the state of exception,[44] the consequence of which is the inoperativity of law and the liberation of 'existential reality'.[45] This rupture in the sovereign's use of the body as the repository of its power is discussed at length in the fittingly titled final volume, *The Use of Bodies*.

By calling on the 'use of self' to negate the non-being of compulsive praxis, 'use' for Agamben becomes 'a new figure of human praxis'.[46] To advance this vision, he opens with the Aristotelian notion of the slave as the absolute identification of use and body, explaining that 'in using the body of the slave, the master is in reality using his own body'.[47] This total internalisation of the slave-other is a statement on the dehumanising attempts at mastering nature in capitalism, and it sets the tone for the final instalment by allegorising the slave-other as an experience of the 'return of the repressed'.[48] The slave only 'represents' but never is,[49] and, as such, is both an apt portrayal of bare life and an ideal starting point from which to contemplate what it means to use the body absent compulsive praxis. Use – not as mastery but as the threshold of undecidability between exploit and habit[50] – is the neutralising factor that keeps intact the potentiality of being and praxis by never exhausting one in the other.[51] Later identifying 'contemplation as use-of-oneself',[52] Agamben does not turn to free will as other Western philosophers do when the self is in crisis,[53] but to contemplation as inoperativity. This contemplative deactivation is necessary so that he can keep intact the being-in-use 'for another's end' of the slave without the compulsive possessiveness of the master.[54]

In the second part of the book, Agamben charges once more on to the battlefield of subjectivity.[55] He reasserts that the effective praxis of being is the basis of existence,[56] and that this becoming of existence (as an effect of the praxis of being) compels a remapping of ontology away from the assumed primacy of the already-existent subject. Instead of rushing to simplify the ambiguity that arises from the futurity of existence and the historicity of being, he delineates the parameters of a 'modal ontology' and exalts ambiguous in-betweenness.[57] Once unfixed from a reductive relation to substance, Agamben explains, being can be rethought as 'mode' and praxis as the modifications of beingness.[58] In the third part of the book, he advances modal ontology as a politics and he ends where the series began: thematising the split between *zoē* and *bios* as 'determinate for the history of Western humanity'.[59] In this finale, Agamben explains potentiality as the *'possibilities* of life'.[60] Through the always becoming of 'form-of-life',[61] the scission between *zoē* and *bios* is abandoned to produce their immediacy and a new triadic modal-point (replacing violence):[62] fracture–threshold–form-of-life.

Throughout the series, the politics that Agamben has in mind is an invite to inoperativity born of non-relation. On multiple occasions, he acknowledges the fascist valence of the realm of the non-relation, where sovereign praxis engenders the non-value of life. What 'determines the bare life of *homo sacer*' is the decisive closure of the original triadic formulation.[63] To break open the absolutism of this functional correlation involves interrupting the compulsive 'duty-to-be', that is, to resist 'the passage from potency to effectiveness'.[64] Principled stasis therefore serves as a break in the fascist circuit that closes the originary fracture, ensuring that the potentiality of the non-relation does not immediately become pure praxis. This modification of the triad entrenches non-relation as the wellspring of potentiality, as Agamben states: '[f]orm-of-life is this ban that no longer has the form of a bond or an exclusion-inclusion of bare life but that of an intimacy without relation'.[65] Come the end of the series, non-relation is ensconced as the generative core of Agamben's politics – having 'neutralized'[66] through abandonment the violence of 'every representation',[67] the compulsive 'duty-to-be' transforms to 'use of self', a form-of-life that entails non-appropriative becoming through contemplative praxis.

Despite its transformative aims, I posit that non-relational inoperativity is not compatible with an anticolonial politics, in part because Agamben's neutralisation schematic assumes a definite experience of the fracture, and, by extension, a specific type of being and praxis. A turn to the writings of Fanon lends weight to this claim.

Radical Relationality as Politics

Fanon identifies a division in existentialist thought between decadent ennui and restive rehumanisation, and he uses these referents to explain the sense of futility that saturates being and praxis in the colonial context. Through trenchant readings of Hegel and Sartre,[68] what emerges is a radical relationality that is the cornerstone of his anticolonial politics. This is not a politics of secreted othering, be it allegorised abandonment or violent appropriation, but a politics that centres the other and commits to working through, with, and towards the human.

Indicative of his own coming into self-reflexive political consciousness,

Fanon exhibits a predilection for Sartrean existentialism in the penultimate section of *Black Skin, White Masks*, which sets the terms of his commentary on Hegel's Master–Slave relation. It occurs during his analysis of the works of Austrian psychologist Alfred Adler, who states that 'the feeling of inferiority arises from a social maladjustment'.[69] Fanon contends that the Adlerian approach internalises and individuates disorders with little attention to the context in which these circumstances arise. To prove this, he applies Adler's framework to the Antilles.[70] This leads him to reject the Adlerian approach because it functions to decontextualise and render chronic the complexes of superiority and inferiority that it purports to diagnose.[71] The cognitive dissonances of Antilleans are shown not to be the result of internalised 'social maladjustment' on an individual basis inasmuch as they are necessitated by the fact of being a racialised and colonised other. He insists that it is society that is maladjusted and argues the necessity of exhuming the longing for whiteness.[72] Through humanist existentialism, Fanon dissects the desire for the *masque blanc* and interrogates how blindness towards the violence of othering abides this self-defeating desire.

For Fanon, Hegel's Master–Slave dialectic is archetypal in this blindness. Hegel explains that over the course of the realisation of mutual recognition between two consciousnesses, that of the self and the other, the pure abstraction from existence demonstrates a willingness to risk one's life to 'raise their certainty of being *for themselves* to truth'.[73] The struggle that ensues between life and death produces recognition of self-consciousness that Hegel insists has an equalising effect on the self in relation to the other. Fanon contends that, following the dissolution of the Master–Slave relation, there still is no reciprocated struggle between the self and the other when this relation is cast in racial terms of black and white.[74] After the master grants the slave's freedom, the entitlements that might flow from this liberty are bestowed on blacks in so far as whites permit them to be. From the outset, blacks come into being according to an alien and self-alienating value system;[75] from this violent othering, their beingness is withheld and their praxis is futile. Whereas Hegel's version of the slave finds freedom – that is, consciousness '*for itself*' as objectivity – in work,[76] Fanon's image of the slave is one that wants to be like the master, as evinced in a desire for the *masque blanc*.

Fanon's revolutionary recasting of the Hegelian Master–Slave dialectic targets the assumptions about consciousness that arise from its separation from contextual specificity and halts the march towards the idealist absolution of the self at the expense of the other. As he continues to sharpen this perspective over the course of his engagement with Sartre, this proves to be fertile ground for a rehumanising politics.[77] Sartre insists against Hegel that being is not a phenomenal representation of a pure essence, but that 'our being is immediately "in situation"',[78] and questions if it is possible to overcome the 'ontological separation' of self and other in a truly reciprocal manner.[79] For Hegel, the only way to unify these two poles in the negation of self-negating alienation is to absolve oneself of any singular perspective so that it is possible to adopt a transcendental consciousness. But, for Sartre, this idealist contortion negates the situatedness of being – '*au contraire*', he argues, 'I must . . . establish myself in my being and pose the problem of the Other from the standpoint of my being.'[80] Where Sartre sees idealist solipsism as generating false truths about being, Fanon sees the violence of this perspective. It is less about an existentialist dispute over the idealist pretensions of the self, and more about making the freedom of the slave conditional on the master's will. Such material differences in power underscore the unequal capacity to engage in othering, which animates Fanon's distrust of recognition as the ends of politics.[81]

Sartre's existentialist position – radical in so far as it universalises the possibility of a will to freedom[82] – cannot account for the overarching factors that differentiate experiences of alienation and complicate appeals to recognition. For this reason, when Sartre asks in 'Orphée noire', '"[w]hat do you expect when you remove the gag from the blacks' mouths? That they would sing your praises? These heads that our fathers made bow to the ground with force, do you think, once they stood upright, you might read adoration in their eyes?"', Fanon responds, 'I do not know, but I say that he who looks in my eyes for something other than perpetual interrogation should look elsewhere; neither gratitude nor hate.'[83] He answers Sartre by being clear about what he will not see in his eyes, precisely those sentiments that unreflexively reproduce the oppressive structure of contingent being and impotent praxis. In other words, Sartre will not see the *masque blanc*. For this to be possible, Fanon devotes himself to 'interrogation perpétuelle' as the beginning and end points of a rehumanising praxis. In pursuit of this objective, he endeavours to situate the individual (as variably a self and an other), and understand the immediate experience, yet connect the individual to the realm beyond the particular.[84]

By treading between universalism and particularism, he differentiates but connects the coloniser and colonised, an approach that resists imperially infused universalist proclivities as well as self-destructive relativism.[85] This is evident in his understanding that neither national consciousness[86] nor negritude are enough to sustain the revolutionary appetite of the masses;[87] as he explains across his writings, emancipatory praxis requires thought and action beyond the regurgitation of imposed universalism and enclosed relativism.[88]

At the end of *Black Skin, White Masks*, he states: '[e]ncouraging man to be *actionary*, while maintaining his respect for fundamental values that constitute the human world, this is the primary urgency for somebody who, after reflecting, learns to act'.[89] Fanon has in mind a specific form of self-reflexive praxis as the universal liberator, but he does not abandon the colonial context. In *A Dying Colonialism* (*L'An V de la révolution algérienne*), he comments that the development of the political consciousness of the oppressed, which takes flight by engaging in the struggle for liberation, cultivates an awareness of one's place in the world.[90] In *Toward the African Revolution*, he contemplates the matter of solidarity among the colonised with a more exacting focus. He argues that the short-sighted analysis of an event tends to lead to contradictory conclusions because not enough attention is given to the 'organic' links that connect that single event to its surroundings within a particular historical context.[91] One example he mentions is the need to connect the liberation of the colonised and the struggles of the exploited working classes on a global scale.[92] He sees the emancipation of both as dialectically related, given that the exploited workers of the imperial countries struggle against the same oppressive agents as do the colonised, but that this is a point that is often overlooked by both sides. By *The Wretched of the Earth*, Fanon writes of 'a sort of collective effort, a common destiny at the level of underdeveloped men',[93] which connects emancipatory struggles across localities. He also offers the firmest declaration that in emancipatory praxis – the unabstracted doing – the colonised 'thing' is rehumanised.[94]

What unites each of these iterations of praxis is the revolutionary import of relationality. Fanon looks to the critical capacity of individuals to make sense of those relations that differentiate and connect the self and the other, and in doing so, summons *interrogation perpétuelle* as multileveled rehumanisation, thus: '[i]t is not enough to fight for the liberty of your own people. During the entire span of the conflict, it is necessary to re-learn about the people and above all else to re-learn about yourself and the full dimension of man.'[95] Engagement in meaningful, far-sighted praxis begins with an understanding of one's place in relation to the immediate context, recognising that this immediacy of being is also global in scope. This amounts to an appeal to act on the basis of one's own experiences but not in a reactionary or reductive manner.[96] What he offers is an existentialism that is informed as much by individuated experiences and shared history as it is by the idea of a common political future: the 'individual must endeavor to assume the universalism inherent in the human condition' at the same time that rehumanising praxis reflects 'place' in a 'most materialist sense'.[97] Because Fanon has an explicit political undertaking in mind, his writings on the universality of human experience are neither idle musings nor without nuance. He is interested in uncovering how the colonised encounter the coloniser from different positions, at the same time making it clear that not every Black will see themselves in these depictions, but nor will every white.[98]

What makes Fanon's politics of relationality radical is the insistence that being is not merely an atomised, interrogating self, but also a humanised, interrogated other. Far from an idealist retreat into the innermost enclosures of self-consciousness, he sees rehumanising praxis as a laborious unravelling of 'partial, limited, unstable truths',[99] an undertaking guided by 'common ends' that operates also as a condition of being in the world. It takes the immediate as a given but not as absolute 'truth',[100] and values a contextualised understanding of what constitutes the specific experiences. The emphasis on the particular calls the individual back to account for how truths prevail in the specific context; this approach is always upsetting and undercutting, and it supports the *interrogation perpétuelle* required by anticolonial politics.[101]

Without this check, parasitic Western values enshrine practices of dehumanisation in a self-alienating logic.[102] Fanon challenges this petrified worldview that expedites its own destruction, writing, '[l]et us decide to not imitate Europe and tense our muscles and our brains in a new direction. Let us attempt to invent a total man that Europe has been incapable of achieving.'[103] The mimetic man would be prone to narcissism because of his uncritical, inward orientation; conversely, far-reaching political praxis must also be rehumanising praxis, and, as such, it cannot be individuated, abstracting or selective. On this, Fanon is insistent while Agamben falters.

The Fracture as Manichaeism

Lost in Agamben's quest to understand the sanctification of the profane (and vice versa) is the correlation between the age of Christian *imperium* and modern biopower.[104] When made explicit, this connection foregrounds the colonial *qua* imperial dimensions of the fracture.[105] For instance, on the order of Emperor Constantine in AD 325, bishops convened and decided that the Son of God, like God, has no foundational being – an interpretation that was affirmed in AD 343 under Constantine II. Agamben elevates this moment, stating that only by understanding 'this original "anarchic" vocation of Christology' is it possible to make sense of 'the history of Western philosophy, with its ethical caesura between ontology and praxis'.[106] As he expounds on the ramifications of this 'theological division between being and praxis',[107] he loses sight of the fact that this split was 'imposed by Constantine',[108] who is recognised in recent scholarship as an innovator of administrative control.[109] Notably,

Constantine appointed 'bishops as instruments of justice by authorizing them to resolve legal disputes',[110] and once he installed himself as the sole emperor of the East and West, his edicts combined with bureaucratic decision-making to help legitimise his authority across the empire.[111] The content of the decision was not necessarily more salient than the form of the decision-making: the spectacle of representative bishops converging for a public debate validated Constantine's authority, while the fracture itself was an imposition of his will as emperor.[112]

In this light, the apparently '"anarchic" vocation of Christology' was the product of a deliberate political decision arrived at as a measure of maintaining *imperium* over feuding religious sects and a culturally heterogeneous empire in decline. Against the notion that Christian theological disputes bestowed an essential even transcendental caesura on Western philosophy, this is evidence that the practical exercise of Christian *imperium* at least facilitated the fracture as a colonial *qua* imperial technique of governance in the first instance. Such techniques matured during the Renaissance-era discovery of the 'New World' and Enlightenment-era writings on civility, which fuelled the shared dehumanisation that motivated enslavement and colonialism alike.[113]

Yet when Agamben discusses the camp as a foremost example of fascist biopower, he continues to overlook such historical context as well as conceptual continuities. Camps are pure effect, a corollary of the fabrication of a 'pure race'.[114] Persuasive arguments exist that connect these racialised tactics of the Third Reich to its colonial roots and ambitions,[115] which is crucial context for comprehending this instance of the fracture between the human and the inhuman. Likewise, it is significant that mere pages after Agamben explains the 'specificity of the National Socialist concept of race', he turns his attention to the 'Third World':

> today's democratico-capitalist project of eliminating the poor classes through development not only reproduces within itself the people that is excluded but also transforms the entire population of the Third World into bare life. Only a politics that will have learned to take the fundamental biopolitical fracture of the West into account will be able to stop this oscillation and to put an end to the civil war that divides the peoples and the cities of the earth.[116]

Like the camp, 'Third World' is 'pure praxis' or extreme effectiveness. Perceived here as an undifferentiated, passive mass, the 'Third World' is a consequence of Western 'development', which pitches the fascistic (if even *in potentia*) ontology of the 'biopolitical fracture of the West' on a global, emphatically colonial scale. From his understanding of the origins of the fracture, Agamben is right to say that a minimum requirement for meaningful politics is a reckoning with the dehumanising effects of this

Western blight. But to prove Agamben right is to show that the way he takes this world historical fracture 'into account' corresponds to the limits of his anti-humanist politics: without the humanism of radical relationality, it is difficult to address the persistent insidiousness of a colonial logic.

Agamben essentialises the fracture as a transcendental event, which he describes as the 'original "anarchic" vocation of Christology'. This elevates the fracture into a suprahuman realm, an ahistorical interpretation that entrenches the fracture, invites fatalism and undermines efforts to reverse the fascistic ontology at its root. The consequences of this timid reckoning with the colonial dimensions of the fracture are evinced in four shortcomings.

First, suspension is not eradication, but, given the transcendentalised nature of the fracture, it is the best that Agamben can offer. Each iteration of the fracture entails a break between being and existence, which induces and is induced by a disaffecting praxis.[117] Contemplative deactivation is meant as an antidote to its most violent effects, and although it produces the conditions for the liberation of 'existential reality', the suspension also safeguards the fracture in the first instance – the same fracture that, in its 'modern' enactment, has as its core the colonial scission between the human and inhuman. For non-relation to enshrine the potentiality of inoperativity as a politics, it must take the originary fracture as a given if only to suspend it through contemplative deactivation. This gets to the illusory facet of Agamben's politics: inoperativity does not eliminate the fracture, so the fracture persists in an absolute sense even if its extreme effectiveness is deactivated. The indistinguishability that makes inoperativity possible therefore assumes the fracture. Fanon describes this type of violent, irrepressible split as Manichaean,[118] which is the term he uses when describing the spatial divide between the coloniser and the colonised. That Agamben renders the fracture integral to political praxis amounts to a Manichaeism taken to its ends through internalisation and stasis: the fracture becomes internalised as an existentialist quandary, suspended through contemplation while leaving the actual historical and political conditions of the divide unaccounted for. Because the colonial scission between the human and the inhuman persists in Agamben's schematic, this raises new questions about the source, scope and purpose of inoperativity.

Second, suspension as a political praxis is not realisable by those deemed 'inhuman' by the fracture – this is evident in Agamben's inclusive exclusion of the slave and the 'Third World'. Inoperativity as 'use-of-self' is pointless for those whose praxis is impotent because – per the provenance of the originary fracture – the inhuman has no self. Fanon refers to this as the white's imposition of an 'existential deviance' on Blacks,[119] and describes liminality not as potentiality but as damnation ('[n]ot yet white, no longer entirely black, I was damned').[120] In this light, the fracture and the praxis of principled deactivation may be the condition of potentiality for the human-self, but it is an immediate and redoubled damnation of the inhuman-other.

Third, if the integrity of the fracture precludes the political praxis of the non-being, then contemplative deactivation recentres the self in service of the self, and the political beingness of the other is akin to their dehumanisation in that it is a pure effect. The self's 'contemplation as use-of-oneself'[121] is what aborts the appropriative use of the inhuman-other.[122] Devoid of a direct pathway towards political praxis through their own agency, the inhuman-other's non-beingness cannot be suspended except secondarily, that is, as an effect of the Western self's praxis of contemplative deactivation. Useful as cautionary tales that lend ethical clout to Agamben's appeal for potentiality, allegorised non-beings remain pure effect even in his prescription for political praxis. The non-being of the other as pure effect of the fracture remains 'coiled, plundered'[123] and their praxis is futile awaiting the Western self's inoperativity. This is antithetical to the basic imperatives of an anticolonial politics, namely the demand to be seen, the necessity of seeing and the impulse to act.

Fourth, transcendental idealism obscures the exclusivity of Agamben's politics, which circuitously reinstates its universalisability. By insisting on the non-relational, he solicits the potentiality of the transcendental in a manner that forsakes situatedness in the name of idealism. This move vitiates the particularities intrinsic to the fracture and elevates, through a deactivation of relationality, potentiality as a universalisable politics. In conflict with its genealogical provenance, this assumes that all experiences of the biopolitical fracture lead to the type of pure interiority that (*ipso facto*) certifies inoperativity as a universalisable politics.[124] The only way to achieve this is to enclose the self within the fractured condition, making the ontologically impossible 'uncomplicated' perspective appear possible while falsely universalising 'the privilege of being "pure subject"'.[125] Fanon indicts the underlying duplicity of such thinking: 'bourgeois ideology, which proclaims an essential equality among men, self-corrects to stay logical with itself by inviting the sub-humans to humanize themselves according to the type of Western humanity that it embodies'.[126] Like Hegel and Sartre, Agamben voids that 'most materialist' specificity that Fanon speaks of as the foundation for rehumanising praxis. If the ontological condition of the possibility of inoperativity is the non-relation, then the politics of inoperativity has a colonial essence: it goes beyond what Sartre identifies as the white's freedom of 'seeing without being seen';[127] it comes down to not being seen and not having to see. To produce the conditions necessary for inoperativity, the realm of the non-relation must remain a paradigm of non-value achievable only through pure interiority.

Through 'contemplation as use-of-oneself', the aporia between being and praxis becomes reconfigured as the possibility of 'form-of-life', the result of deactivated self-negation in the name of 'properly human life'.[128] From within this rarefied realm, however, there is little room for the other to act on the self; the beingness of the other remains suspended and praxis futile – an imposed undecidability necessitated as a corollary of the self's inoperativity. This pure interiority runs contrary to humanist existentialism. Humanism of this variety expresses an ethical universalism,[129] specifically that the freedom of the self is reciprocally dependent on the freedom of the other, as Sartre states: 'it is not in turning inward, but always by searching outside of himself for that goal that is liberation, such a particular realization, that man will realize himself precisely as human.'[130] Given Agamben's anti-humanist tendency, one wonders what he considers 'properly human life' and whether the inward focus of his existentialism can deliver a comparable vision of liberation – one that can challenge both the colonial reach and the fascistic ontology of the West's 'biopolitical fracture'. Despite the volumes devoted to deactivating the circuits of the fascistic non-relation, non-relationality as 'form-of-life' remains, at best, a politics fit for a narrowly conceived liberal juridical subject in the West;[131] at worst, it offers no significant role for the other that is not primarily in service of the self, making it antithetical to human solidarity[132] and, likewise, unfit for far-reaching, anticolonialist politics.

Instead of interrogating the source and ends of the fracture itself, Agamben indulges the essential othering it entails, idealising as a playful impotence the violent potency of a universalised self. Along the way, he neutralises the colonial inheritance of the fracture, which allows him to exalt the aporia as potentiality, but it has the effect of disinheriting the inhuman-other of their agency. While his politics glorify the self's ability to assign new meaning to non-value, this quest to re-signify negation is why he does not take 'into account' the extent to which othering remains a colonial albeit obscured corollary of pure interiority. The principled stasis he champions is akin to that which Fanon rebukes:

> today, we are assisting in a stasis of Europe. Let us flee, comrades, this immobile movement where the dialectic, little by little, transforms itself into the logic of the status quo. Revisit the question of man. Revisit the question of intellectual reality, the intellectual mass of all humanity that must multiply its connections, diversify its networks, and rehumanize its messages.[133]

Complicity in the stasis of Europe is complicity in the coloniser's logic, that is, the logic of non-relation that is a condition of not having to see or be seen. For Agamben, 'immobile movement' is the goal of his politics; for Fanon, the task 'of all humanity' is to 'multiply its connections, diversify its networks' – to fortify, not obviate human relationality. He argues the need to move past imposed antinomies and any complicit logic that both pathologises and glorifies the desire for the *masque blanc*.[134] An anticolonialist taking 'into account' of the fracture exposes the connection between complicit logic and dehumanising Manichaeism – a Manichaeism that safeguards the damnation of being and impotence of praxis.

Conclusion

Agamben shows that reactionary politics can arise from the compulsive 'duty-to-be';[135] he notes the role of race in demarcating the human from the inhuman;[136] and he finds that when sovereign power takes the biological being as immediately political, such is the foundation of 'modern' biopolitics.[137] But beyond the obvious paradox of attempting to render operative (through application to colonial contexts) the purposeful inoperativity that is the cornerstone of Agamben's politics, the hazards of doing so run deeper.

The experience of a fractured self need not be thought of as one that is exclusive to the Western individual – the title *Black Skin, White Masks* proves as much – yet the historical contextualisation of that experience matters. The limit of Agamben's politics is that he takes as a given that which drives the dehumanising imperatives of Western excess and elevates it as the bedrock of a political praxis: the non-relation. Agamben's inoperativity does not meet the minimum requirements for an anticolonial politics: the condition of its universality is the erasure of situatedness; its driving force to safeguard the realm of non-relation is inimical to solidarity-building; and it trades on a dangerous complicity with the realm of non-relation that is also the wellspring of fascism. Against Fanon's radical relationality, the perilous complicity of Agamben's politics is evident.

Notes

1. Robert Bernasconi, 'Situating Frantz Fanon's Account of Black Experience', in *Situating Existentialism: Key Texts in Context*, ed. Jonathan Judaken and Robert Bernasconi (New York: Columbia University Press, 2012), p. 338.
2. Because I focus on anticolonialism (rather than postcolonialism) and their divergent politics, there are affinities between Agamben and Fanon that I do not discuss, such as necropolitics, for which see Achille Mbembé, 'Necropolitics', trans. Libby Meintjes, *Public Culture* 15.1 (2003) and Marcelo Svirsky and Simone Bignall (eds),

Agamben and Colonialism (Edinburgh: Edinburgh University Press, 2012). If read as a theoriser of dehumanisation, Agamben's work can illuminate aspects of colonial relations, but the arc of coherence across his series is debatable when reconsidered through the lens of his politics, as I argue herein.
3. Giorgio Agamben, *The Kingdom and the Glory: For a Theological Genealogy of Economy and Government*, trans. Lorenzo Chiesa and Matteo Mandarini (Stanford: Stanford University Press, 2011), p. 53.
4. Ibid.
5. Giorgio Agamben, *Opus Dei: An Archaeology of Duty*, trans. Adam Kotsko, vol. II, 5, *Homo Sacer* (Stanford: Stanford University Press, 2013), p. 81. An example Agamben cites is the priest and his duties: he becomes a priest in performance of duties, while dutiful acts arise from his being a priest. One is not a priest if not performing priestly duties.
6. Ibid. p. 59.
7. Edward Said, *Culture and Imperialism* (New York: Vintage Books, 1993), p. 268.
8. 'Unexceptional' in the sense of undifferentiated, but I use this term also to underscore the thematic of the indistinguishability between rule and the exception that appears across Agamben's works.
9. This 'anti-humanism' is the bedrock of poststructuralism and postmodernism, which focus less on individual agency in favour of a deconstructive or genealogical analysis of the structural and discursive foundations of power. Post-colonialists likewise adopt this critique in response to Fanon's humanist politics; see, for example, Homi K. Bhabha, 'Remembering Fanon: Self, Psyche, and the Colonial Condition', in *Rethinking Fanon: The Continuing Dialogue*, ed. Nigel Gibson (Amherst, NY: Humanity Books, 1999).
10. This borrows from Ato Sekyi-Otu's 'partisan universalism', in which 'human requirements and possibilities' are 'the first and last word in our moral and political judgement'; see *Left Universalism: Africacentric Essays* (New York: Routledge, 2018), p. 82.
11. The realm of non-relation is the product of a type of fracture that appears in difference guises across Agamben's nine volumes, such as the fracture between *zoē* and *bios* (*Homo Sacer: Sovereign Power and Bare Life*, trans. Daniel Heller-Roazen (Stanford: Stanford University Press, 1998), p. 90), law and fact (*State of Exception*, trans. Kevin Attell (Chicago: University of Chicago Press, 2005), p. 1), or being and praxis (*The Kingdom and the Glory*, p. 59). This liminal zone is defined by undecidability and immediacy and is the source of both violence and potentiality throughout the *Homo Sacer* series. Because I focus on the connection between fascism and colonialism in this essay, I do not attend to the non-relation as the basis of sovereign power in (liberal) democratic contexts – although it is a subject that I explore in detail in my other publications on Agamben.
12. Agamben, *Homo Sacer*, p. 11.
13. Ibid. p. 153.
14. Ibid.
15. Ibid. p. 90.
16. William E. Scheuerman, 'Critical Theory and the Law', in *The Routledge Companion to the Frankfurt School*, ed. Peter E. Gordon, Espen Hammer and Axel Honneth (New York and London: Routledge, 2019), p. 489.
17. Agamben, *Homo Sacer*, p. 153.
18. Elsewhere, I brand this double negation a 'regressive logic', which in his earlier works produces a 'meaningless authenticity'; see Susan Dianne Brophy, 'Agamben and the Political Act: Traces of a Regressive Logic', *Constellations* 22.4 (2015); 'Meaningless Authenticity: The Ethical Subject in Agamben's Early Works', *Critical Horizons* 16.3 (2015). To a significant degree, this chapter is a continuation of both lines of thought.
19. Agamben, *State of Exception*, p. 35.

20. Ibid. p. 73.
21. Ibid.
22. Ibid. p. 37.
23. Ibid. p. 88.
24. Giorgio Agamben, *Stasis: Civil War as a Political Paradigm*, trans. Nicholas Heron (Edinburgh: Edinburgh University Press, 2015), p. 16.
25. Ibid. p. 37.
26. Ibid. p. 54.
27. Giorgio Agamben, *The Sacrament of Language: An Archaeology of the Oath*, trans. Adam Kotsko (Stanford: Stanford University Press, 2011), p. 50.
28. Ibid. p. 70.
29. Agamben, *The Kingdom and the Glory*, p. 64.
30. Ibid. p. 134.
31. Ibid. p. 141.
32. Ibid. p. 64.
33. Agamben, *Opus Dei*, p. xii.
34. Ibid. p. 55.
35. Ibid. p. 107.
36. I elaborate on the role of Kantian philosophy in the *Homo Sacer* series elsewhere; see Susan Dianne Brophy, 'Freedom without Being: Kant's Corrective as the Philosophical Crux of Agamben's "Homo Sacer" Series', *European Journal of Political Theory* 18.2 (2019).
37. Giorgio Agamben, *The Time That Remains: A Commentary on the Letter to the Romans*, trans. Patricia Dailey (Stanford: Stanford University Press, 2005), p. 28.
38. Giorgio Agamben, *Remnants of Auschwitz: The Witness and the Archive*, trans. Daniel Heller-Roazen (New York: Zone Books, 2002), p. 55.
39. Ibid. p. 75.
40. Ibid. p. 134.
41. Ibid. p. 146.
42. Ibid.
43. Giorgio Agamben, *The Highest Poverty: Monastic Rules and Form-of-Life*, trans. Adam Kotsko (Stanford: Stanford University Press, 2013), p. 107.
44. Ibid. p. 115.
45. Ibid. p. 136.
46. Giorgio Agamben, *The Use of Bodies*, trans. Adam Kotsko (Stanford: Stanford University Press, 2016), p. 30.
47. Ibid. p. 14.
48. Ibid. p. 21.
49. Ibid. p. 23.
50. Ibid. p. 87.
51. Ibid. p. 65.
52. Ibid. p. 64.
53. Ibid. p. 62.
54. Ibid. p. 75.
55. Ibid. p. 172.
56. Ibid. p. 137.
57. Ibid. p. 161.
58. Ibid. p. 175.
59. Ibid. p. 199.
60. Ibid. pp. 207–8.
61. Ibid. p. 227.
62. Ibid. p. 223.
63. Agamben, *Homo Sacer*, p. 153.
64. Agamben, *Opus Dei*, p. 128.

65. Agamben, *The Use of Bodies*, p. 236.
66. Ibid. p. 276.
67. Ibid. p. 237.
68. This is a selective sampling of existentialist philosophy and it reflects neither the breadth nor depth of Fanon's engagement with the field. Robert J. C. Young, 'Fanon, Revolutionary Playwright', in *Alienation and Freedom*, ed. Jean Khalfa and Robert J. C. Young, trans. Steven Corcoran (London, Oxford, New York, New Delhi and Sydney: Bloomsbury Academic, 2018), p. 13.
69. Alfred Adler, *The Science of Living* (Garden City, NY: Garden City Pub. Co, 1929), p. 64.
70. Frantz Fanon, *Peau noire, masques blancs* (Paris: Point, Éditions du Seuil, 1952), p. 171.
71. Ibid. p. 173.
72. Ibid. p. 179, especially 9n.
73. G. W. F. Hegel, *Phenomenology of Spirit*, trans. A. V. Miller (Oxford: Oxford University Press, 1977), p. 114.
74. Fanon, *Peau noire, masques blancs*, p. 176.
75. Ibid. p. 178.
76. Hegel, *Phenomenology of Spirit*, p. 119.
77. Nigel Gibson, *Fanon: The Postcolonial Imagination* (Cambridge and Oxford: Polity, 2003), p. 16.
78. Jean-Paul Sartre, *L'Être et le néant: Essai d'ontologie phénoménologique* (Paris: Éditions Gallimard, 1943), p. 74.
79. Ibid. p. 282.
80. Ibid.
81. Young, 'Fanon, Revolutionary Playwright', p. 43.
82. Jean-Paul Sartre, *L'Existentialisme est un humanisme* [1946], http://www.danielmartin.eu/Textes/Existentialisme.htm
83. Fanon, *Peau noire, masques blancs*, p. 23.
84. Lou Turner, '(E)Racing the Ego: Sartre, Modernity, and Fanon's Theory of Consciousness', *Parallax* 8.2 (2002): 50.
85. Ato Sekyi-Otu, *Fanon's Dialectic of Experience* (Cambridge, MA, and London: Harvard University Press, 1996), p. 21.
86. Christopher L. Miller reads Fanon as maintaining 'a context in which the confines of a nation are not problematic and in which everything is subordinate to national liberation'; see *Theories of Africans: Francophone Literature and Anthropology in Africa* (Chicago: University of Chicago Press, 1990), 47. This view stems from a discomfort with the way that Fanon negotiates the tension between universal humanism and colonial particularism, resulting in the perception that Fanon privileges the national at the expense of the universal. But it is not prudent to foist upon Fanon's work a reductive dimension where one does not exist; see Sekyi-Otu, *Fanon's Dialectic of Experience*, p. 33. While Fanon sees it as irresponsible to avoid the 'national question', this does not lead him to a reductive stagism; to read Fanon otherwise is to ignore the dialectical dimensions of his ontology and politics.
87. Aimé Césaire, *Cahier d'un retour du pays natal*, ed. Abiola Irele (Columbus: Ohio State University Press, 2000), p. 23. Negritude offers a scathing commentary on colonial racism and as an initial way of thinking through the confines of race relations in the French colonies. In *Peau noire*, Fanon disagrees with Sartre's dismissal of negritude as the black's negation of a negation, as only a 'weak' intermediary stage in the greater dialectic, Sartre, 'Orphée noir', p. xii. In *The Wretched of the Earth*, he concedes that there is a degree of political futility embedded in the perpetual retreat to nativism. Fanon's critical reworking of the Hegelian dialectic in 1952 leads him to eventually agree with Sartre on this point by 1961; see Azzedine Haddour, 'Sartre and Fanon: On Negritude and Political Participation', in *Sartre Today: A Centenary*

Celebration, ed. Adrian van den Hoven and Andrew N. Leak (Oxford and New York: Berghahn Books, 2005), p. 293.
88. Paul Nursey-Bray, 'Race and Nation: Ideology in the Thought of Frantz Fanon', *The Journal of Modern African Studies* 18.1 (1980): 140.
89. Fanon, *Peau noire, masques blancs*, p. 180.
90. Frantz Fanon, *L'An V de la révolution algérienne* (Paris: François Maspero, 1959), p. 51.
91. Frantz Fanon, *Pour la révolution africaine* (Paris: François Maspero, 1964), p. 167.
92. Ibid.
93. Frantz Fanon, *Les Damnés de la terre* (Paris: François Maspero, 1961), p. 150.
94. Ibid. p. 30.
95. Ibid. p. 224.
96. Fanon, *Peau noire, masques blancs*, pp. 9–10.
97. Ibid. p. 8. See also Sekyi-Otu, *Fanon's Dialectic of Experience*, p. 16.
98. Fanon, *Peau noire, masques blancs*, p. 9.
99. Fanon, *Les Damnés de la terre*, p. 150.
100. Sekyi-Otu, *Fanon's Dialectic of Experience*, p. 35.
101. Fanon, *Peau noire, masques blancs*, p. 23.
102. Fanon, *Les Damnés de la terre*, p. 224.
103. Ibid. p. 240.
104. For an account of the connections among settler-colonialism, Christianity and biopolitics from the sixteenth century, see Scott Lauria Morgensen, 'The Biopolitics of Settler Colonialism: Right Here, Right Now', *Settler Colonial Studies* 1.1 (2011): 61.
105. This is not a conflation of imperialism and colonialism, but an endorsement of Said's nuanced definitions: '"imperialism" means the practice, the theory, and the attitudes of a dominating metropolitan center ruling in a distant territory; "colonialism," which is almost always a consequence of imperialism, is the implanting of settlements on distant territory', *Culture and Imperialism*, p. 9.
106. Agamben, *The Kingdom and the Glory*, pp. 58–9.
107. Ibid. p. 60.
108. Ibid. p. 58.
109. John Dillon, *The Justice of Constantine: Law, Communication, and Control* (Ann Arbor: University of Michigan Press, 2012), p. 5.
110. Ibid. p. 10.
111. Hans A. Pohlsander, *The Emperor Constantine*, 2nd edn (London and New York: Routledge, 2004), p. 48; Dillon, *The Justice of Constantine*, p. 97.
112. David Potter, *Constantine the Emperor* (Oxford: Oxford University Press, 2015), pp. 233–4.
113. Aimé Césaire, *Discours sur le colonialisme* (Paris: Presence africaine, 1962); Norbert Elias, *The Civilizing Process: The History of Manners*, vol. 1 (New York: Blackwell, Oxford, and Urizen Books, 1978); Walter D. Mignolo, 'The Darker Side of the Renaissance: Colonization and the Discontinuity of the Classical Tradition', *Renaissance Quarterly* 45.4 (1992); Said, *Culture and Imperialism*; Anne McClintock, *Imperial Leather: Race, Gender, and Sexuality in the Colonial Contest* (New York: Routledge, 1995); Stuart Hall, 'The West and the Rest', in *Modernity: An Introduction to Modern Societies*, ed. Stuart Hall et al. (Cambridge, MA: Blackwell, 1996); Domenico Losurdo, *Liberalism: A Counter-History*, trans. Gregory Elliott (New York and London: Verso Books, 2011); Lisa Lowe, *The Intimacies of Four Continents* (Durham, NC, and London: Duke University Press, 2015).
114. Agamben, *Homo Sacer*, p. 146; see also Agamben, *Remnants of Auschwitz*, p. 85.
115. Patrick Bernhard, 'Colonial Crossovers: Nazi Germany and Its Entanglements with Other Empires', *Journal of Global History* 12.2 (2017); Thomas Kühne, 'Colonialism and the Holocaust: Continuities, Causations, and Complexities', *Journal of Genocide*

Research 15.3 (2013); Shelley Baranowski, *Nazi Empire: German Colonialism and Imperialism from Bismarck to Hitler* (Cambridge and New York: Cambridge University Press, 2010); Mark Mazower, *Hitler's Empire: How the Nazis Ruled Europe* (New York: Penguin Books, 2009).

116. Agamben, *Homo Sacer*, p. 180.
117. Captured by the claim that in the state of exception, 'existence is not a real predicate', see Agamben, *State of Exception*, p. 66.
118. Fanon, *Peau noire, masques blancs*, p. 36.
119. Ibid. p. 11.
120. Ibid. p. 112.
121. Agamben, *Use of Bodies*, p. 64.
122. Agamben, *Homo Sacer*, p. 180.
123. Frantz Fanon, *Les Damnés de la terre* (Paris: La Découverte, 2002), p. 52.
124. So all experiences of bare life are assumed to be the same in terms of non-relational value, which reflects the point I make in the introduction regarding unexceptional experience; see note 8.
125. Sekyi-Otu, *Fanon's Dialectic of Experience*, p. 71. This term 'uncomplicated' appears in Sekyi-Otu's book as a quoted translation of Jean-Paul Sartre's 'Orphée noir'. Sartre's original text refers to the white man as benefiting from 'regard pur'; Jean-Paul Sartre, 'Orphée noir' [1948], in *Anthologie de la nouvelle poésie nègre et malgache de langue française*, ed. Léopold Sédar Senghor, 5th edn (Paris: Quadrige/Presses universitaires de France, 2001), p. ix.
126. Fanon, *Les Damnés de la terre*, 2002, p. 158.
127. Sartre, 'Orphée noir', p. ix.
128. Agamben, *Use of Bodies*, pp. 273, 277–8. See also Susan Dianne Brophy, 'Immanuel Kant', in *Agamben's Philosophical Lineage*, ed. Adam Kotsko and Carlo Salzani (Edinburgh: University of Edinburgh Press, 2017), p. 168.
129. Sekyi-Otu, *Left Universalism*, p. 4.
130. Sartre, *L'Existentialisme est un humanisme*.
131. I offer this qualifier of 'narrowly conceived' because the Western provenance of the state of exception is, by definition, not universal. As such, the notion of 'bare life' that accompanies it has an historically and politically narrow range of applicability. For more on the essential contingency of Agamben's politico-legal subject (and, by extension, his politics), see Susan Dianne Brophy, 'Lawless Sovereignty: Challenging the State of Exception', *Social & Legal Studies* 18.2 (2009): 215; 'Freedom, Law, and the Colonial Project', *Law and Critique* 24.1 (2013): 43; 'Freedom without Being', p. 204.
132. On this point, Agamben's recent statements about the global pandemic are revealing. Unmindful of how the shared threat to existence can unite 'all humanity' and 'multiply its connections' (per Fanon), he asserts that '[b]are life – and the danger of losing it – is not something that unites people, but blinds and separates them'; see 'Giorgio Agamben: "Clarifications"', trans. Adam Kotsko, *An und für sich* (blog), 17 March 2020, https://itself.blog/2020/03/17/giorgio-agamben-clarifications/. While he is right to be concerned about the consequences of authoritarian fiats, his inattentiveness to the other means ignoring the practices and potential of human solidarity – that which is the wellspring of resistance to the very outcomes he fears – see Panagiotis Sotiris, 'Against Agamben: Is a Democratic Biopolitics Possible?', *Viewpoint Magazine* (blog), 20 March 2020, https://www.viewpointmag.com/2020/03/20/against-agamben-democratic-biopolitics/.
133. Fanon, *Les Damnés de la terre*, 2002, p. 303.
134. Fanon, *Peau noire, masques blancs*, p. 6.
135. Agamben, *Opus Dei*, p. 107.
136. Agamben, *Remnants of Auschwitz*, p. 85.
137. Agamben, *Homo Sacer*, pp. 47, 153.

Chapter 12

Dis/Belief in Agamben and de Silentio

Marcos Antonio Norris

Wading my way through Agamben's corpus some years ago, I was taken with the philosopher's treatment of Christian sources, both classical and scholastic. When taken together, Agamben's various engagements with the Christian tradition present an image of God that at first struck me as counterintuitive, an a/theistic depiction of divine nothingness that conflated the deity with a pure potentiality at the heart of language. My study of Agamben coincided with my study of Søren Kierkegaard who, under the pseudonymous authorship of Johannes de Silentio, presents Abraham as the exemplary father of faith. To my surprise – given the two authors' distance from each other as theoreticians, one being a nineteenth-century Protestant theologian and the other a twentieth-century political philosopher – I found that *Fear and Trembling* shared with Agamben's 2005 study *The Time That Remains* remarkable similarities in their portrayal of the Abrahamic faith. In particular, Agamben and Silentio share an understanding of *the universal* – for what Silentio describes in Danish as *sædelighed* Agamben identifies with the Greek *nomos* – and both view *the absolute* as an unmediated relationship with God.

This is significant because, in *Fear and Trembling*, Abraham forms a direct relationship with the absolute 'by means' of the universal, and it is likewise 'by means' of the universal that Abraham suspends (*aufheben*) the universal.[1] To my knowledge, this crucial detail – that both tasks are accomplished *by means* of the universal – is unaccounted for in the scholarship surrounding *Fear and Trembling*. According to Merold Westphal, the standard reading of *Fear and Trembling* is that Abraham chooses a direct relationship with the absolute *over against* the universal (which he describes as the laws and customs of normative society), not *by means* of the universal, and, likewise, it is through a teleological suspension of the universal that Abraham *circumvents* rather than *travels through* the universal in order to access the absolute, which cannot be mediated, Silentio asserts, by means of the universal. But the standard reading exemplified by Westphal fails to explain an ostensible contradiction: namely, how does Abraham access the absolute *by means* of the universal when the universal cannot mediate Abraham's relationship with the absolute, which is to say, how does Abraham access the absolute *by means* of the universal when the universal is explicitly *not* the means by which Abraham gains access to the absolute? According to the standard reading, the absolute cannot be mediated by the universal, and in fact the universal must be suspended for Abraham to access the absolute, as the two are fundamentally at odds, but, as Silentio very clearly states in *Fear and Trembling*, it is *by means* of the universal that Abraham forms a direct relationship with the absolute. Westphal and others overlook this crucial and as yet unaccounted-for detail that, in my judgement, unlocks a deeper understanding of Silentio's text. As readers of this chapter will discover, Agamben's reading of the Abrahamic faith in *The Time That Remains* explains how Abraham forms a direct relationship with God *by means* of the universal, and at the same time suspends the universal as the very means through which Abraham forms a direct relationship with the absolute. Agamben's insights help to explain what Kierkegaardian scholarship has no explanation for, opening a path into *Fear and Trembling* that transforms how we understand Silentio's treatment of the Abrahamic faith.

Considering the Ethical Universal as *Nomos*

For practical purposes, I begin with a discussion of *the universal*. As Silentio describes in Problem 1 of *Fear and Trembling*, Abraham is a knight of faith because he violates the universal in his obedience to the absolute. This is in contrast to Agamemnon, Jephthah and Brutus who, in their infinite resignation as tragic heroes, sacrifice their children for the greater good of society. Agamemnon sacrifices his daughter so that the Greeks can win the Trojan War, Jephthah sacrifices his daughter so that God will help him conquer the Ammonites, and, in similar manner, Brutus executes his sons for plotting against the state. In each of these cases, the so-called knight of infinite resignation prioritises the wellbeing of society over the individual lives of father and child because the universal is superior to the individual, who has an ethical obligation to the entire community. In this manner, the knight of infinite resignation violates one ethical obligation in the service of a higher ethical obligation and so 'remains within the ethical', Silentio writes; 'He lets one expression of the ethical find its *telos* in a higher expression of the ethical. The ethical relation between father and son, or daughter and father, he reduces to a sentiment which has its dialectic in its relation to morality.'² The *universal* thus refers to our highest ethical calling, a universal responsibility, that is, to serve society in the greatest possible way. 'The ethical is the universal', Silentio writes.³ The two are one and the same.

This distinction matters because, as Westphal explains in *Kierkegaard's Concept of Faith*, the 'main point' of *Fear and Trembling* 'comes in the contrast between the ethical and the religious, or, more concretely, between Abraham and Hegel'.⁴ For Hegel, the individual realises authentic selfhood within the ethical contours of society. But for Kierkegaard, who was both a student and fierce critic of Hegel, the individual's singularity dissipates within the ethical, which is fundamentally at odds with authentic selfhood. Mark C. Taylor rightly observes that '[w]hat Hegel sees as self-realization Kierkegaard sees as self-alienation, and what Hegel interprets as self-estrangement is for Kierkegaard self-fulfillment'.⁵ In Kierkegaard's *Stages on Life's Way*, the aesthetic way of life is succeeded by the ethical which is then succeeded by the religious. So, too, in *Fear and Trembling* does the individual restore authentic selfhood by establishing his singularity over against the ethical way of life, in which, for both Hegel and Kierkegaard alike, the individual dissipates. Thus, it is only by suspending the ethical universal that the single individual can form a direct relationship with the absolute, according to Silentio, who gives voice to this common Kierkegaardian theme. 'In fact, throughout his labyrinthine *oeuvre* Kierkegaard has given his readers ample and recurrent opportunities to understand his philosophy as essentially subjectivist,' Leo Stan writes, observing further that:

> One need only recall the metaphysical slogan of the *Concluding Unscientific Postscript*, 'subjectivity is truth;' or the famous diary entry where a restless young Kierkegaard decides to aim solely at that 'truth that is truth *for me*, [. . .] the idea for which I am willing to live and die.' Equally unforgettable is the fideistic axiom of *Fear and Trembling*, whose philosophical transposition purports that within the bounds of Judeo-Christianity 'the single individual is higher than the universal.'⁶

Understanding the ethical universal in contrast with the single individual is therefore of the utmost importance. The Abrahamic faith is a paradox for Silentio, precisely because it stands in conflict with the ethical universal, of which the child sacrifices carried out by Agamemnon, Jephthah and Brutus are the highest possible expression. Agamemnon, Jephthah and Brutus find ethical fulfilment within the universal, but Abraham is called to a higher task.

De Silentio uses the Danish equivalents *det sædelige* and *sædelighed*, respectively, for Hegel's *das Sittliche* and *Sittlichkeit*, both of which are ordinarily translated into English as 'ethical life'. *Sittlichkeit* is a nominalisation of *sittlich*, the adjectival or adverbial form of 'customary', and stems from *Sitte*, which can be translated into English as 'custom' or 'convention'. Reading Hegel's *The Phenomenology of Spirit, Philosophy of Right* and *Philosophy of Spirit*, Westphal defines the ethical life further as 'the laws and customs of one's people', noting that Silentio uses *Sædelighed* in reference to 'the nation, the state, society, the church, and the sect', such that 'ethical life', in Silentio's usage, refers to laws and customs both secular and sacred.[7] Hegel's English translator Terry Pinkard says that *Sittlichkeit* is a colloquial German word usually rendered as 'morality' by Kant's translators, but that, unlike Kant, Hegel deliberately uses *Sittlichkeit* in opposition to *Moralität*, which also translates as 'morality', in order to draw an important conceptual distinction.[8] *Sittlichkeit* does not refer to Kantian ethics, Platonic forms or natural law, which are all metaphysical in nature. Rather, 'Silentio wants to concentrate our attention, not on some generic notion of the ethical,' Westphal observes, 'but on that specific variety that makes the laws and customs of a particular society the highest norms for its members and seeks to transubstantiate this particularity into a universality.'[9] This is why Abraham's journey to Mount Moriah distresses Abraham, in Westphal's opinion; it is not because Abraham knows child sacrifice is morally wrong on metaphysical grounds, but because he is socialised to believe that child sacrifice is wrong. As Westphal writes, 'The world in which what [Abraham] intends is condemned as murder is a world in which he still lives.'[10] Murder may not actually be wrong in an absolute, metaphysical sense, but Abraham *believes* it to be wrong, and this is the critical distinction.

Himself a critic of Kantian ethics, Hegel argues that so-called categorical imperatives are themselves historically contingent societal constructs. Kierkegaard and Silentio agree with Hegel on this point, and this, according to Westphal, is why Kierkegaard's work is sometimes framed as an ideological critique. Westphal writes that:

> Marx and Engels will later put it this way: 'The ideas of the ruling class are in every epoch the ruling ideas, i.e. the class which is the ruling material force of society is at the same time its ruling intellectual force.' The only (crucial) difference between Marx and Engels on the one hand and Hegel and Kierkegaard on the other is that the latter pair, while thinking that 'reason' is always a reflection of a historically particular world, and therefore neither 'pure' nor utterly universal, do not put this in terms of economic classes but leave open the possibility of a wide variety of conditioning factors.[11]

Kierkegaard generalises ideological critique beyond a purely economic framework in much the same way that the Marxist critic Louis Althusser does in 'Ideology and Ideological State Apparatuses'. According to Althusser, the ideas of the ruling class are propagated not only through *Repressive State Apparatuses* like 'the police, the courts, the prisons; . . . the head of State, the government and the administration', but also through *Ideological State Apparatuses* like 'Churches, Parties, Trade Unions, families, some schools, most newspapers, [and] cultural venues, etc.'.[12] In Althusser's assessment, ideology pervades legal and state institutions in addition to a wide variety of discursive institutions and beyond, appearing in its purest form as *discourse* per se, the encompassing cultural narratives of our epoch.

In this sense, ideology is not simply *false consciousness*, as Marx would have it, which can be understood as a false perception or misunderstanding of the way things actually are, but instead refers, in Althusser's account, to beliefs that have been naturalised as self-evident, beliefs, in other words, that we immediately recognise as ahistorical and universally true. Moreover, ideology, for Althusser, is not something that one can escape, as it is the very basis of subjectivity, generating personhood through an immersive socialisation process that he refers to as the subject's *interpellation* or *hailing*. '[Y]ou and I are *always already* subjects, and as such constantly practice the rituals of ideological recognition, which guarantee for us that we are indeed concrete, . . . irreplaceable subjects', Althusser writes; 'The writing I am currently executing and the reading you are currently performing are also in this respect rituals of ideological recognition, including the "obviousness" with which the "truth" or "error" of my reflection may impose itself on you.'[13] Tracing the legacy of Hegel's *Sittlichkeit* through Marx and Althusser presents us with a more thorough understanding of the challenges facing Abraham. The single individual is subordinate to the universal because, in the borrowed words of Althusser, he is always already interpellated as a subject within the ethical, where child sacrifice automatically appears to Abraham as incontrovertibly wrong. The social construction of morality is naturalised in such a way that it appears to Abraham as ahistorical and universally true. For this reason, Abraham must suspend (*Aufhebung*) the universal if he is to obey God's call to sacrifice Isaac, through which he forms a direct relationship with the absolute.

As we have already established, the ethical universal, or Hegelian *Sittlichkeit*, is at odds with the absolute, which Silentio presents as an unmediated relationship with God, so readers of Silentio cannot simply reduce the absolute to an everyday religious experience, where, for example, the individual's encounters with divinity are mediated by such things as the church, its sacraments and liturgy, and the sacred scriptures. For Silentio, the absolute exists beyond religion as a cultural experience and even beyond culture as a semiotic system as something beyond our representational constructs altogether, be they secular or sacred in nature. Westphal defines *Sittlichkeit* as a 'historically particular community to which individuals belong and whose laws and customs are the norms for their lives'.[14] Hegel himself presents *Sittlichkeit* as the cultural matrix of laws, customs and conventions through which individuals realise their personhood as part of a collective consciousness.

Sittlichkeit overlaps with Agamben's use of the Greek term *nomos* (νόμος), which similarly translates into English as 'law', 'convention' or 'custom', and Agamben opposes *nomos* to the Greek term *physis* (φύσις), which translates into English as 'nature', to draw a distinction between nature and culture, law and lawlessness, that leaves his readers with an encompassing view of jurisprudence. Generally speaking, *nomos* refers to the legal systems of particular governments and organisations, but, on a more fundamental level, *nomos* refers to *difference*, in Agamben's use of the term, to language as a system of differences, and, concomitantly, to the representational divisions that give structure to our world. Given the remarkable similarities between *nomos* and *Sittlichkeit*, it should come as little to no surprise that Agamben credits Hegel with first unveiling the exclusionary nature of representation, which in turn founds the sovereign division of citizen and bare life. As Agamben writes in *Homo Sacer: Sovereign Power and Bare Life*:

> Hegel was the first to truly understand the presuppositional structure thanks to which language is at once outside and inside itself and the immediate (the nonlinguistic) reveals itself to be nothing but a presupposition of language. 'Language', he wrote in the *Phenomenology of Spirit*, 'is the perfect element in which interiority is as external as exteriority is internal.' . . . We have seen that only the sovereign decision on the state of exception opens the space in which it is possible to trace borders between inside and outside and in which determinate rules can be assigned to determinate territories.[15]

All laws are culturally constructed representations that contain the seeds of their own undoing, the pure potentiality concealed within our representational constructs that Agamben and Hegel identify here with a presuppositional structure. It is only when this linguistic system of differences is mistaken for a transparent description of the way things actually are that culturally constructed representations of the world are wrongly perceived as legally binding metaphysical truths. Under this mistaken perspective, sovereignty authorises its own vision of the world as lawful. 'Language is the sovereign who, in a permanent state of exception, declares that there is nothing outside language and that language is always beyond itself', Agamben writes, but '[t]he particular structure of law', and of representational difference, which should be carefully understood, in light of its political consequences, is that legal authority rests 'in this presuppositional structure of human language. It expresses the bond of inclusive exclusion to which a thing is subject because of the fact of being in language, of being named. To speak [*dire*] is, in this sense, always to "speak the law," *ius dicere*.'[16] Cultural representations marginalise their victims through an inclusive exclusion that carries the force of law under this metaphysical domain, but all laws conceal within themselves a presuppositional structure that threatens their undoing and deauthorisation. *Sittlichkeit* – or the laws, customs and conventions of normative society – is for Hegel, as *nomos* is for Agamben, the organising force of communal life and the primary determinant of an individual's subject formation. Drawing a comparison between *Sittlichkeit* and *nomos* is useful in this regard, for it establishes the grounds for even further comparison between Agamben and Silentio. In the pages that follow, I will show how the comparison between *Sittlichkeit* and *nomos* opens the way to a new understanding of Abraham, for whom the ethical universal at first appears as lawfully binding.

The Paradoxical Nature of Abraham's Faith

I turn now to a summary explication of Abraham's faith, which Silentio says is 'utterly unthinkable' by virtue of the absurd.[17] The *Oxford English Dictionary* defines the absurd as 'without reason or propriety', while the Latin root *absurdus* literally means 'out of tune', but the ambiguity of these definitions reflects the basic disagreement found among Kierkegaard scholars. If, on the one hand, the absurd means to be without reason then Abraham's faith is irrational; if, on the other hand, the absurd refers to a lack of propriety then Abraham's faith deviates from the normative standards of moral behaviour. In the latter case, Abraham's faith is 'unthinkable' in a figurative sense, whereas, in the former case, Abraham's faith is literally 'unthinkable' because of its illogic. But, in order to retain the paradoxical aspect here, there must be something illogical, not simply improper, about trusting God's command to sacrifice Isaac, for there is nothing paradoxical about deviating from a cultural norm if that norm is indeed recognised as merely *cultural*, especially not if God commands one to do so. To better understand the issue, let us turn to Silentio's own explanation: 'Faith is precisely the paradox that the single individual as the single individual is higher than the universal', he writes, that the individual 'is justified before [the universal], not as inferior to it but as superior' to it.[18] The paradox lies in the fact that Abraham is made 'higher' than or 'superior' to the universal law that he violates in the binding of Isaac. On this basis, we can gather that Abraham is 'justified' before the ethical universal when he ought to be condemned by it, that he is superior to the ethical universal when he ought to be subject to its legal authority. Silentio continues:

> it is the single individual who, after being subordinate as the single individual to the universal, now by means of the universal becomes the single individual who as the single individual is superior, that the single individual as the single individual stands in an absolute relation to the absolute.[19]

We can deduce from this sentence that the individual is ordinarily subject to the universal but becomes superior to the universal by forming a direct relationship with the absolute. Moreover, the individual forms a direct relationship with the absolute 'by means of the universal', in Silentio's account, so it is somehow *through* the universal that Abraham becomes superior to the universal, and likewise it is somehow *through* the universal that Abraham forms a direct relationship with the absolute.

The paradox emerges in that '[t]he ethical is the universal, and as such it is also the divine. Thus it is proper to say that every duty is essentially [a] duty to God.'[20] Earlier in the text, Silentio identifies the universal with 'social morality', but, in Silentio's reading of Hegel, social morality can be 'traced back to God', so the universal must also be identified with the divine if we are to adopt a Hegelian understanding of *Sittlichkeit*.[21] Thus, it is not merely a cultural norm that Abraham violates by choosing to sacrifice Isaac but one that has been divinely authorised by the deity as morally binding. In response to this claim, readers may object that Silentio ironically adopts a divinely authorised vision of *Sittlichkeit* to further illustrate how incompatible Hegelian philosophy is with the Abrahamic faith, but readers must remember that Silentio at no point corrects or qualifies this statement, so there is simply no reason to rule out the view that *Sittlichkeit* mediates the divine, even if Abraham becomes superior to the universal through an *unmediated* relationship with the absolute. For the paradox of Abraham's faith lies not in the conflict between social ethics and divine morality for Silentio, but between a mediated relationship with the absolute and an unmediated relationship with the absolute, both of which are divinely authorised. Certainly, in Silentio's account of the Abrahamic narrative, the knight of faith regards the sacrifice as a murderous, sinful act by society's standards, and he also regards the sacrifice as a murderous, sinful act by his own standards, as someone socialised under the ethical universal; it must be acknowledged, however, that, in addition to these truths, Abraham views the murder-sacrifice as a direct violation of God's covenantal command in Genesis 17:9 to preserve Isaac's life. In choosing to obey God's subsequent command in Genesis 22:2 to murder-sacrifice Isaac, Abraham violates a social norm, in Silentio's view, but he also violates his covenant agreement with God, who vowed to make Abraham the father of nations through Isaac, who 'was born', Paul says, 'through the promise' (Galatians 4:23 NRSV). The ethical universal, or *Sittlichkeit*, a historically particular community bound together by shared laws and customs, refers specifically, in this context, to the *Abrahamic* community, the patriarch's family and tribe, all of whom were foreigners in the land of Canaan but were bonded together in their own local community under the covenant of circumcision, a customary practice that marked out its members as God's chosen people. In the book of Genesis, God makes explicit the terms of his covenant with Abraham:

> This is my covenant, which you shall keep, between me and you and your offspring after you: Every male among you shall be circumcised. You shall circumcise the flesh of your foreskins, and it shall be a sign of the covenant between me and you. Throughout your generations every male among you shall be circumcised when he is eight days old, including the slave born in your house and the one bought with your money from any foreigner who is not of your offspring. Both the slave born in your house and the one bought with your money must be circumcised. So shall my covenant be in your flesh an everlasting covenant. Any uncircumcised male who is not circumcised in the flesh of his foreskin shall be cut off from his people; he has broken my covenant. (Genesis 17:10–14 NRSV)

Circumcision as a legal custom is established as the founding practice of the covenantal community, so Abraham circumcises the members of his tribe, including his son Isaac, through whom the covenant was promised. Just a few chapters later, God orders Abraham to sacrifice Isaac, committing an act that violates the ethical universal, as well as the founding legal custom of the covenantal community, which is to be indefinitely administered to Isaac's descendants. As an act that revokes the very basis of communal life, the murder-sacrifice of Isaac must be carried out in private by the single individual, Abraham, who is unable to explain his paradoxical obedience to the absolute will of God. We can conclude on this basis that Abraham gains access to the absolute by violating a divinely authorised cultural law, an ethical universal which is 'also the divine'. So it is not simply that Abraham's faith causes him to violate merely cultural standards regarding child sacrifice; it is that Abraham's faith is truly irrational, for he remains committed to his covenant agreement with God at the same time that he chooses to violate it, and likewise, he agrees to preserve Isaac's life at the same time that he agrees to murder him.

It would be a mistake to attribute Silentio's views to Kierkegaard himself, who adopted a handful of pseudonyms to explore various and sometimes contradictory viewpoints that did not always agree with his own, but Kierkegaard should nevertheless be trusted as the author of Silentio, a kind of fictional character, let us say, whose perspective was in fact created by Kierkegaard himself. For this reason, Kierkegaard should be trusted as a reader of *Fear and Trembling*, though not necessarily as the author of *Fear and Trembling*, who can accurately comment on Silentio's perspective. We should take as authoritative Kierkegaard's comments on the paradoxical aspects of *Fear and Trembling*, then, when he writes in a journal entry that 'the collision' or conflict, forming the basis of Abraham's faith, 'is not a collision between God's command and man's command but [a collision] between God's command and God's command'.[22] To reduce Abraham's faith to a breach of propriety – reducing the ethical universal to the merely cultural – is to miss the point. Abraham's faith is not simply a conflict between social morality and the absolute, but rather, as Silentio writes and Kierkegaard later confirms, it is a conflict between God's command to sacrifice Isaac and God's command to preserve Isaac's life, through whom the covenant was made. The universal ethics Abraham violates in his demonstration of faith is therefore also a divine ethical mandate.

This preliminary reading of *Fear and Trembling* shows us that the paradox of Abraham's faith lies in the fact that Abraham must violate God's will in order to obey God's will, that he must sin against God in order to prove to God that he is righteous. 'The ethical expression for what Abraham did is that he meant to murder Isaac', the text reads; 'the religious expression is that he meant to sacrifice Isaac – but precisely in this contradiction is the anxiety that can make a person sleepless, and yet without this anxiety Abraham is not' the father of faith.[23] Commenting further on this point, Silentio explains in the book's exordium why he will never comprehend the story of Abraham. He writes that

> It was a quiet evening when Abraham rode out alone, and he rode to Mount Moriah; he threw himself down on his face, he prayed God to forgive him his sin, that he had been willing to sacrifice Isaac, that the father had forgotten his duty to his son. He often rode his lonesome road, but he found no peace. He could not comprehend that it was a sin that he had been willing to sacrifice to God the best that he had, the possession for which he himself would have gladly died many times; and if it was a sin, if he had not loved Isaac in this manner, he could not understand that it could be forgiven, for what more terrible sin was there?[24]

We see, on the one hand, that Abraham so deeply loves Isaac that he is unable to comprehend the murder-sacrifice as a sin. But we see, on the other hand, that Abraham's decision to sacrifice Isaac is nevertheless a murder by ethical standards, so Abraham prays that God will forgive him for carrying out the sinful act. Returning to our definition of the absurd as either impropriety or a lack of reason, it appears that we must side with the latter definition, since there is nothing paradoxical in deviating from a merely cultural norm, especially not if God commands one to do so. If that cultural norm is also the ethical will of God, however, then Abraham's decision to sacrifice Isaac is simultaneously the decision to murder Isaac, meaning that his obedience to God is simultaneously his disobedience to God. Abraham is not condemned as a murderer because his decision to sacrifice Isaac, by which he forms a direct relationship with the absolute, makes him 'superior' to the universal will of God. The paradox of Abraham's faith lies in the absurdity of this statement, which, by virtue of its illogic, is literally beyond comprehension.

But there is still more to be accounted for in this reading of Abraham's faith. As we saw earlier, the single individual is made higher than the ethical will of God 'by means' of the universal law that he violates, as if it were the violation itself – which can only take place as a violation *within* the universal – that places Abraham in a direct relationship with the absolute. We learn, in addition, that '[f]aith itself cannot be mediated into the universal, for thereby it is canceled', meaning that Abraham's faith must remain 'for all eternity a paradox, impervious to thought' because 'all mediation takes place only by virtue of the universal'.[25] But there is an important question here that has yet to be answered. We know that the essential paradox of Abraham's faith lies in the 'collision . . . between God's command and God's command', as Kierkegaard states, but we are not told why Abraham's decision to violate the universal will of God results in a teleological suspension of the ethical.[26] We may certainly argue that a direct, unmediated relationship with God takes priority over a relationship that is mediated by the universal, but this explanation does not account for the rather tricky detail that Abraham forms a direct relationship with the absolute 'by means of the universal' law that he violates.[27] The following pages compare the readings of Westphal, Jerome Gellman, John Caputo and Jacques Derrida in search of an explanation, for this particular detail must be accounted for if we are going to properly identify the nature of Abraham's faith. There is unquestionably more research available on Silentio's text, but I focus on the readings of Westphal, Gellman, Caputo and Derrida because their insights and – more significantly – their shortcomings progressively lead us to Agamben, who is best able to show how the single individual forms an unmediated relationship with the absolute *by means* of the universal.

Critical Approaches to *Fear and Trembling*

As we have already seen, Westphal challenges irrationalist readings of *Fear and Trembling*, arguing that Abraham chooses to obey God's divinely revealed command to sacrifice Isaac over against the ethical universal. But, in Westphal's view, *Sittlichkeit* is entirely cultural and should not, for that reason, be attributed to the divine, so Abraham does not embrace a contradiction between God's command and God's command, as Kierkegaard asserts, but a contradiction between God's command and humankind's command. According to Westphal, Abraham suspends his allegiance to the man-made conventions of normative society and conforms to a higher moral calling, choosing to obey God's will rather than a cultural norm. One might argue, in response to this, that conflict still emerges between God's command and Abraham's *belief* in the ethical universal, for if Abraham sincerely believes in the moral authority of *Sittlichkeit* then embracing God's order to murder-sacrifice Isaac would surely strike the patriarch as paradoxical. It is in this sense, however, that Westphal's reading mediates what Silentio says cannot be mediated, for there is nothing paradoxical about deviating from the human conventions of normative society if God commands one to do so. Westphal acknowledges this problem, writing that it would be 'highly unreasonable to elevate merely human norms above the commands of God'.[28]

What makes Abraham's faith irrational, Westphal argues, is that Abraham's belief in the supernatural contradicts the anti-supernatural prejudices of his community. According to Westphal, Silentio has in mind here 'something like a Humean or Kantian understanding of Reason', such that God's miraculous intervention in the life of Abraham is 'outside the realm of possible knowledge', *Sittlichkeit*, or the anti-supernatural beliefs of Abraham's community.[29] Westphal cites Kierkegaard's sermon at Trinity Church in Copenhagen delivered four months after the publication of *Fear and Trembling* as evidence for this position, writing that, for Abraham, 'divine revelation' is 'foolishness, even madness, not intrinsically but in relation to and from the perspective of a merely human standpoint', referred to by Kierkegaard in the sermon as the 'earthly eye'.[30] But there is no indication that the earthly perspective talked about in Kierkegaard's sermon is anti-supernatural. In fact, Kierkegaard writes that the 'earthly eye' was a 'stumbling-block' for the covenantal community of the Jews, who undoubtedly believed in divine intervention.[31] Nor is there any indication that this earthly perspective should be applied to Silentio's idea of a universal ethics. In the pages of *Fear and Trembling*, after all, Silentio equates the universal with 'the divine', which can be 'traced back to God', and he does not qualify or correct these statements in his ostensible critique of Hegelian philosophy.[32] Add to this the fact that the ethical universal prohibiting child sacrifice is backed by the covenantal command to preserve Isaac's life, not to mention the fact that Isaac's survival is inextricably tied, in this case, to the founding command of the Abrahamic community (that is, that all of Isaac's descendants be circumcised), and Westphal's argument falls flat. There is simply no reason to believe that Abraham or his community had anti-supernatural prejudices.

Moreover, Westphal's interpretation totally resolves the paradox of Abraham's faith, which Silentio says is incomprehensible and therefore 'higher than all mediations'.[33] The faithful individual 'simply cannot make himself understandable to anyone', Silentio writes, not because of his community's anti-supernatural prejudices, but because the illogic of Abraham's faith divides God against himself.[34] Either the binding of Isaac is an act of sin, or it is an act of obedience. By logical standards, it cannot be both. But this is precisely what makes Abraham's faith paradoxical, and precisely why Abraham is unable to articulate his condition in a way that people can understand. Westphal's reading skirts around the paradox; it fails to address the contradiction between God's command to sacrifice Isaac and the covenant promised to Isaac's descendants; moreover, it does not properly account for Silentio's rather clear assertion that the universal is also the divine. Perhaps even more to the point, however, is that Westphal makes no attempt whatsoever to explain how the individual gains authority over the universal *by means* of the universal. This is a crucial and as yet overlooked detail that cannot be explained under Westphal's interpretive paradigm. But this detail, perhaps more than any other, needs to be explained if we are to discern the meaning of Silentio's text.

Moving closer to an explanation than Westphal is able to do, Jerome Gellman argues in his 1994 monograph *The Fear, the Trembling, and the Fire* that, in the 'standard interpretation' of *Fear and Trembling*, Abraham is torn between 'conflicting imperatives', a religious imperative to sacrifice Isaac and an ethical imperative to preserve his life.[35] For a time, Gellman appears to equate the ethical, or Hegel's *Sittlichkeit*, with the divine universal, which does not merely 'constrain certain individuals, but pertains to their very essence as persons'.[36] For Hegel, a 'person is first and foremost a "member" . . . of [their] social structures', so the 'morality of *Sittlichkeit* frees the citizens' from the bonds of absolute freedom – what Gellman describes as their indeterminate natures, or 'unbounded subjectivity' – by giving them a socially conscripted identity.[37] The ethical imperative that Abraham should not murder-sacrifice Isaac is a moral principle with universal applicability, for Hegel, who, according to Gellman, equates social reality with metaphysical truth. Viewed from this perspective, Abraham's decision to sacrifice Isaac would be a violation of societal norms, but it would also be a violation of the metaphysical reality that these social conventions are thought to embody.

Gellman compares the binding of Isaac – and what Silentio calls the teleological suspension of the ethical – to the Hasidic concept of *averah lishmah*, a sinful act commanded by God. 'When involved in [a teleological suspension of the ethical], one acts in a way that has the *form* of sin, since sin may be formally defined, ethically speaking, as making oneself an exception to the universal. However, this sin is redeemed', Gellman writes, 'because the vantage point of the ethical, from which the act is seen as sinful, is "suspended." Nonetheless, from the point of view of the ethical the sin remains.'³⁸ Gellman compares the teleological suspension of the ethical to *averah lishmah* in that both concepts refer to a temporary suspension of ethical norms. For Westphal, these norms are the result of their institutionalisation by conventional society, but, when it comes to *averah lishmah*, these norms reflect a covenant made between God and the Jewish community. According to Gellman, then, God's command to murder-sacrifice Isaac is in conflict with the divine universal embodied by the moral precepts of the covenantal community. On these grounds, Gellman appears to support an irrationalist reading of Silentio that casts the binding of Isaac as a type of holy sin – an exceptional command given by God to the individual that violates the general commands already given to the covenantal community. '[T]he greatness of Abraham at the *akedah* was signaled by his having reached the paradoxical state of double-mindedness', Gellman writes; 'Abraham is to be lauded . . . for having risen *ethically* above the universal, into an idiosyncratic privacy of individual definition.'³⁹ Like the *averah lishmah*, a teleological suspension of ethical norms would appear to bring God's general will into conflict with God's special will, thus prompting Abraham to commit a holy sin.

But Gellman qualifies his claims, resolving the ostensible conflict between God's command and God's command. '[*Averah lishmah*], as we shall see, is in accordance with the *will* of God, as opposed to His set commands, and is justified only in individual instances', Gellman writes; 'In performing [*averah lishmah*], a person commits a deed that is formally a sin, but a sin that God *wants* her to perform, the act not being generalizable to anyone else.'⁴⁰ Gellman relativises the will of God so that it applies differently in different circumstances. This means that the ethical will of God applies to most people most of the time, but it also means that there are exceptional circumstances that preclude a universal application of God's 'set commands' to every individual throughout all time. For this reason, the sin committed in *averah lishmah* is not morally wrong in a metaphysical sense. God's covenant with the Jews institutionalises a set of general practices, but it does not enforce metaphysical principles with universal applicability. Under the right circumstances, God's will can change, just as it changed for Abraham, who chooses to obey God's command to murder-sacrifice Isaac over against the institutionalised moral precepts that structure his social existence within the covenantal community. For Silentio 'to speak of Abraham within the ethical is to speak of him enmeshed within the network of moral relationships immanent in social institutions', but Silentio 'rejects Hegel's claim that selves are to be *defined* as members of those social structures which embody the ethical'.[41] In recognising that the ethical universal will sometimes align with God's moral will, Gellman provides us with a fuller, more accurate account of Silentio's text, but, in a similar manner to Westphal, Gellman reduces the ethical universal to a set of institutionalised cultural conventions that do not always align with God's moral will; he fails to recognise that God's order to murder-sacrifice Isaac contradicts the covenantal command to circumcise Isaac's descendants, who will never be born if Isaac is killed; and, most importantly of all, he makes no attempt to explain how Abraham becomes superior to the universal *by means* of the universal law that he violates, and this detail, more than any other, still must be accounted for.

Yet there are other philosophers who embrace the paradox for what it is. John Caputo, for example, refuses to see the binding of Isaac as anything other than a heinous act of child murder. He presents Abraham's faith as irrational because it results in a decision that blatantly contradicts the moral will of God. Caputo writes that:

> Kierkegaard's rejoinder to the Hegelians is a salient counter-example: the faith of Abraham, whose greatness lies in being willing to do something that makes no human sense. It is one thing if the 'absurd' simply means a 'marvel' that exceeds human reason, something of which an omnipotent God is capable but which is beyond our understanding, like making Sarah pregnant again at an advanced age. But it is quite another thing (and this is the problem with *Fear and Trembling*) to approve of a divine command to kill an innocent child, which seems to be absurd in a stronger sense, not simply exceeding reason but flatly contradicting all reason. To a modern reader this paradigmatic example of an act of faith, killing an innocent child, represents what de Silentio himself calls an 'appalling' violation of an inviolable law of morality, which makes its perpetrator a murderer from an ethical point of view.[42]

Caputo draws a distinction between a faith that exceeds reason and a faith that flatly contradicts it. The divine command to murder-sacrifice Isaac violates an inviolable law of morality, an ethical certainty that Caputo identifies with the universal. Abraham's faith is absurdly irrational, in this sense, because it puts God into conflict with the divine laws, or 'set commands', as Gellman called them, that the deity himself created and sustains. The contradiction here between 'God's command and God's command' opens the space for an entirely new ethical category that deauthorises the 'inviolable' laws of morality, for Caputo, who identifies this category with the teleological suspension of the ethical, which he explains in terms of Jacques Derrida's deconstruction of representational law.

> A more fruitful reading of *Fear and Trembling*[, he states,] was proposed by Jacques Derrida, who gave Kierkegaard's conception of the religious exception a postmodern sense. In *The Gift of Death*, Derrida argued that instead of defending a religious exception to ethics, Kierkegaard's point is best served by defending the exception as itself an ethical category. Ethics may be redescribed in such a way that no ethical obligation may be reduced to the mechanical application of a universal rule, as if making ethical choices is like running a computer program. As a postmodern category, singularity implies the uniqueness of each and every being . . . In postmodernity Kierkegaard's category of the exception is widened beyond its religious scope – or perhaps it is better to say that his religious category is granted a wider sweep and significance.[43]

In Caputo's reading of Derrida, the deauthorisation of universal law during Abraham's teleological suspension of the ethical results from Abraham's readiness to embrace God as an absolute singularity that lies forever beyond the horizon of his cultural representation. According to Silentio, Abraham becomes superior to the universal *by means* of the universal, as it is paradoxically through his violation of the universal prohibition against murder-sacrifice that Abraham forms a direct relationship with the absolute. How Abraham forms a direct relationship with the absolute becomes clear from a Derridean perspective that casts the ethical universal in terms of representational law and the absolute in terms of the *absolutely other*, or that which lies forever beyond our cultural representations as a pure potentiality. For there is a sense in which the undecidable nature of our representational forms is actually more essential to our ontological condition than the forms themselves. Understanding this aspect of Derrida's work also sets the stage for my analysis of Agamben, whose parallel study of the Abrahamic faith provides the key for unlocking Silentio's peculiar use of the phrase 'by means'.

According to Derrida, Abraham violates the universal by attending to the otherness of God, who appears to Abraham in an unrecognisable form; for God commands Abraham to murder-sacrifice Isaac, which Abraham knows is morally wrong, so his obedient response to God paradoxically amounts to a loss of faith, as it requires Abraham to suspend his belief in God's promise and, with it, his belief in who God is. Derrida will argue that Abraham is open to the antinomies of God's cultural representation, which is to say, in other words, that Abraham is open to the deity's contraries, or that which is expressly *not* God. So Abraham's faith, in this sense, is also, paradoxically, his lack of faith, a willingness to attend to the otherness, or pure potentiality, that lies forever beyond the horizon of God's juridical representation. 'God is the name of the absolute other as other', Derrida writes, and as 'soon as I enter into a relation with the absolute other, my absolute singularity enters into relation with his on the level of obligation', but there are even more 'others, an infinite number of them', in fact, 'to whom I should be bound by the same responsibility, a general and universal responsibility [that] Kierkegaard calls the ethical order'.[44] The paradox, for Derrida, lies in a conflict between the singular and the universal, the same and the other, the included and the excluded, the law and its deconstruction. The other must be approached as a singularity, he argues, not as a universal. As a result, a person is only made conscious of the other *by means* of the representational exclusions that originally mark the other as exterior, ever beyond the canons of intelligibility.

Unlike Westphal and Gellman, Derrida is able to explain, on this basis, how the single individual is made higher than the universal *by means* of the universal – the primary interpretive challenge facing all readers of Silentio's text, in my opinion. The juridical representation of God is always threatened by its antinomic structure, the undecidable nature of which gives rise to Abraham's paradoxical dis/belief. For Abraham believes, on the one hand, that God commands him to sacrifice Isaac, but he continues to believe, on the other hand, that doing so is a sinful act, a violation of the covenant through which Abraham will become the father of nations. By attending to the alterity of God, Abraham forms a direct relationship with the absolute, not because he trades a false representation of the deity for a true representation, and certainly not because he circumvents juridical representation (*Sittlichkeit*) altogether for unmediated access to the deity, but because he embraces alterity as such, a passage between the possible and the impossible, the represented and the unrepresentable, that forces Abraham into a state of contradiction, or permanent undecidability. This is how the individual is made higher than the universal *by means* of the universal, and this is why Abraham's faith must take the form of an irresolvable paradox. The absolute emerges in the deconstruction of our representational boundaries, the dark spaces of alterity that lie forever beyond the horizon of God's canonical representation, which is always, for Derrida, in the process of deconstruction.

The teleological suspension of the ethical – which is to say, the suspension, or deauthorisation, of representational law as a binding, juridical force – brings the subject into a new ethical relation with God and others that Derrida will describe, in conversation with Emmanuel Levinas, as a form of hospitality. This hospitality results in, what Colby Dickinson calls, a *messianic* undoing of juridical representation. But, as Dickinson explains, the deconstruction of our juridical forms does not result in the obliteration of law as such but, rather, in its deauthorisation, a suspension of the metaphysical authority believed to undergird its exclusionary structures. 'Derrida's readers have . . . often mistaken him as advocating a complete dismissal of the canonical form', Dickinson writes; 'His attempt to stay within the confines of representation, however, meant that his deconstructing of canonical forms, in the end, equally sought for their preservation.'[45] All of this is to say that the suspension, or deauthorisation, of juridical representation – which refers more generally to language, or *nomos* – makes one superior to the universal *by means* of the universal, as it is paradoxically *through* language that its deauthorisation takes place, for it is only by excluding the other through a representational act that structural alterity first becomes a threat to legal authority, drawing attention to the instability – the potential for change – that deauthorises our representational laws from within.

Agamben's Portrayal of the Abrahamic Faith

Agamben casts the divine nature similarly in *The Time That Remains*, where *Jesus Messiah* – the nominal syntagma used by Paul throughout his letters in reference to the risen Lord – signifies a teleological suspension of constative representation during *ho nyn kairos*, or the time remaining between the Messiah's ascension and his final, apocalyptic return. The peculiar phrasing of *Jesus Messiah* – rather than, say, *Jesus the Messiah* or *Jesus is the Messiah* – was carefully chosen by Paul. Agamben notes that '*Messiah* is not a predicate tacked onto the subject *Jesus*, but something that is inseparable from him, without, however, constituting a proper name.'[46] While the constative syntagma *Jesus is the Messiah* says something about the nature of Jesus in terms of his identity and ontological existence, the nominal syntagma *Jesus Messiah* revokes the constative function of the statement and instead draws attention to its performative operation, suspending the constative logic of non-contradiction and, with it, the distinction between true and false representations of our world. '[T]he performative bears witness to a phase in human culture in which – contrary to what we are used to thinking – language does not merely refer to things on the basis of a constative or truth relation, but', Agamben writes, 'through a very particular kind of operation, in which the word swears on itself, it itself becomes the fundamental fact'.[47] In other words, language does not form a relation to the world that can be tested as true or false, in Agamben's view. Rather, it gives meaningful shape to the spaces we inhabit by creating juridical divisions that exist not because of their internal, metaphysical validity but because of their temporal performance as *nomos*, or universal law. The nominal syntagma *Jesus Messiah* suspends this normative, denotative function of representation and marks a distinction between *langue* and *parole*, potentiality and its actualisation by drawing attention to the taking place of language itself, which is to say, in other words, to the mere fact of existence before its differential articulation as universal law.

English-language translator and scholar of Agamben's work Adam Kotsko argues that Paul uses *nomos* in reference to an 'overarching category of legal systems that includes both the Greco-Roman and Jewish legal traditions'.[48] We know this, Kotsko asserts, because Paul uses the word when addressing the Galatians, a community of uncircumcised Gentiles who were never subject to the Jewish laws from which their Christian faith is supposed to have freed them. 'Paul has presented himself as a faithful Jew', Kotsko writes, but 'we have no indication that the Galatian community is made up of anything but "pagans" subject to Roman law'.[49] Thus, when Paul speaks about their shared liberation from *nomos* – referring to both a Gentile liberation from Roman law in addition to his own, Jewish liberation from the Torah – he must have in mind the representational divisions that characterise both legal traditions, not in regard to their shared content (as they are very different juridical systems with different practical purposes), but in regard to representation itself, or the constative operation of language.[50] 'Only in this way', Kotsko writes, 'can we make sense of the notion that Christ came to set both Jews and Gentiles free from the curse of the law', for both Jew and Gentile are subject to the exclusionary violence of *nomos*, the constative, universal truth claims that capture the world in its representation.[51]

Agamben advances a similar reading of *nomos* in *The Time That Remains*, arguing that '[e]ach revelation is always and above all a revelation of language itself, an experience of a pure event of the word that exceeds every signification and is, nevertheless, animated by two opposing tensions'.[52] The first, 'which Paul calls *nomos*, attempts to encapsulate the excess by articulating it in precepts and in semantic contents', writes Agamben; 'The second, which coincides with *pistis*, is oriented, on the contrary, toward maintaining it open beyond any determinate signification.'[53] As I discussed in the introduction to this volume, Agamben articulates the difference between *pistis* and *nomos* in *Language and Death* as the difference between *langue* and *parole*, potentiality and its actualisation. The indeterminate pronoun, like the performative utterance *Jesus Messiah*, alerts one to the pure potentiality that lurks within and thus threatens to destabilise those representational laws that 'encapsulate' the absolute nature of God. Just as in *Fear and Trembling*, however, this does not mean that the juridical representation of God in the form of universal precepts – *Sittlichkeit* or the ethical universal – is illegitimate; it simply means that mediated representations of the deity are subordinate to the absolute, unmediated nature of God as a pure potentiality. On Agamben's reading of Paul, faith is not a belief in God's juridical representation, but that which moves beyond the constative logic of non-contradiction to reveal the nothingness, or pure potentiality, concealed within our representational constructs. What Silentio calls a direct relationship with the absolute, Agamben describes as 'dwelling near the word'.[54] But in order to truly *dwell* in pure potentiality and thereby form a direct relationship with the absolute, one must suspend the constative operation of language that actualises in order to conceal this potentiality within the legal boundaries of divisive universals, for there 'is no such thing as a content of faith, and to profess the word of faith does not mean formulating true propositions on God and the world. To believe in Jesus Messiah', Agamben writes, 'does not mean believing something about him.'[55]

We established earlier that Abraham gains access to the absolute *by means* of the universal law that he violates. If the absolute in this context refers to *langue* – or God before and beyond his mediation as *parole* – and the ethical universal refers not simply to cultural normativity but to constative representations of the deity's moral will – then one should conclude, on this basis, that Abraham gains access to the absolute through a violation that suspends the exclusionary articulations of *parole*. Silentio – whose name translates into English as *John of Silence* – writes that 'Abraham cannot be mediated' in that 'he cannot speak', for '[a]s soon as I speak, I express the universal', a constative utterance that divides the world into true and false representations, but 'if I do not [speak]', Silentio writes, 'no one can understand me'.[56] Abraham is rendered silent by a violation that suspends the constative logic of non-contradiction, bringing him into a direct relationship with the absolute, unmediated nature of God that Agamben identifies with the negative ground of ontology, *langue*, or language before its differential articulation as *parole*. But as our earlier analysis demonstrated, Abraham does not gain access to the absolute by circumventing the universal; nor does he gain access to the absolute through a violation that – *as a violation* – authorises the universal divisions of *parole*. Rather, Abraham's faith violates the divisions of *parole* in a way that suspends the constative logic of representation as such, a deeper level violation that moves beyond true and false representations of the deity to the alterity, or pure potentiality, that, in the face of contradiction, is laid out before the faithful in its purest form. Abraham's silence results from his decision to violate the universal as such, a deeper level violation that enacts a '*removal of the voice*'.[57]

Abraham's faith is a violation of God's will that is also, paradoxically, an act of faith. We saw earlier that '[t]he ethical expression for what Abraham did is that he meant to murder Isaac', while 'the religious expression is that he meant to sacrifice Isaac'.[58] Abraham obeys a God who contradicts the universal representation of his own divine ethics through a murder-sacrifice that divides the deity against himself, thereby forcing Abraham, who now finds himself similarly divided, into a paradoxical state of dis/belief. In other words, because Abraham's decision to sacrifice Isaac is simultaneously his decision to murder Isaac, and because Abraham's decision to trust God is simultaneously his decision to abrogate God's promise to Isaac's descendants, the patriarch's obedience to God is likewise his disobedience to God. This is why Kierkegaard himself describes Abraham's faith as a contradiction 'between God's command and God's command', a holy sin that inherently violates the constative logic of *parole*, or *Sittlichkeit*, the differential representations that bind a community together. 'Speak he cannot', Silentio writes, because 'he speaks no human language. And even if he understood all the languages of the world, even if those he loved also understood them, he still could not speak', for Abraham 'speaks in a divine language, he speaks in tongues'.[59] For Agamben, this divine language is revealed by the performative utterance *Jesus Messiah*, the *nomen tetragrammaton*, and even the indeterminate pronoun of medieval theology. Like Silentio, Agamben describes the Christian faith as Abrahamic, or the result of a contradiction that violates in order to suspend the constative divisions of *parole* – what he describes as a *division of division itself* in his ground-breaking study of Paul's Letter to the Romans.

This fundamental Pauline gesture is similar to the binding of Isaac in that it contradicts the covenant promised by God to Abraham and his descendants through Isaac. According to Silentio, Abraham's faith is accompanied by an attitude of infinite resignation because he must sacrifice both the covenant and his beloved son to commit the murder. We read in Genesis 17:14 that the covenant is marked by circumcision in order to distinguish the Jew from the non-Jew, the descendants of Isaac from pagan unbelievers, such that any male 'who has not been circumcised in the flesh, will be cut off from his people'. According to Agamben, the division of Jew and non-Jew is the very foundation of Judaic law, but Paul introduces a new division between flesh and spirit that cuts across, in order to deauthorise, juridical divisions of any kind, for the division of division itself marks a deeper level violation that embraces contradiction in order to suspend the constative logic of *parole* and, with it, all forms of *nomos*, Jewish or otherwise. 'The criteria for how this division works is both clear (circumcised/foreskin) and exhaustive, for it divides all "men" into two subsets', Agamben explains; 'Paul cuts this division in two via a new division, that of the flesh/breath. This partition does not coincide with that of the Jew/non-Jew, but it is not external to it either; instead, it divides the division itself.'[60] Believing in the gospel means no longer observing the law of circumcision. As Paul asserts in Galatians 5:2, 'if you let yourself be circumcised, Christ will be of no value to you.' But this does not mean that the promise – which was originally 'transposed onto [legal] works and mandatory precepts' – is abolished, for faith in *Jesus Messiah* renders 'these works inoperative' by giving 'potentiality back to them in the form of inoperativity and ineffectiveness. The messianic', Agamben explains, 'is not the destruction but the deactivation of the law, rendering the law inexecutable.'[61] The messianic validates in order to *invalidate* mutually exclusive ethical precepts, thereby suspending their juridical authority, or the power to exclude. This suspension of legal authority forces the faithful into an undecidable state, where the conflict between God's command and God's command divides each and every division from within to reveal a pure potentiality at the heart of *Sittlichkeit*, *nomos* or our representational constructs.

Paul's theology thus renders the law inoperative without abolishing it, giving the faithful individual, who is both inside and outside of the law, authority over its juridical force. 'To the extent that the sovereign [individual] has the legitimate power to suspend the validity of the law, he is both inside and outside [of] the law', Agamben observes, for 'in the state of exception, the law is in force in the form of its suspension, being applied in disapplying itself', so that *nomos* now 'includes', by virtue of an irresolvable contradiction in God's will, 'that which is rejected from itself'.[62] This is why Silentio describes faith as 'utterly unthinkable', for it renders our conceptual categories unintelligible and thereby deprives Abraham of the ability to speak.[63] The patriarch withdraws from the representational divisions of *parole* – which God himself brings into conflict – to dwell in the pure potentiality of *langue*, a 'divine language' that both Silentio and Agamben associate with the absolute.[64] In this sense, Abraham is made higher than the universal *by means* of the universal, as it is only *through* the universal – or the constative operations of *parole* – that contradiction as such can logically occur. When the opposing ends of a contradiction are divinely authorised, forcing a 'collision', as it were, 'between God's command and God's command', the faithful individual is brought into a direct relationship with the absolute, deauthorising juridical representations of the divine through a division of division itself, a deeper level violation that unveils God as a pure potentiality.

In Genesis 22, God commands Abraham to sacrifice Isaac even though it violates the covenantal command given to Abraham in Genesis 17. Instructed to perform contradictory tasks, Abraham is confronted, in this moment, with two versions of God. Obeying the God of Genesis 22,

Abraham chooses to murder-sacrifice Isaac even though it violates the covenant already formed with God in Genesis 17. But this transition does not reflect the transference of Abraham's belief from one version of God to another. Rather, Abraham continues to believe in the promise of Genesis 17 despite God's revocation of the promise in Genesis 22. This transition marks the difference between sacrifice and murder, but, on this point, Silentio is clear: for Abraham, the sacrifice is *also* a murder; the patriarch, like the deity, is divided against himself. Agamben makes a parallel argument in his reading of Paul's Letter to the Romans, for Paul instructs the faithful to transgress without abolishing the covenant of circumcision just as Abraham did. This new command contradicts the original command that divides the world into Jew and non-Jew. Embracing the contradiction, the children of Abraham knowingly violate the ethical universal, suspending the exclusionary logic of *parole* through a division of division itself. Those who dwell near the word – or the pure potentiality of God – are likewise suspended between belief and disbelief, internally divided against themselves in a state of faithful disobedience. The Pauline faith, like the Abrahamic faith, is forever beyond mediation, as paradoxical dis/belief like Abraham's can never truly be explained in a logical way. We may certainly identify the nature of this faith, and we may even understand how the pure potentiality of God is revealed through a suspension of *parole*, but contradiction is nevertheless incomprehensible to the conscious mind in that it violates the representational divisions that make our world intelligible.

Only through a deeper level violation of the ethical universal, which appears as a violation only under the legal authority of the ethical universal, does Abraham become superior to the ethical universal through its teleological suspension. Traditional readings of *Fear and Trembling* do not adequately explain how this is possible. Instead, they present Abraham as circumventing the ethical universal rather than passing through it, but as we have already clearly established, Abraham becomes superior to the ethical universal *by means* of the ethical universal, which is preserved in its very suspension. This long-overlooked detail is one that Kierkegaard scholars and readers of Silentio fail to acknowledge, much less explain, and yet it stands at the centre of Silentio's depiction of the Abrahamic faith. Only by superimposing central tenets from *The Time That Remains* upon the central tenets of *Fear and Trembling* do we discover crucial overlaps that provide a way into understanding this mysterious detail. Through his Pauline reading of the Abrahamic narrative, Agamben elucidates one of the founding documents of existentialism in a truly unprecedented way.

De Silentio confronts us with an existential figure – the single individual – whose will to rise above the ethical universal is, for many, an archetype of sovereign, lawmaking decisionism.[65] When viewed from Agamben's perspective, however, we find that Abraham's leap of faith is one that deactivates its own lawmaking authority through a teleological suspension of *nomos*, a deeper-level violation of the law that, when taken as archetypal, casts a shadow of doubt over longstanding metaphysical depictions of the existentialist tradition. So it may very well be that Silentio, as one of the reputed founders of existentialism, marks a suspension, rather than a continuation, of Western metaphysics.

Notes

1. Søren Kierkegaard, *Fear and Trembling/Repetition*, ed. Howard V. Hong and Edna H. Hong (Princeton: Princeton University Press, 1983), pp. 55–6.
2. Ibid. p. 69.
3. Ibid. p. 78.
4. Merold Westphal, *Kierkegaard's Concept of Faith* (Grand Rapids, MI, and Cambridge: William B. Eerdmans Publishing Company, 2014), p. 43.
5. Mark C. Taylor, *Journeys to Selfhood: Hegel and Kierkegaard* (Berkeley and Los Angeles: University of California Press, 1980), p. 14.
6. Leo Stan, 'From Singularity to Universality and Back Kierkegaard's Clandestine Religion', in *Revista di Filosofia Neo-Scolastica* 105.3/4 (2013): 612.
7. Westphal, *Kierkegaard's Concept of Faith*, p. 43.
8. Georg Wilhelm Friedrich Hegel, *The Phenomenology of Spirit*, ed. and trans. Terry Pinkard (Cambridge: Cambridge University Press, 2018), p. xliii.
9. Westphal, *Kierkegaard's Concept of Faith*, p. 47.
10. Ibid. p. 51.
11. Ibid. p. 47.
12. Louis Althusser, 'Ideology and Ideological State Apparatuses', in *The Norton Anthology of Theory and Criticism*, ed. Vincent B. Leitch (New York and London: W.W. Norton & Company, 2001), p. 1489.
13. Ibid. p. 1503.
14. Westphal, *Kierkegaard's Concept of Faith*, p. 43.
15. Giorgio Agamben, *The Omnibus* (Stanford: Stanford University Press, 2017), p. 21.
16. Ibid. p. 22.
17. Kierkegaard, *Fear and Trembling/Repetition*, p. 71.
18. Ibid. p. 55.
19. Ibid. pp. 55–6.
20. Ibid. p. 68.
21. Ibid. pp. 55, 68.
22. Ibid. p. 248.
23. Ibid. p. 30.
24. Ibid. p. 13.
25. Ibid. pp. 71, 55, 56.
26. Ibid. p. 248.
27. Ibid. p. 55.
28. Westphal, *Kierkegaard's Concept of Faith*, p. 95.
29. Ibid. p. 91.
30. Ibid. p. 88.
31. Ibid.
32. Kierkegaard, *Fear and Trembling*, p. 68.

33. Ibid. p. 66.
34. Ibid. p. 71.
35. Jerome Gellman, *The Fear, the Trembling, and the Fire: Kierkegaard and the Hasidic Masters on the Binding of Isaac* (Lanham: University Press of America, 1994), p. 2.
36. Ibid. p. 8.
37. Ibid. pp. 8–9.
38. Ibid. p. 46.
39. Ibid. p. 77.
40. Ibid. p. 47.
41. Ibid. p. 9.
42. John D. Caputo, *How to Read Kierkegaard* (New York and London: W.W. Norton & Company, 2008), p. 53.
43. Ibid. p. 55.
44. Jacques Derrida, *The Gift of Death* (Chicago and London: Chicago University Press, 1995), p. 68.
45. Ibid. p. 57.
46. Giorgio Agamben, *The Time That Remains: A Commentary on the Letter to the Romans*, trans. Patricia Dailey (Stanford: Stanford University Press, 2005), p. 128.
47. Ibid. p. 133.
48. Colby Dickinson and Adam Kotsko, *Agamben's Coming Philosophy: Finding a New Use for Theology* (London and New York: Rowman & Littlefield, 2015), p. 232.
49. Ibid.
50. Ibid.
51. Ibid.
52. Agamben, *The Time That Remains*, p. 135.
53. Ibid.
54. Ibid. p. 137.
55. Ibid. p. 136.
56. Kierkegaard, *Fear and Trembling*, p. 60.
57. Giorgio Agamben, *Language and Death* (Minneapolis: University of Minnesota Press, 1991), p. 30.
58. Kierkegaard, *Fear and Trembling*, p. 30.
59. Ibid. p. 114.
60. Agamben, *The Time That Remains*, p. 49.
61. Ibid. p. 97.
62. Ibid. p. 105.
63. Kierkegaard, *Fear and Trembling*, p. 71.
64. Ibid. p. 114.
65. Jean-Paul Sartre describes Kierkegaardian decisionism as lawmaking in 'Kierkegaard: The Singular Universal', *We Have Only One Life to Live: The Selected Essays of Jean-Paul Sartre 1939–1975*, ed. Ronald Aronson and Adrian van den Hoven (New York: New York Review of Books, 2013). And Carl Schmitt famously models the sovereign exception after Kierkegaardian figures in *Political Theology*, trans. Charles Schwab (Chicago and London: The University of Chicago Press, 1985).

Chapter 13

The Existential Situation and Christian Experience: Messianism and Eschatological Salvation

Daniel Minch

The broad strokes of the development of Christian 'eschatology' are often portrayed as beginning with an immanent expectation of the Parousia in early Christ-believing communities, transformed into an institutionalised and formalised hope for an afterlife in the wake of disappointment with the 'delay' in Jesus's return. As the church itself became a 'permanent' and 'worldly' institution, the early expectations of the community became more individualistic, primarily focused on the salvation of the individual souls after death. I do not find this account of Christian eschatology to be particularly accurate, but it is a compelling image that many, including Giorgio Agamben, have largely adopted to criticise Christian faith as the codification of an originally dynamic spiritual experience into a formal institution.[1] The hope for eschatological salvation is, indeed, one of the cornerstones of Christian faith, and this hope has endured in various forms throughout two millennia of tradition. From a Christian perspective, it is rooted in the fundamental experience of salvation that the first believers encountered in their own experiences with the living Jesus of history.

The expression of Christian eschatology is today, and always has been, very much dependent on the 'existential situation', or the place in history in which human beings find themselves, including our contemporary experience of time. Johann Baptist Metz notes that, despite the fact that 'every theological statement about being is endowed with a temporal index, there is hardly anything in theology that is so little cultivated as an authentic, unborrowed understanding of time'.[2] Metz fears that, without an adequate theological understanding of history consonant with our own historical, existential situation, time devolves into 'an empty, internalized eschatology that transpires in a time that has no limit or end'.[3] Likewise, Agamben makes the point that 'every culture is first and foremost a particular experience of time, and no new culture is possible without an alteration of this experience'.[4] Agamben's reflections on messianism and messianic time contain very important insights into the nature of our existential experience of time, and for Christians the experience of messianic time in relation to salvation. However, because much of his work draws on the Christian theological tradition, it is necessary to place his work in a constructive dialogue with elements of more contemporary eschatology and biblical theology.

The years prior to and following the Second Vatican Council constituted a recovery of elements of eschatological theology and the restoration of eschatology to a central place in contemporary Catholic thought. Here, I will utilise insights from the work of the modern theologians Johann Baptist Metz, Karl Rahner and Edward Schillebeeckx, who were all instrumental in this eschatological recovery. Their theologies were shaped by Thomism, *Ressourcement* theology and modern philosophy. Rahner was heavily influenced by Martin Heidegger, while Schillebeeckx attended lectures by Maurice Merleau-Ponty and Albert Camus in Paris. After Vatican II, Schillebeeckx integrated existential hermeneutics and critical theory in a productive dialogue with Catholic faith.[5] In particular, Schillebeeckx's attention for the 'existential situation' of contemporary people was a key part of his development of an eschatological framework for evaluating experience – both the experience of suffering and experiences that mediate salvation.

My concern here is to examine Agamben's account of messianic time in relation to Christian eschatology and the existential situation. The full task of Agamben's biopolitical project is beyond the scope of this reflection, as is his focus on language, but these will be touched upon in places. Agamben has mined texts and ideas from the Christian tradition in service of 'the coming philosophy', and it is certainly fair to do the opposite from the Christian perspective. Agamben can, at times, provide remarkable insight into the Christian tradition – the kind of insight that one attains only from hearing the impressions of an 'outsider' to the tradition. Even so, we remain within our rights to correct the places where he has misread things, deliberately or otherwise. The existential content of Agamben's time-analysis can be better clarified by contextualising it within the framework of Christian eschatology – the experience of salvation coming from God, as Schillebeeckx often identifies it. The existential situation is revealed in the experience of messianic time and time-consciousness, but its transformative potential lies – from the Christian perspective – not in a pure transcendence of time and history, but in a radical commitment to the world. Therefore, salvation, messianism and grace must be considered in connection with temporality and lived history. Contemporary existential experience and interpretation affect our ability to meaningfully identify the 'Messiah', and the salvific content of messianism. Such an eschatological identification also proves to be decisive for any praxical appropriation of the messianic, which is integral to Christian faith of any era.

Agamben's Examination of Paul and Messianic Time

In examining the contemporary experience of temporality, much of Agamben's inspiration has come from his continued engagement with the work of Walter Benjamin, and in particular Benjamin's assertion that 'we have been endowed with a weak Messianic power, a power to which the past has a claim'.[6] Messianism and an analysis of 'messianic time', stemming from Benjamin's use of the terms in his 'Theses on the Philosophy of History', has also been a topic of interest among postmodern philosophers, especially those adhering to the various forms of deconstructionism and Lacanian thought.[7] Agamben has been perhaps the most successful of those looking to appropriate Benjamin's 'messianic' legacy in the field of political philosophy with a specific focus on cultivating a new concept of temporality. He has, however, also drawn heavily on the writings of Saint Paul in order to explicate the 'original messianic force' that is at work in Paul's writings and which, Agamben asserts, was watered down and suppressed by the institutional church. His is a project of recovery, to find what has been lost in Paul due to an alleged collusion between the church and Judaism to 'expunge it from its originary messianic context'.[8] Agamben's ultimate goal is political. He wants to re-evaluate the construction of contemporary society and its reliance on sovereign power and violence. It is also 'biopolitical', however, since he detects in humanity a lost or squandered original potential that has been given over to the violent representations of language, producing not life as such but a manufactured 'human life' that is artificially and violently separated from 'bare life'.[9] The messianic, according to Agamben, is opposed to this system of violent exclusion, and he therefore seeks to develop its potential.

Eschatology or Messianism?

Christian eschatology, the study of the *eschaton* (ἔσχτος) or the 'last things' (ἔσχατα), involves a fundamental tension between the transcendent and the immanent, that which occurs in history and that which has occurred in Christ. This is not an oppositional or dualistic sense of 'two times', wherein the present age is followed by the stopping of time, or its extension in paradise after the end/*eschaton*. Rather, the 'end', the salvific presence and activity of God as 'all in all' (1 Cor. 15:28) is present in history without being fully available to it. The tension between the 'already' and 'not yet' forms the basis of genuine Christian eschatology. This is important because it qualifies the way in which Agamben understands Paul's use of 'messiah', as well as tempers his implicit claim that Paul's radical messianism was extraordinary and needed to be diluted to serve the church as it grew as a religious power structure.

Agamben opposes messianic and eschatological time, since he understands eschatology to be a perversion of messianism.[10] Essentially, this involves mistaking 'the time of the end [messianism] for the end of time [eschatology]'.[11] He identifies eschatology with canonicity and with the later codification of a specific Christian belief structure, while messianism is the originary dynamic source. The first problem with this is that, in Judean and Christ-believing communities of the first century, multiple eschatological frameworks existed, many of which interacted on various historically irretrievable levels.[12] Paul did not write alone or in a vacuum. Paul addressed specific communities and was influenced by multiple traditions. Even his 'Christology' is not so primitive as some might imagine, but neither is it a fully developed systematic conciliar theology.[13] Second, Agamben describes eschatology as a projection from the end of time into the present: 'It sees the end fulfilled and describes what it sees.'[14] He emphasises that eschatology redirects our attention from the messianic 'now' moment to the future apocalypse. The contemporary, or the existential, situation of the subject is already circumscribed by a predetermined end. Agamben argues that eschatological salvation is entirely oriented towards 'a final end', and eschatology risks mistaking 'the time of the end for the end of time'.[15] This is a fundamental misreading of Christian eschatology, or at least a very outdated view of it.

Although neo-scholastic theology perhaps made the error identified by Agamben, having largely relegated eschatology to a theological 'appendix' consisting of speculation on 'the last things' – the nature of heaven, hell, purgatory and the state of the soul after death – neo-scholasticism was only the theological 'mainstream' for a relatively short time. Neo-scholasticism gained prominence after Vatican I but it effectively died as a dominant methodology in the first debates at Vatican II. As Metz observes, neo-scholastic eschatology lacked 'vital relationship to the whole of theology' and therefore also failed 'to be related to the theology of the world'.[16] This eschatology, in Catholic thought, had been under fire since at least the French worker priest experiments in the 1940s, and in scholarly debates throughout the 1950s, culminating in the promulgation of the Pastoral Constitution on the Church in the Modern World, *Gaudium et spes*, at the final session of the Second Vatican Council in 1965.[17]

Properly understood, eschatology has much more in common with the messianism discerned in Paul than it does with apocalypticism, or more precisely, what Karl Rahner named 'false apocalypticism'. In an important article, Rahner draws a distinction between apocalypticism and eschatology, saying: 'To extrapolate from the present into the future is eschatology, to interpolate from the future into the present is apocalyptic.'[18] Reading the present *into* the future presents great hermeneutical challenges for the contemporary context, especially in putting up bulwarks against falling into ideological speculations and idealisations of the *eschaton*. Eschatology is a fundamentally hermeneutical undertaking, directly opposed to the 'false apocalyptic' identified by Rahner. Uncritical apocalypticism presupposes that the 'end' is objectively seen ahead of time and imposed on the present in an ideological fashion. In one way, apocalypticism so envisioned does not posit a substantial difference between the present and the future. Potential for the genuinely new, either in the lived present or expected future, is limited or even non-existent. The future will be because of the present; the present *is this way* (typically, this is a negative evaluation on the present) because of the coming future. From Metz's perspective, however, only from 'the eschatological horizon of hope does the world appear as history'.[19] Eschatological hope is experienced only in and through history, the existential situation of human beings in the world, and it should not be simply placed 'at the end' of history.

Pauline Eschatology and the Contraction of Time

What interests Catholic theologians who begin from eschatology is, in fact, precisely what is interesting to Agamben: 'the time that remains between time and its end'.[20] Messianic time is 'that part of secular time which undergoes an entirely transformative contraction', guided by Paul's assertion that time has been shortened (1 Cor. 7:29), or Agamben's translation of the first-person nominative singular middle/passive participle (συστέλλω, συνεσταλμένος), 'time contracted itself' and begins to end.[21] What is revolutionary about Paul's eschatology is not the 'eschatological' expectation of a new age, but the 'tension' that arises from the intermingling of the old and new ages, the being both 'in Adam' and 'in Christ'. What is new in Paul is the *tension* between the already and not-yet elements of salvation that are present in history.[22] This brings to mind the distinction between a 'realised eschatology' and a 'final eschatology'; the latter indicates that all salvific activity is concentrated in the Parousia and not available outside of Jesus of Nazareth, while the former assumes some kind of salvific presence whether Christological or pneumatological within history that will be fully available at the Parousia. The gospels in particular exhibit a gradual shift towards a realised eschatology that places the Parousia at a far-off distance from the present accompanied by partial salvation present within the Christ-believing communities. Paul's eschatological expectation is not necessarily about impending immanence, but simply that 'the last days had begun'.[23] It is not just that there is a profound change or shift from one epoch to another, but that God's final salvific purpose is in the process of being revealed. God's plan is definitively *in motion*.

Based on Paul's 'body of the lord' ecclesiology, Paul can be identified with a type of 'realised eschatology' in development, which places the risen Christ's activity within the earthly ministry of the church.[24] This notion is not present in Mark's Gospel, but it is discernible in the earliest strata of the Q tradition, although in a very different form.[25] For this tradition, it is the heavenly Jesus who is active through Christian prophets and who is also identified with the coming 'son of man', but the suffering and death of Jesus do not figure into this creedal formula as they do for Paul.[26] The nuances inherent to content of the earliest creeds and Christological titles of the Christ-believing communities, including Paul's, show that there is already an *eschatological* understanding of Christ's activity in the time before the Parousia – the heavenly Christ, who comes as the Son of Man is active in the *world now*, and for Paul this is Jesus as the Christ or messiah.

Agamben's translation of συνεσταλμένος as 'time contracted itself' is quite deliberate. He decides against the generally accepted 'passive' meaning of the verb, which would indicate an agent who does the contracting. Instead, he opts for a reading whereby time 'contracts itself', which is grammatically possible but contextually implausible. God would be the generally accepted agent of a passive verb (thus the 'theological passive' literary convention), especially if the subject/agent involved is *transforming* an object/theme, which in this case is time (καιρός). Time is a cosmic element over which only God could be expected to have control in first-century Judaism, leading to the likely conclusion that time *has been contracted* by God as the agent.[27] It is in the contraction of time (whether by an agent or by the agency of time/καιρός itself) that we begin to see the emergence of 'messianic time', inaugurated by the messianic event that starts with the resurrection of Jesus.[28] Paul's theology exhibits a clear understanding of progression. We are moving towards the Parousia, and it is nearer than it was at the start of Paul's faith in Christ. However, he is not surprised by the death of those faithful in Thessaloniki before Christ's return. There is no 'crisis' in Paul's letters caused by the delay of the Parousia, and this presumed 'delay' probably did not drive development in Paul's theology.[29] There are not two events – a resurrection and a Parousia as a beginning and a deferred end. For Agamben, the notion of deferral introduces a kind of 'transitional time' in between two events, the result of which is, 'as with any transition, [the Parousia] tends to be prolonged into infinity and renders unreachable the end that it supposedly produces'.[30] Instead, Agamben proposes a 'uni-dual' structure to the messianic event composed of two 'heterogeneous' times.[31]

Rather than an infinite deferral of the Parousia as something that 'comes later', it is already present in the Pauline expression 'the time of the now' (ὁ νῦν καιρός) – what Agamben identifies as a 'technical term' for the messianic event.[32] The 'now' moment is of supreme importance for Agamben's project since 'the reference of messianic time is no longer the future or the past, but the very present moment itself'.[33] Grammatically, this seems to be borne out in Paul's use of the aorist and present tenses. Paul expresses his theory of salvation, his soteriology, in both the aorist ('denoting a decisive event in the past') and the present tense ('an ongoing process').[34] Salvation is a process for believers, which has its definitive beginning in a once-and-for-all event in the past, or what Paul calls the 'beginning of salvation'.

Breaking Down Purely 'Linear' Time

In order to access the 'now' moment, Agamben juxtaposes two concepts of time, each expressed linguistically in Greek: χρόνος and καιρός. Chronotic time, χρόνος, is what Agamben understands as 'secular time', or the easily representable time as a straight line that roughly breaks down to the formula 'time = rate/distance'. This is a spatially representable form of time composed of infinitely divisible points or instants.[35] This is the empty, homogenous and infinitely progressive form of temporality that comprises the contemporary understanding of history: linear, and extending from beginning to end. In this time there is no pure 'present', since the 'pure present is always on the point of sliding into the past'.[36] Agamben identifies this as 'something perfectly *representable*, but absolutely *unthinkable*', since thinking it always entails its passing away.[37] This corresponds roughly to the Judaean conception 'that history runs only once – from creation to a grand climax'.[38] This view contrasts with the 'Greek' understanding of time, or at least the predominant Stoic version of it. Hellenism was no monolithic entity (and Paul was a Hellenised Jew), so, as Agamben himself notes, it is inaccurate to say there was one 'Greek' way of representing time.[39] However, there was an influential Stoic view which postulated that '"history" runs in cycles, each ending in a great conflagration, which is followed by a new beginning'.[40] The representative term here is 'καιρός', which Agamben understands in terms of 'occasion', and this is accurate, especially in Koine usage where it indicates the time when something is to be done: 'season' of the year, opportunity or period.[41] Hence, in Mark 11:13, Jesus approaches the fig tree, but it was not the καιρός for figs, forming the first part of an intercalation that is ultimately about the καιρός of the temple (comprised of parts: a, 11:12–14; b, 11:15–19; a, 11:20–25).[42] What we are left with is a time, καιρός, that is thinkable and understandable, but according to Agamben it is not representable despite encompassing our real experience of temporality.[43]

To explicate more clearly what καιρός is, Agamben takes recourse to the work of the linguist Gustave Guillaume.[44] Guillaume's concept of 'operational time' attempts to 'inscribe temporalization within spatial representation'.[45] The chronological time that is representable by a straight line is a time image produced independently from that image.[46] The 'operational time' that does not accord with this linear scheme is *the time that the mind takes to realize a time-image*, giving rise to a 'chronogenetic' or three-dimensional temporal schema.[47] As such there is something, operational time that is 'alongside' the linear time image and does not fully correspond to it.[48] According to David E. Johnson, the principle of unity between linear chronological time and this 'operational' time, the time it takes to comprehend a time-image, is that language 'refers to its own taking place, to a pure instance of discourse in action' through a mental operation.[49] The inherently linguistic mental operation of thinking takes time to realise itself, and in so far as it refers to itself, it introduces a separation in the temporal structure of subjectivity. Every thought, or mental operation, 'implies an operational time', and therefore, 'even referring to the instance of discourse in action would imply a certain time, and chronothesis, or time-positing, would contain within itself another time that introduces a disjointedness and delay in the "pure presence" of the enunciation'.[50]

From here we can see two 'times', one linear and one that is not, but that is both connected to and disjointed with linear time. Our linear, and easily represented time is χρόνος, while καιρός is the designation for 'operational time'. It is also equivalent to 'messianic time', or *'the time that time takes to come to an end . . . the time we take to bring to an end, to achieve our representation of time'*.[51] The 'ending' described by Agamben is also 'beginning', however, since each linguistic operation represents part of a series of operations. Even so, the point for him is not the series, since that would be to consider only the chronological flow of 'one thing after another', but the operating and non-coincidence itself. The messianic time is also not simply 'another time . . . a supplementary time added on from outside to chronological time'.[52] It springs forth from within the chronological temporal existence itself, meaning that the two, χρόνος and καιρός, are not opposed to one another, but interpenetrating. Messianic time is καιρός that is 'not another time, but a contracted and abridged *chronos*'.[53] Hence, time has been contracted (or, for Agamben, 'contracted itself'), opening up a space for the messianic event to enter, which entails allowing for the positing of an absolute messianic 'now moment' of non-coincidence. Agamben is not always so irenic about the coexistence of the two forms of time, however, as he sometimes sets them explicitly over against one another. He considers chronological time to be the source of an 'empty, continuous and infinite time of vulgar historicism'.[54]

Nevertheless, the two are bound together, especially since καιρός is essentially composed of concentrated χρόνος.[55] The two times never quite coincide with one another, and as such the 'now moment', the existential situation, can 'never fully coincide with a chronological moment internal to its representation'.[56] This leads us to two preliminary conclusions. First, the inbreaking, or interruptive messianic event is somehow immune to transience and the passage of time.[57] It is not one point on a line, nor is it an event in the past awaiting fulfilment. Yet, Agamben wants this messianic to be something that is immanent, something that does not fall into the problems of onto-theological categories of transcendence and immanence. The singularity of the messianic event is in its presence to every moment for the experiencing subject (immanent to chronological, secular time), without coinciding with it. Thus, messianic time 'implies an actual transformation of the experience of time that may even interrupt secular time here and now'.[58] This is why the resurrection and Parousia are not considered to be two events, one in the past and one at the end of time. It is in the 'ending' of the representative moment that both are essentially already present, founding the moment but disappearing in its definitive representation. Second, there is something perfectly generic, universally available in the messianic, but not graspable; something prior, but not at the chronological 'beginning'.[59]

Messianic Time, History and the Existential Situation

For Paul, the messianic event inaugurated by the resurrection is not simply 'past'. It is reopened in the contemporary disjunction between past and present through which another concentrated form of time emerges. The messianic as 'the time that remains between time and its end' cannot be separated out into 'resurrection' here, and 'Parousia' there.[60] The interpenetrating relationship, where one is constituted in the other is the messianic itself.[61] What I think is significant in Agamben's account of messianic time is the way that he characterises the messianic event, the Christ-event, as having penetrated time and history. It is something that is present in every lived moment of history, and not merely a far-off utopian expectation or a dead event in the past. Its very 'pastness' is an important aspect of the Christ-event as what brought it into history in the first place, but the fact that it is reopened in all subsequent moments of time and history means that it refuses closure and refuses to be fully determined. Second, the non-correspondence between time and the language that represents it implies a certain time consciousness, which in turn must give way to questions of meaning and ultimately the meaning of history.

Eschatology and History

Edward Schillebeeckx wrote that eschatology 'is the expression of the belief that history is in God's hands, that the history of the world can reach its fulfilment [sic] in communion with God and that it will be brought to this fulfilment [sic] in Christ who embodies God's promise'.[62] This is not out of step with the 'messianic' as posited by Agamben, although it does require that we bring God back into the conversation. The present – the 'time of the now' – is very much the site where God's relationship with humanity is experienced historically, and as such it is the hermeneutic principle for the interpretation of religious experience and expectations of the future.[63] The person of Jesus of Nazareth, continues to be present in his resurrected form in each moment of time. Paul's identification of salvation as both ongoing and a 'once and for all' event engenders this Christological insight and shows that, despite Jesus's having been condemned, crucified and executed, his story is not finished by death. It is God, and not death or the humans who murdered Jesus, who has the last word on what his life and ministry meant. That Jesus is raised from the dead and continues to be effective in history as salvation coming from God is the culmination of Israel's own process of self-understanding as the recipients of God's promise.

As such, there is no separation between a 'Jesus Messiah' and Jesus of Nazareth, since the former is the recognition in faith of the continued, living and salvific presence of the latter. Israel's history is a process of coming to recognise God's faithfulness in the face of tragedy and defeat, to the point where the people eventually came to believe in a transcendent salvation that was more powerful than death. Therefore, the hope for resurrection is not the *source* of the Yahwistic faith, but something that was only able to be formulated after many centuries of reflection and devotion.[64] Paul's affirmation of Jesus as 'the gospel of God' (Romans 1:1) is in continuity with God's plan and the history of Israel, not something totally unexpected.[65] The intrinsic openness of the messianic within chronological time presents God's original promise to creation that God has the last word on the meaning of history – the closure of history through death is not, in fact, what it seems. The experience of messianic time holds out to us in our time consciousness the possibility of salvation beyond the systems of linguistic representation and violence which inevitably close off possibilities for the future. To affirm the resurrection as Paul does is to affirm God's judgement on creation and history as already present, but this is a reality that empowers us to act in ways which are consonant with the salvific reality encountered in Jesus. For Paul, the appearance of the messiah also means the in-breaking of the new creation (2 Cor. 5:17; Gal. 6:15), so our understanding of messianism and messianic time must be related to creation theology.[66]

While apocalypticism places the *eschaton* at the end of history and bends everything in the present towards it as what is truly important – as the site of definitive salvation – 'Christianity has put [the *eschaton*] within history itself.'[67] This both orients humanity towards history in and through the existential situation of the present, while also pointing towards the future promise of eschatological salvation that is still to be achieved. This must be in continuity with the past as well, since an understanding of the present is always based on the history that stands behind that present. Thus, eschatology is a fundamental orientation towards 'the world', and a rejection of apocalyptic flight from the world. Certainly, for contemporary Catholic theology, the 'watchword is no longer flight from the world, but flight with the world towards the future, a taking of the world itself with us in our christian [*sic*] expectation of the future, which is already transforming the earth here and now'.[68] The recognition of the importance of 'the world' and the present does not strip us of a critical voice or impetus. Rather, it intensifies the demand for realising salvation within the present through

> a saving Christian presence, the forerunner of that hope in a 'new heaven and a new earth,' a hope which *revolutionizes* our efforts for a better future on earth and one in which, at the same time, every socio-political order that already exists becomes of *relative* value inasmuch as it is not yet the new world of God's promise.[69]

The openness of the messianic presence in time allows for the relativisation of the status quo in favour of what *should* exist, and which Paul believed was coming into being in the 'time of the end'.

Meaning and Existential Situation

The uni-dual nature of time as more than just chronological progression means that humanity's 'experience does not simply run on in time, with an undercurrent of "becoming", but implies an element of time-consciousness'.[70] Being conscious of embodied temporality, and its operational linguistic expression allows for a certain kind of transcendence of time from within time itself. This transcendence does not allow us to leave reality behind or escape the confines of finite embodied existence, but it allows us to have an understanding of 'wholeness', imparting a preunderstanding and even expectation that the chronological fragments add up to more than just fragments – in essence it allows access to existential freedom through self-transcendence. This is both part of the engine that drives human experience and an affirmation of the hermeneutic nature of all experience, stemming from the encounter with otherness, and primarily the otherness within messianic time that presents an eschatological fullness that cannot be fully expressed through language. Existential time-consciousness carries the expectation of meaning with it into the human subject, and in lived experience this turns into a concrete question about the meaning of events – their place within the expected whole. This, in turn, becomes a question about the meaning of history itself, both in the sense of personal histories ('what does *my* life mean?') and universal history ('what does *our collective* history amount to?'). From here, it is a short step to the existential question, 'why is there something rather than nothing?'; time-consciousness has a kind of natural theology implicit within it in so far as it directs our gaze to the meaning of existence.

Something that is experienced as meaningful has the potential to affect the existential situation of a person in the world because it affects every aspect of our being. Each experience of meaning adds to our hermeneutic framework for interpretation, changing the character of our being-in-the-world. Such changes can be small or large, relative to the type of meaning encountered. What is encountered in the revelation in Jesus of Nazareth is an eschatological fullness that has the potential to transform the one who receives it. Revelation 'presents itself as *full of meaning* because it is *full of being*'.[71] Therefore, it is the reality of the risen Christ's presence to creation within each moment that is the content of revelation. What is handed on and continuous is the *experience* of as resurrected presence, not merely a set of doctrines about Jesus or the resurrection.[72] This experience, however, is only accessible in continuity with the historical Christ-event which conditions and makes possible our access to the eschatological reality that it inaugurated. It is only on this basis that we can experience, with any degree of clarity, God who is identified as the future of humanity.

Conclusion

Although there is much to criticise in Agamben's work, particularly in his rather ahistorical appropriation of Christian sources and ideas, his assumptions regarding the relative importance of complex etymologies, and especially his rather uncritical assumption that Paul was uninterested in the Jesus of history, he does present genuine insights for theological reflection. His explication of the uni-dual structure of time, and the 'weak messianic power' inherent within it, is clearly meant to further his own project of profanation of law and undoing violent linguistic power structures. His philosophical project, and especially his *Homo Sacer* series, has helped political theology to reach new insights, and he has helped to enable what amounts to an 'economic turn' in contemporary political theology. Agamben has recovered and even further refined Carl Schmitt's 'secularisation thesis' that all political concepts are really secularised theological concepts. Agamben argues that 'contemporary politics is founded on the secularisation of eschatology', meaning that 'what are secularised, today, are essentially eschatological concepts'.[73] Although his understanding of 'eschatology' is quite impoverished and, as we have seen above, does not correspond to developments in Catholic theology in the twentieth century, it remains an important insight that warrants further theological reflection. Schillebeeckx's work in particular has a conceptual dynamism that corresponds far more with 'the messianic' than with the false apocalypticism identified by Rahner and which Agamben takes at face value. Although Agamben claims that 'the Church has lost the messianic experience of time that defines it and is one with it', the eschatological element that he has identified in temporality seems to argue otherwise.[74] The 'messianic experience' was the encounter with Jesus in which people experienced God's offer of salvation. This experience continues to be present in the church, but is not and never was 'one' with it, since the existential experience of the present cannot be equated with the Rule of God. The Rule of God, the general resurrection of the dead, the new creation, and definitive salvation – powerful symbols of God's promise – are only *eschatologically* present in the world and in the church, which are interpenetrating, but not coterminous, realities.

Notes

1. See, especially, Giorgio Agamben, *The Church and the Kingdom*, trans. Leland de la Durantaye (London and New York: Seagull Books, 2012).
2. Johann Baptist Metz, 'Suffering unto God', *Critical Inquiry* 20.4 (1994): 620.
3. Ibid.
4. Giorgio Agamben, 'Time and History: Critique of the Instant and the Continuum', in *Infancy and History: The Destruction of Experience*, trans. Liz Heron (London and New York: Verso, 1993), p. 91.
5. See Anthony J. Godzieba, 'Schillebeeckx's Phenomenology of Experience and Resurrection Faith', in *T&T Clark Handbook of Edward Schillebeeckx*, ed. Stephan van Erp and Daniel Minch (London: T&T Clark, 2019), pp. 86–105.
6. Walter Benjamin, 'Theses on the Philosophy of History', in *Illuminations*, trans. Harry Zohn (New York: Schocken Books, 1986), p. 254.
7. Colby Dickinson, 'Canon as an Act of Creation: Giorgio Agamben and the Extended Logic of the Messianic', *Bijdragen, International Journal in Philosophy and Theology* 71.2 (2010): 136.
8. Giorgio Agamben, *The Time That Remains: A Commentary on the Letter to the Romans*, trans. Patricia Dailey (Stanford: Stanford University Press, 2005), p. 2; Colby Dickinson, *Agamben and Theology*, Philosophy and Theology (London: T&T Clark, 2011), p. 94.
9. Dickinson, *Agamben and Theology*, pp. 12–19, 66–7.
10. Agamben, *The Time That Remains*, pp. 62–3; Job De Meyere, 'The Care for the Present: Giorgio Agamben's Actualisation of the Pauline Messianic Experience', *Bijdragen, International Journal in Philosophy and Theology* 70 (2009): 175.
11. Agamben, *The Time That Remains*, p. 63.
12. Raymond E. Brown, S.S., 'Not Jewish Christianity and Gentile Christianity but Types of Jewish/Gentile Christianity', *Catholic Biblical Quarterly* 45.1 (1983): 74–9.
13. Among the different Christological themes in Paul there is a particularly strong 'Adam Christology'. See James D. G. Dunn, *The Theology of Paul the Apostle* (Grand Rapids, MI: Eerdmans, 2008), pp. 203–4.
14. Agamben, *The Time That Remains*, p. 62.
15. Ibid. p. 63.
16. Johann Baptist Metz, 'The Church and the World', in *The Word in History: The St. Xavier Symposium*, ed. T. Patrick Burke (New York: Sheed & Ward, 1966), p. 77.
17. See James M. Connolly, *The Voices of France: A Survey of Contemporary Theology in France* (New York: The Macmillan Company, 1961), pp. 149–53.
18. Karl Rahner, 'The Hermeneutics of Eschatological Assertions', in *Theological Investigations*, trans. Kevin Smyth, vol. 4 (London and New York: Seabury Press, 1974), p. 337.
19. Metz, 'The Church and the World', p. 78.
20. Agamben, *The Time That Remains*, p. 62.
21. Ibid. p. 68.
22. Dunn, *Theology of Paul*, p. 465.
23. Ibid. p. 240.
24. See 1 Cor. 12:12–28; Rom. 12:4–5; Eph. 4:11–16. Edward Schillebeeckx, *Jesus: An Experiment in Christology*, trans. Hubert Hoskins and Marcelle Manley, Collected Works of Edward Schillebeeckx, vol. 6 (London: Bloomsbury T&T Clark, 2014), p. 387 [423]. Citations from the Collected Works series include the original English pagination in brackets.
25. Schillebeeckx, *Jesus*, pp. 386–7 [421–3].
26. Ibid. pp. 376–7 [411–12].

27. Compare De Meyere, 'The Care for the Present', p. 176: 'The Greek words suggest a reflexive and active verb . . . It is time which itself begins to end and starts to finish.' De Meyere is incorrect. The verb presents several possibilities, but the context decides.
28. Agamben, *The Time That Remains*, p. 126.
29. Dunn, *Theology of Paul*, pp. 311–12.
30. Agamben, *The Time That Remains*, p. 70.
31. Ibid. pp. 70, 100.
32. Ibid. pp. 61, 63.
33. De Meyere, 'The Care for the Present', p. 168.
34. Dunn, *Theology of Paul*, p. 319.
35. Agamben, *The Time that Remains*, pp. 64–6; Agamben, 'Time and History', p. 93.
36. Schillebeeckx, 'The Interpretation of the Future', *The Understanding of Faith: Interpretation and Criticism*, trans. N. D. Smith, Collected Works of Edward Schillebeeckx, vol. 5 (London: Bloomsbury T&T Clark, 2014), p. 3 [4]; Agamben, 'Time and History', pp. 93–4, 104.
37. Agamben, *The Time That Remains*, p. 64; emphasis original.
38. E. P. Sanders, 'Paul between Judaism and Hellenism', in *Paul among the Philosophers*, ed. John D. Caputo and Linda Martín Alcoff (Bloomington and Indianapolis, IN: Indiana University Press, 2009), p. 83.
39. Agamben, 'Time and History', pp. 91–4.
40. Sanders, 'Paul between Judaism and Hellenism', pp. 82–3.
41. Agamben, *The Time That Remains*, p. 69.
42. However, Paul's quotation from Gal. 4:4a uses χρόνος: 'But when the fullness of time had come . . .' This does not help Agamben's argument but it does not *necessarily* cut too far against it either.
43. Agamben, *The Time That Remains*, p. 64.
44. Ibid. pp. 65–6; David E. Johnson, 'As If the Time Were Now: Deconstructing Agamben', *South Atlantic Quarterly* 106.2 (2007): pp. 274–5.
45. Johnson, 'As If the Time Were Now', p. 274; Agamben, *The Time That Remains*, p. 65.
46. Agamben, *The Time That Remains*, pp. 65–6.
47. Ibid. p. 66; emphasis original.
48. De Meyere, 'The Care for the Present', pp. 177–8; Agamben, *The Time That Remains*, p. 70.
49. Johnson, 'As If the Time Were Now', p. 275. Agamben refers to Émile Benveniste's theory of 'enunciation', or the 'pure instance of discourse in action'.
50. Agamben, *The Time That Remains*, p. 66.
51. Ibid. p. 67.
52. Ibid.
53. Ibid. pp. 68–9.
54. Agamben, 'Time and History', pp. 104–5.
55. Agamben, *The Time That Remains*, pp. 68–9.
56. Ibid. p. 70.
57. Patrick O'Connor, 'Redemptive Remnants: Agamben's Human Messianism', *Journal for Cultural Research* 13.3–4 (2009): p. 338.
58. Agamben, *The Time That Remains*, pp. 68–9.
59. O'Connor, 'Redemptive Remnants', pp. 339–40.
60. Agamben, *The Time That Remains*, p. 62.
61. Ibid. p. 74.
62. Schillebeeckx, 'The Interpretation of the Future', p. 9 [10].
63. Ibid.
64. Ibid. pp. 8–9 [9–10].
65. Dunn, *Theology of Paul*, p. 169.
66. Ibid. p. 180.
67. Schillebeeckx, 'The Interpretation of the Future', p. 10 [11].

68. Schillebeeckx, 'Christian Faith and Man's Expectation for the Future on Earth', *The Mission of the Church*, trans. N. D. Smith (New York: Seabury Press, 1973), p. 71.
69. Edward Schillebeeckx, 'The Church as the Sacrament of Dialogue', *God the Future of Man*, trans. N. D. Smith, Collected Works of Edward Schillebeeckx, vol. 3 (London: Bloomsbury T&T Clark, 2014), p. 84 [138].
70. Schillebeeckx, 'The Interpretation of the Future', p. 3 [3].
71. Edward Schillebeeckx, *The Eucharist*, trans. N. D. Smith (London and New York: Burns & Oates, 2005), pp. 18–19.
72. Edward Schillebeeckx, 'Towards a Catholic Use of Hermeneutics', *God the Future of Man*, trans. N. D. Smith, Collected Works of Edward Schillebeeckx, vol. 3 (London: Bloomsbury T&T Clark, 2014), p. 23 [34].
73. Giorgio Agamben, *Stasis: Civil War as a Political Paradigm*, Meridian: Crossing Aesthetics (Stanford: Stanford University Press, 2015), p. 67.
74. Agamben, *The Church and the Kingdom*, p. 4.

Index

Abed, Azzam, 90–1
Abraham, 5, 12, 37–42, 46, 53–5, 57, 130, 212–28, 231–5
absolute, divine, 191
absolute, the, 31, 37, 39–44, 101, 104, 118, 122, 127, 140, 194–6, 212–14, 216, 219–22, 227–8, 230–1, 233
absolute, transcendental, 41
actuality, 1, 4–5, 10, 11, 14, 27–8, 30–1, 69, 74–5, 140, 175, 182–3, 185
Adorno, Theodor W., 48, 112
anomie, 1
anti-humanist, 191–3, 203, 205
Arendt, Hannah, 91, 140, 145–7, 176
Aristotle, 91, 140, 145–7, 176
atheism, 2, 12, 17, 91, 103, 107–8, 117, 120

bare life, 8, 10, 14–16, 19, 33, 35–6, 41–2, 51–2, 54, 65–7, 75–6, 139, 144, 147, 150, 157, 169, 175, 196–7, 202
Bartleby, 19, 178–80, 183–4
Being, 5, 14, 17, 71, 104–6, 112, 126, 163, 195
beings, 11, 19, 38, 41–2, 65, 70, 77, 88, 90, 94, 102, 104, 106, 112, 147, 155, 162, 174–5, 177–9, 182, 185–7, 237

being-there, 3, 104, 160–1
being-towards-death, 141–3, 145, 159–61, 163–4, 169
Benjamin, Walter, 13, 15, 26, 33–6, 41–2, 132, 180, 239
Benveniste, Émile, 5, 162
biopower, 15–16, 51, 201–2
bios, 54, 56, 83–5, 92, 156, 193–4, 196–7

Camus, Albert, 2–3, 7, 11–12, 115, 118, 175, 182–7, 238
Caputo, John D., 222, 226
category, animal, 75
category, ethical, 226–7
category, pronominal, 75
colonialism, 30, 193, 202
Constantius, Constantine, 8, 28–32, 37, 40, 42, 48–50, 69
crypto-Gnostic, 175, 180, 182, 185, 187

Dasein, 3–4, 18–19, 104, 124, 126, 140–1, 143, 160–4, 169
de Beauvoir, Simone, 2, 7, 18, 101, 139
de Silention, Johannes, 20, 37–42, 53–4, 212–16, 218–21, 223–7, 231–5
deactivation, contemplative, 196, 203–4
decionism, 13, 194, 235

decionism, sovereign, 10, 13, 15, 69–70, 77
Deleuze, Gilles, 2, 71, 74, 168
Derrida, Jacques, 51, 102, 222, 227–8
division of division, 2, 12–13, 232–4

Engels, Friedrich, 49, 215
eschaton, 129, 132–3, 239, 241, 247
exception, existential, 43
exception, Kiekegaardian, 8–9, 12, 15–16, 48–50, 56–7
exceptionalism, sovereign, 13, 15
exclusionary truth, 2
existential becoming, 54–5
existentialism, 2, 6–8, 11–15, 17–20, 83–4, 102–3, 110–11, 120, 192, 205, 234–5
existentialism, humanist, 198, 205
existentialism, Sartrean, 198

Fanon, Frantz, 2, 19–20, 191–2, 197–201, 203–6
figure, existential, 66, 71, 72, 76, 78, 234
finitude, 10–11, 141, 145, 149–50, 155, 160–1
form-of-life, 1, 3, 6, 10, 13, 16–17, 65–6, 71–7, 86, 88, 93, 95, 111–12, 196–7, 205
Foucault, Michel, 51, 85
fracture, 107, 124, 192–5, 197, 201–6
fracture, biopolitical, 202, 204–5
fracture, originary, 193, 197, 203

Gould, Rebecca, 68
ground, negative, 3, 5, 9, 12, 231

Hegel, G. W. F., 124, 142–3, 197–9, 204, 214–15, 217–19, 224
Heidegger, Martin, 2, 3, 7–8, 11–12, 16–19, 26, 48–9, 74, 84, 86, 108, 110–12, 124, 140–4, 155, 159–64, 238

immanence, 35–6, 43, 70–1, 107, 112, 242, 245
immanence, absolute, 2–3, 65–70, 107–8
immanent, T/the, 2, 112, 239
im-potentiality, 19, 74, 181
impotentiality, 1, 144, 157, 168, 178–9
infinite, the, 16, 75, 121, 142, 149
infinitude, 10–11
inhuman, 195, 203–6
inoperativity, 19, 71–3, 83, 85–7, 88–90, 92, 178–81, 187, 193, 196–7, 203–6, 233
interiority, 30–1, 204–5, 217

Jesus Messiah, 5–6, 10, 12, 130–2, 229–33, 246

Kierkegaard, Søren, 2, 8–12, 14–16, 20, 25–32, 37, 41–4, 46–52, 54–9, 65, 68–71, 73–7, 212, 214–15, 218, 220–3, 228, 232, 234
Kotsko, Adam, 2, 33, 230

langue, 5, 10, 124, 230–1, 233
Levinas, Emanuael, 228
liminality, 195, 203
logos, 102, 106, 126–7, 131, 142
Löwith, Karl, 49, 215–16

Manichaeism, 203, 206
Marx, Karl, 49, 215–16
masque blanc, 198–9, 206
Master-Slave dialectic, 198
messianic form, 133
messianic time, 20, 128–9, 132–3, 238–9, 241–5, 247–8
messianic weakness, 132
messianism, 20–1, 133, 180–1, 238–41, 247
metaphysics, 3, 7, 17, 84, 86, 88, 101–6, 111, 113, 123–7, 140, 142–3, 146–8, 235

Metz, Johann Baptist, 237–8, 240
Mills, Catherine, 127, 144
mimetic man, 201
monads, 71, 73, 76–7

natal negativity, 139, 145
negative, the, 18, 139–40, 142–5, 147–8, 151
negative theology, 18, 104, 125
Negri, Antonio, 176, 181
Nietzsche, Friedrich, 2–3, 8, 11–13, 16–17, 20, 74, 83–6, 90–6, 103–5, 107–8, 111, 116–17, 120, 129, 133–4
nihilism, 17, 20, 84, 86, 103–7, 109, 111–12, 116–17, 123, 126, 129, 133–4, 141–4, 148
nihilism, imperfect, 13
nihilism, perfect, 13
nomos, 1, 5, 131, 212–13, 217–18, 229–30, 232–3, 235
non-relation/relationality, 72, 74, 192–5, 197, 203, 205–6

ontology, 3–5, 9, 12, 17, 53–5, 72, 75, 85, 104, 107, 111–12, 124–5, 140–1, 156, 160, 169, 196, 201–2, 231
ontology, fascistic, 192, 203, 205
ontology, modal, 9, 17, 51, 72, 112, 196
ontology, negative, 1, 13
ontotheology, 14, 104, 111, 142
othering, 76–7, 191–2, 198–9, 205

parole, 5, 10, 124, 230–4
particularism, 199
perptual interrogation/*interrogation perpétuelle*, 199, 200–1
philosphy, decisionist, 9
philosophy, existential, 26–7, 29
philosophy, political, 8, 19, 27, 192, 195, 239
pistis, 5, 131, 230
polis, 58, 75, 194

politics, 12, 16, 19, 25–6, 53, 57–8, 65, 67, 70–3, 75, 90, 118, 123, 133, 144, 176–7, 180, 182–4, 187, 191–206, 249
potential, destituent, 19, 174–5, 177–8, 180, 182–3, 185, 187
potentiality, 1–2, 3–6, 9–12, 14, 19, 26, 30, 44, 73–6, 108, 131–2, 140, 142, 144, 147, 155–7, 159, 161–2, 164, 167–9, 178, 180–1, 183, 193–7, 203–5, 212, 217, 227, 230–1, 233–4
power, constituent, 174, 176–8, 182, 184, 185
power, constituted, 19, 174, 176, 178, 180, 184
power, sovereign, 2, 59, 66, 110, 176–8, 179, 187, 192–4, 206, 217, 239
profanation, 2–3, 106, 112, 249

referent, transcendent, 76
relationality, 65, 200–1, 204, 206
relationality, radical, 192, 197, 203, 206
repetition, 16, 29, 37, 39, 49, 66, 68–74, 76–8, 93, 143, 163

Sartre, Jean-Paul, 2–3, 7, 10–12, 14–15, 17–18, 20, 100–4, 106–7, 110–11, 115, 117–24, 128, 134, 156, 165–8, 197–9, 204–25
Schillebeeckx, Edward, 20, 238, 246
Schmitt, Carl, 1, 8–10, 12–16, 25–9, 31–4, 42, 47–9, 51, 55–6, 65–70, 77, 132
Shifter, 4, 161–3
Siedentop, Larry, 108
Signification, 4, 7, 132, 162–3, 230
silence, 54, 122, 126, 143, 231
singularities, 14, 38, 65, 71, 74, 77
singularity, 17, 38–44, 65, 68–70, 72, 77, 111, 157, 168, 214, 227–8, 245
situatedness, 199, 204, 206

situation, existential, 20, 237–8, 240–1, 245, 247–8
sovereign, 1–2, 7–10, 12–17, 26–9, 31–6, 42, 47, 50, 56–7, 59, 66–70, 75–7, 102, 108, 110–11, 146, 151, 175–7, 179, 181–2, 187, 192–4, 196–7, 206, 217, 233, 235, 239
sovereignty, 8–9, 16, 18, 29, 33, 48, 58, 65–8, 106–8, 110–11, 130, 156, 174, 176–7, 181–3, 187, 193–4, 217
subject, existential, 3, 14
suspension, 8–9, 12–13, 18, 32, 38–9, 56–7, 67, 130, 156–7, 194, 203, 212, 221, 224–9, 233–5

Taubes, Jacob, 8, 12, 15–16, 25, 48–50, 68
totality, self-referential, 32
Trace, the, 143
Transcendence, 13, 18–19, 35–6, 43, 70–1, 94, 107, 112, 118–19, 124, 156, 158, 164, 166, 238, 245, 248
Transcendental, the, 166–7, 204

Universal, the, 8, 10, 12, 28–9, 30–6, 38–40, 48, 50–1, 56, 68, 181, 200, 212–14, 216, 218–19, 221–9, 231–3
Universalism, 53, 192, 199–200, 205

violence, divine, 34–6
violence, mythical, 36
violence, original, 36, 42
violence, sovereign, 33–5, 181
Voice, T/the, 5, 125–7, 162–4, 231

Westphal, Merold, 212–15, 217, 222–6, 228

zoé, 1, 54, 56, 83, 85, 88, 90, 92–3, 156, 193–4, 196–7

EU representative:
Easy Access System Europe
Mustamäe tee 50, 10621 Tallinn, Estonia
Gpsr.requests@easproject.com